Understanding Local Area Networks

A Practical Approach

ARTHUR THOMPSON

Prentice Hall
Upper Saddle River, New Jersey *Columbus, Ohio*

To Vicki: Your patience with my bouts of concentration continues to amaze and astound.

Library of Congress Cataloging-in-Publication Data
Thompson, Arthur (Arthur William)
Understanding local area networks : a practical approach / Arthur Thompson.
p. cm.
ISBN 0-13-921222-1
1. Local area networks (Computer networks) I. Title.
TK5105.7.T56 2000
004.6'8—dc21 99-20147
CIP

Publisher: Charles E. Stewart, Jr.
Production Editor: Rachel Besen
Design Coordinator: Karrie Converse-Jones
Text Designer: STELLARViSIONs
Copyeditor: Laura Larson
Cover Designer: Dan Eckel
Production Manager: Matt Ottenweller
Electronic Text Management: Marilyn Wilson Phelps, Karen L. Bretz, Melanie N. King
Illustrations: Christine Marrone
Marketing Manager: Ben Leonard

This book was set in Dutch 801 and Franklin Gothic by Prentice Hall and was printed and bound by R.R. Donnelley & Sons Company. The cover was printed by Phoenix Color Corp.

Printed in the United States of America

10 9 8 7 6 5 4 3 2

ISBN: 0-13-921222-1

Prentice-Hall International (UK) Limited, *London*
Prentice-Hall of Australia Pty. Limited, *Sydney*
Prentice-Hall of Canada, Inc., *Toronto*
Prentice-Hall Hispanoamericana, S. A., *Mexico*
Prentice-Hall of India Private Limited, *New Delhi*
Prentice-Hall of Japan, Inc., *Tokyo*
Prentice-Hall (Singapore) Pte. Ltd., *Singapore*
Editora Prentice-Hall do Brasil, Ltda., *Rio de Janeiro*

Preface

Connectivity is the buzzword these days. Any business with the need for more than one computer can derive significant benefits if its computers are connected together. Everything from two personal computers in the family home to the global Internet are being connected. This book offers an introduction to the knowledge required to understand networking and telecommunications. The book provides practical considerations for installation, administration, and maintenance of networks. Each chapter is designed to provide fundamental theoretical knowledge and practical application tips plus practical projects you may wish to do to solidify your understanding of the chapter. Also included in each chapter is a troubleshooting section to enable you to recognize and solve common network problems using tools that are common to network troubleshooting.

Understanding Local Area Networks includes detailed information on the four most common local area network protocols: Ethernet, Token-Ring, ARCNET, and FDDI. A brief introduction to common network operating systems is presented, including Novell NetWare, Microsoft NT, Banyan Vines, and Apple Computer's AppleTalk.

Although this book deals primarily with local area networks, an introduction to telecommunications and wide area networking is also provided, including a chapter devoted to the Internet protocol, TCP/IP. An introduction to public carrier protocols such as ISDN, ATM, Frame Relay, and ADSL is also presented. Additional chapters cover small network design considerations, network security, troubleshooting, and performance tuning.

This book is most appropriate for use by community college, technical college, or vocational school network technology programs or as an introductory overview course at the university level. Every attempt has been made to minimize prerequisites; however, an understanding of the binary numbering system and familiarity with personal computer operating systems and the use of personal computers would be helpful.

I would like to thank the following people for reviewing this book in manuscript form: Robert Morris (DeVry Institute of Technology), Shivakont Mishra (University of Wyoming), Frank Whetten (Embry-Riddle University), Judy Serwatka (Purdue University), and Michael Miller (DeVry Institute of Technology).

Trademarks

Every effort has been made to acknowledge the numerous trademarks used throughout this book. In the event that one has been overlooked, I hope you will accept my sincere apologies and give me an opportunity to correct any omissions in future editions.

Trademark	***Registered Owner***
Apple, Appleshare, and AppleTalk	Apple Computer, Inc.
ARCNET	Datapoint Corporation
DEC	Digital Equipment Corporation
Ethernet	Xerox Corporation
EtherTalk	Apple Computer, Inc.
IBM	International Business Machines Corp.
Intel	Intel Corporation
IPX	Novell, Inc.
LAN	Novell, Inc.
LANalyzer	Novell, Inc.
MS-DOS	Microsoft
NetBIOS	International Business Machines Corp.
NetBEUI	International Business machines Corp.
NetWare	Novell, Inc.
NT	Microsoft
PC (Personal Computer)	International Business Machines Corp.
Pentium	Intel Corporation
Proliant	Compaq
SPX/IPX	Novell, Inc.
SNA	International Business Machines Corp.
Sniffer	Network General Corporation
SystemPro	Compaq
Token-Ring	International Business Machines Corp.
UNIX	UNIX Systems Laboratories
VINES	Banyan Systems, Inc.

Contents

1

Beginning with the Basics

HISTORICAL PERSPECTIVE

Networks existed long before computers became a reality. In 1846 Samuel F. B. Morse created a digital code using a series of dots and dashes. Soon after, a network of wires was strung throughout parts of the country to facilitate the exchange of coded information. This network was called the telegraph. Using Morse code, the first "electronic mail" messages could be sent and received. Figure 1.1 shows the basic code.

Throughout this book I will refer to the term *protocol*. In its most general form, the term *protocol* is used to define a set of rules for communication over a specified medium. The Morse code protocol involved the code for a letter or number. For example, the letter *A* is represented as a single dot followed immediately by a single dash.

Dashes are equal in time to three dots; a space between characters is equal to two dot times. So long as all operators used the same protocol, rapid and reasonably accurate data could be broadcast and shared.

An additional rule had to be added to the protocol because of the construction of the network itself. There was only one wire used for transmission. Although data could flow in either direction, only one operator could transmit at a time. Each operator had to listen for traffic and transmit only when the line was clear. This one-at-a-time mode of transmission is called *half duplex*. In the chapter on the local area network protocol known as Ethernet, the method used today for a single-wire, half-duplex transmission protocol is explained.

On March 7, 1876, Alexander Graham Bell patented the telephone. Less than two years later, on January 28, 1878, the city of New Haven, Connecticut, opened the first voice network in the United States. American Telephone and Telegraph was formed in 1885 and eventually absorbed the Bell Company. It is AT&T that is primarily responsible for the nationwide voice network that exists today. The Regional Bell Operating Companies (RBOCs) have been broken free from AT&T control and set up as independent companies to provide local dialing area service. The important point to remember is that the telephone network is extensive and provides a very convenient *backbone* that can be used to send data to a very large area of the world. (*Backbone* is the networking term used to describe the transmission medium used to connect multiple networks.)

Almost from the beginning of computing, there has been a need for more than one user to be connected to the same centrally located computer. The computer and its peripheral devices such as printers and disk drives for data storage were much too expensive to stand idle waiting for a single user to need access. It was thought that access to valuable information could be more carefully controlled if the information only resided in one place. So also is the physical security of the central controlling computer better controlled from a central location (see Figure 1.2).

The idea of multiuser access was first implemented in mainframe computers and quickly followed by their smaller minicomputer cousins. A great many of the world's networked computers are connected to mainframes and minicomputers. Of course, as soon as more than one user is connected, some method must be developed to allow multiple users to share the same programs, data, and hardware. Normally, each user is given a small space in the host computer's environment. Then, in turn, each user is allowed access to the host computer's resources on a time-shared basis.

COMMON TERMINOLOGY AND CONVENTIONS

Networking is a very detailed subject. You will spend a great deal of time learning the terminology, nearly all of which is expressed in mnemonic or acronym form. Table 1.1 is a list of a few of the basic terms that the text assumes you are familiar with. The IBM or IEEE dictionaries of electronic, computer, and networking terminology are excellent references. The back of this book also contains a glossary.

Figure 1.1 Morse Code

.-	A	--.	G	--	M	...	S	-.--	Y	.....	5
-...	B	....	H	-.	N	-	T	--..	Z	-....	6
-.-.	C	..	I	---	O	.--	U	.----	1	--...	7
-..	D	.---	J	.--.	P	...-	V	..---	2	---..	8
.	E	.-.	K	--.-	Q	.--	W	...--	3	----.	9
--.-	F	.-..	L	.-.	R	-..-	X	.----	4	-----	0

Figure 1.2 Typical Host-Centric Computer Installation: HP 3000 Minicomputer Installation

WHY NETWORK?

Perhaps the single most important reason for multiuser computing is to *reduce costs* by sharing expensive resources such as data storage devices and printers. Mini- and mainframe systems accomplish sharing by putting all processing capability in a centrally located processor called the *host*. In contrast to the concept of centralized mainframe control is the personal productivity gained by the stand-alone personal computer. The alternative to centric hosts is to distribute the processing to the users by replacing host-controlled terminals with personal computers and allowing most of the processing to be done in the PC. Connecting personal computers together will accomplish our cost reduction goal in the same way as minis and mainframes, by the sharing of peripheral devices.

From the very beginning of electronic computers, connecting remotely located devices such as terminals and printers has been a necessity. Primarily, networks are tools for communication. The well-known RS-232C/D (*RS* means "Recommended Standard") was created to provide a common method for connecting data terminals to modems so that information in the form of data could be communicated over the telephone network to and from remote sites. Expanding communications needs for business, government, and the general

Table 1.1 Commonly Used Terminology

Term	Description
0123h	Notation used in which the lowercase *h* denotes that the number is a hexadecimal value.
11001001b	Notation used in which the lowercase *b* denotes that the number is a binary value.
Analog	Electrical signals that are continuously variable in frequency and amplitude.
Digital	Electrical signals that have two amplitude states only: logical 0 and logical 1.
Address	The location of data or devices in a computer or network. Two types of addresses exist: addresses within a device and the address of a device connected to a network.
Bit	A single unit of data equal to a binary value of 0 or 1. Usually expressed as either logical 0 or logical 1. The speed of a data transfer is usually expressed in bits per second (bps).
Byte	A group of eight bits. This may also be referred to as an *octet* because *byte* is often associated with characters, and an ASCII character byte may be only seven bits.
Baud	The rate at which a modem sends data. Defined as 1/bit-cell-time (or time period of a bit).
Flag	A defined bit or group of bits used to identify specific functions. In networking, the beginning and ending bits that signify the start and end of a frame.
Node	A single addressable hardware device connected to a network.
Protocol	The set of rules used to define the syntax and semantic format for communication.
Server	The node on a network that contains a network operating system responsible for controlling shared resources and providing network services and security. Servers may be shared workstations or dedicated microcomputers, minicomputers, or mainframes.
Workstation	Workstations are user-controlled nodes attached to a network and are usually microcomputers.

public are driving the growth of networking. Application and user requirements driving the need for networking include the following:

- *Resource sharing*—Often, computing equipment is very expensive. Any equipment that can be shared by people who use a computer system will drive the need for a network. Printers, plotters, modems, and shared databases are ideal candidates for networking.
- *Security*—Although resource sharing may be a valuable asset, maintaining the security of data and programs becomes a potential liability. Storing valuable databases in a central location offers the opportunity to protect the data and to control access to it. Users may share access, but under controlled circumstances. Users may have access to programs but are unable to copy or alter them if they are confined to a centrally located and controlled device.

  As databases of "mission-critical" data have grown, corporate information managers have begun, once again, to rethink the value of centralized data storage. Given the immense value of a company's data and the large amount of revenue that would be lost should the data be compromised, damaged, or destroyed, many databases are being *distributed* across networks to be stored in many different locations. Truly critical data are replicated on storage devices in many different locations; other data are stored in locations where it is actually needed and used.

- *Electronic data services*—Computer networks have contributed significantly to the ability of users within an organization to communicate more effectively with each other. Services such as **E-mail** (electronic mail) and scheduling programs are commonplace on most networks. Each user is assigned an E-mail account name that becomes an address in the local network's "post office."

E-mail is electronic mail.

- *Video data services*—Increasingly, multimedia voice and video communications are taking place over networks. As you shall see in later chapters, this often requires large volumes of data that must be sent in real time. If the capability exists, a computer workstation can become a teleconferencing platform capable of receiving and sending real-time voice and video. These services are already available for use in your home over the global network known as the Internet. Companies such as Microsoft are actively engaged with manufacturers of home entertainment equipment and the public telephone and cable television operators to provide interactive voice and video services to the home. Almost a certainty is the change in television from its current analog transmission mode to some form of high-resolution digital medium. Satellite TV from DSS and DirectTV is already digital. For example, to have a pay-for-view movie turned on, you merely connect the satellite receiver to the telephone line and click the remote control to cause the satellite to open the movie channel to your receiver.
- *Voice data services*—Nearly all of the United States' telephone systems are currently digitized between the phone companies' central offices. The connection on the outside wall of your house is known as a *Point of Presence* (POP). *Customer Premise Equipment* (CPE) is connected to the *Central Office* (**CO**) of your local telephone company beginning at the POP. This voice-quality line is the only analog link still left. As these old analog links are replaced with higher-capacity transmission media, the opportunity to provide high-speed digital communications to anyone who has a telephone is a realistic possibility.

CO stands for Central Office.

Many of the RBOCs already offer *Integrated Services Digital Network* (**ISDN**). Basic-rate ISDN is a totally digital service that is offered over your old analog telephone lines. You may already have one of these services known as caller identification. Many companies are installing ISDN equipment in their employees' homes so that the employee can "telecommute." Although previously too expensive for most private use, recent trends in price reductions are making ISDN increasingly attractive.

ISDN is Integrated Services Digital Network.

There seems to be a trend to convert all phone company services, including your analog telephone, to full-digital connections. With the Telecommunications Act of 1996, cable TV companies are beginning to offer digital services to the home in addition to the current multichannel analog services. At present, the bandwidth available throughout the TV cable is roughly 300 times that of even ISDN. This competition has provided the RBOCs with additional incentive to upgrade their old analog lines using a new technology called *Asynchronous Digital Subscriber Line* (ADSL). A more thorough treatment of both ISDN and ASDL comes up in later chapters.

ADSL means Asynchronous Digital Subscriber Line.

NETWORK TYPES

Local Area Networks

Simply stated, a *network* is a group of devices that have been connected together so that devices on the network may communicate with each other and share resources. Computer networks, defined as local, are usually confined to a single building or closely assembled group of buildings. This is due to limitations on the length of cables that are used to connect the components of the network together. *Local Area Networks* (**LAN**s) may be connected by devices designed to increase cable distances; however, LANs rarely cross public boundaries such as roads or highways.

LANs are Local Area networks.

In 1974 IBM introduced a mainframe host-centric computer network named *System Network Architecture* (**SNA**). SNA networks are designed around mainframe computers that control all network activities. This concept is known as *host-centric* because the mainframe host is implemented as the central controlling and processing device. A terminal wishing to send a message to another terminal must wait to be *polled* by the mainframe before it is allowed to send a message to the mainframe, which would in turn create a transaction that sends the message to the desired destination. These networks are transaction oriented in that all data transfers, whether message traffic or file transfers, are dealt with on a transaction-by-transaction basis. Even though proprietary (IBM wholly owns and controls SNA), SNA is used by a great many network users in the United States.

SNA is System Network Architecture.

Even though it clearly has a vested interest in mainframe-oriented networks, IBM has recognized the need for connectivity between isolated and independent computing systems. *Token-Ring* is a method for interconnecting stand-alone workstations in a *peer-to-peer* mode that allows each workstation to act as its own transaction device. One of the workstations acts as a monitor to control timing and the token-passing process. This concept eliminates the need for an expensive central controller such as IBM's 3745, an understandable reason for IBM's delay in bringing Token-Ring to the market. An upcoming chapter will provide the details for Token-Ring operation.

In the early 1970s, Xerox Corporation introduced a different networking concept called *Ethernet.* Ethernet is designed to run on a single transmission line to which all stations are connected. As with Token-Ring, Ethernet is peer-to-peer; however, no monitoring device is required. Unlike Token-Ring, Ethernet does not require that stations wait for a token to be passed before transmitting. Stations are able to connect directly to each other and pass data any time there is no activity on the network.

A third, though less popular, LAN protocol has been developed by the Datapoint Corporation to allow the use of cheap twisted pair cable. Also peer-to-peer, *ARCNET* requires no controller but does pass tokens in a manner somewhat similar to Token-Ring. In following chapters, these three popular local area network protocols, Ethernet, Token-Ring, and ARCNET, will be explained in detail. Additionally, an all–fiber optic cable LAN protocol known as *Fiber Distributed Data Interface* (**FDDI**) will be presented.

FDDI means Fiber Distributed Data Interface.

In the current market, we may correctly state that SNA still occupies a large share of networked users. Ethernet is installed in the majority of the LANs not using mainframes. It should be noted that, with recent price reductions, demand for Token-Ring products seems to remain competitive but only shares about 5 percent of the market. ARCNET has clearly lost favor as the protocol of choice, although enough installed ARCNET LANs still exist to warrant a chapter in this book.

Metropolitan Area Networks

Metropolitan Area Networks (**MANs**) cover an area large enough to exceed the copper-based cabling distance limitations of most LANs. MANs are often connected with fiber optic cable and are usually confined to distances of up to fifty kilometers. You may also hear MANs referred to as *Campus Area Networks* (CANs) because many of them are installed on large, multiple-building campuses. MANs often combine LAN protocols with protocols that are used in wide area networks, which makes the distinction between a MAN and a WAN difficult.

MANs are Metropolitan Area Networks.

Wide Area Networks

When a network extends itself beyond the cabling limits of LAN protocols to include public or private carrier systems such as the telephone system, the overall network needs to be reclassified as a *Wide Area Network* (**WAN**). A WAN would include two or more LANs connected by WAN equipment, protocols, and transmission medium. WANs know no boundaries. Perhaps the most well-known WANs are the telephone companies and the Internet. Chapter 12 will discuss wide area and internetworking concepts. One very clear distinction between LAN and WAN is that all devices on a LAN must use the same protocol. WANs

WAN is a Wide Area Network.

are designed to allow LANs with differing protocols to connect and communicate. A new term, *Global Area Networks* (GANs), has appeared in articles referring to the global Internet. GANs are still WANs and use the same techniques, protocols, and equipment.

VPN is Virtual Private Network.

Where a global organization might find it cheaper and more convenient to use the Internet to connect its far-flung enterprise, it is possible to cause the network to appear to a user as though it is a private network. You will see the term *Virtual Private Network* (**VPN**) used to describe a WAN that appears private yet uses public networks to connect the truly private LANs together.

STANDARDS AND PROTOCOLS

Standards

Of primary importance to networking is the requirement for all stations connecting to the network to conform to an agreed-on set of standards. Even the slightest deviation from the standards will cause a device to be unable to communicate with other devices on a given network. Without an agreement on standards, it would be necessary to design a separate interface between each device and between each network to communicate, an extraordinary expense.

A wide variety of interests must be included in the development of the standards. Numerous standing committees exist whose members represent the interests of vendors, contractors, government agencies, and the academic community. Users, manufacturers, and governments must be routinely consulted during the development of a standard. As technology improves, changes must be made to existing standards, and these changes must be introduced in such a way as to preclude users of older units from being forced to replace their equipment every time a small part of a standard is changed.

Some of the most important contributors to standards are the users. Users quickly learn to avoid vendors whose products do not conform to accepted standards. Attempts to change standards are often involved in a rather vicious circle. Vendors will be only too happy to change the standard if users will sign up to buy it. Users, of course, are reluctant to buy unless the new product is demonstrated to improve productivity or reduce costs, and the proof is often only available after the product has been accepted in the marketplace.

Protocols

As previously mentioned, *protocol* is probably best defined as a set of rules that have been agreed on to facilitate communication. These rules, as they pertain to networking, may include

- a definition of the *syntax* (specific software instruction or hardware command format) that will be used,

- the *semantics* (the meaning of words and symbols) that are part of the protocol,
- specifications for unique hardware construction, and
- specifications for unique software construction.

Protocols will be presented in this book that describe the most commonly used methods for connecting networks together, including the popular LAN protocols: Ethernet, Token-Ring, FDDI, and ARCNET and the WAN protocol TCP/IP. A detailed understanding of the protocols used in networking is essential if one is to truly understand how a specific network functions.

Proposed new standards are often begun by generating a *Request for Comment* (**RFC**) published by the company or organization that has developed the new standard. Interested parties may then respond with their concerns. This approach was implemented during the early research to develop the Internet. It was so successful that in many cases, RFCs have become de facto standards long before the official standards bodies pronounced them "standard." Many universities and commercial organizations maintain data banks that contain known RFCs and make them available to the Internet so that all interested parties can have access to this very valuable information.[1]

RFC stands for Request for Comment.

STANDARDS ORGANIZATIONS

International Standards Organization (ISO)

The ISO was originally an international body composed of users, vendors, and service providers who volunteered their time to the creation and maintenance of networking and communications standards that could be used by the international community. It is currently incorporated into the *International Telecommunications Union* (ITU). Insofar as networking is concerned, the ISO *Open Systems Interconnect* (OSI) reference model, originally created by *the Open Systems Foundation* (**OSF**), will form the basis for all of the different kinds of networks and protocols that are presented in this book. Without the OSIRM, it is quite likely that networks would have retained proprietary ownership by the companies that created them. By embracing the international OSI model, a multitude of vendors has been able to create conforming products that prevent users and service providers from being "locked in" to proprietary systems. Vendors are free to improve their products, usually by making them faster or by offering more features. In fact, manufacturers of networking products are often the driving force behind new or improved standards.

OSF is *the* Open Systems Foundation.

[1] At the time this text was written, a list of RFC repositories was presented at http://www.isi.edu/in-notes/rfc-retrieval.txt.

American National Standards Institute (ANSI)

IEEE is the Institute of Electrical and Electronic Engineers, *EIA* is the Electronic Industries Association, and *CBEMA* is the Computer and Business Equipment Manufacturers Association.

ASCII stands for American Standard Code for Information Interchange.

ANSI (pronounced "ann-sea") is the North American standards body that defines standards for both industrial and electrical/electronic purposes. It participates in the International Standards Committee under the auspices of the United Nations. Organizations that contribute proposed standards to ANSI include the Institute of Electrical and Electronic Engineers (**IEEE**), the Electronic Industries Association (**EIA**), and the Computer and Business Equipment Manufacturers Association (**CBEMA**).

You may already be familiar with the ANSI standards for computer terminal symbols referred to as **ASCII** (American Standard Code for Information Interchange) and extended ASCII graphic symbols. Most computer users are familiar with the EIA standard for the hardware used in serial data transmissions called RS-232C/D. In this book the IEEE 802.x standards will be dealt with in detail. These standards define the specific protocols for the different types of local, metropolitan, and wide area networks presented in this book and are included as a part of the OSI reference model.

IEEE Standards

In February 1980, the IEEE formed a committee to implement standards for local area networking. This committee became appropriately known as the *Project 802* Committee. The following standards have since been established and are adhered to by most vendors associated with LAN products:

> *802.1 Higher-Layer LAN Protocols Working Group.* Among other items, this standard defines the "Spanning Tree" protocol and is concerned with connectivity and management issues between networks. Spanning Tree is the protocol used to connect similar LANs together and is explained in Chapter 4.
>
> *802.2 Logical Link Control Working Group (Inactive).* Defines the half of the Data Link Layer that is concerned with the connection points between specific devices on a network and the second half of layer 2 known as the MAC sublayer. The 802.2 standard is described in detail in Chapter 2.
>
> *802.3 Ethernet Working Group.* This is the so-called Ethernet protocol. In truth, 802.3 describes a method for detecting errors that are the result of data collisions that can occur on a common bus network. Standard 802.3 is presented in detail in Chapter 4. Subsets of 802.3 include the following:
>
> 802.3aa: 100 BaseT for using twisted pair at 100 Mbps
>
> 802.3ab: 1,000 BaseT also known as "Gigabit Ethernet"

802.4 Token Bus Working Group (Inactive). Standard 802.4 is not commonly implemented. ARCNET, described in Chapter 6, is in part a token-passing bus scheme.

802.5 Token-Ring Working Group. Chapter 5 presents Token-Ring.

802.6 Metropolitan Area Network Working Group (Inactive).

802.7 Broadband TAG (Inactive). This standard refers to broadband LAN standards such as 10broad36. Broadband standards are not dealt with in this book.

802.8 Fiber Optic TAG.

802.9 Isochronous LAN Working Group. ISDN is the specific standard referred to in 802.9.

802.10 Security Working Group

802.11 Wireless LAN Working Group. Includes infrared light, microwave, and spread spectrum.

802.12 Demand Priority Working Group. This is the 100VG-AnyLAN standard originally developed by Hewlett Packard.

802.13. Not used.

802.14 Cable Modem Working Group

CONSULTATIVE COMMITTEE FOR INTERNATIONAL TELEGRAPH AND TELEPHONE

The Consultative Committee for International Telegraph and Telephone (**CCITT**) as its name implies, sets standards for the various international telephone and telegraph systems. In 1996, the CCITT was absorbed by *the International Telecommunications Union* (ITU). CCITT standards are of particular importance in wide area networking where the public telephone systems are used to connect networks.

CCITT is the Consultative Committee for International Telegraph and Telephone.

Internet Engineering Task Force

The Internet Engineering Task Force (IETF) is a committee of representatives from academic, government, and commercial organizations whose function is to establish the standards and protocols used on the Internet. Many of the RFCs issued by the IETF are the basis for definitions used throughout this text. Each RFC used will be identified in the chapter in which it is used.

TROUBLESHOOTING

Perhaps the only troubleshooting needed for this chapter is my grammar and spelling. However, because the book emphasizes troubleshooting, this section will explain the format for the troubleshooting sections of the book. The word *troubleshooting* implies that something has gone wrong and needs to be restored to proper working order. In that spirit, the troubleshooting sections will attempt to offer tips that will apply to the subject matter in each chapter, to help you prevent such problems.

Good troubleshooting requires good methodology and a logical thought process. Good troubleshooters are therefore methodical and above all knowledgeable. You are reduced to guessing if you have not mastered the technology you are trying to repair.

Most of the chapters offer case study options. Having access to a real working network will make your study of this book much more realistic. Being able to see the troubleshooting tools used in networking is a plus as well. Good troubleshooters also keep good records. You should immediately develop the habit of carrying a notebook with you in which you will record settings for hardware and software, solutions to problems, and anything you note that might be valuable in the future.

I will discuss several troubleshooting instruments and software programs in this book. If you can begin now to arrange for access to similar tools, try to have them available when the book covers them. Among the more popular troubleshooting tools are

- a cable tester,
- a network analyzer (both hardware and software),
- time domain reflectometer,
- LED indicator lights, and
- multimeter to measure resistance and voltage.

You will soon discover that meticulous record keeping is a must. This paragraph offers a partial list of records that should be kept. Do not be concerned at this time if you do not recognize some of the terminology; it will be explained as the book progresses. For now, keep in mind that good records will include

- hardware settings for IRQ, DMA, memory, and so forth;
- software settings for addressing and configuration, which might include routing tables and IP addresses;
- physical locations of all network devices including network cables,

- a network cable log showing wiring diagrams, connector and cable run locations, patch panel settings, and periodic cable quality test results;
- a disaster recovery procedure in the event of catastrophic failure.

The chart in Figure 1.3 may be used to guide you through a logical thought process when troubleshooting a network problem. Keep it handy as you review the troubleshooting sections at the end of each chapter.

CHAPTER REVIEW

- Networking in the United States began with Morse code and the telegraph system.
- Early network developers include IBM (Token-Ring and SNA), Xerox (Ethernet), Datapoint Corporation (ARCNET), and AT&T (the telephone network).
- Networks exist to share resources and data and to provide electronic communications.
- LANs are confined to local areas such as buildings, floors, or rooms. MANs connect buildings and campuses but rarely extend beyond a 50-kilometer radius. WANs know no boundaries.
- Standards provide the necessary conformity that users, vendors, and service providers demand.
- Protocols are the rules by which communication can take place. They include semantics, syntax, and construction specifications for hardware and software.
- Standards organizations include the ITU, ISO, CCITT, ANSI, IEEE, EIA, CBEMA, and IET.
- Common standards include OSI, EIA RS-232C/D, IEEE 802.1 through 802.6, and they are often introduced through RFCs.

REVIEW QUESTIONS

1. Give an example of a LAN, and briefly justify your example.
2. List three reasons for networking computers.
3. Briefly describe the characteristics of a MAN.
4. Briefly describe the characteristics of a WAN.

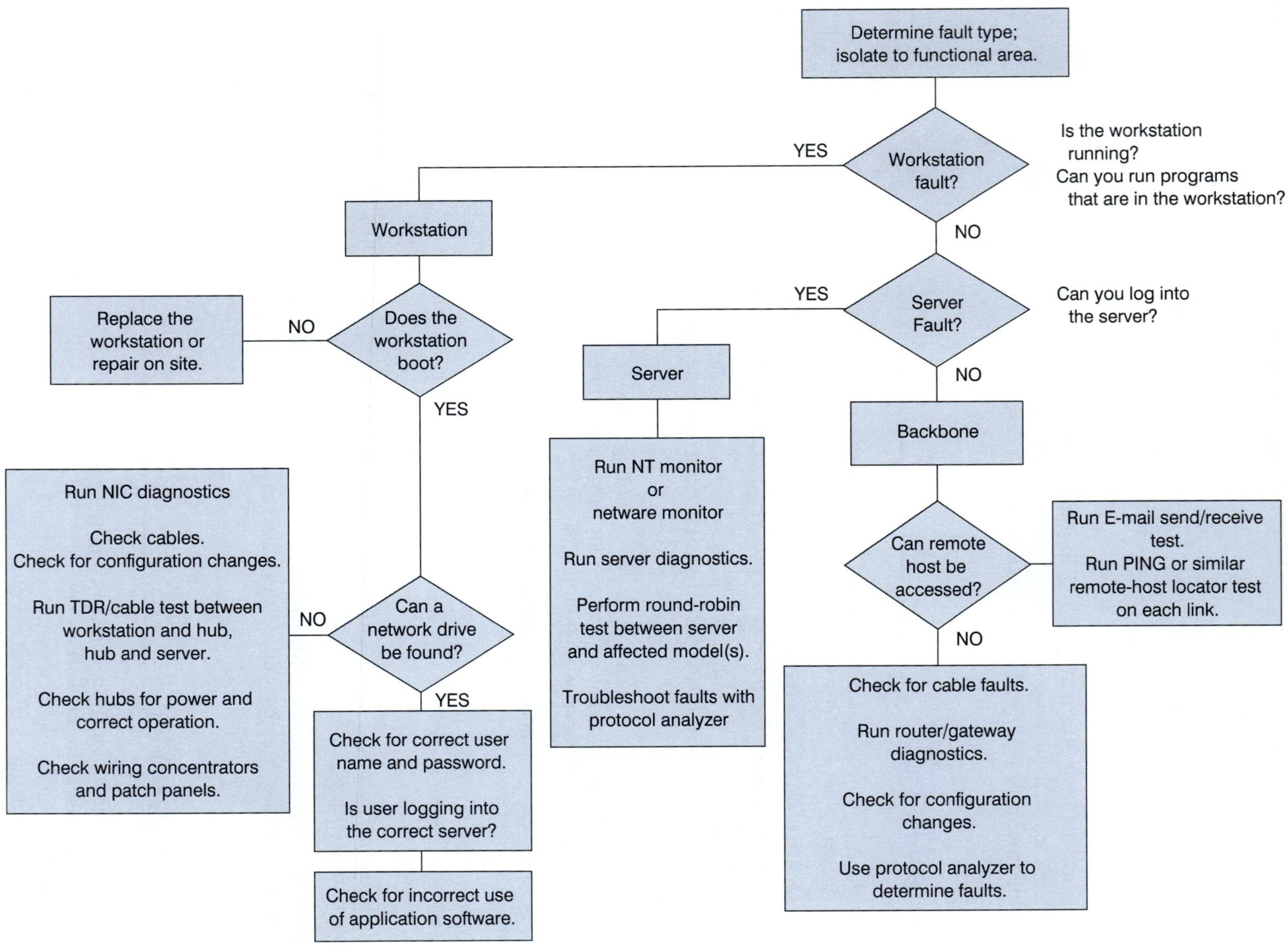

Figure 1.3 Network Troubleshooting Chart

5. What is SNA?
6. Describe a peer-to-peer network.
7. Why are standards and protocols necessary to networking?
8. In your own words, define the term *protocol.*
9. What useful purpose does an RFC serve?
10. List the Project 802 standards and provide a brief description of each standard.

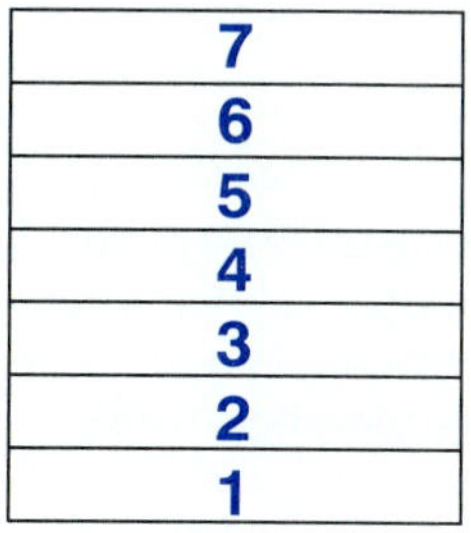

2

Open Systems Interconnect Reference Model

INTRODUCTION

ISA is Industry Standard Architecture.

It is particularly important to recognize that communication among computing devices can only take place when every device connected to a common network conforms to a common set of protocols. IBM's release of the specification for Industry Standard Architecture (**ISA**) provided the opportunity for standardization of microcomputers using the PC or MS-DOS operating system. Yet, even though two DOS-based machines "speak the same language," to transfer information from one DOS-based machine to another, one had to laboriously copy the data to a floppy disk, carry the disk to the second DOS-based machine, and copy the data into the new machine. This has been referred to, humorously, as the "NikeNet." If both machines could be electrically connected together, however, the process of transferring data could be done much more easily.

Most personal computers usually have either a parallel printer port or a serial communications port. These ports are relatively easy to connect and are often used to pass data from one computer to another. Unfortunately, only two computers may be connected in this fashion. In addition, both serial and parallel ports are limited to the maximum speed at which the typical ISA I/O bus can operate, typically 8 to 10 MHz.

Parallel ports can effectively transfer about 9,600 characters per second. This data transfer rate would be suitable for many applications. Unfortunately, parallel port cables are constrained to less than 20 feet because of the 5-volt signal levels, construction of the cables and connectors, and radiation regulations imposed by the Federal Communications Commission (FCC).

By the time the data actually get transferred across a serial interface card, throughput is down to a maximum of 115.2 Kbps (bits per second, not characters), owing to the 64550a/b serial universal asynchronous receiver transmitter (UART) chips used on most serial interface ports. Currently, the primary method used to connect a home PC to the Internet is through the use of a modem (modulator-demodulator) connected between a PC serial port and the analog telephone line.

If voice-quality telephone lines and analog modems are used between computers, data speeds are further limited to real-time data rates of about 2,400 bps. This is because AT&T determined that sufficient quality of the human voice could pass over very inexpensive twisted pair wire that had a maximum range of frequencies between 300 and 3,400 Hz.

We can apply some electronic phase-shifting techniques to get four bits of data out of each bit time. This approach allows data speeds of up to 9,600 bps. Using mathematical data compression, we can increase 9,600 bps to 33.6 Kbps, still too slow for any meaningful data transfer beyond simple file transfers. To remain technically accurate, it should be pointed out that analog modems nearly always require error correction because of the inherent noise in voice-quality lines and are only able to achieve their highest speeds under the most ideal conditions. The data rate from a CO to an analog subscriber is currently limited to 53 Kbps.

Any truly meaningful network, particularly when more than two users are connected, must be fast, reliable, and versatile. Data rates should be fast enough to prevent noticeable delay in response to user requests, certainly greater than 1 megabit per second. Data transfers should have guaranteed, error-free delivery. The network should be flexible enough to allow additional users to connect at any time without disturbing existing users. In the chapters on LAN protocols you will discover that the most popular LANs operate between 2 and 16 Mbps.

THE SEVEN-LAYER OSI MODEL

Many networking models have been developed. Perhaps the best known and most adhered to model is that developed by the International Standards Organization (ISO) known as the Open System Interconnect (OSI) reference model. The OSI model has become the international model for interconnecting data processing systems.

Figure 2.1 is a graphical representation of the OSI model. Note that the model has seven layers, each defined for the type of use it is expected to have. Figure 2.1 has been labeled to show some of the currently popular protocols used in each of the layers. The OSI model is an open model in that it merely defines the purpose for the layer rather than any specific usage or protocol. In this manner, manufacturers can be creative in their designs yet still conform to the OSI model. Unfortunately, this also means that users must be aware that conformance to the OSI model does not necessarily mean that two LAN nodes

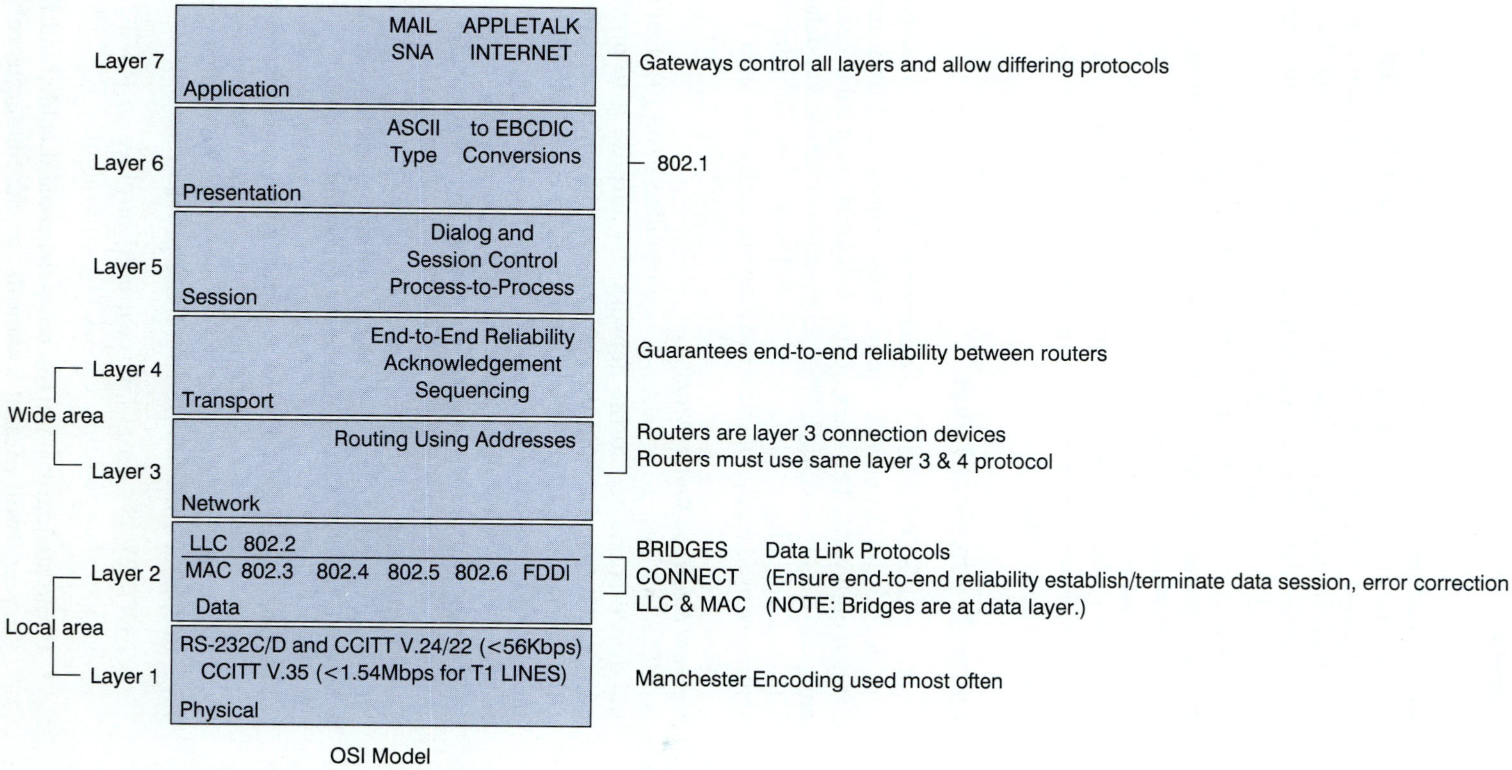

Figure 2.1 Open Systems Interconnect Reference Model

are compatible. For compatibility to occur, both nodes must also conform to identical protocols that, in turn, conform to the OSI model.

During your study of the OSI model, keep in mind that we are not talking about something physical. The model is merely a graphical representation to which we can reference the various functions that are required to connect different devices together. Each protocol is a software program, running at specified addresses in the memory of a computer, that directs the processing of data as it passes through the layer associated with the protocol.

A protocol, running in memory, may also contain software *device drivers* used to control a specific piece of hardware. When all of the protocols used on a specific network device are installed, they must then be bound to the hardware devices they control. Binding combines the hardware device drivers and protocol programs.

Layer 1: Physical Layer

Layer 1 of the OSI model is concerned with the physical medium used to connect devices on a network. Connectors, cables, and transmission modes are defined on layer 1. The sizes, shape, and location of cable connectors and their pin locations are specified. Physical medium construction details are specified. The data encoding method, voltage and current magnitudes, and timing characteristics used on the physical medium are defined in layer 1.

Network Interface Cards (NICs)

NIC is Network Interface Card.

A **NIC** is the layer 1 hardware device installed in or attached to each computing device connected to the network. Its purpose is to provide an interface between the network and the software running in the computer in which the NIC is installed. NICs normally provide service for both layer 1 and layer 2 of the OSI model. That part of a NIC that is used on layer 1 includes service for setting the electrical characteristics of the data transmission and the physical connection of the computing device to the physical medium.

Layer 1 Standards

Numerous standards are associated with the physical layer. Some of the more commonly used standards include the following:

- RS-232C/D—serial interface used with data speeds less than 56 Kbps. RS-232C is most commonly connected to network device communications (comm) ports and the lines running to modems connected to the telephone company (telco) service provider.
- CCITT V.35—serial interface used in place of RS-232 for data speeds greater than 56 Kbps. The CCITT equivalent to RS-232C is V.34.
- Cable standards—for twisted pair, coaxial cable, and fiber optic cable. Chapter 3 will present standards for the numerous cable types that are

used in connecting the physical layer components. Additional techniques exist to implement the physical layer over radio waves, microwave, satellite, and both infrared and laser beams.

Layer 2: Data Link Layer

Layer 2 is responsible for the transmission of data between devices on a network. It provides the mechanism for access to the physical medium and higher layers. In addition to providing the connection to layer 1 physical media, NICs also contain the layer 2 devices that provide the mechanism for creating *frames* of data that add fields of information to the raw data for addressing, frame control, and error detection.

According to RFC1122, *frame* is defined as "the unit of transmission in a [data] link layer protocol that consists of a [data] link layer header followed by a packet [of data bits]." The detailed construction of data frames is presented in the chapters for each of the layer 2 protocols: Ethernet, Token-Ring, ARCNET, and FDDI. Layer 2 has been further defined by IEEE standard 802.2, which will be presented in detail later in this chapter. Specific packet assembly details are included in the chapters that deal with the network and transport layers of the OSI model.

Layer 3: Network Layer

IEEE standard 802.1 defines layers 3 through 7 and internetworking between networks using different layer 2 protocols. Layer 3 protocols assemble packets of data and determine packet routing between networks. According to RFC1122, *packet* is defined as "the unit of data passed across the interface between the [network] layer and the [data] link layer." When referring to data on layer 3 and higher, use the term *packet*. When referring to data on layers 1 and 2, use the term *frame*.

Because the destination of the data may be on a different LAN altogether, it falls on the network layer to deal with routing from network to network, switching to connect to different points, and congestion on busy network devices as packets are sent from source node to final destination.

Because the protocols used on layers 3 and 4 are the same on all devices, it is possible for local area networks to use different protocols. For example, on the global Internet, every device that connects to the Internet uses TCP at layer 4 and IP at layer 3. My local area network can then use Ethernet on layers 1 and 2, whereas your LAN uses Token-Ring. The most important point to remember is that all devices must use the same TCP/IP protocol.

A hardware device called a *router* is used to determine the path used to transfer packets of data between networks. Routers may also be used to provide the connection point between networks that use different protocols on layer 1 and layer 2. My Ethernet LAN has a router that uses Ethernet to connect to devices on my LAN using layers 1 and 2, but it employs a wide-area public telephone system protocol such as Frame Relay or ATM to connect to the router that is on your Token-Ring LAN. Of course, the Token-Ring router must use the same public telephone system protocol as the Ethernet router, and both routers and all devices needing to connect to both networks must use the same transport and network layer protocols, as shown in Figure 2.2.

To summarize, layers 1 and 2 provide for data frame flow between network devices that use the same protocol. Layers 3 and 4 deliver packets of data between network devices using different protocols.

Layer 4: Transport Layer

The transport layer provides for the end-to-end reliability, sequencing, and acknowledgment of packets sent across the network. Because it is possible for packets to arrive at their destination out of sequence owing to multiple paths available through a given network, layer 4 protocols add a sequence number to the packet. This allows the destination device to reassemble packets in the correct order. In addition, an acknowledgment of the receipt of a packet or group of packets is expected. If a packet arrives at its destination with an error in it, a no-acknowledgment is returned to the sender, and the packet may be resent. In this way, layer 4 protocols ensure that packets are correctly received by the intended destination device.

Common protocols associated with layers 3 and 4 that will be explained in more detail in upcoming chapters are

- Novell NetWare's IPX/SPX,
- the Internet protocol TCP/IP (TCP is the transport layer and IP the network layer), and
- IBM's NETBEUI (the default protocol used by Microsoft NT).

Layer 5: Session Layer

When two network nodes "connect," it is the session layer that manages the dialogue between the nodes. Protocols running at layer 5 open a dialogue ses-

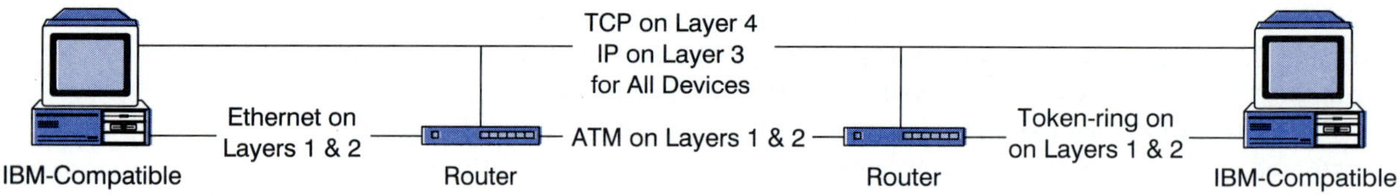

Figure 2.2 Connecting Networks Using Different Protocols

sion and terminate it when finished. A dialogue session should not be confused with the layer 2 functions that send data frames from source to destination node. Node names and addresses are translated at the session layer, and the necessary synchronization functions between nodes is provided.

Layer 6: Presentation Layer

Layer 6 provides the translation required to send the correct syntax for screen presentations and data passed between nodes. The presentation layer also provides data encryption and compression, if used. MS-DOS and the core protocols of network operating systems such as Novell NetWare, IBM LAN Server, and Microsoft NT and LAN Manager operate at the presentation layer.

Layer 7: Application Layer

Application programs run in the application layer. Network services such as electronic mail, remote or shared databases and resources, and file transfers are provided to end users by programs run in the application layer. When a user logs into a network, it is a program running in the application layer that is "seen" by the user. The reader should understand that all programs running in a computer technically operate at the application layer. In networking, we refer to software that is controlling lower layers as running on the layer being controlled. TCP, for example, is said to be a layer 4 protocol because it is controlling the layer 4 functions.

DETAILED LAYER SPECIFICATIONS

IEEE 802.2

Now that you have seen the basics of the seven-layer model, we can begin to fill in the details. Layer 2 of the OSI model has been divided into two sublayers by the IEEE 802.x standards. Standard 802.2 deals directly with the Logical Link Control (**LLC**) sublayer, and the 802.3, 802.4, 802.5, and 802.6 standards describe the specific protocols for the Media Access Control (**MAC**) sublayer. The 802.3 through 802.5 standards will form the basis for the chapters on the various protocols for LANs such as Ethernet and Token-Ring.

LLC is Logical Link Control.

MAC is Media Access Control.

LLC Sublayer

The concept of an LLC sublayer was introduced with the original Token-Ring. Its purpose is to provide access and throughput between the MAC sublayer protocol and the network layer. Additionally, it is the function of the LLC to open and close a session between nodes. Do not confuse an LLC session with the session layer—they are two different kinds of sessions.

There are three types of LLCs:

Figure 2.3 LLC Protocol Data Unit

DSAP ADDR 8 bits	SSAP ADDR 8 bits	Control 8/16 bits	Information *N*-8/16 bits

N is a function of the method used to control MAC access where a value of 0 or greater determines the number of bits used.

- *Type 1*—unacknowledged, connectionless services. These are simple broadcast or datagram services that are sent in the blind with no expectation for response or acknowledgment.
- *Type 2*—connection-oriented services. These are logically connected services that provide sequencing and acknowledgment, error control, and flow control. Type 2 LLCs must be connected before data are sent and disconnected at the end of a data transfer session, which makes them very reliable.
- *Type 3*—acknowledged connectionless services. Datagram-oriented services, similar to type 1 but with acknowledgment of receipt. No attempt is made to provide error control or flow control.

SAPs are Service Access Points.
DSAP stands for Destination Service Access Point.
PDU is Protocol Data Unit.
SSAP is Source Service Access Point.

Access between layers 2 and 3 is provided via *Service Access Points* (**SAPs**). A SAP is nothing more than an address, sometimes called a *port* for a specific type of service within a given protocol. Figure 2.3 shows a typical LLC *Protocol Data Unit* (**PDU**). The PDU begins with two 8-bit fields for *Destination Service Access Point* (**DSAP**) and *Source Service Access Point* (**SSAP**), respectively.

Table 2.1 lists commonly used SAP values. In most cases, the SAP value in both source and destination would be identical for a given event since both nodes must use the same protocol. To be in conformance with the OSI model, designers must use the correct SAP.

Table 2.1 SAP Descriptions

HEX	Description	HEX	Description
00	Null	E0	NetWare
02	Individual LLC (sublayer management)	F0	NETBIOS (Lanmanager, NT)
03	Group sublayer management	F4	LAN management (individual)
04	SNA path control (individual)	F5	LAN management (group)
05	SNA path control (group)	F8	IBM remote program load
06	IP	FE	ISO network layer
80	3COM XNS	FF	Global
AA	SNAP (TCP/IP)		

An LLC PDU can take one of three forms:

- *Information* (I)—used to provide sequential data transfers. I format contains a sequence number that is used to sequence packets and an acknowledgment bit to confirm data transfers. It is used for type 2 LLC only.
- *Supervisory* (S)—supervises the exchange of I frames; also used for type 2 LLC only.
- *Unnumbered* (U)—used to connect and disconnect the logical link and issue simple broadcast frames

MAC Sublayer

As previously stated, the MAC sublayer is defined by the specific protocol being used. Common MAC protocols include the following:

- 802.3—Ethernet
- 802.4—Token Passing Bus (ARCNET conforms, in part, to 802.4.)
- 802.5—Token-Ring
- 802.6—MAN, fiber-based Dual Queue Dual Bus (DQDB).

Figure 2.4 shows the generic format for a MAC frame. As shown, the MAC frame is only a part of the total frame. Both Ethernet and Token-Ring begin a MAC frame with timing and control information followed by destination and source addresses. Additional control information may be added for protocol-specific purposes following the addressing. The data field is next, followed by yet additional control information and a frame check sequence field used to ensure that the frame was passed correctly.

ENCAPSULATION

As data packets pass down through the layers of the OSI MODEL, each layer adds its own information in the form of a *header*. In most protocols the LLC PDU, with all of the higher-layer headers attached, is completely *encapsulated* or encased within the MAC frame. At this point, the frame can be sent across the physical media to its intended destination.

MAC Frame 802.x

Timing	Control	Destination Address	Source Address	Control	Data	Control (opt)	Frame Check Sequence

Figure 2.4 Generic MAC Frame

For example, an E-mail application might send a message to a network user. The message is divided into conveniently sized packets of data. Packet size is determined by the protocol in use. The protocol installed at the application layer 7 adds its header to the data packet so that layer 6 knows where the data came from, how to process the data, and to which layer the data should next flow. Each lower layer, in turn, adds its own information until the original block of data arrives at its intended destination. By the way, it is not always necessary for a packet to use all of the layers if no protocol is installed for a given layer.

Conversely, as frames are passed from lower to higher layers, each layer strips its header off, decodes the information contained therein, and passes the frame on to the next higher layer. In our E-mail example, this process would take place when the destination user received the packet of data and passed it up the layers to its own E-mail program. The end result might produce a message on your screen notifying you that you have mail. Figure 2.5 demonstrates the concept of encapsulation.

At this juncture, a very important point should be repeated. Within a LAN, *all* nodes must conform to the same MAC layer protocol. For devices using differing protocols to communicate, both the LLC and MAC information must be removed, and only the data link layer PDU passed on to the net-

Figure 2.5 Encapsulation of Frames

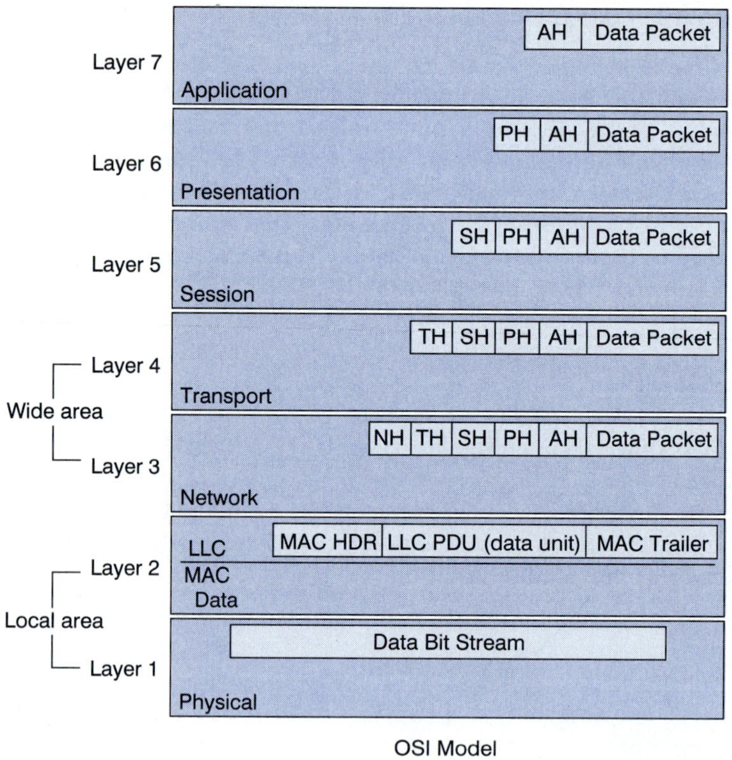

work using a different protocol. This function is usually accomplished by routers that transmit a frame from one network node to a node on a different network. When the router forwards the data to another router, the data packet is encapsulated in the new data link layer protocol.

Because it appears, at the data layer, that the network layer header is placed inside of the MAC header, the encapsulation process is sometimes called *tunneling*. Additional details on the subject of routing will be provided in later chapters.

TOPOLOGIES

Topology is the term used in networking to provide a physical or logical description of the layout of a given network. The physical components of topologies consist of similar basic components:

- The physical cabling or *medium* used to transport the data signals from point to point within the network
- An NIC that encodes data frames for transmission on the physical medium and decodes incoming frames. In both Ethernet and Token-Ring, two forms of a technique called *Manchester coding* are used for this purpose.
- A protocol that determines the format in which packets are assembled and disassembled, the form that addressing of nodes will take, and the method used to control events on the network. In most cases the protocol is implemented by a software driver that controls a chip set on the NIC.
- Hardware platforms such as user workstations (personal computers), network servers, bridges, routers, and gateways that contain the NIC. Each of these devices will be dealt with individually throughout the book.

Manchester Coding

Figure 2.6 shows a wave form diagram of the Manchester coding technique used in Ethernet. Note that each bit cell time is identical and set to the transmission rate defined in the protocol being used (in practice, how fast the NIC sends and receives data). Logical ones and zeros are determined by detecting wave form transitions in the center of the cell. If the transition is from zero to one, the bit is a logical one; conversely, a one to zero transition is a logic zero. Because a wave form transition occurs in each cell at a precise time, the transitions can be used for timing purposes. NICs are thus required to generate timed data when transmitting only. Receiving stations need only adjust to the timing of the sending station.

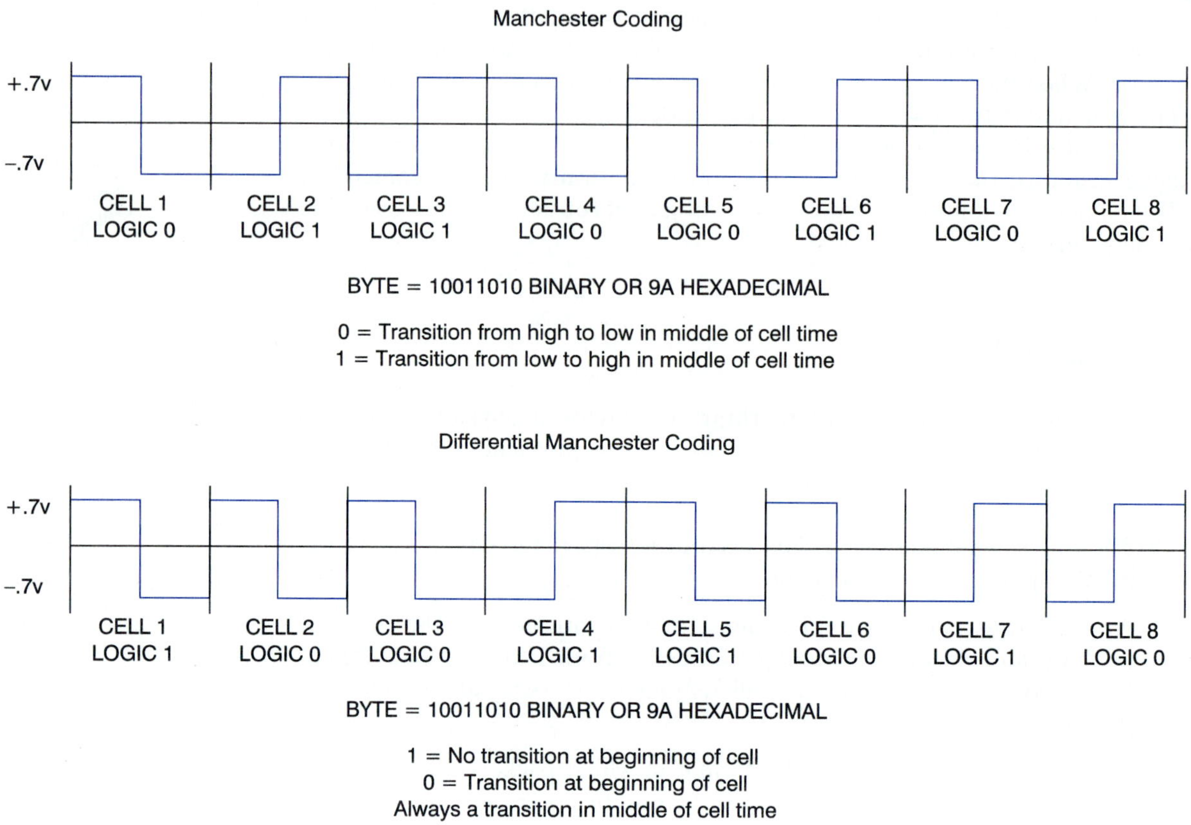

Figure 2.6 Manchester Coding Example

A modification called *differential Manchester coding* is used in Token-Ring. Differential Manchester coding results in a transition for all logic ones, but no transition change takes place for a zero. Note that there is a transition in the middle of every cell, but the transition that is used for determining the logic of a bit occurs at the beginning of a cell. Causing a transition in the middle of each cell improves the ability to maintain timing synchronization.

Star

Figure 2.7 shows a generic star topology. Note that all of the network nodes are connected to a central hub that may or may not provide control functions. Nearly all protocols can be implemented, at least in part, in a star topology. It is a common practice to "stack" hubs by connecting them in a daisy chain fashion (see Figure 2.8). This is done either to extend the distance between hubs or to allow more workstations to connect to the LAN.

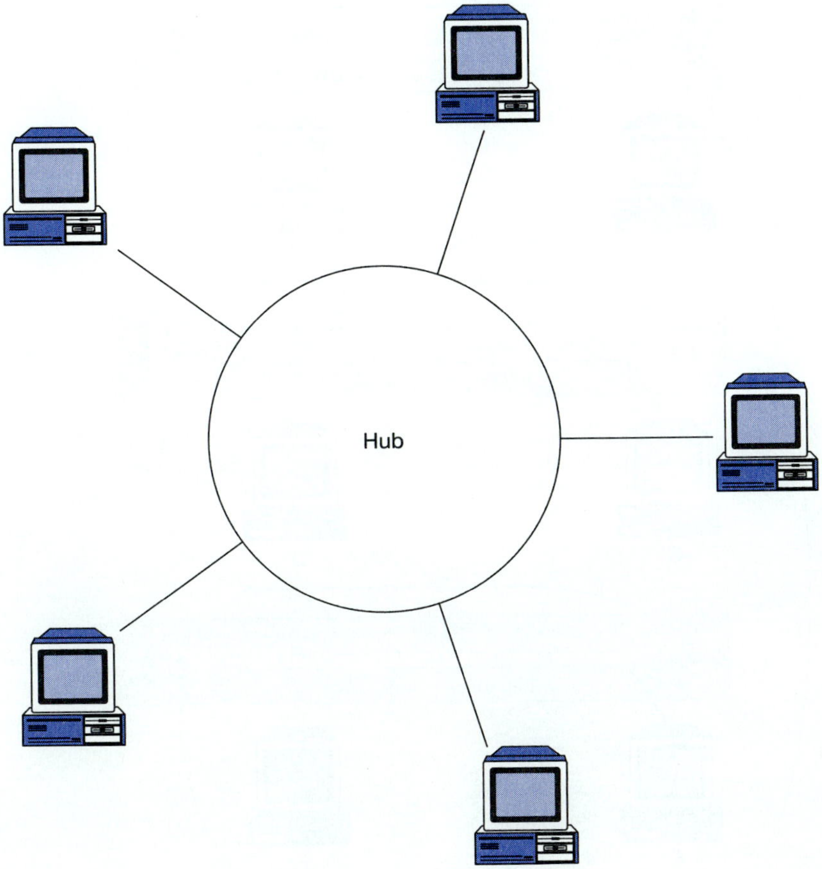

Figure 2.7 Star Topology

Ring

Figure 2.8 diagrams a ring topology. In a ring, one of the nodes acts as a controller to initiate and maintain timing. Each node on the ring must wait for its turn to access the physical medium. Perhaps the most common implementation of the ring topology is the Token Passing Ring. Note, however, that while the "ring" portion of Token-Ring is implemented through the hub and all NICs, nodes may appear connected in a star fashion, making Token-Ring appear a hybrid topology.

Common Bus

Figure 2.9 depicts a common bus topology. In common bus any node may attempt access to the physical medium at any time. Because the likelihood of data "collisions" due to multiple access is high, some method must be created

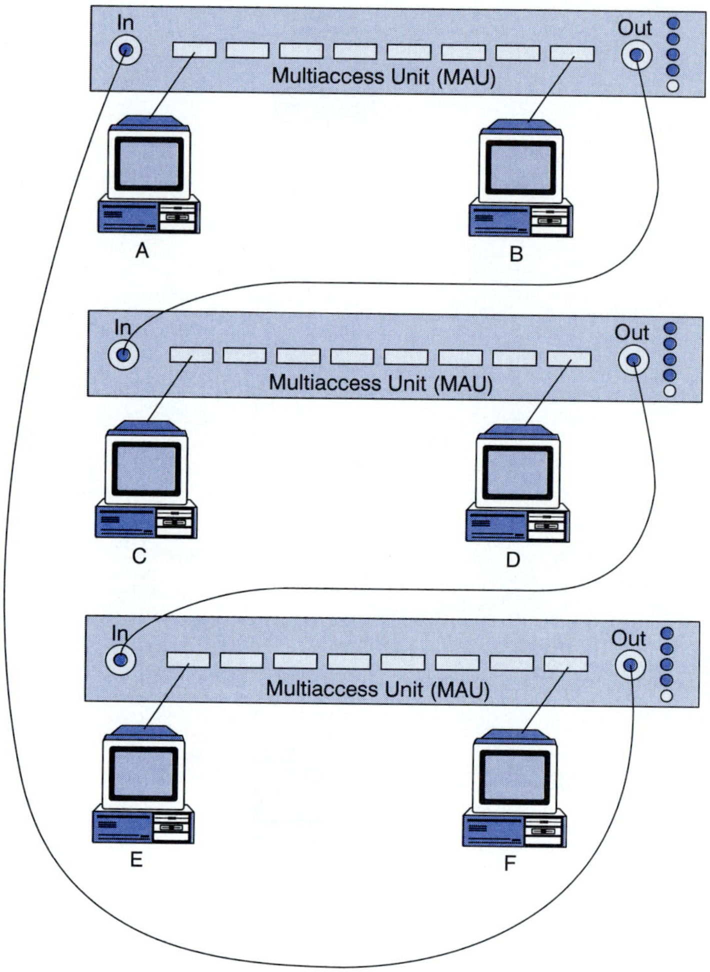

Figure 2.8 Ring Topology

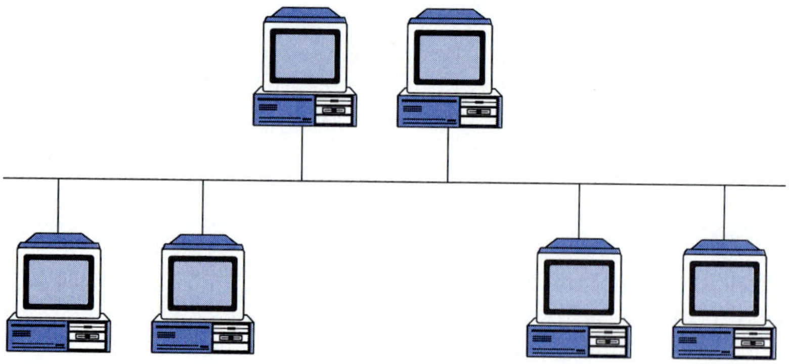

Figure 2.9 Common Bus Topology

to test the bus for activity before access is attempted. Two of the common techniques are *Carrier Sense Multiple Access/Collision Detection* (CSMA/CD) implemented in Ethernet and the Token Passing Bus scheme used by ARCNET. Each of these protocols will be analyzed in later chapters.

BRIDGING

A device called a *bridge* is used to connect LANs using identical protocols. Figure 2.10 is a diagram that shows two ring topology LANs being connected. The primary goal of a bridge is to pass only those frames that are not on a local segment to the bridged segment. In this manner, large and congested LANs may be segmented to reduce congestion. There are actually three bridging techniques that are commonly used, each of which is described in the following sections.

Transparent Bridges

Transparent bridges use the Spanning Tree Protocol defined in IEEE 802.1D. These bridges contain tables of addresses of known nodes in the LANs connected to them. At periodic intervals of about 30 seconds, transparent bridges will broadcast their table contents to each other, thus sharing the addressing information. The process used to create the address tables begins with a workstation sending a broadcast message to determine whether a destination node is active. An example might be \\LAN_TECH_SERVER, a server in another LAN. Because the bridge, initially, has no such entry in its address table, it will pass the frame and copy the address to its table if \\LAN_TECH_SERVER answers by sending a frame back to the source workstation. If the requested node fails to respond, the bridge terminates the frame to prevent an endless broadcast storm. The originating workstation eventually times out waiting for a response and reports the unavailability to the user.

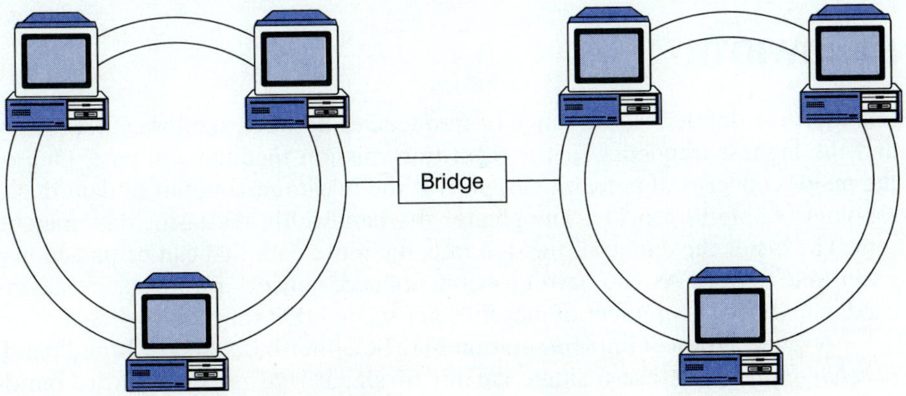

Figure 2.10 Diagram Showing Two Bridged LANs

Source Routed Bridge

RIF is Routing Information Field.

This technique requires a *Routing Information Field* (**RIF**) in the MAC frame. It falls to the workstation to enter the routing information into the RIF field. In this manner, the bridge need only insert the bridge address in the RIF field and pass the frame to the addressed LAN node without taking the time to look up the path in a table. To prevent endless looping in the event the destination node is not available, the bridge will terminate the frame if it sees its own address in the RIF field.

Translational Bridge

This bridge is used to connect LANs with differing protocols. As its name implies, the bridge translates the MAC protocol information from source to destination. As of the writing of this text, only the IBM 8209 bridge offers protocol translation.

Path Control

An important distinction should be made to determine which layer controls the path that a frame or packet will take. Figure 2.11 shows a diagram of three connected LANs. Two of the LANs are bridged Token-Ring LANs and the third, an Ethernet LAN, connected by routers. Within LANs of identical protocols, up to the input port of the router, data delivery is controlled by the LLC sublayer. Between LANs of differing protocols or LANs connected by routers, sequencing and acknowledgment of data packets is controlled by the network and transport layers. Remember, however, between routers there must also be a data link layer protocol controlling the routing path and delivery mode between routers just as there would be on any network. Routers therefore have the ability to connect to data/physical layers using two different protocols: one for the router port connected to the LAN and another for the router port connected to another router or routers.

BANDWIDTH

Bandwidth is defined as the range of frequencies between the lowest frequency and the highest frequency that a given transmission medium will pass. One of the major concerns of network designers is the maximum amount of data that a topology is able to provide. The greater the bandwidth, the faster data may be sent. The faster the data transmission rate, the more data that can be passed in a given time period. As you have probably noticed, network protocols are advertised, in part, by the number of megabits per second that they can process.

A given protocol implementation may be either baseband or broad band. *Baseband* protocols use a single carrier or signal that uses the entire band-

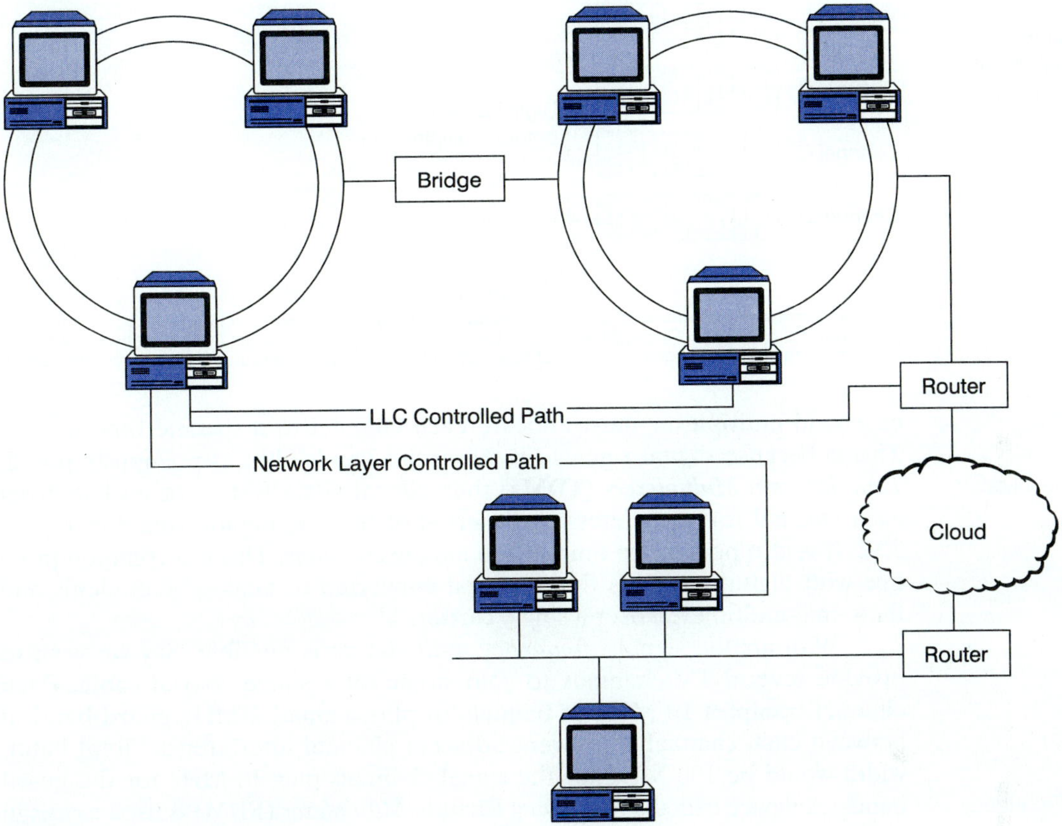

Figure 2.11 Path Control

width. Baseband protocols are primarily digital, and digital protocols are always baseband. Packets or frames may be sent at the fastest speed that the physical medium is capable of, but only one packet at a time may be sent on a baseband network. Examples of baseband implementations are the common Ethernet and Token-Ring.

A *broadband* topology has sufficient bandwidth to allow multiple channels to run on the same physical medium at the same time without interfering with each other. An example of a broadband implementation is CATV, in which a broadband coaxial cable is used to transmit multiple television channels simultaneously. Broadband protocols will always be analog.

Multiplexing

In both baseband and broadband, it is possible to pass multiple channels of information across the medium using techniques known as *multiplexing*. A

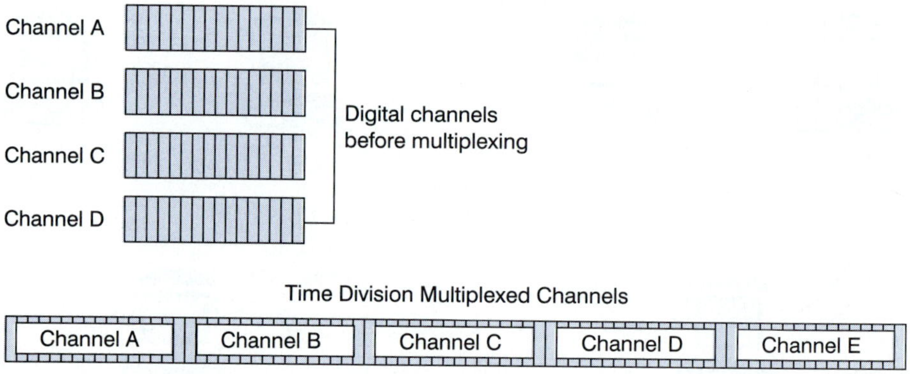

Figure 2.12 Time Division Multiplexing. Note that each channel is repeated at the correct time.

TDMs are Time Division Multiplexers.

baseband multiplexer must allocate each channel to a specific time period. This is because digital signals fill the entire bandwidth, as previously noted. *Time Division Multiplexers* (**TDMs**) then allocate data frames or packets from each channel for a predetermined period of time, as demonstrated in Figure 2.12. It is also possible to time-divide analog channels. This is a common practice with digital channels that are first converted to analog by modems and then time-multiplexed over a single carrier.

FDM means Frequency Division Multiplexer.

With analog signals, *frequency multiplexing* is possible. Say we wish to provide several TV channels to your home on a single coaxial cable. Each channel occupies 10 MHz of bandwidth plus a small 2-MHz guard band in between each channel to prevent adjacent channel interference. Total bandwidth would be 100 MHz for the signal channels plus 18 MHz for the guard bands. A device called a *Frequency Division Multiplexer* (**FDM**) is used to assign each channel and guard band to the correct band of frequencies within the overall bandwidth. Figure 2.13 shows how each channel is assigned. In the case of both time and frequency division multiplexers, appropriate demultiplexers are used to convert or divert the channels to their original time or frequency.

CHAPTER REVIEW

- OSI seven-layer reference model

  Layer 1—physical layer

  Includes cables, connectors, transmission encoding/decoding.

  Layer 2—data link layer

  Is responsible for reliable end-to-end delivery of data in a LAN

  The 802.2 standard defines Logical Link Control to guarantee sequencing and acknowledgment of data transfers and the Medium Access Control that consists of the specified protocol.

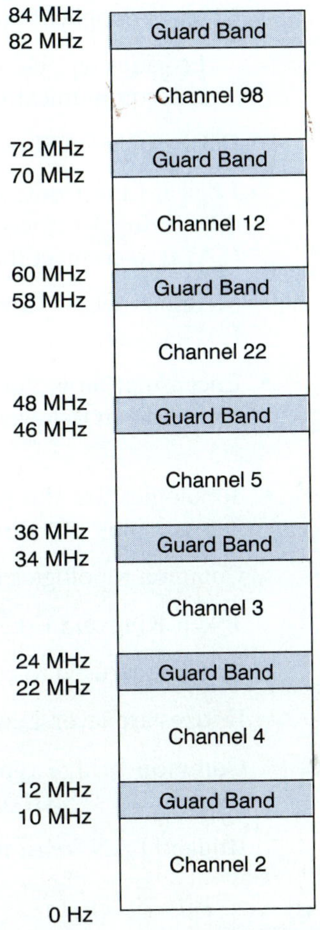

Figure 2.13 Channel Assignments for Broadband CATV Using Frequency Multiplexing

Layer 3—network layer

Is responsible for routing packets between layers

Routers are the layer 3 devices.

Layer 4—transport layer

Provides the sequencing and acknowledgment for data packets transferred between networks

Layer 5—session layer

Opens and terminates dialogue sessions between network nodes

Layer 6—presentation layer

Provides translation and screen form services

Layer 7—application layer

Provides shared services such as E-mail, log-in, databases, printing, and communications

- IEEE 802.2—defines the layer 2 LLC and MAC sublayers

  Logical Link Control (LLC) provides the end-to-end delivery of frames containing Protocol Data Units (PDUs) plus Service Access Points (SAPs) to connect the MAC sublayer to the network layer.

  Medium Access Control (MAC) is the specific protocol chosen for the LAN.

- Encapsulation is the technique that adds headers to packets as they are passed down to lower layers or stripped off when passed up to higher layers

- Topologies are the physical methods used to interconnect devices on a network plus encoding and decoding of data on the physical medium.

  Common topologies include ring, star, and bus.

  Token-Ring and Ethernet use Manchester coding.

- Bridges are used to connect LANs together.

  Bridges are layer 1 and 2 devices.

  Common bridge types include Transparent "Spanning Tree," source route bridges (SRBs), and translational bridges.

  Bridged LANs *must* use identical protocols or use translational bridges.

APPLICATION PROJECTS

Project 1

Make an appointment with the LAN administrator in your school or company to take a tour of a LAN implementation. As you make your tour, answer the following questions:

1. What topology does the LAN use?
2. What protocol does the LAN use?
3. What is the LAN's physical medium?
4. Is the physical medium baseband or broadband?

5. What kinds of devices are connected to the LAN?

   Workstations

   Hubs

   Printers

   Routers

   Bridges

   Repeaters

   Switches

   Other

6. Is the LAN connected to other LANs? If so, how?
7. What is the LAN's main purpose?
8. What services does the LAN provide users?
9. What resources are shared by users on the LAN?
10. If the LAN has a server, what operating system does it use?

Project 2

This project assumes that students are familiar with the use of MS-DOS or Windows and the use of serial ports, which are not covered in this book. The objective is to connect two microcomputers together via their serial ports. Using the Interlink programs that are supplied with MS-DOS 6.x or any other serial link programs, copy a large file from one computer to the other. (This may also be done using Apple computers. See your Apple manuals for specific requirements.) Measurements may be taken to evaluate the time necessary to transfer a known quantity of data.

1. Set the serial ports to the fastest setting your computers are capable of. This will be 9,600 bps for 8250-based serial cards or 115 Kbps for 16550-based cards. It is critical that both computers run their serial ports at the same speed. You must consult your computer's manuals to determine what serial port speeds your PCs will run at.

2. Connect the machines to each other. **Caution:** Be certain *not* to connect the interface cable to any IBM-style female ports. To do so will destroy those ports. IBM compatible serial ports are male 25 pin or 9 pin only. The serial interface cable must be a "null modem" cable. Apple users must use appropriate null modem cables for the Apple serial interface.

3. The file transferred should be at least 1 Mb in size to allow a reasonably easy time interval to measure. A series of files could also be transferred, but be certain to retain the same files, in their original sizes, to be used in later projects.
4. Carefully measure the time that is required to actually transfer the file (do not include setup time).
5. Create a report document that details your experiment. This report can be used later to compare timing with different LAN protocols. Your report should include
    - a diagram of the connection between computers,
    - setup specifications for the serial ports,
    - names of file or files that are transferred and the order of the transfers, and
    - a record of time measurements of at least three identical transfers.

TROUBLESHOOTING

Troubleshooting a problem with conformance to the OSI model generally falls into two categories:

- One or more of the hardware components of a network is not in conformance with one or more of the standards used in a given network.
- One or more of the software components of a network is configured for a protocol that is not compatible with other devices.

Careful attention to protocol conformance during the design and procurement phases will most often prevent nonconformance. Other suggestions include these:

- Ensure that all NICs on a given LAN segment are the identical brand and model. This is particularly true when mixing brand names. Slight differences in timing can produce unanticipated results.
- Most of the common protocols have evolved over time. Ensure that you are using the same version of each protocol. This problem is usually discovered when a newly installed machine fails to connect properly.
- Ensure that your new machine has all of the protocols in use on your network installed in it.
- Ensure that each protocol is correctly configured and that each device on your network has a unique address.

REVIEW QUESTIONS

1. What is the function of the ISO?
2. Briefly describe the purpose for the OSI model.
3. List each of the seven layers of the OSI model, and briefly describe the function of each layer.
4. List two common standards used in OSI layer 1.
5. How does Manchester coding improve the ability to accurately send data?
6. List at least three major standard-setting bodies, and describe the types of standards they deal with.
7. What is an NIC?
8. Briefly discuss the difference between a frame and a packet.
9. Define the term *LLC,* and list the three types of LLCs.
10. What is a SAP?
11. How is layer 2 divided?
12. List four of the IEEE standards that define MAC sublayers.
13. Discuss the concept of encapsulation.
14. What is the difference between baseband and broadband?
15. List the commonly used LAN topologies.
16. List three common protocols used in LANs.
17. Briefly describe the three kinds of bridges.

3

Installing the Physical Layer

INTRODUCTION

Most local area networks have a few things in common. Before installing a network, the designer must, for example, select a protocol that will meet the requirements of the organization as well as the individuals and applications using the network. The chosen protocol will determine the topologies that are available. Environmental factors such as distance between workstations, electrical interference, and building codes will determine the physical layer interconnect medium. If a file server is to be used, its operating system must be capable of supporting the LAN protocol.

This chapter will present selection considerations and requirements for

- building codes;
- cable selection and wiring;
- wire closets;
- cable trays, ducting, and conduit;
- bandwidth;
- environment;
- distance limitations; and
- network interface cards.

We will also touch on installation and testing processes for

- raceways, ducting, and conduit;
- initial wire runs;
- connectors;
- wiring concentrators and hubs; and
- servers.

BUILDING CODES

Most towns and cities have imposed strict requirements on the installation of wiring and cables. In some cities, network cable installers must be licensed low-voltage wiring installers. A licensed installer will have passed an examination and perhaps demonstrated competency on the job as an apprentice. The National Electric Code, available through the Government Printing Office, specifies acceptable standards for wiring. Article 800 lists communications cable requirements for telephone, telegraph, PBX, burglar alarms, and so forth, as well as code requirements for such things as physical separation between power and signal lines, insulation and sheathing, grounding, and lightning protection. Article 700 deals with fiber optic code requirements.

Some of the more common code requirements include the following:

- Vinyl insulation coating is rarely allowed in plenum (return air) spaces, which are often the easiest places to install wiring. Plenum cable using flame-retardant and nontoxic insulation such as Teflon® is usually required.
- Vertical shaft wire runs between floors may allow cheaper vinyl-coated cable, but at any point where the cable or conduit penetrates a floor or ceiling, your local fire code may require fire-stopping material to plug any holes.
- Increasingly, city building codes are requiring licensed, low-voltage installers to run network cables.
- Check both the National Electric Code and your local codes!

Marking codes required for cable include these:

- **CM**—Communications cable
- **CMR**—Riser rated cable (vinyl-covered cable used in vertical shaft wire runs)
- **CMP**—Plenum rated wire (usually Teflon® coated for use in the heating and air conditioning air return spaces in ceilings and overheads that is called the plenum air space)

See color insert Figure 1 for a photograph of cables and connectors.

CABLE SELECTION AND WIRING

The choice of cable type will be based on a number of factors:

1. Each LAN protocol only supports specific topologies and a specific topology only supports certain cable styles. Details of cable and connector construction will be presented as the book progresses.
2. Environmental factors must be considered such as
   - Electro Magnetic Interference (EMI) from motors, generators, engine spark plugs, and so forth;
   - Radio Frequency Interference (RFI) from transmitters, video displays, and other electronic equipment; and
   - Ground soil conductivity for equipment grounding and shielding.
3. External and underground cable and conduit should be suitable for their physical environment. In particular, underground cable should be "filled" to prevent corrosion.
4. Bandwidth requirements will further determine the types of cable that may be used.
5. Distance limitations of cable types will influence the choice of cable.

Topologies

- Star topologies are most often implemented in either *Unshielded Twisted Pair* (**UTP**) or *Shielded Twisted Pair* (**STP**), although the ARCNET protocol sometimes uses daisy-chained coax in a star fashion. FDDI workstations can be starred to a single device in which the FDDI ring topology is implemented. Only fiber optic cable is used in FDDI installations.

UTP is Unshielded Twisted Pair; *STP* is Shielded Twisted Pair.

- Ring topologies are usually implemented entirely within multistation access units, wiring concentrators, or hubs. A wiring concentrator is really just a single location, usually a rack-mounted box, in which most of a network's wiring is terminated so that it can be connected in the appropriate manner.
- Common bus topologies are most often implemented in coaxial cable although ARCNET and Artisoft's Lantastic® are capable of connecting workstations together in a daisy chain using twisted pair. Ethernet hubs are common bus internally.

Cable Standards

Cable selection is directly tied to the selected protocol as well as the environment in which the network must operate. Future chapters will explain the commonly used protocols in detail. For now, it is only important for you to associate the various cabling techniques and standards with the protocols they are used with.

There are a number of commonly used specifications to measure the quality of wiring for networking.

- *Impedance* is the measurement of the resistance to the flow of the data signals. Impedance is important because all of the devices connected to a network, including all points along the length of the cable plus any open ends of a cable, must have the same impedance. Otherwise, signals can be reflected back down the cable at any point where there is an impedance mismatch, causing distortion and loss of data.
- *Bandwidth* is the measurement that expresses the maximum range of frequencies that a cable is able to pass. Bandwidth is normally expressed in Hertz (Hz).
- *Data rate* is the rate, expressed in bits per second (bps), that data are sent down a cable.
- *Distance* refers to the maximum length of a cable segment that allows the maximum-rated bandwidth.
- *Gauge* describes the diameter of the metal conductor(s) in the cable using American standard wire gauge (AWG) sizing.

Commonly used cabling includes the following:

- *Unshielded Twisted Pair* (UTP) cable used to connect LAN devices. ANSI/EIA-586 rates UTP copper wire cable by category for speed and distance limitations. Impedance is 100 ohms. Typical wire gauges are 24 and 26; however, 22-gauge wire will sometimes allow small increases in the 100-meter distance limitation. Twisting the signal wire with a signal ground wire is done to improve the noise immunity of the pair. By carefully controlling the number of twists per inch and the way that multiple pairs are twisted around each other, the manufacturer can significantly improve the bandwidth of each pair.

POTS is Plain Old Telephone System.

Category 1—Voice and low-speed data only. Sometimes referred to as *Plain Old Telephone System* (**POTS**). US West, for example, sets a nominal distance limitation of 18,000 feet for voice grade pairs but limits bandwidth to 3,300 Hz. Analog modems are commonly used to achieve up to 9,600 bps real time, and up to 56 Kbps using data compression.

Category 2—Data to 4 Mbps (IBM does not recommend for Token-Ring)

Category 3—Voice and data to 10-Mbps Ethernet or 4-Mbps Token-Ring and up to 100 meters per segment.

Category 4—Voice and data to 20 Mbps and up to 100 meters per segment.

Category 5—The highest level rated at 100 Mbps over distances to 100 meters. Categories 3, 4, and 5 use four pairs in a single outer cladding. It should be noted that gigabit Ethernet is now being run over category 5 cable at up to 100 meters using all four pairs.

- *Shielded Twisted Pair* (STP) cable with characteristics similar to UTP but with the added protection from EMI and RFI provided by the conductive braided shield that encases the cable. Impedance is 150 ohms.
- *10BaseT*—10-Mbps baseband twisted pair; four-pair UTP or STP cable terminated in eight-pin RJ-45 connectors similar to the four-pin RJ-11s used on household telephones. Data rates to 1,000 Mbps are possible using category 5 UTP. 10BaseT installations are limited to a maximum distance of 100 meters per cable segment.
- *10Base2*—10-Mbps baseband coaxial cable. RG-58 coaxial cable terminated in BNC connectors. This is sometimes called “Thinnet” or “Cheapernet.” RG-59 (75-ohm) cable is used for ARCNET when installed in CATV networks. RG-62 (93 ohm) is used with ARCNET when installed in microcomputer-based networks. Cable segments are limited to 185 meters.
- *10Base5*—10-Mbps baseband 50-ohm coaxial cable terminated in either SO-239 or type N connectors. This is sometimes called “Thicknet.” “Ethernet” cable can be specified that is double-shielded and marked every 2.5 meters to show the precise locations for connection to the cable. RG-8 cable is a single-shielded, unmarked cable that may be used as a less expensive substitute. Cable segments may be up to 500 meters in length with a maximum of three segments unless using the IEEE 802.3 standard, in which case up to five segments may be used.
- *100BaseF*—100-Mbps baseband fiber optic cable and connectors. There are several different specifications available for fiber optics. Two cable types are used: multimode cable with LED transmitters and single mode with laser transmitters. Data rates in excess of 2 Gbps and distances to 50 miles are possible using single mode with laser transmitters. Fiber is also impervious to electromagnetic interference since light and not electricity is the transmission medium.

See the insert for color insert Figure 2, an RJ45 connector; color insert Figure 3, a 10Base2 “Thinnet” BNC connector and coaxial cable; and color insert Figure 4, a 10Base5 “Thicknet” type N connector on double-shielded “Ethernet” coaxial cable.

Cable Selection Based on Protocols

- Ethernet, covered in Chapter 4, supports either common bus or star topologies. Within a common bus, either 10Base5 Thicknet or 10base2 Thinnet are possible. IEEE 802.3 originally specified coaxial cable in a common bus but was later expanded to include twisted pair cable using 10BaseT in a combination of star and common bus.
- Token-Ring, covered in Chapter 5, is a hybrid protocol because it combines two different topologies. The ring topology is always implemented within the multistation access units (MSAUs). All other nodes such as workstations and servers are connected to the MSAU in what appears to be a star fashion using UTP or STP. The electrical ring, however, is maintained out through each node and returned to the MSAU.
- ARCNET, covered in Chapter 6, can be implemented as a combination of common bus or star in either RG-62, 93-ohm coaxial cable or twisted pair.
- Fiber Distributed Data Interface (FDDI) is implemented with fiber optic cable in a dual counterrotating ring topology only. Chapter 7 discusses FDDI.

Additional Considerations

- *Wire closets*—It is usually desirable to locate routers, gateways, servers, wiring concentrators, and multistation and media access units in centrally located, secure, and environmentally controlled rooms. These rooms, often called *wire closets*, should be centrally located, where possible, to minimize the length of wire runs. In multifloored buildings, the elevator shaft is often the best vertical access to floors. A middle-level floor should be selected and the wire closet located near the elevator shaft. The wire closet should contain adequate air flow and temperature control to prevent overheating of electronic equipment such as servers, routers, and concentrators. In addition, the wire closet should be a secure room with access limited to authorized personnel only.
- *Punchdown blocks*—At each workstation it is common to install a wall plate that contains an RJ-45 (*RJ* stands for "recommended jack") and a wire termination device called a *punchdown block*. Punchdown blocks are designed to speed the installation of multipaired cable. Each wire is pressed, using a *punchdown tool,* onto a lug type connector that is nothing more than two knife edges that cut through the insulation on each side of the wire and make electrical contact with the conducting wire itself. Color insert Figure 5 shows voice-/telephone-grade "66" punchdown blocks; color insert Figure 6 shows data-grade "110" punchdown blocks (photos courtesy AutoDesk, Inc.). Color insert Figure 7 shows well-designed and -installed data punchdown blocks and wiring.

TECHTIP

A note of caution about elevators. The motors and electrical systems that control elevators are excellent sources of RFI and EMI as well as noticeable vibration. It is advisable to use shielded cable or fiber and shock mounting for any equipment that is next to an elevator shaft.

- *Cable trays, ducts, raceways*—These devices are often installed in factories or industrial buildings that have open ceilings. The primary consideration in planning is to ensure that no cable is required to exceed its minimum bend limit. Low-voltage wiring should never be installed in the same trays, ducts, or raceways with high-voltage wiring. Prudent designers will plan for excess space in wire runs to allow for as much as 25%–50% growth. Unless required by code or security considerations, conduit should be avoided simply because even large conduit is difficult to pull long cables through, and only a relatively few cables can be run in each conduit. Conduit also adds significantly to the cost of the wiring plant.
- *Bandwidth*—Ethernet operates at 10 Mbps, 100 Mbps, or 1 Gbps; ARCNET at 1 to 2 bps; Token-Ring at 4, 16, or 100 Mbps; FDDI at 100 Mbps. Category 3-5 twisted pair, both Thicknet and Thinnet coaxial cable, and fiber optic cable will meet bandwidth requirements for Ethernet, ARCNET, and Token-Ring, although IBM does not recommend category 3 for 16-Mbps Token-Ring. If 100-Mbps fast Ethernet or Token-Ring are to be used, only category 5 twisted pair, coaxial, or fiber will handle the 100-Mbps speeds. FDDI requires fiber optic cable only.
- *Environment*—Electrical noise is a primary consideration. Environments that contain electrical motors and generators or radio transmitters will probably eliminate twisted pair as a reliable choice. Double-shielded 10base5 "Ethernet" coaxial cable provides adequate shielding in most cases. Although expensive, fiber optic cable is clearly the best choice for electrically noisy environments.

An additional environmental problem is encountered whenever a cable leaves a building. Specially waterproof coated and filled cable should always be used in underground runs even if the cable is in conduit. You would be amazed at the water standing in "sealed" underground conduits.

Care should be taken to adhere to the minimum specified radius of bends in cable runs. Fiber and coaxial cable are particularly sensitive to tight bends and abrasion. Kinks in any cable or scuffed insulation "shin-

TECHTIP

A seldom considered installation requirement is an adequate ground attachment. A poorly grounded network is highly susceptible to unwanted electrical noise particularly when cable segments are long. A well-grounded network is particularly important if you expect to connect your network to the telephone system.

A solid earth ground may be obtained by driving a solid copper rod at least 8 feet into the ground outside the building. In dry climates or in sandy soils, be certain to water your ground rod at least once each week. The metal I-beams used in commercial buildings are often a good ground.

Connect all metal duct, raceway, conduit, equipment chassis, and rack-mounted cabinets to the ground point with the largest diameter stranded or braided wire you can find. Relatively inexpensive 4-inch-wide copper grounding strap is also available and ideal for this purpose. Try to keep the connection from the ground point to equipment bays as short as possible. The longer the run, the fatter the cable or strap required. Inspect and clean ground connections yearly, more often in humid and salt air environments.

ers," where the braided copper shield or conductors are exposed, cause changes in the characteristic impedance that result in unpredictable null spots on the cable where signals cannot be received properly.

- *Distance*—It should be noted that distance limitations are established by the protocol being used. As new protocols and signaling techniques are developed, both distance and bandwidth are increasing. As implemented in 10BaseT, twisted pair is limited to 100 meters or less. Thinnet (RG-59 coaxial cable) allows 185 meters per segment and up to five segments for a total distance of 925 meters. Thicknet (RG-8 or double-shielded Ethernet coaxial cable) allows the same five segments, but with each segment at 500 meters, the total distance is increased to 2.5 km. Fiber comes in two forms, single mode and multimode. Distances between stations can be as much as 2 km for multimode and 100 km for single mode. A 30-station multimode fiber segment could be as long as 60 km; 3,000 km using single mode.

INSTALLATION PROCESSES

NIC Selection and Installation

Your selection of a network interface card will be driven by four criteria that must all be in conformance with each other:

- *Link Layer Protocol*—Ensure that the NIC is capable of running the protocol that your network uses and at the speed your network runs at.
- *Topology*—Match the connectors and impedance of the NIC to the cable system in use.
- *Workstation architecture*—Ensure that your workstation will support the I/O interface of the selected NIC.
- *Bandwidth*—Be certain to select a NIC that is able to run at the same speed as other devices on the network using the same protocol.

Most Ethernet and Token-Ring network interface card manufacturers adhere to a global addressing convention that ensures no two NICs will have the same address. This is particularly important if the NIC is connected to wide area networks or the Internet so that only one router will accept the NIC address, thus ensuring that the data are sent to the correct destination. If the global (also called *universal*) address convention is maintained, merely record the address and proceed with the installation. ARCNET is an exception in that ARCNET NICs have a switch that must be set for the NIC address. Care must be taken to ensure that no two NICs have the same address.

NICs also have settings for Interrupt ReQuest (**IRQ**), Direct Memory Access (**DMA**) channel, base I/O address, and sometimes the base address for a data buffer in memory. An interrupt request is sent to the CPU whenever the NIC needs to access the MAC layer. Using interrupts prevents the CPU from having to poll a NIC constantly to find out if it needs service.

IRQ means Interrupt ReQuest.
DMA stands for Direct Memory Access.

TECHTIP

- Settings for NICs used to be done with removable jumpers. Without a manual or well-labeled circuit board, this task was nearly impossible. Today's NICs are software-programmable. Without the manufacturer's diskette, the task may be totally impossible.
- If your NIC is using a PCI slot, there will be no setting for DMA because the PCI bus was designed to connect directly to the main memory bus.
- IRQ values are dynamically allocated by the PCI BIOS. PCI slots can be set to assign IRQ automatically; however, it may be preferable to configure your CMSO setup to allocate IRQ values manually. Ensure that the IRQ sharing feature is disabled. This lets you guarantee that there will be no conflicts with other cards.
- In PCs using MS-DOS and Windows 3.x, use MSD.EXE to discover settings on other system boards; in Windows 95, use the System Resources tab in the control panel; in Windows NT, use the diagnostics program in the Administration Tool Set.

When an interrupt request is granted by the CPU, data may be transferred directly to a memory data buffer. The DMA controller makes the direct connection between the NIC and memory so that data may be transferred directly to memory without having to be processed by the CPU.

The MAC layer software communicates with the NIC via its I/O address. Control information is sent to the NIC to tell it what to do. Once you have correctly configured the settings for your NIC, be certain to record the address and the location of the workstation in which the NIC is installed, plus the settings for the NIC.

When purchasing NICs, ensure that their connectors conform to your topology and cable requirements. A note of caution is in order to ensure that no other cards in a workstation use the same IRQ and DMA values. A conflict is created when more than one device uses the same IRQ number or DMA channel at the same time.

Cables and Wiring

With cables and wiring, preventive maintenance is the best insurance you can buy to guarantee that your wiring plant will perform correctly and continuously. The following tips will help ensure that your wiring plant will operate reliably.

- It is usually best to install cable trays, raceways, ducting, and conduit before any other equipment is installed. This approach will prevent damage to equipment if tools or parts are dropped by installers working above. Wall boards and punchdown blocks can usually be installed at the same time cables are being run. Baseboard ducting is a common technique where false ceilings are not available or where cables cannot be run inside walls.
- Pretest all cable while it is still on the reel. This ensures that you can exchange it under warranty.
- Ensure that cable runs have no sharp bends or kinks.
- Use care to prevent abrasions to insulation or braided shield.
- Ensure that connectors and punchdown blocks are correctly installed.
- Test installed cables for continuity and conformance to characteristic impedance prior to final connection to equipment.
- Once cables are run, all of the electronic equipment may be installed including servers, workstations, concentrators, and so forth.

Use the wiring diagrams for modular connectors as shown in Figure 3.1. Note that in most Ethernet LANs EIA/TIA standard 568B is used by patch panel manufacturers. Patch panels are used to allow components of a network

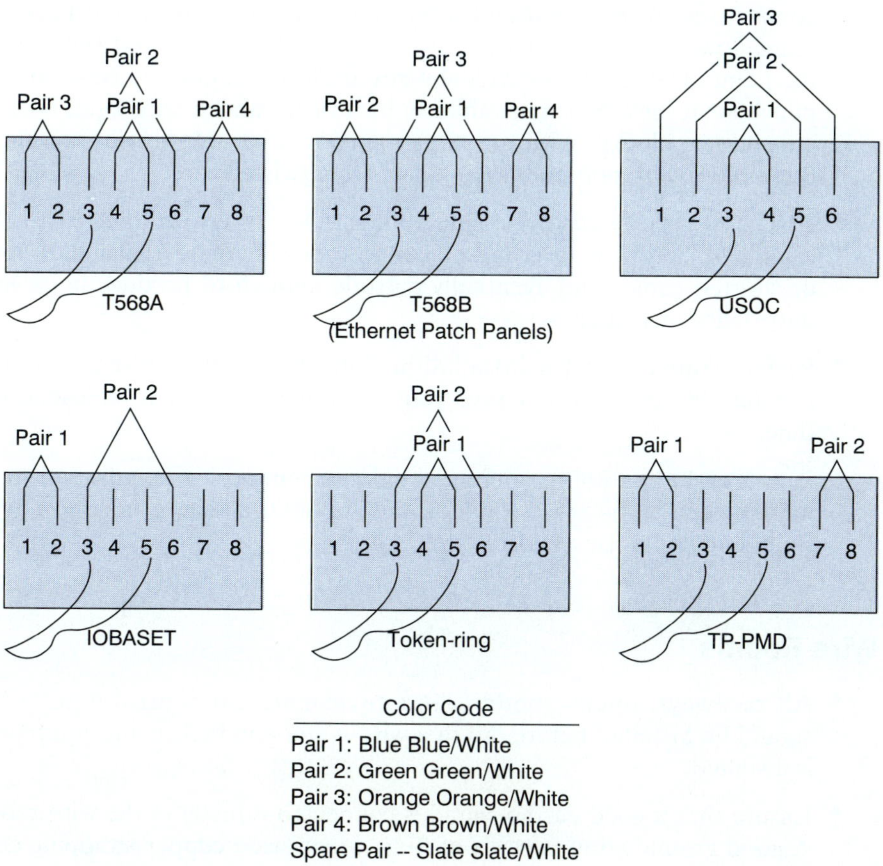

Figure 3.1 EIA/TIA Wiring Standards

to be easily connected at a central location by simply plugging in a short section of cable between the desired connections. If using patch panels, you must wire connectors to match the panel wiring scheme. You may often hear that an Ethernet LAN is wired to 10BaseT. Check the connector wiring to make certain it really is. There is a distinct difference between the wiring color code for 10BaseT and EIA586.

Connectors

Perhaps the single largest contributor to network failure is poorly installed connectors. Punchdown blocks are nearly as prone to mistakes. Particular attention should be paid to the following tips.

- The spacing and number of twists per inch in twisted pair cable is what determines the bandwidth and noise immunity factors. Great care *must* be taken to minimize the amount of wire that is untwisted when RJ-45 connectors are installed and when the outer cover is peeled back for punchdown block installation. Twists should be maintained right up to the point at which the individual wires are inserted into the RJ-45 or the punchdown lugs. Not more than ½ inch of untwisted wire is allowed at punchdown blocks. With practice, you should be able to wire a punchdown block with not more than ½ inch of untwisted wire.

- BNC and type N coaxial connectors should always be *soldered* to the cable end. Screw-on or crimp-on connectors will create a plague of open or shorted cables and eventually corrode enough to produce noise and impedance mismatches.
- Perfect your connector installation skills before attempting your first installation, and you may save yourself a great deal of troubleshooting time.
- Pay careful attention to minimum and maximum cable lengths and spacing between stations on common bus topologies. These measurements should be as precise as is practical.

Wire Rooms

- All raceways, ducts, conduit, and environmental control equipment should be installed before the first wire is run and before any equipment is installed.
- Ensure that a good earth ground is connected directly to the wire room. A good ground strap consists of 3- to 4-inch-wide copper strapping connected between the building ground plane and a 2- to 3-inch copper grounding bar that is run around the wire closet above the tops of the equipment bays. The ground plane should consist of solid copper rod(s) sunk to a minimum of 8 feet in normally moist earth or a buried copper mesh that covers as large a square footage as is possible. All equipment cases, raceways, ducting, and conduit should be connected to ground as well as any earth or chassis grounds on equipment.
- A common wire room installation technique is to install ¾- or 1-inch plywood on the wall(s) where media or multistation access units and punchdown blocks are to be installed.
- Servers, concentrators, and routers may then be installed in racks or cabinets bolted to the floor. Shock mounting is recommended near elevators or where there is noticeable vibration from heavy equipment or vehicles.
- You may wish to consider installing security devices to control entry and to warn of unauthorized access.

In the photograph in color insert Figure 8, you can see a nearly complete rack-mount installation. While the patch panels appear somewhat messy, if you look carefully, you will note that every cable is carefully labeled at *both* ends. This practice should be followed religiously with the cable numbers carefully recorded in the cabling master record. New installations often begin with the cable plan master record from which the installer must choose the correct number for each cable as it is installed and labeled.

In color insert Figure 8 you will also note the telephone sitting on the lower left-hand shelf. This should be an analog phone, connected to its own modem and telephone line and nothing else. Should the power go down for the building, knocking out all servers and the digital telephone system, you will still be able to communicate through an analog modem to remote sites. This is because the power for analog lines is supplied by the telephone company, whereas power for digital lines is supplied by the user.

Hand Tools

Most networks and PCs can be assembled and maintained with a few simple hand tools. Table 3.1 lists the necessary items. In all cases ensure that your tools are nonmagnetic. Although not suited for professional use, some very inexpensive "computer" tool kits are available that will do for the occasional repair job.

Table 3.1

Item	Description
Phillips screwdrivers	#3 (medium-sized and both long and short shafts) and #1or #2 (small "tweaker" size for connector and plug screw-downs).
Flat-blade screwdrivers	Same sizes as the Phillips.
Nut drivers	¼″, 3⁄16″, and 5⁄16″. A ¼″ socket set is a good substitute.
Torx screwdrivers	#4, #6, and #8 sizes are usually sufficient.
Wire strippers	One set for 22 to 30-gauge wire and another set for coaxial cables.
Wire cutters	One small pair and one "lineman" style for large cables.
Grabber	This is the long flexible tool used to "grab" the small screws, nuts, and other parts that are dropped into equipment.
Soldering iron	A small temperature-regulated iron is sufficient. Use resin-core solder only. Do not attempt to use unregulated irons—they are much too hot for small wire work.
Punchdown tool	Have one die for each style punchdown block.
Crimper, RJ-45, RJ-11	Dies for both RJ-11 and RJ-45 should be available. A second crimper is needed for coaxial connectors with dies for each size and style of cable to be used.

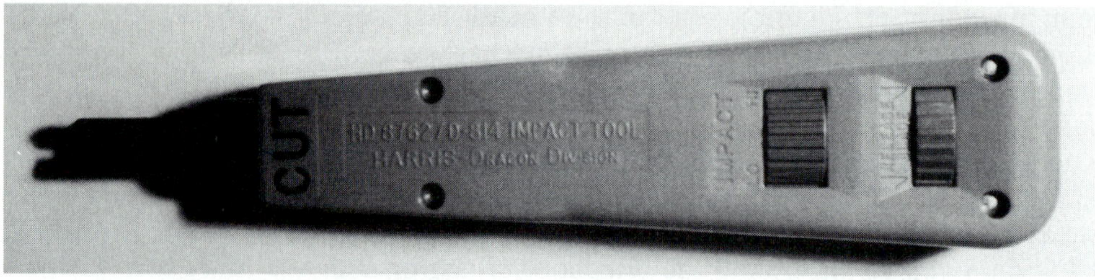

Figure 3.2a Punchdown Tool

Figure 3.2b Cabling Tools: left, coaxial cable crimpers with "Thinnet" dies; right, RJ crimpers. Dies are changed for each style of connector.

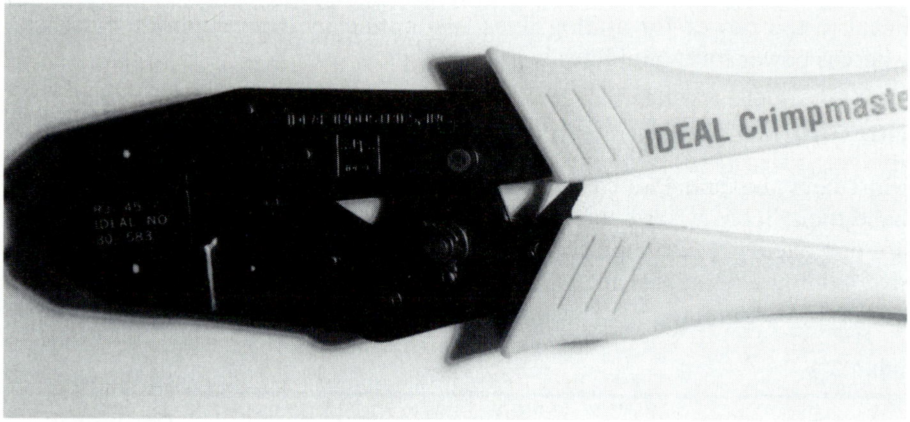

Figure 3.2a shows a punchdown tool. Figure 3.2b shows the crimpers used for BNC coaxial and RJ-45 connectors. These are nearly mandatory unless you are willing to outsource all of your network maintenance. For the most part, the crimpers are easy to learn to use, but practice on some old scraps of cable before you take on the real thing. A truly professional installation should only be done by experienced installers. To do otherwise will almost certainly result in unnecessary maintenance down the road.

The photographs shown in color insert Figures 9, 10, and 11 are of typical network installations.

Figure 3.3 diagrams a typical Ethernet installation in which the server NIC is connected to a hub with RG-58 coax and BNC connectors. The workstations are connected with UTP and RJ-45 connectors. By using BNC T connectors at the hub, additional hubs could be daisy-chained to accommodate additional workstations. Note that the open ends of the coaxial cable are terminated with 50-ohm terminators.

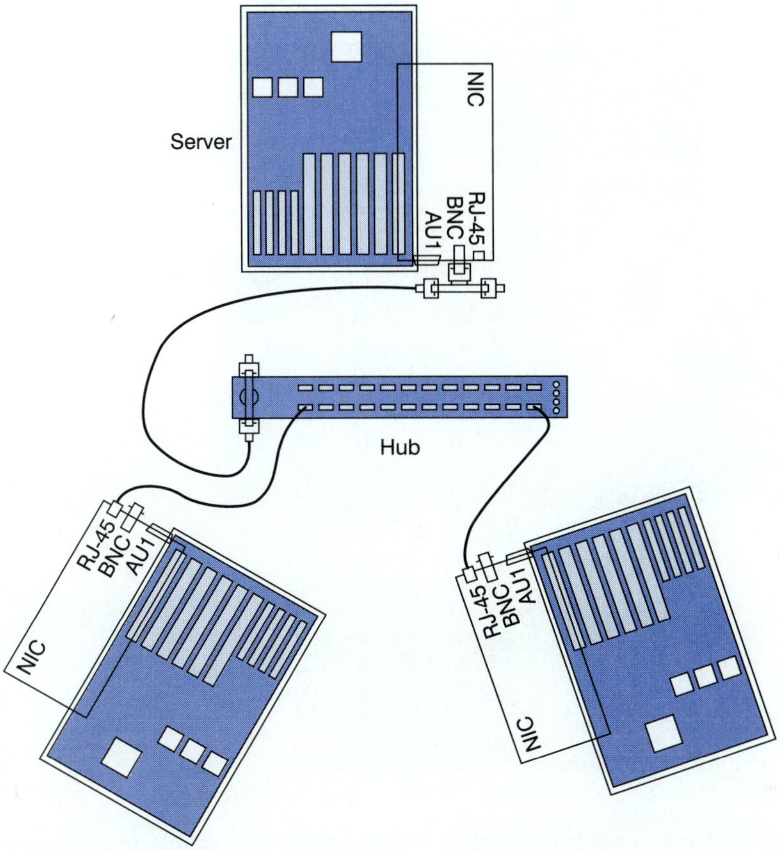

Figure 3.3 Typical Ethernet Installation

TESTING

Cable Testers

Numerous companies supply hand-held cable testers. Cables may be tested for continuity (good electrical connection from end to end), impedance (resistance to alternating current), and quality (the ability to transfer actual data). The following section lists some of the more common tools and methods for testing cables.

Breakout box. This tool is designed to allow the user to select the correct cable wiring for the RS-232 standard used between modems and the computer serial port. Breakout boxes may also be used to monitor activity on a serial

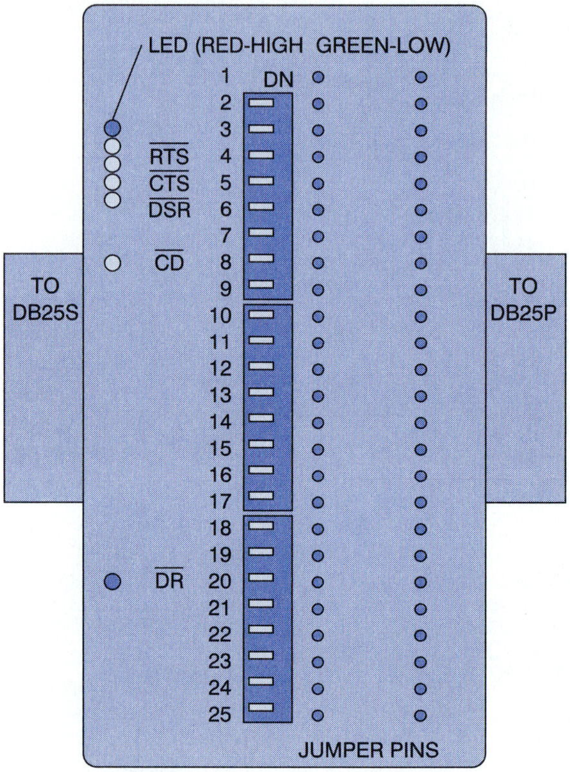

Figure 3.4 Breakout Box

port. A *smart cable* is simply a breakout box that is able to automatically determine the correct wiring for the equipment it is connected to. Figure 3.4 diagrams a simple breakout box.

BERT is Bit Error Rate Tester.

BERT. *Bit Error Rate Testers* (**BERTs**) are used to compare a known bit pattern to the reflected pattern that is the result of transmitting the pattern down the cable or cable network. A BER is calculated by dividing the number of error bits reflected by the total bits reflected. It is usually recommended that several measurements be taken at random intervals, along the cable, to ensure that a single measurement is not merely reflective of a single error that never reoccurs.

BKERT stands for Block Error Rate Tester.

EFS is for Error-Free Second.

BKERT. *Block Error Rate Testers* (**BKERTs**) provide a test based on the number of blocks of data that are reflected with a *bit* error in them. An additional test that may be made is to calculate the number of seconds in which no bit errors occurred. The *Error-Free Seconds* (**EFSs**) test is used by companies such as AT&T to measure a guaranteed line quality.

TDR is Time Domain Reflectometer.

TDR. *Time Domain Reflectometers* (**TDRs**) are used to provide a visual record of a cable or network of cables. These are analog instruments that send an electrical pulse of known timing and voltage down the cable and then record any changes that occur in the reflected signal. Faults such as shorts, opens, kinks, and shiners (abraded insulation) are easily seen. By measuring the time between the start of the pulse and the time at which waveform distortion occurs, the TDR will tell you where on the cable an error exits.

Cable analyzers. Today's cable analyzers are often handheld units that range from inexpensive continuity testers to expensive models that provide a combination of tests for a variety of cable types and protocols.

Standardized Test Procedure

Testing a new installation should be done at each stage of the installation and any problems corrected before the installation proceeds. The following is a time-tested methodology:

1. Test entire cable reels for continuity and with a TDR, if possible, before running any cable. Then test each cable for proper continuity as the connectors or punchdowns are installed. If a TDR is available, now is a very good time to use it.
2. Connect workstations, one at a time, and run the test that comes with the NIC software or your own commercial testing programs.
3. If you have access to a TDR, you can run a test of each completed cable run and the completed network installation before power is applied to any of the equipment. It is usually recommended that the results of this initial TDR measurement be recorded and filed as a reference against which future measurements may be compared. A good TDR will have a serial port so that it can be connected to a PC. This enables nearly automatic storing of TDR readings.
4. Leave each station connected and running as you connect the cable to the next station. It is not uncommon for a poorly installed connector to work with one workstation but not work when additional stations are added to the network. When the last workstation has been connected, perform a final check of all workstations to ensure that all are functioning correctly.

CHAPTER REVIEW

- Building codes

  National Electric Code Article 800 covers copper communications cable standards; Article 700 deals with fiber optic standards.

Use plenum-rated cable for all plenum air spaces. Vinyl insulation is used for risers, but many cities are requiring fire-resistant, nontoxic, insulation materials for all communications cabling. Fire-stopping material is required for all breaks in risers.

- Planning your installation

  Choose cable style and gauge to match: bandwidth, distance of cable runs, protocol, building codes.

  Locate hubs or wiring concentrators in centralized locations.

  Locate servers, routers, and security-sensitive equipment in secure environments.

  Ensure that wire trays, raceways, ducts, and conduit are installed to ensure that minimum cable radii are not exceeded.

  Use shielded twisted pair, coaxial, or fiber for electrically noisy environments.

  Use fiber for long distances and high bandwidths.

- Rating baseband and broadband designs

  Baseband refers to digital signals that occupy the entire bandwidth. Broadband refers to analog signals where there may be more than one signal, each occupying a small portion of the total bandwidth. The quality of a given cable is rated by impedance, bandwidth versus distance, and sized by gauge.

  100BaseT—Baseband twisted pair to 100 Mbps. Current standards include 100BaseT4, 100BaseTX, and 100BaseVG.

  1000BaseT—Not yet a standard, gigabit Ethernet is being sold that runs over the same 10/100BaseT, category 5 cable installation.

  10Base2—Baseband small-diameter, coaxial "Thinnet" to 10 Mbps

  10Base5—Baseband large-diameter, coaxial "Thicknet" to 10 Mbps

  100BaseF—Baseband fiber optic to 100 Mbps

  Broadband—Analog signals varying in bandwidth depending on application

- NIC considerations

  NIC connectors must match the cable connectors and the chosen protocol.

  Ensure that NIC IRQ and DMA settings do not conflict with other devices in the workstation.

Choose NICs that conform to the universal/global addressing conventions, or set addresses that do not conflict with other devices on the network.

Ensure that the NIC software is installed on the workstation.

- Installation procedures

  Test the cable before taking it off the reel, then test and label each cable run as the connectors are installed.

  Do not exceed minimum-turn radius, and prevent shiners.

  Install servers, hubs, wiring concentrators, routers, and gateways in secure rooms that have sufficient air conditioning, grounding, and protection from EMI, RFI, and power fluctuations and interruptions.

TROUBLESHOOTING

Test Equipment

There is no substitute for experience and proper test equipment when troubleshooting or tuning networks. Techniques that work well for a given installation may not provide the same results in an installation using different topologies or protocols. Keep in mind that changes to one parameter of a network may improve the observed parameter yet adversely affect another. Much of the time, particularly in the absence of proper test equipment, the network troubleshooter is reduced to a "best guess" at parameters such as user and cable activity.

When the measurement of actual "real-world" results cannot be accurately compared to calculated results, or when it is not possible to calculate a result accurately, empirical testing must be done. To produce empirical data, one should calculate a result based on the best data available, then compare measured results to the calculations. Make a modification to an observed parameter, and then observe and record the results a second time. Continue empirical testing until you have produced the desired result. With common protocols such as Ethernet, Token-Ring, and TCP/IP, a great deal of empirical data already exist that may be used to guide your efforts.

Let me repeat, for emphasis, that there is no substitute for proper test equipment. Small office networks might get by with a simple cable tester, but a properly equipped network manager would also have a time domain reflectometer to periodically observe coaxial and fiber optic cable and compare results to previous observations to enable early detection of deteriorating cable. A multiprotocol analyzer that is capable of capturing data for each protocol should also be used periodically and results compared to previous observations. These are not inexpensive items. Expect to pay more than $3,000 for a professional-quality cable tester or TDR and $15,000 to $35,000 for your protocol analyzer. The cost justification for expensive test equipment should be based on an estimate of the cost of downtime when the network fails (and it will!), plus the cost of lost opportunity and productivity when a user sits idly by waiting for you to return a workstation to service.

REVIEW QUESTIONS

1. List the five ANSI/EIA-586 categories for twisted pair, and discuss the characteristics of each category.
2. Which cable types should be used in electrically noisy environments?
3. Discuss the characteristics of the following:
   - 10BaseT
   - 10Base2
   - 10Base5
   - 100BaseF
   - 36Broad2
4. You are planning the installation of a new LAN on the fifth floor of an office building. Discuss the pros and cons of using the telephone wire room that is next to the elevator shaft.
5. Where would you expect to most easily run cables between floors in a building?
6. What type of cable is *plenum* cable, and where would it be used?
7. What license is often required to install communications cables?
8. What is a shiner? What can you do to prevent a shiner?
9. Discuss the importance of grounding.
10. Discuss the importance of the master cable record.
11. What are the following instruments used to measure?
    - TDR
    - BERT
    - BKERT
    - Breakout box

4

Ethernet

INTRODUCTION

This chapter covers the theory and practical applications of the Ethernet protocol. Topics presented include

- physical layer topologies,
- specifications and capabilities,
- collision detection and prevention,
- the IEEE 802.3 specification,
- connecting Ethernet segments together, and
- advantages and disadvantages of Ethernet.

OVERVIEW

Ethernet is characterized in three different ways. At the physical layer, all LAN devices have simultaneous, probabilistic access to the network bus. Because simultaneous transmissions would result in data collisions, the Ethernet protocol must include a resolution to a collision problem. This also means that two or more stations may attempt to transmit simultaneously, making precise access timing a problem of chance rather than mathematical calculation. The second characteristic of Ethernet is the protocol that governs construction of the frames of data that are transmitted on the physical layer. Ethernet may also be characterized by its baseband, 10-, 100-, or 1,000-Mbps data transfer rate.

In practical applications, Ethernet is most commonly implemented on either a coaxial cable in a common bus topology or on twisted pair using the

10BaseT format in a star topology. In the early years of Ethernet, coaxial cable using 10Base5 "Thicknet" or 10Base2 "Thinnet" was the specified cable as the technology, at the time, did not allow the implementation of high-speed data on twisted pair. In recent years, a great many new installations have gone to the 10BaseT twisted pair cable. Category 3 or 4 cable is easily capable of the 10 Mbps of Ethernet. Category 5 UTP offers opportunity for growth as higher-bandwidth Ethernet applications become available.

There are also implementations of Ethernet in a wireless topology using radio, LED, and laser technologies. In the mid-1990s, wireless LANs were being implemented in increasing numbers where it is impractical or impossible to install wire runs. Infrared LED or laser light beams are ideally suited to the portable notebook computer in such environments as conference rooms and factories where electrical interference is high. No cables need be run, nor does the portable workstation need to be "plugged in." Ultrahigh-frequency radio waves are able to go through walls that do not lend themselves to the easy installation of cable runs. By controlling power levels, the physical area of the LAN can be confined to small enough areas that interference to other radio spectrum services is minimized.

THEORETICAL CAPABILITIES AND SPECIFICATIONS

The Ethernet protocol is implemented on layers 1 and 2 of the OSIRM and is therefore considered a LAN protocol. Specifications for the physical interconnect and the encoding of data transmission are defined in layer 1. Layer 2 defines the Ethernet frame format and the method for passing data to and from higher layers.

Physical Layer Specifications

Common bus topology.

- 10Base5—Sometimes called "Thicknet," 10Base5 uses 50-ohm coaxial cable that conforms to RG-8 specifications. You will often see the cable simply labeled "Ethernet Cable." This cable is very often double shielded and marked at 2.5-meter intervals to show the correct placement of nodes on the cable. As shown in Figure 4.1, in a Thicknet installation, open ends are terminated in the characteristic impedance of 50 ohms. Each of the transceivers connected to the cable is also terminated in 50 ohms.

  Each workstation network interface card (NIC) is connected to a transceiver unit through an interface cable called an *Attachment Unit Interface* (AUI). AUI cables are terminated in DB-15 connectors. The transceiver is connected to the Thicknet cable by clamping the transceiver to the cable in a manner that allows an insulated center conductor to penetrate the outer cover and shield of the coaxial cable and make

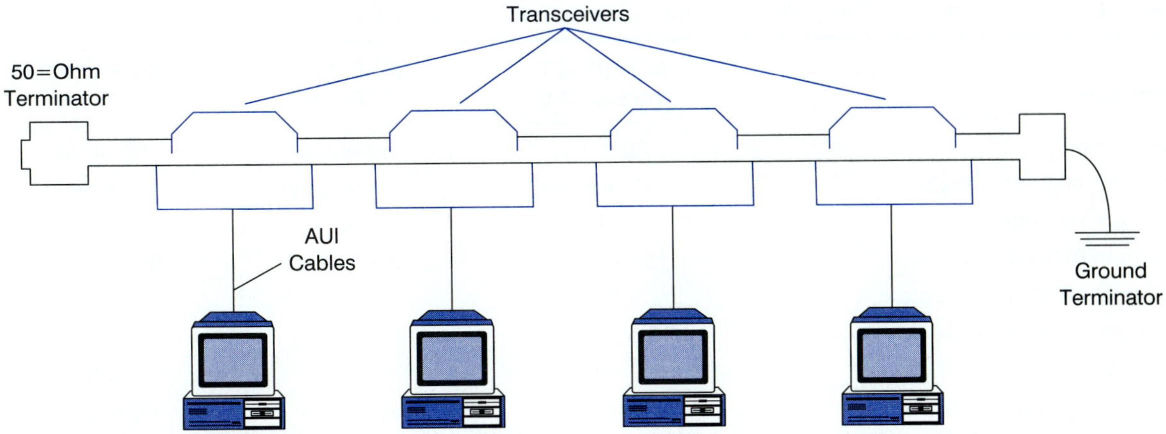

Figure 4.1 Typical 10Base5 "Thicknet" Installation

contact with the inner conductor. An additional insulated conductor connects to the braided shield of the coaxial cable. The transceiver is, itself, terminated in the 50-ohm impedance and controls all of the functions necessary to pass data to and from the cable. In some cases, the cable is cut to smaller lengths that are multiples of 2.5 meters, and each end is terminated in a type N connector screwed directly onto the transceiver. Transceivers, also known as *Media Access Units* (MAUs), are placed at a minimum of 2.5 meters apart along the length of the cable. (Color insert Figure 12 shows a 10Base5 transceiver.)

Thicknet cables have a maximum length of 500 meters, although individual 500-meter segments may be connected to each other through repeaters or bridges to extend the total length of the LAN. A maximum of two repeaters is allowed unless the IEEE 802.3 protocol is used, in which case up to four repeaters may be used. AUI cables have a maximum length of 50 meters between workstation and transceiver. Finally, 10Base5 allows for not more than 100 transceivers per 500-meter cable segment.

- 10Base2—Sometimes called "Thinnet" or "Cheapernet," 10Base2 is implemented in 50-ohm cable with characteristics similar to RG-58. Because of its physically smaller size, 10Base2 is limited to 185 meters in length, and the minimum distance between attachments is 0.6 meters. All other specifications are identical to Thicknet. 10Base2 is most often implemented without the transceiver unit. Cable segments are terminated with BNC connectors and attached directly to workstation NICs using BNC "T" connectors. In such cases, the NIC has all of the transceiver functions built in. Table 4.1 is a summary of the layer 1 specifications for Ethernet using coaxial cable.

Table 4.1 Summary of the Ethernet Physical Layer Specifications for Coaxial Cable

Parameter	ETHERNET Version 2.0	IEEE 802.3 10Base5	IEEE 802.3 10Base2
Impedance	50 ohms	50 ohms	50 ohms
Maximum segment length	500 meters	500 meters	185 meters
Maximum repeaters	2	4	4
Maximum network span	1500 meters	2500 meters	925 meters
Maximum transceivers/segment	100	100	30
Minimum distance between transceivers	2.5 meters	2.5 meters	0.6 meters
Connector type	N	N	BNC
Maximum AUI cable length	50 meters	50 meters	50 meters

Star topology.

- 10BaseT—The 10BaseT standard is most commonly implemented in a star topology. Wiring hubs or concentrators are used to form the base of the star with workstation NICs connected directly to the hubs using four pair cable and RJ-45 connectors. When Ethernet runs at 10 Mbps, category 3, category 4, or category 5 cable should be used. Figure 4.2 shows a typical star configuration.

Cable runs in 10BaseT are limited to 100 meters. When installing RJ-45 connectors or installing twisted pairs on punchdown blocks, care

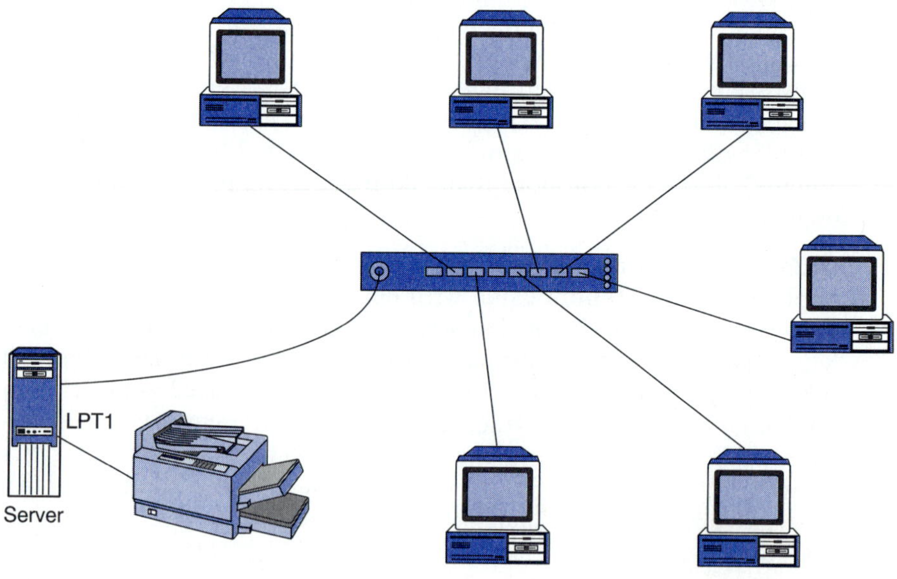

Figure 4.2a Star Topology Using Eight-Port Hub (note the 10Base2 connection to the server)

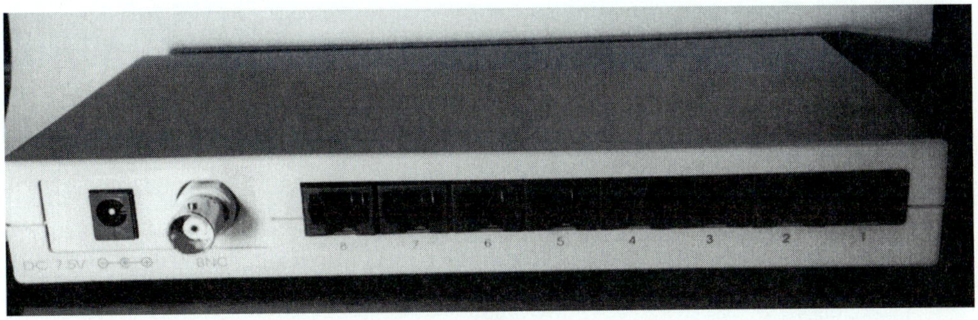

Figure 4.2b Photo of Ethernet Hub Using 10Base2 and 10BaseT (note the 50-ohm BNC terminator)

Figure 4.2c Ethernet Network Interface Card (NIC)

should be taken to maintain the twists, in their original shape, right up to the termination point. Breaking the twists out more than ½ to ¾ inch away from the termination point will result in lower bandwidth and increased sensitivity to noise interference.

- 100BaseF—Where very high bandwidth requirements such as 100-Mbps fast Ethernet or electrically noisy environments are encountered, fiber optic cables and connectors may be used. Special NICs are required to convert the light signals into electrical signals used by workstations.

TECHTIP

When choosing an Ethernet transmission medium, consider the following guidelines:

Environment

- Where electrical or radio frequency interference is high, coaxial or fiber optic cable is preferred. Fiber is totally immune to electrical and RF interference but is more expensive than coax, particularly the optical to electrical interfaces.

Bandwidth

- The highest bandwidths and longest segment distances are obtainable with fiber optics. Bandwidths to 1 Gbps are available for Ethernet. Large increases in distance for single LAN segments may also be achieved.
- Coaxial cable also has high bandwidth, well into the hundreds of Mbps. In many cases, a backbone such as might be used to connect LAN segments between floors in a building would use coax to ensure noise immunity and increase segment length even though the individual floors only require twisted pair.

- 100BaseT—This is the so called "fast Ethernet" specification for copper-based 100-Mbps bandwidth. It currently comes in two modes: 100BaseT and 100BaseVG. 100BaseT is very near standardization within IEEE 802.3. 100BaseVG is an industry standard supported by Hewlett-Packard and is being considered for standardization as IEEE 802.12.

The Ethernet Frame Format

Ethernet was developed long before the IEEE 802 project established the 802.3 standard. Unfortunately, this means that you may encounter Ethernet networks that are not compatible with each other. As of this writing, the data layer protocols Ethernet II and the IEEE 802.3 standard are still supported by vendors. One characteristic, shared by both protocols, is the Manchester physical data encoding method. Figure 4.3 demonstrates Manchester encoding. A logical bit is established by a voltage transition in the center of a data bit cell time. A transition from –0.7 vdc (volts direct current) to +0.7 vdc is taken as a logic one, and a transition from +0.7 vdc to –0.7 vdc generates a logic zero.

We will begin our discussion with the Ethernet frame format as developed by Digital Equipment Corporation, Intel, and Xerox followed by a comparison to the 802.3 standard set by the IEEE. Figure 4.3 shows the frame construction for Ethernet type I.

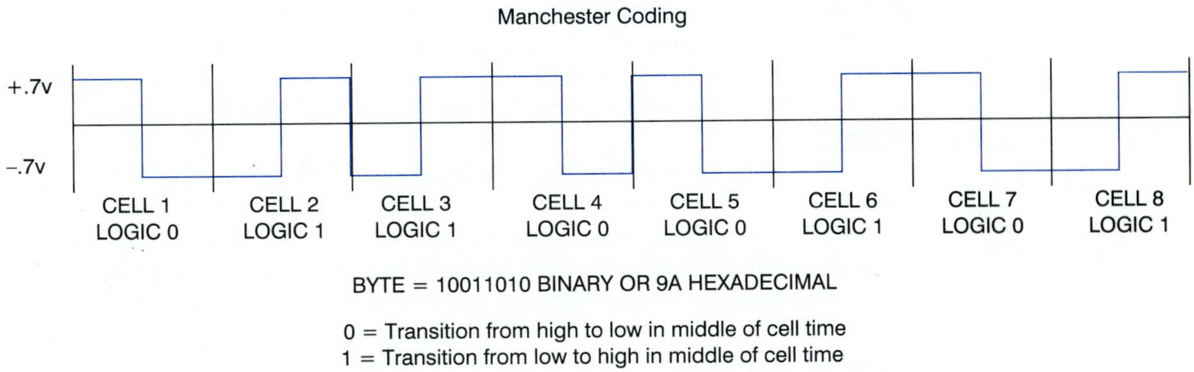

Figure 4.3 Manchester Encoding Scheme

An Ethernet frame consists of six *fields*, each of which performs a specific function. Frames are sent serially at the 10-Mbps rate specified for Ethernet. Each frame begins with an eight-octet *preamble* field consisting of a binary 101010 . . . pattern that ends in 1011. The preamble is generated by a sending station to synchronize clock timing on the network. All other nodes will receive the preamble, synchronize their clocks to the sending station, and prepare to read the destination address contained in the second field.

The second field is a six-octet *destination address*. This address is normally the address of the station to which the frame is sent. Setting LSB=1 causes the address to be seen as a *multicast* address that can be used by network administrators to address groups of workstations. Setting the destination address to all ones (FFFFFFFFFFFFH) results in a *broadcast* frame that is read and copied by all receiving stations.

Field 3 is a six-octet *source address*—that is, the address of the sending station. In most cases, the address of a NIC is burned into a ROM on the NIC by the manufacturer so that no two NICs, worldwide, will have the same address. The least significant bit, as shown in Figure 4.4, is set by the manufacturer (LSB=0), to indicate a unique physical address.

By convention, octets 1 to 3, of the source address, are assigned by the IEEE, and octets 4 to 6 are assigned by the manufacturer. The ROM chip can sometimes be removed, when a NIC is defective, and installed in a new NIC so that the workstation retains its original address. It is also possible for administrators to set their own addresses, in internal registers, that do not conform to IEEE standards. One should have a very good reason for abandoning the unique address, for to do so will result in increased administration time and

Preamble	Destination	Source	Type	Data	FCS
1 Octet	6 Octets	6 Octets	2	45–1,500 Octets	4

Figure 4.4 Ethernet Frame Format

potential addressing problems if the network is ever connected to the Internet or other WANs that may have duplicate addresses.

A two-octet *type* field follows that designates the higher layer protocol destination for the data. Examples might be TCP/IP (0800H) or Novell's IPX (8138H).

User data are sent in a variable-length *data* field that must be at least 46 octets long and may contain as many as 1,500 octets. Frames with less than 46 octets must be padded with enough octets to make the total size of the data field 46 octets. Frames with data fields of less than 46 bytes are often called *runts*. This condition is the result of a defective NIC. Runts must be discarded by all receiving stations, and if a NIC is continuously sending runts, it should be replaced.

FCS is Frame Check Sequence.
CRC means Cyclical Redundancy Check.

The final *Frame Check Sequence* (**FCS**) field is composed of a four-octet error checking value. This 32-bit *Cyclical Redundancy Check* (**CRC**) number is the remainder of a division calculation based on the sum of the values in the address, data, and type fields and a constant used as the divisor. Any frame whose CRC value does not conform to the actual bits received by the destination station is discarded and must be resent.

IEEE 802.3 MAC Frame

SFD is Start Field Delimiter.

Figure 4.4 shows the IEEE 802.3 MAC frame. Immediately following the preamble is a one-octet *Start Field Delimiter* (**SFD**) of the value 10101011B. In 802.3, the preamble is only seven octets; however, the combined result of the preamble and SFD is identical to Ethernet type I. Destination and source addresses may be either two or six octets, as shown in Figure 4.5. The I/G bit indicates the *individual/group* address, which provides the same function as the Ethernet P/M bit. The *universal/local* bit indicates an IEEE/manufacturer universal address or an address set by the local administrator.

Whereas Ethernet uses a type field (refer to Figure 4.3), 802.3 uses a *length* field to specify the length of the data field. Access to higher layers is done using *Service Access Points* (SAP) in the 802.2 LLC sublayer. 802.3 also adds a *pad* that ensures the minimum 46-octet data field length. Ethernet relies on the network layer to provide padding functions.

CSMA/CD

Access to an Ethernet bus is considered *probabilistic* owing to the possibility of simultaneous transmission by more than one station. Access times cannot be accurately calculated because of the possibility of data frame collisions and true network performance must be monitored over long periods of time if accurate predictions are to be made. If network activity was sparse, collisions might be rare enough to be tolerated. However, the prevention of collisions will significantly improve the performance of the network.

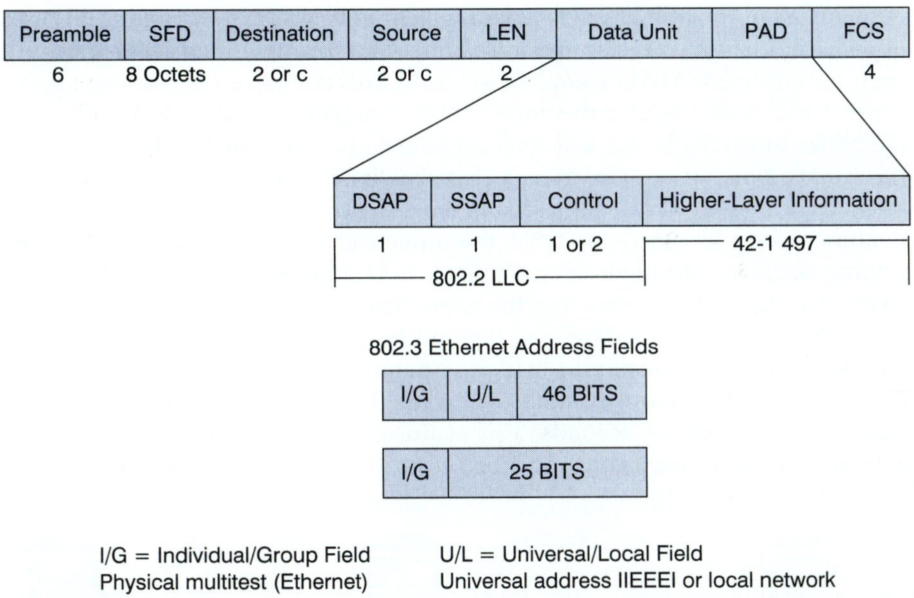

Figure 4.5 IEEE 802.3 MAC Frame

Carrier Sense Multiple Access/with Collision Detection (**CSMA/CD**) is the protocol used to control access to an Ethernet bus. CSMA/CD is implemented in two parts. A workstation wishing to transmit a frame will first monitor the bus in an effort to detect (sense) a carrier($\pm$0.7 vdc). If no voltage is detected within the time that it would take for a frame to transit the entire length of the cable system, the station will transmit its frame. Any station that senses a carrier will wait until the bus is clear before sending its data frame. Because of the distances between workstations, more than one workstation could easily sense no carrier and go ahead and transmit at the same time, producing a collision.

CSMA/CD stands for Carrier Sense Multiple Access/with Collision Detection.

Collision detection (not available on all NICs) is done by sensing incorrect voltages that would be caused by a data collision or by detecting data bits on the bus that do not conform to the timing synchronization. Stations detecting a collision will then wait a random length of time before attempting access to the bus a second time.

TRANSPARENT BRIDGING

Bridging is used either to break large and overloaded LANs into smaller segments or to connect LAN segments together for such things as shared resources and E-mail. An important distinction of bridges is that they only run on layers 1 and 2. Because of the lack of a routing information field in the Ethernet/802.3 frame, only transparent bridges, in which the routing information is supplied by routing tables learned by the bridge, will be seen on Ethernet LANs. Each bridge monitors all of the frames on its LAN segment to learn the destination addresses of nodes not on the LAN. Transparent bridges, sometimes called *learning bridges,* then look at each MAC frame destination and compare the address to the learned addresses stored in the bridge. If the destination address does not exist in the bridge table, the bridge will copy the address to its internal table but not pass the frame. This, of course, means that the first frame sent to a station in a bridged segment must be sent a second time. If, however, the bridge has the destination address in its routing table, the frame will be passed. Because all of the routing decisions are made by the bridge, workstations need not, and are not, aware that the bridge exists—thus the name "transparent" (see Figure 4.6).

A *BPDU* is a Bridge Protocol Data Unit.

The *Spanning Tree Protocol*, defined by IEEE 802.1D, is often used by manufacturers of transparent bridges. Spanning tree adds a *Bridge Protocol Data Unit* (**BPDU**) that is passed to all of the bridges on a multisegment LAN approximately every 30 seconds. This protocol allows spanning tree bridges to communicate with each other for the purpose of determining which bridge is

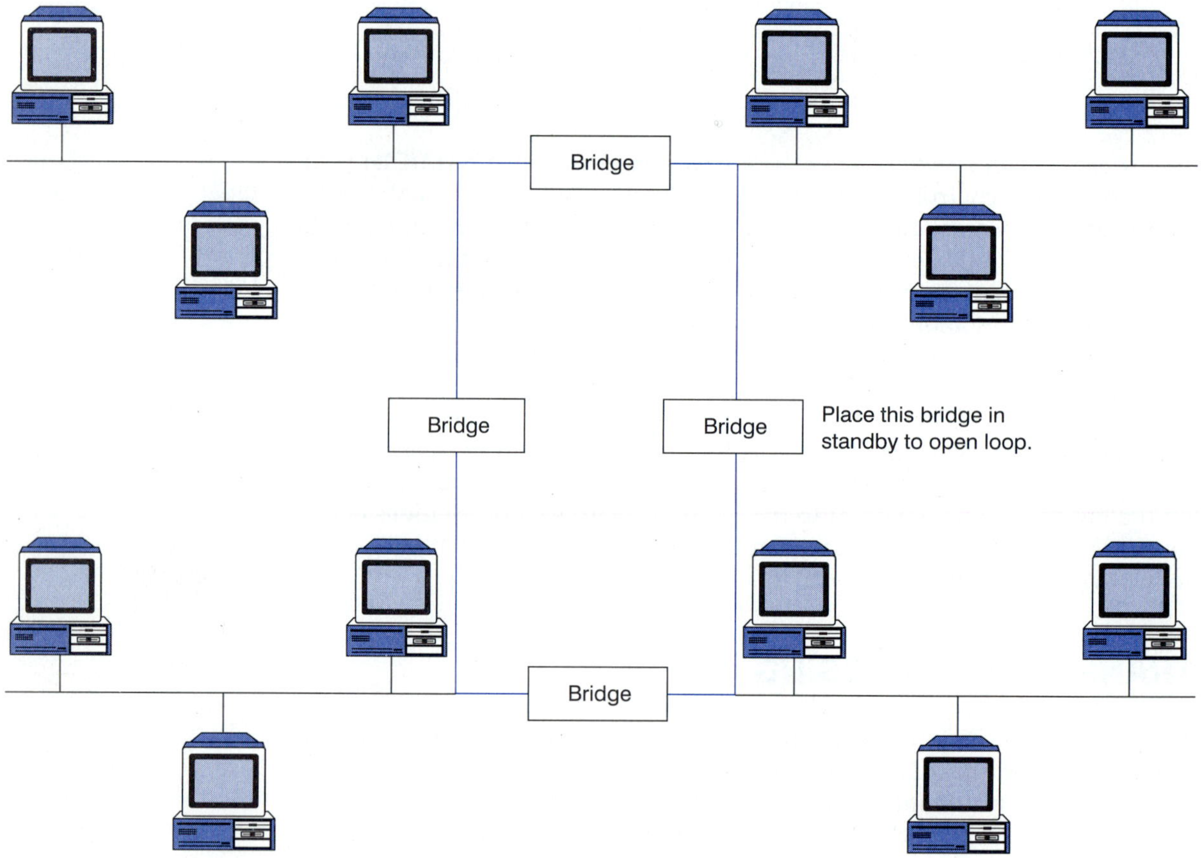

Figure 4.6 Transparent Bridging with Spanning Tree

the last bridge in a closed loop of bridged segments. Once determined, the last bridge goes into a standby mode so that frames will not be continuously passed in an endless closed loop.

SWITCHING

Bridging has a major disadvantage in that it becomes a bottleneck to data flow between segments. The bottleneck is produced by the need to store frames of data while the bridge looks up destination addresses before a frame can be forwarded. In addition, bridges are single-port devices shared by all nodes on a LAN segment. A newer methodology for connecting or segmenting LANs is being implemented that not only replaces bridges, it also replaces multiport 10/100BaseT hubs with devices called *switches*.

Switches are capable of connecting any two nodes on a network directly together through the switch. Ordinary 10/100BaseT hubs connect all nodes together in a common bus (internally). In a switch, only two nodes are connected and effectively isolated from the rest of the network. The two connected nodes are now able to use the entire available bandwidth because there is no longer any need to share a common bus. In addition, switches are able to make their connections at very nearly the same speed that the data are passed.

It is quite common to see switches connected to each other by a single port on each switch. Using such a configuration provides the bridging capability but without the bottleneck that bridge protocols create. This configuration is often referred to as a *backbone.*

In a shared bandwidth Ethernet segment using ordinary hubs, the maximum utilization rate peaks at about 40%. Usage beyond the 40% level results in too many collisions which in turn reduce efficiency. At 40%, the average data transmission rate for a given node is approximately 3.7 Mbps. These numbers clearly indicate a disadvantage to shared bandwidth. Switches, on the other hand, allow connected nodes to achieve as much as 96% utilization because there is no possibility of collision with only two nodes connected. This will be just as true for LAN segments with 2 users or 200 users. The only disadvantage of using switches is that it takes twice the number of ports on each switch that ordinary hubs would use and they are significantly more expensive on a per-port basis.

Switches, like bridges, must read the destination address in a frame before the frame can be passed to its intended node. Most switches are able to employ a method called *cut through* that connects the source port to the destination port with a latency of less than 40 microseconds. You will hear the term *wire speed* used to indicate that frames are passed through a switch with this very small latency delay.

An added value to the use of switches is their ability to connect pairs of nodes in parallel. This simply means that up to half the ports on a switch may connect to the other half simultaneously. Of course, no two ports may transmit to each other at the same time.

TECHTIP

As a practical matter, most PCs have a local memory bus that runs at 33 MHz, a significant processing bottleneck even with full 32-bit data transfers. Also available are 66- and 100-Hz bus machines but at significantly greater cost. NICs running at 100 Mbps (12.5 bytes/second) should be in a PCI slot to take full advantage of the network's available bandwidth and minimize the impact to CPU processing time. If in an 8-MHz ISA slot, even using all 16 data bits, the maximum data rate is 128 Mbps. The result is that the CPU will be spending a significantly greater percentage of its time processing data to and from the NIC. In a busy server, both a higher memory bus and I/O bus speed are desirable.

Many manufacturers of Ethernet NICs and switches offer products that are able to run at either 10 or 100 Mbps. This technique would allow a device to take full advantage of the higher speed of a switched backbone, when connected, yet remain compatible with older 10-Mbps LAN segments.

FAST ETHERNET

In an effort to improve bandwidth and provide for a migration from 10Base(x) Ethernet LANs to 100Base(x), two competing standards have emerged. *100BaseT* has been standardized by the IEEE and incorporated into the 802.3 standard. 100BaseT retains the CSMA/CD collision management format and can be made compatible with legacy LANs using 10Base(x). 100BaseT is composed of five parts:

- *Media Access Control*—The MAC layer is still based on CSMA/CD and conforms to the requirements of IEEE 802.3.
- *Media Independence Interface*—An MII layer has been implemented to define a standard interface between the MAC sublayer in IEEE 802.2 and any of the three physical layer implementations. Figure 4.7 shows the relationship between the physical and MAC layers.
- *100BaseTX*—This is the physical layer definition for 100-Mbps Ethernet over UTP category 5 or STP type 1. In both cases two pairs of wires are used. One pair is used for transmit and the other for receive. Wire connections are identical to 10BaseT.
- *100BaseT4*—By using all four pairs of wires, 100BaseT4 allows the use of UTP category 3, 4, or 5 cable. Three pairs are used for transmit and receive while the fourth pair monitors for collisions.

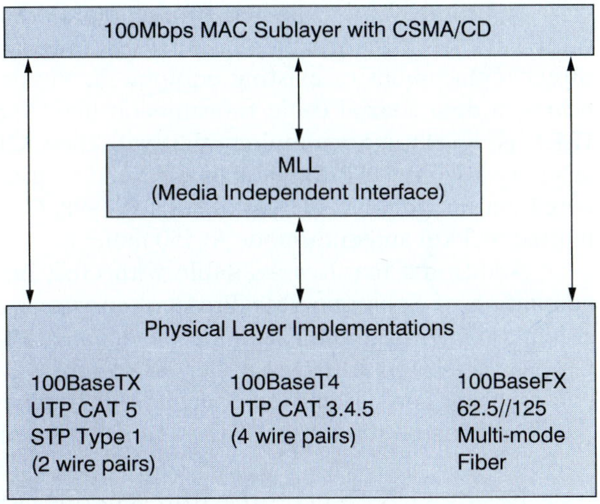

Figure 4.7
100Base(x) MAC and Physical Layers

- *100BaseFX*—This is the multimode fiber specification for fast Ethernet; 62.5/125-micron fiber is used. (Additional detail on fiber optic cable is provided in Chapter 7 on FDDI.)

Not surprisingly, distances are much more limited with fast Ethernet. Using copper, the maximum span including repeaters is limited to 205 meters compared to the 500 meters of 10BaseT. Cable distance from workstation to hub is retained at 100 meters (163 meters for fiber). Where longer spans are required, FDDI backbones (see Chapter 7) may be required with local segments using fast Ethernet.

GIGABIT ETHERNET

Current switching technology can provide data throughput rates of up to OC48 (2.4 Gbps). Predictions indicate speeds as high as OC192 (9.6 Gbps) as early as 1998. Current Ethernet switching technology is available at up to 1 Gbps. Given these very high speeds, switches are proving ideal candidates for backbone applications. A common example might be two or more 10-Mbps LAN segments, each connected to a switch that contains a fiber optic port running at 100 Mbps or more. This scenario allows the switches to connect to each other using the 100 Mbps in a shared bandwidth mode. Following the rule of thumb of 40% saturation of shared bandwidth would provide up to 40 Mbps on the switch backbone.

IEEE 802.3z is expected to become a standard for Gigabit Ethernet (GbE) in 1998. Conformance to existing frame sizes is expected that will allow direct replacement of existing equipment. Physical media include fiber and *twinax*, a dual coaxial cable transmission line. The 802.3ab working group at IEEE is developing technology that will allow Gigabit Ethernet to run over category 5 UTP. UTP for GbE is expected to use the full 100-meter segment length on category 5 cable. As of August 1998, GbE, even single-mode fiber, is limited to 3 km and multimode to 550 meters.

Additional features available with GbE include layer 3 switching. An adaptation of Spanning Tree Protocol known as *Spanning Forrest* allows the switch to perform routing functions when used with IP (Internet Protocol; see Chapter 13 on TCP/IP). Latency through a GbE switch is measured in microseconds compared to milliseconds for routers.

Anticipated standards for Gigabit Ethernet include the following:

- 1000BaseCX—This is the truly amazing, soon to be new standard for Gigabit Ethernet over category 5 copper. Current distance is limited to 20 meters; however, when fully standardized, each of the four pairs is expected to carry a half duplex signal at 125 Mbps at up to 100 meters.
- 1000BaseSX—Multimode fiber optic standards using 850-nm wavelength (SX) and 1,330-nm wavelength (LX). SX spans up to 300 meters, LX up to 500 meters.
- 1000BaseLX (single-mode fiber)—Increases maximum distance to 3,000 meters.

ADVANTAGES AND DISADVANTAGES OF ETHERNET

The primary advantage of Ethernet is cost. Compared to Token-Ring, presented in the next chapter, an Ethernet LAN is noticeably less expensive. If need for bandwidth does not exceed 40% saturation, access to the shared bus is more efficient than Token-Ring because there is no wait for a free token. Unfortunately, common access also results in collisions that can produce a serious inefficiency on normally active Ethernet LANs where 40% saturation is exceeded. An additional weakness in Ethernet is the lack of management functions unless expensive intelligent hubs are used. The use of switches, although expensive, has enabled more efficient use of shared bandwidth. Fast Ethernet protocols may be used to increase bandwidth to 100 Mbps.

TROUBLESHOOTING

Defective Cabling

This problem includes miswired connectors, open or shorted wires, shiners, and kinks. A good cable tester will detect all of these problems. A time domain reflectometer is required to find the exact location of defects. Review the Chapter 3 "Troubleshooting" section for details on physical layer troubleshooting.

Defective NICs

NIC problems include

- jabbering;
- timing due to mixed manufacturers or models;
- duplicate addresses;
- incorrect settings for IRQ, DMA, and base I/O address;
- totally inoperative function;
- mixed Ethernet standards—all three 10-Mbps Ethernet modes may be run simultaneously; however, a common server must be configured for all of the modes used if all nodes are to be able to connect to each other.

Troubleshooting most NIC problems can be prevented by proper installation and specifying that all of the NICs on a given LAN be the same make and model. Choose a reliable vendor that is not going out of business soon, and keep a couple of spares on hand. As for truly defective NICs, substitution with a known good device is a common method. This, however, can be time-con-

> **TECHTIP**
>
> NICs that are used in PCI slots in PCs have a potentially unique configuration problem. Most current BIOS configurations default to auto-assign an IRQ value beginning with PCI slot one. Set this feature to manual and assign IRQ values yourself.

suming. To rapidly discover a defective NIC, you must be able to analyze the individual data frames that are on the cable. The next section describes the use of a network protocol analyzer used to read frames directly off the cable.

Bandwidth Overload

Symptoms of this problem occur when performance of the LAN begins to deteriorate with no obvious problem such as a jabbering NIC. The cause is usually growth in either the number of nodes connected or the level of activity of existing nodes. Running a full server backup at the same time accounting is closing the yearend books can easily exceed the peak saturation rate of an Ethernet LAN segment. Saturation statistics can be compiled using a protocol analyzer.

Overload can be cured in three different ways:

- Breaking the existing LAN into two separate segments connected by a bridge
- Creating a backbone and then breaking the LAN into multiple segments connected to the backbone
- Replacing hubs with switches

Protocol Analyzer

A protocol analyzer, commonly referred to as a *sniffer*, is really a software application that is able to decode and identify the different fields of the various frames and packets that are present on the transmission medium (see Figure 4.8). A portable model usually comes in a laptop or notebook computer that contains one or more NICs that are configured to operate in *verbose* mode. *Verbose* simply means that, regardless of destination address, all packets and frames may be captured and stored in the sniffer's memory for analysis.

Protocol analyzers are generally capable of identifying each of the fields in an individual frame, compiling selected statistics about the data being passed on the network, and identifying damaged frames and packets. With a protocol analyzer, one could capture statistics such as peak load and peak load times, peak users, and network saturation. Maximum and average frame size could be monitored and recorded. Overhead statistics could be analyzed to determine the percentage of the traffic that is local compared to that of packets from other networks. One could determine the statistics for router delay, internetwork response time, or the average number of unacknowledged packets, or time-outs on transmitted packets.

Perhaps the greatest value provided by a protocol analyzer is the identification of defective frames and packets. A jabbering Ethernet NIC, for exam-

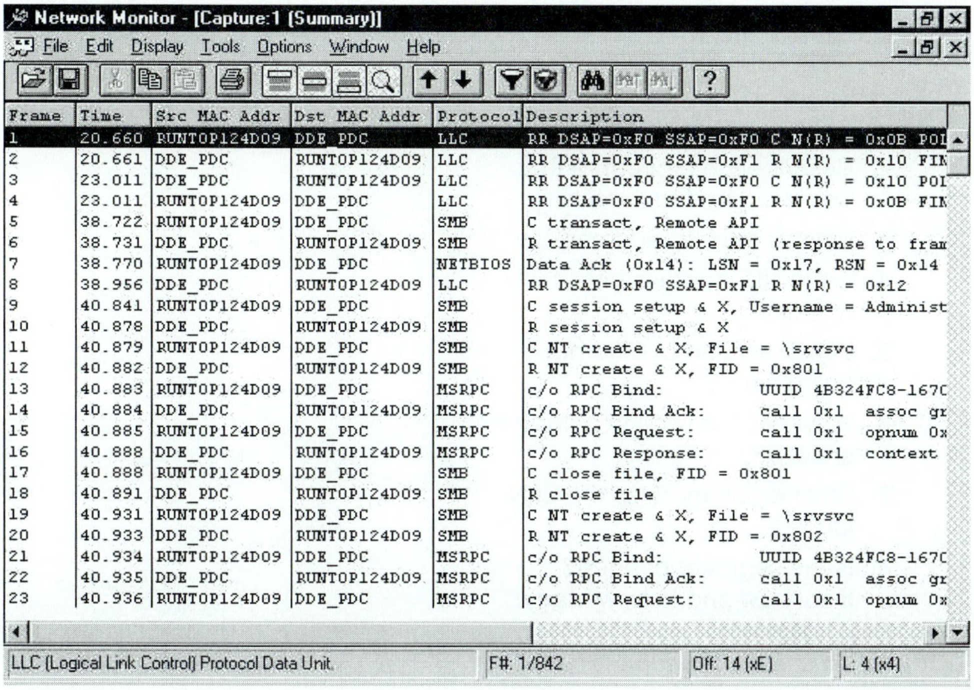

Figure 4.8 Protocol Analyzer

ple, could be identified quickly and its node ID displayed on screen. Beaconing, common to Token-Ring, can be easily traced to the offending workstation. Packets containing encapsulated frames can be displayed to determine which of the protocols is responsible for a transmission error. In the hands of a skilled operator, the protocol analyzer is a truly formidable instrument.

APPLICATION PROJECTS

Project 1

The best possible practical installation application is to participate in an actual Ethernet installation. If your school or company has an Ethernet LAN, ask the network manager to allow you to attend the next workstation installation. Take notes during the installation so that you can complete the following lab form.

Item	Observed Result
1. What cable is used? Do you know why this cable was specified?	
2. Describe the procedure that was used to install the NIC.	
3. What is the NIC address?	
4. Is the NIC address universal or local?	
5. Which version of Ethernet is being used?	
6. Why was the version of Ethernet chosen?	
7. What topology does the LAN use?	
8. Is the segment bridged? If so, how and to how many segments? What kind of bridge is used?	
9. Is the LAN peer-to-peer or client/server?	
10. What is the file server operating system, if any?	

Project 2

Design an Ethernet LAN to service a small office composed of an accountant, a receivables bookkeeper, a payables bookkeeper, and a general ledger bookkeeper. Your design should include

- specifications for cables, connectors, NICs, and workstations;
- drawings to show wiring and equipment placement; and
- a list of all equipment required.

REVIEW QUESTIONS

1. What topologies are suitable for Ethernet?
2. Describe each of the fields for an IEEE 802.3 MAC frame.
3. Discuss the differences in frame construction between Ethernet II and IEEE 802.3.
4. Briefly discuss CSMA.
5. Briefly discuss CD.
6. What is the maximum length of a 10Base5 Thicknet segment?
7. How many stations can be connected to a single Thicknet segment?
8. Discuss the differences between 10Base5 Thicknet and 10Base2 Thinnet.
9. When installing a coaxial cable segment, how are the open ends of the cable terminated?
10. What layers of the OSIRM is Ethernet implemented on?
11. How does an Ethernet frame designate a broadcast frame?
12. What is the data encoding technique used by Ethernet and what are its characteristics?
13. What is the primary reason for using transparent bridging on Ethernet?
14. What is the maximum practical limit to the number of workstations on a single Ethernet segment? Why?
15. Briefly discuss the advantages and disadvantages of Ethernet.
16. Define the term *latency*.
17. What technique is available to improve the latency of bridges?
18. What is the method used by most switches to reduce latency?
19. You have installed a 16-port Ethernet switch. How many transmitting workstations may simultaneously connect to their intended destinations?
20. With respect to the switch in question 19, what is the maximum number of sending stations that may be connected at the same time?

5

Token-Ring

INTRODUCTION

This chapter will cover the theory and practical application of the IEEE 802.5 Token-Ring. Areas of discussion will include

- physical layer implementation,
- 802.5 MAC frame,
- active monitor functions,
- neighbor notification,
- ring access,
- bridging rings, and
- advantages and disadvantages.

OVERVIEW

In 1985 IBM introduced a local area network protocol known as *Token-Ring*. The development of the Token-Ring technology can be traced to work done by Farmer and Newhall (1969), Bell Laboratories, the University of California Irvine (Loomis, 1973), and MIT (Clark et al., 1978; Saltzer and Pogran, 1979). A European, von Willemjin, in 1972 began his work on a token passing ring and obtained patents in Europe and the United States. That gentleman was highly successful in his attempts to force IBM into lucrative license and royalty payments for a number of years, although he showed no interest beyond the development stage and is now reported to be doing raw material research. More than any other individual or group, however, IBM was the driving force behind IEEE adoption of their 802.5 standard for Token-Ring that is currently in use. The obvious gap between development and introduction by IBM is probably due to IBM's dedication to the SNA system and mainframe sales.

Token-Ring is characterized by its implementation in a token passing ring topology, its 4- or 16-Mbps baseband operating speed, and its *deterministic* access process. A single station on the ring assumes the role of active ring monitor and provides timing and control of ring functions. All other stations assume standby monitor functions in case the active monitor should fail for any reason. A special frame called a *token* is passed around the ring, beginning with the active monitor and passing to each station in turn. Any station wishing to transmit must wait for a free token to pass to it. Because ring timing and access are precisely controlled, access to the ring by any station may be determined by mathematical calculation.

PHYSICAL LAYER IMPLEMENTATION

An *MSAU* is a Multistation Access Unit.

As you noted in the overview, Token-Ring is a physical layer token passing ring topology. The earliest versions physically connected each node to its neighbor in a ring topology. More recently, Multistation Access Units (**MSAUs**) are used to connect all nodes at a common location, the MSAU. The ring is maintained within the MSAU and extended through any node that connects to the MSAU. All nodes are connected to the MSAU in a physical star topology. The term *MSAU* should not be confused with the Medium Attachment Unit (MAU) specified in IEEE 802.3d applications as the wiring hub or concentrator used in Ethernet.

Copper-based installations are usually done with four-pair UTP or two-pair STP cable in either 22 or 24 gauge. UTP is terminated in RJ-45 modular connectors and STP in a four-conductor hermaphroditic (genderless) connector at the MSAU and a standard DB9 at the NIC. Figure 5.1a shows the color code used to wire the STP connectors and 5.1b the RJ-45.

IBM designed the hermaphroditic connector to be both genderless and simple to install. Care should be taken to match color coding during assembly and when testing completed cables. Be certain to note the internal shorting bars in the hermaphroditic connector.

Where IBM equipment using coaxial cable interfaces is in use, balun transformers (not shown in Figure 5.1) are installed to provide the impedance match between the ring cable and the coaxial cable. Unmatched impedances can cause the signals to be reflected back into the cable. The result of reflected signals is a collision between the original signal and its reflection, thus destroying the data.

Available from IBM, the baluns are constructed as part of the hermaphroditic connector. Red baluns are intended for IBM 3270 terminals and green for 5520 terminals.

Figure 5.1 Token-Ring Connector Wiring

Hermaphroditic/DB9

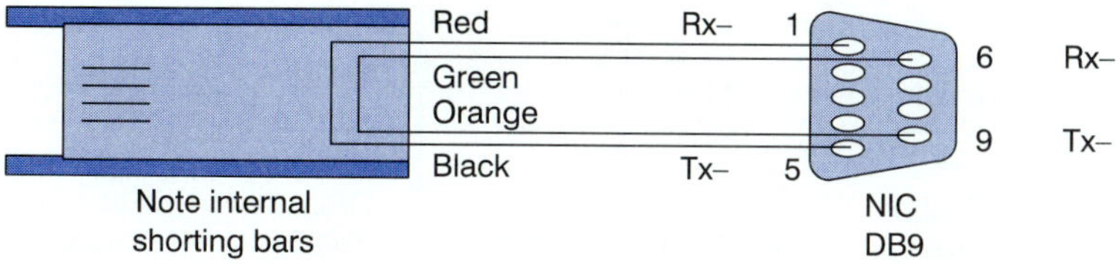

(a)

Color Coding

Transmit	(Tx–): Orange
Transmit	(Tx–): Blue or Black
Receive	(Rx–): Red
Receive	(Rx–): Green

RJ–45

← Pin Number →

1	2	3	4	5	6	7	8
NC	NC	Tx	Rx	Rx	Tx	NC	NC

(b)

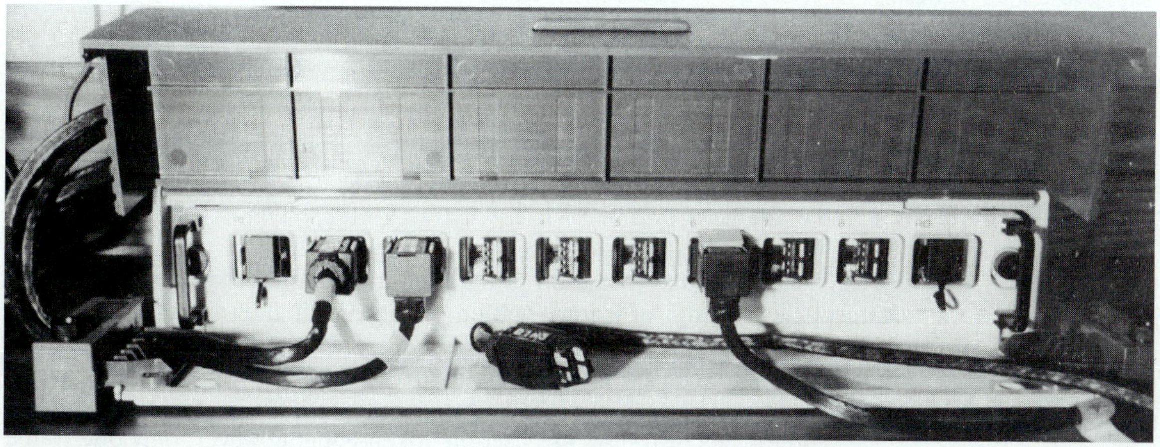

IEEE 802.5

Physical layer data encoding is done with a variation of the Manchester code called *differential Manchester*. Figure 5.2 diagrams the differences between Manchester and differential Manchester coding. Note that differential Manchester causes a transition in the center of every cell time and uses the beginning of a cell time to determine the logic state of a bit. Clock timing may now be accurately synchronized in every cell and is independent of the data transi-

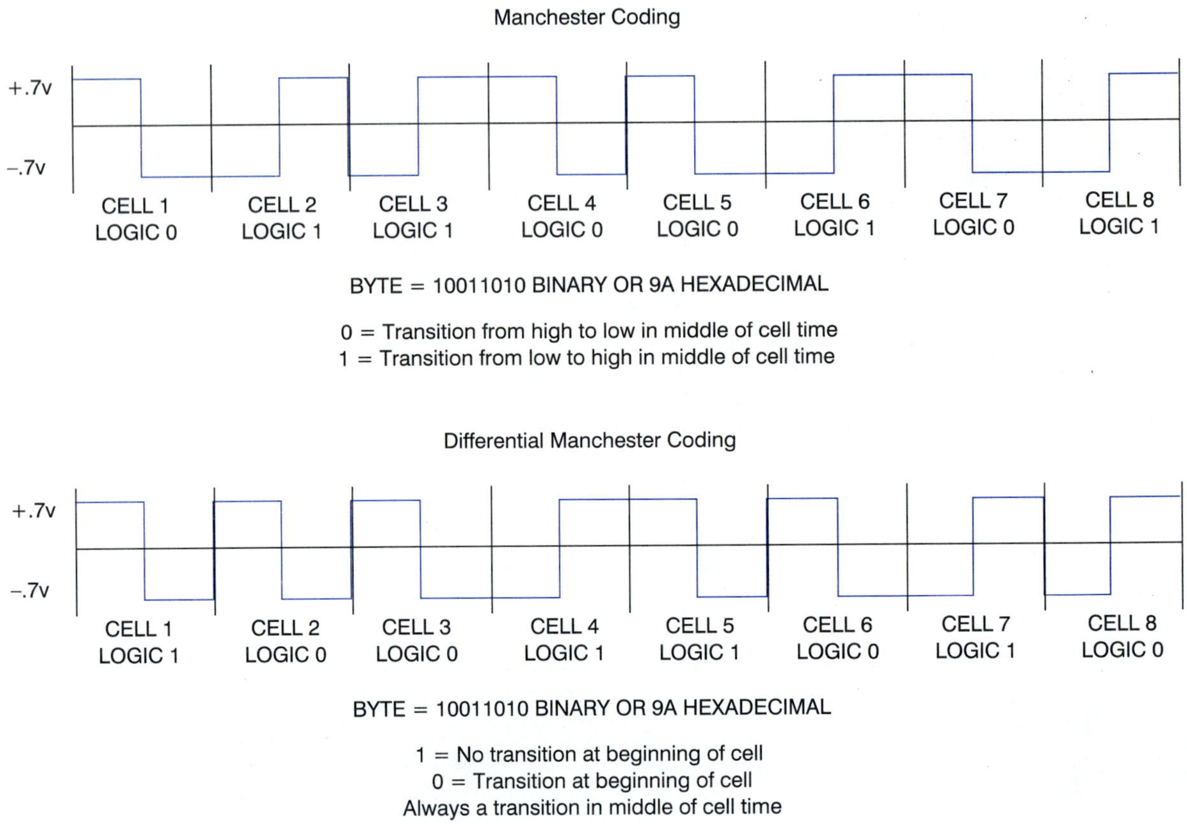

Figure 5.2 Differential Manchester Compared to Manchester Coding

tions. Using the edge transition of a data bit is a more reliable test of a logic state. A clear change of voltage, within the time limit allowed, must take place for a logic state to be recognized. Measuring the static voltage level to determine logic state can produce ambiguity when voltages are near the change over point between a logic one and a logic zero.

Three kinds of frames are used in Token-Ring; however, only one frame at a time may be on the ring. A free *token* is initiated by the active monitor to indicate that the ring is free. Any station that receives the token may take it, add its source address and the address of the destination station, and create the second type of frame by attaching a frame containing user data or ring management information and commands. The third frame type is the *abort token* that contains only the beginning and ending fields of the token. An abort token is sent by any station that detects a faulty token or a correctable ring error.

Refer to the simplified diagram of an installed Token-Ring shown in Figure 5.3. Whenever a data frame is sent, each station examines the destination address as it is received. If the station sees its own address, it copies the frame to its internal data buffer and modifies it to indicate that the frame has been copied. The frame is then passed to the rest of the ring stations, one at a time, until the frame returns to the sender. The sending station removes the frame from the ring, examines it to determine whether the frame has been copied by the receiving station, and places a free token back onto the ring. In this manner, no station may send more than one frame without releasing the token back to the ring.

The passing of tokens and frames will occur as follows:

1. Assume that station A is the active monitor.
2. Station A would place a free token on the ring, which would be passed to station B. Note that none of the unused MSAU ports between A and B are in use and are automatically bypassed by relays inside the MSAU.

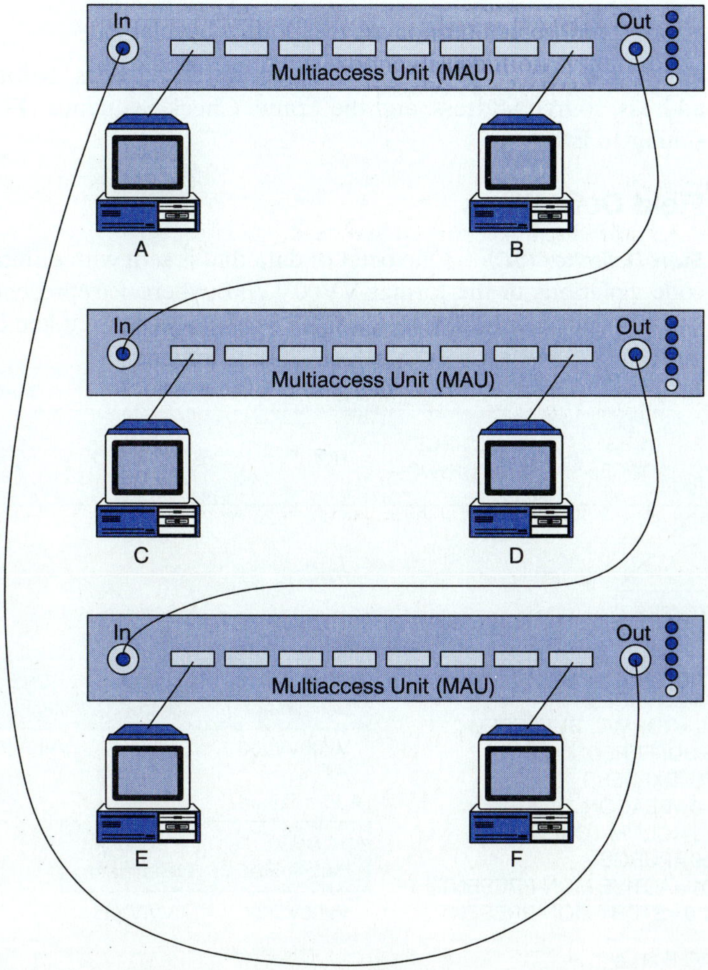

Figure 5.3 Typical Token-Ring Installation

3. If station B wishes to send a frame, it copies the token to its internal data buffer, adds the frame it wishes to send to the token, and sends the frame on to station C.
4. The frame will continue to be passed from station to station until its destination address is recognized by one of the ring stations or until it returns to station B, the sender, unrecognized.
5. If the destination address of the frame sent by station B were station D, D would copy the frame to its internal buffer, modify the frame to indicate that it both recognized its address and copied the frame without error, then pass the frame on. When the frame returned to station B, it would see that the address recognize and frame copied bits were set and remove the frame from the ring, replace the free token, and pass it to station C.

802.5 Frame Construction

FCS stands for Frame Check Sequence.

Figure 5.4 displays the IEEE 802.5 frame and tokens. Notice the destination address, source address, and the Frame Check Sequence (**FCS**) fields that are similar to Ethernet.

Field Definitions

Start Delimiter (SD). One octet of data that is sent with differential Manchester code violations in the format VV00VV00 (where *V* represents a violation bit). The SD field is only used to notify the ring that either a token or frame follows.

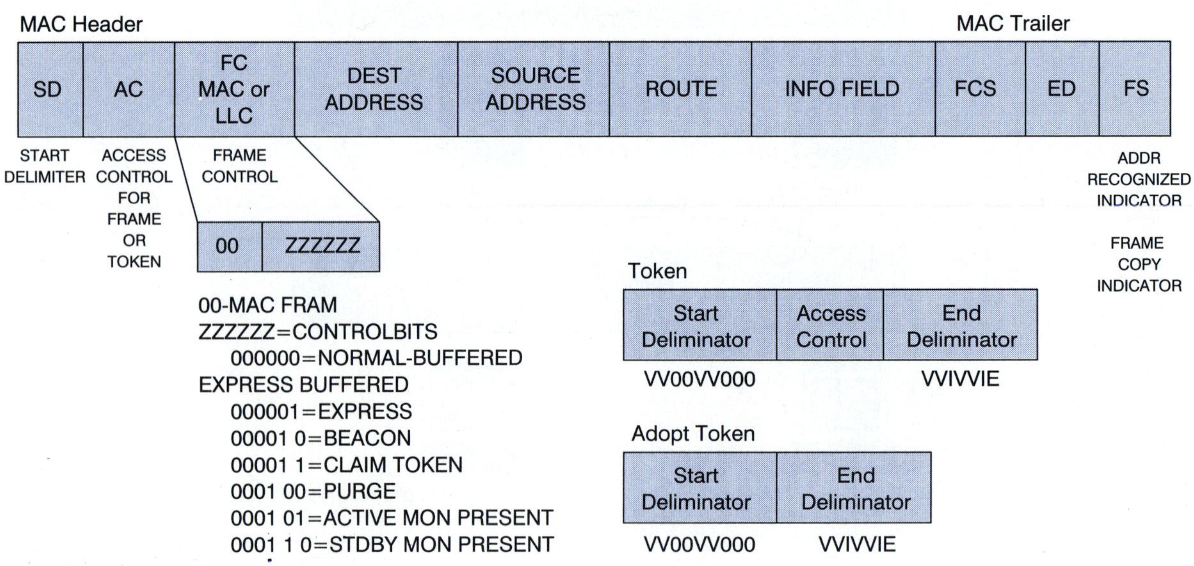

Figure 5.4 Token-Ring MAC Frame

Access Control (AC). A one-octet field used to determine ring access using format PPPTMRRR. The format of bit functions follows:

- PPP—Three bits used to set priority, where 000 is lowest priority. Administrators must set an NIC's priority to higher values if needed. File server NICs or perhaps routers or bridges might warrant higher priority to prevent congestion.
- T—T=1 indicates a data frame; T=0 indicates a token.
- M—When the active monitor station sees an M=1 bit, it will assume that the sending station failed to remove a token or frame after a single pass around the ring. The active monitor will remove the token or frame, initiate a ring purge to clear the ring, and issue a new token.
- RRR—Three bits used by a station to reserve priority for the next available free token.

Frame Control (FC). A one-octet field used to determine the frame format. Only the first two bits have significance:

- *00 = MAC frame*—A full data frame that contains ring information for management and control of the ring. MAC frame functions include the following:

  Active monitor present—This function is performed at regular intervals as a test of the functional integrity of the ring. An active monitor present frame is sent, and the neighbor notification routine is initiated.

  Standby monitor present—In practical application, a timer that is reset by the active monitor unless an active monitor or ring error occurs.

  Ring purge—Initiated by the active monitor whenever a faulty token is encountered.

  Remove station—A frame that is sent to direct a station to disconnect itself from the ring. This frame is often sent by the file server operating system.

  Claim token—A procedure that is used to select the active monitor.

  Duplicate address test—When a station wishes to connect to the ring, it goes through a process that includes a test to determine that its address is not duplicated by another station on the ring.

  Beacon—If a token or frame is not received within a predetermined period of time, a station will begin sending beacon frames to notify the ring that there is a break in the ring between the beaconing station and its upstream neighbor.

- *01 = LLC frame*—A frame that contains user data
- *1x = Reserved for future use*

DA means Direct Address.

Destination Address (DA). This field may be either two or six octets that are the address of the receiving station. IBM uses six octets only.

- Bit 0 (U/L) indicates a universal address (B=0) or locally set address (B=1).
- Bit 1 (I/G) indicates an individual address (B=0) or a group address (B=1).
- An address of all zeros, called a *test address,* may be sent but not received and is removed when a free token is placed on the ring.
- Broadcast frames of destination FFFFFFFFFFFFh are received by all stations.

SA stands for Source Address.

Source Address (SA). This field may be either two or six octets that form the address of the sending station. All destination and source addresses, on a given ring, must be identical lengths. Most applications, particularly where WAN access is required, use the six-octet format.

- Bit 0 (U/L) indicates a universal address (B=0) or locally set address (B=1).
- Bit 1 (I/G) indicates an individual address (B=0) or a group address (B=1).
- As with Ethernet, NIC addresses are unique, with IEEE assigning global addresses and manufacturers assigning the remaining bits.

Addressing in Token-Ring also allows for function-dependent addressing that is implemented by setting bit 0 in octet 2 of an address and setting the remaining bytes for one of 31 possible functions as defined by IBM.

RIF is Routing Information Field.

Routing Information Field (RIF). An optional 0- to 30-octet field inserted by the sending station when the final destination address is beyond the local ring and must be sent through a source route bridge or a router. Each router or bridge that is passed through is called a *hop*. With a field length limit of 30 octets, the number of hops is limited to seven. As the frame passes through the bridge, it adds its bridge number plus the ring number of the next ring to the RIF field (RA+B1+R2) so that the final destination will have a complete set of values for return acknowledgments.

Information Field. This is the field that contains either MAC or LLC frames. It is variable in length from 32- to 32-K octets. Figure 5.5a shows the construction of the MAC *protocol data unit* (PDU) and 5.5b, the LLC PDU.

In the MAC PDU, fields for length and class precede the command and parameter field. There are 25 different types of MAC frames divided into the following five classes:

- *Medium control*—Network reliability functions
- *Station initialization*—The process for connecting to the ring
- *Error monitoring*—Looks for soft errors
- *Network management*—Ring configuration and station parameters

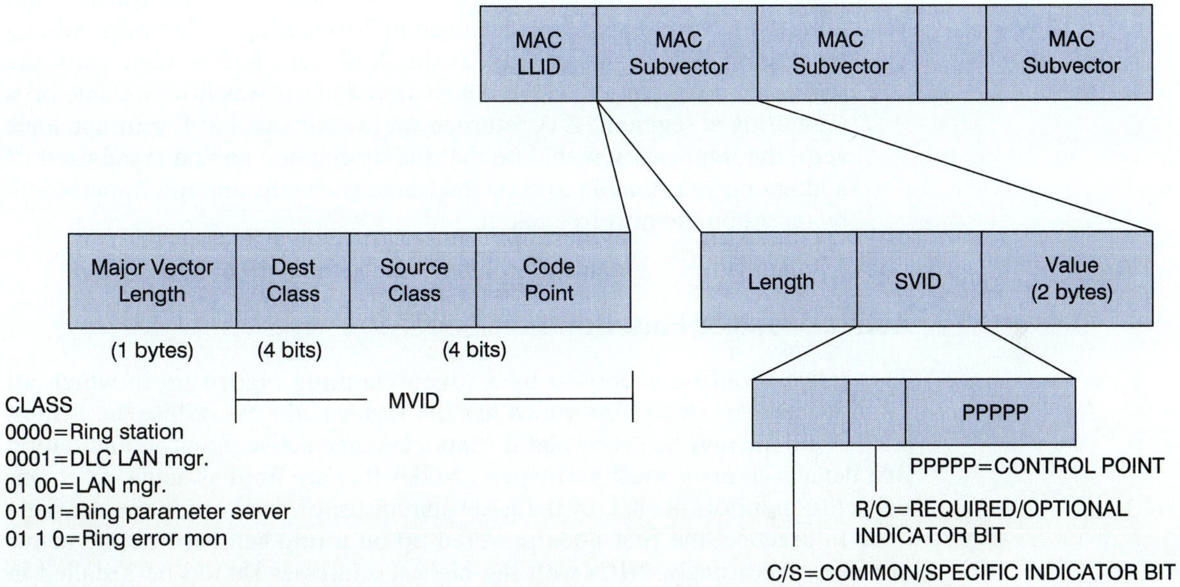

Figure 5.5a 802.5 Token-Ring MAC PDU

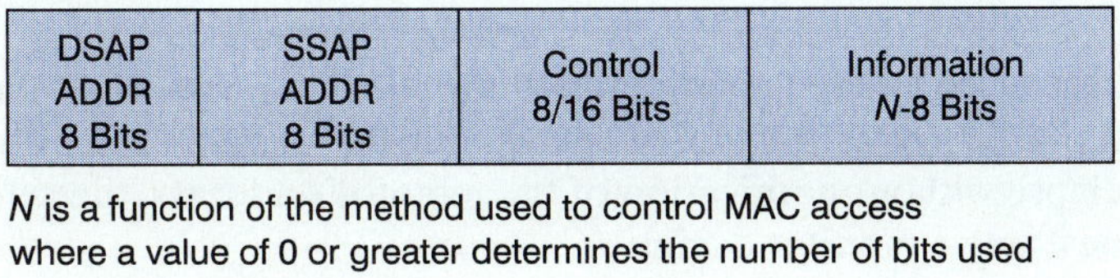

Figure 5.5b 802.5 Token-Ring LLC PDU

Frame Check Sequence (FCS)

Similar to Ethernet, the FCS field is a four-octet (32-bit) CRC value used to check for errors in a frame transmission.

End Delimiter (ED). ED is an end of frame Manchester code violation in the format VV11VV1E, where *E* represents a deliberate error bit.

Frame Status (FS). The FS octet follows the convention AFrrAFrr:

- *Address Recognize*—This bit (A) is set by a station that recognizes its own address.
- *Frame Copied*—This bit (F) is set by the receiving station to indicate that the frame has been copied into the station's data buffer.
- The sending station knows that its frame was recognized and copied if the A and F bits are both set when the frame completes a full pass around the ring. This is an advantage to Token-Ring in that acknowledgment frames need not be sent. If the A bit returned as logic zero, the sender could assume that the destination address was not available or is on a bridged segment. If A returned set to logic one but F returned logic zero, the implication would be that the destination station recognized its address but was unable to copy the frame correctly, and the frame would be resent on the next free token.

Active Monitor Functions

The active monitor is chosen by a token claiming algorithm in which all standby monitors determine which has the highest address. While the default state of a node may be set so that it cannot become active monitor, any station that detects an error must participate. Nodes that are used as active or potential active monitors are set, by the LAN administrator, to override the default.

In practice, the first node powered up on a ring will become the active monitor. Accordingly, NICs with the highest addresses should be installed in those stations designated for active monitor duty because the process of selecting a new active monitor is disruptive to users on the ring. Administrators often power up a station, such as a server, that is normally never turned off before any other stations to prevent unwarranted disruptions.

Each standby monitor contains a "receive notification timer" that is set and synchronized by the active monitor to notify ring stations of the active monitor's address approximately every 7 seconds. If more than 15 seconds elapse without notification of the monitor's address, the selection process for a new active monitor begins.

The primary functions of the active monitor include error-checking functions such as these:

- Missing or faulty tokens or frames
- Prioritized tokens or frames that pass around the ring more than once
- More than one active monitor

Additional active monitor functions include the following:

- Ensure minimum ring length of the three octets of a token (this is done so that a complete token can pass around the ring before it can overwrite itself). To accomplish this task, the active monitor sets aside a buffer area of the number of bits needed to maintain ring length.
- Monitor master clock and control timing.
- Synchronize all ring timers to master clock.
- Monitor transmission of tokens and frames.
- Initiate and monitor the neighbor notification procedure.
- Clear ring when errors are detected and issue new token.

Ring Access

Whenever a station is turned on or connected to the MSAU, a specific series of events must be undertaken so that the station can join the ring in an orderly way that does not interfere with ring functions. A noticeable number of seconds are required, and users should expect to see some delay before connecting to the ring.

1. *Lobe test*—This is a test of the cable (called a *lobe*) connecting a station to the MSAU. A special MAC frame is issued with destination address zero. If the station receives the frame back, it assumes the cable to be intact. The frame must also be issued at voltage levels that are low enough to prevent the MSAU relay from connecting the lobe to the MSAU ring. An additional check is done to ensure that the NIC can receive frames addressed to it.

   At this point, the station connects to the MSAU by issuing a "phantom voltage" that is used to activate the MSAU relay.

2. *Active monitor present test*—Following connection, the station sets its T timer and waits for an active or standby monitor present frame. If no MAC frame is received before the timer expires, the station assumes it is the only active station and initiates the token claiming procedure to become the active monitor.

3. *Duplicate address test*—If a proper monitor present frame is detected, the station will conduct a duplicate address test. If the frame is returned with

ARI set to logic one, the station must immediately disconnect itself. Unfortunately, no warning messages are given to notify a user; the station simply doesn't connect to the ring.

4. *Participate in neighbor notification*—If the duplicate address test is successful, the station participates in the next NAUN procedure (see the next section).
5. *Request insertion*—The station now requests parameters for ring speed (monitor clock) and timer settings if a timing server is in use, and it begins normal operation.

Neighbor Notification

NAUN is Next Addressable Upstream Neighbor.

Approximately every 7 seconds, the active monitor timer issues a highest-priority active monitor present frame. The next station on the ring receives this frame, copies the frame to its internal buffer, and sets the frame copied and address recognized bits to logic one. The station next stores the source address, which becomes its *Next Addressable Upstream Neighbor* (NAUN). If more than 15 seconds were to go by without a frame from the NAUN address, the station would know that there was a potential break in the ring. This would be the point at which the station would begin to send beacon frames.

Once the ARI and FCI bits are set and the NAUN copied, the station sends the active monitor present frame on around the ring and sets a 20-second timer. Because the ARI and FCI bits are set, no other station will copy the frame, and the active monitor will remove it. When the 20-second timer expires, the station will send a standby monitor present frame with ARI and BRI cleared to logic zero so that its downstream neighbor can use the frame to discover its NAUN.

The procedure thus continues until the active monitor receives a standby monitor present frame from its NAUN. If the active monitor ever sees a monitor present frame with BRI or FCI cleared to logic zero, it will assume that it is the only station on the ring. The active monitor will also assume that if no monitor present frame is received within a fixed period of time, there is a break or defective station in the ring.

BRIDGING RINGS

SRB is Source Route Bridging.

An *RIF* is a Routing Information Field.

Although Token-Rings are perfectly capable of using transparent bridging, the more common method is *Source Route Bridging* (**SRB**). The primary difference between SRB and transparent bridging is that source route bridges contain no address tables. All routing information is controlled by workstations. Stations must maintain their own address tables and insert Routing Information Fields (**RIFs**) in frames that are sent to bridged rings. Figure 5.6 shows the structure of the RIF. The control field is used to designate

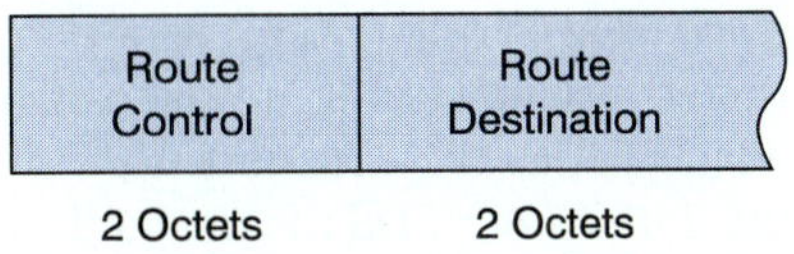

Figure 5.6 Routing Information Field (RIF)

- broadcast type,
- direction,
- length of RIF field, and
- maximum transmittable frame length.

As shown in Figure 5.6, each of the seven possible route designation fields lists the source ring, the current bridge designator, and the next ring in a format: (RingA-Bridge1-RingB) and so forth. Designator fields are strung together to include all of the hops that exist in the path between the source and destination addresses. This method requires that bridges only be programmed to know their own designators and the ring numbers of the adjacent rings. Given the 30-octet limit of the RIF field, a maximum of seven hops is possible.

SWITCHES FOR TOKEN-RING

Switching technology is available for Token-Ring. Because Token-Ring is limited to 16 Mbps, obtaining higher bandwidth would require forklifting an entire Token-Ring network and replacing it with Ethernet. Such an undertaking could be prohibitively expensive. Replacing MSAUs with Token-Ring switches provides a less expensive solution. IEEE 802.5r provides for a *Dedi-*

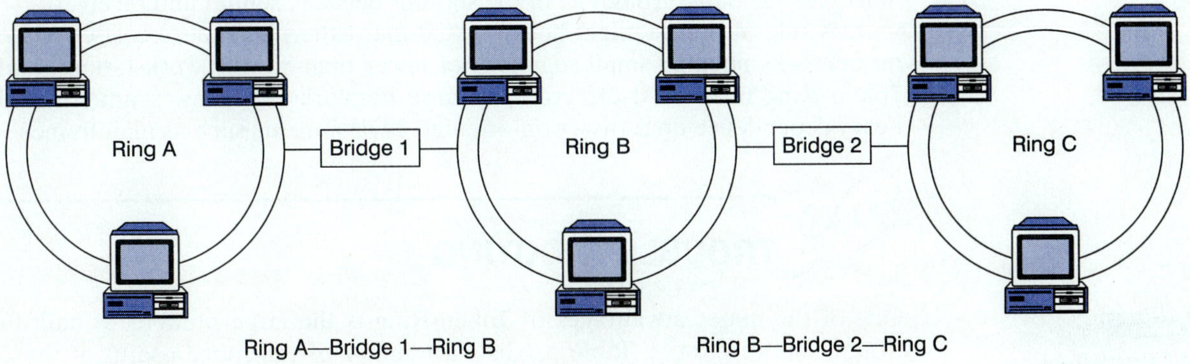

Figure 5.7 Route Designators in a Source Route Bridge Configuration

cated Token-Ring (DTR) in which NICs normally connected to MSAUs can be directly connected to a Token-Ring switch that supports C-port. Such a switch would act as the concentrator for the ring. An additional feature called *Transmit Immediate* (TxI) is available that provides full duplex transmission, effectively doubling the 16-Mbps bandwidth.

Token-Ring switches can also be equipped to learn the MAC addresses of both source route bridged stations (RIF field present) and transparent bridged stations. The result of this feature is that an Ethernet segment can be connected to a Token-Ring segment through a switch. Older Token-Rings can be kept in place and newer, faster Ethernet segments added to the overall network plan.

ADVANTAGES AND DISADVANTAGES

Token-Ring's primary advantage is its deterministic access. Where Ethernet develops significant collision problems at 30%–40% of peak load, Token-Ring actually improves its efficiency up to as much as 90%–95% of peak load. Up to 260 workstations can operate on a single ring, with as many as 150–200 active stations not exceeding the peak efficiency. In addition, Token-Ring operates at 16 Mbps compared to 10 Mbps on Ethernet. Another advantage of Token-Ring is its built-in ring management tools. Other than collision management, Ethernet has no such tools making it more difficult to troubleshoot.

The primary disadvantage of Token-Ring is its relatively high cost. NICs and MSAUs are significantly more expensive than other protocols. Still, if high workstation count per segment or high data transfer volumes or large data file transfers are common on a network, Token-Ring might well be the most cost-effective choice of protocols.

Token-Ring stations wishing to transmit must wait for a free token. Ethernet stations may transmit as soon as a clear cable is detected and will pass data in real time, directly to the receiving station. Token-Ring sending stations must pass the data through all of the stations between sender and receiver.

A rule of thumb might be suggested that Ethernet is more cost-effective on networks needing small segments of fewer than 50–100 workstations, and Token-Ring more cost-effective on large networks with few segments and heavy dependence on transaction-oriented environments such as mainframes.

TROUBLESHOOTING

One of the major advantages of Token-Ring is the large number of built-in troubleshooting tools. Table 5.1 lists a number of the more useful of these functions. If you are equipped with a protocol analyzer, these frames can be monitored to determine the health of a Token-Ring network.

Table 5.1 Built-in Token-Ring Troubleshooting Functions

MAC Control Frames

Token-Ring provides 25 media access control frames that are responsible for (1) ring insertion by any station joining the ring, (2) physical ring control, (3) network management, and (4) error monitoring. These frames are contained within the chip set on NICs and may be analyzed by a protocol analyzer to monitor the health of the ring.

All Token-Ring NICs contain a network management product that is composed of a *Ring Error Monitor* (REM), a *Configuration Report Server* (CRS), and a *Ring Parameter Server* (RPS). A network management agent, resident in each NIC, uses REM, CRS, and RPS to provide such features as error monitoring, NAUN, configuration details, and ring parameter control.

Ring insertion frames.

- *Duplicate Address Test*—Guarantees a unique address for all stations or insertion cannot take place
- *Initialize Ring Station*—Used by the Ring Parameter Server (RPS) to send the ring parameters to the inserting station. RPS service is provided in every Token-Ring NIC.
- *Lobe Media Test*—Tests the condition of the physical media before a physical connection to the ring can take place. Unfortunately, if there is no station message generated, the station simply cannot connect.
- *Request Initialization*—Generated by inserting station to request the ring parameters

Physical layer control frames.

- *AM Present (Active Monitor Present)*—Transmitted every 7 seconds and at the end of Ring Purge to notify all stations of its active presence
- *Beacon frames*—Transmitted whenever a station detects that either a signal has been lost from its neighbor or a streaming data condition exists (similar to a jabbering Ethernet NIC) in which a continuous stream of unformatted data is present
- *Claim token*—A procedure initiated by any station that detects the absence of the active monitor. The station with the highest address wins.
- *Ring purge*—Used by the active monitor to clear the ring and generate a new token whenever it detects an error on the ring
- *Standby Monitor Present*—Generated during NAUN by all standby monitors to acknowledge Active Monitor present

continued

Table 5.1 *continued*

Network management frames

- *Change Parameters*—Used by the configuration report server (CRS) to modify NIC parameters
- *Remove Ring Station*—Used by CRS to eject a station from the ring
- *Report New Active Monitor*—Generated by a new AM following a token claiming process
- *Report SUA Change*—Generated following NAUN by stations whose Stored Upstream Address (SUA) has changed since the last NAUN determined the address of the NIC's next upstream neighbor on the ring

Error monitoring frames

- *Report Error*—A count of the soft errors from higher-layer protocols that are potentially recoverable
- *Report Monitor*—Generated by any station that detects a problem with either the AM or a token-claiming process
- *Report NAUN Incomplete*—Generated when a station does not hear from its upstream neighbor during NAUN

Token-Ring Troubleshooting Chart

Figure 5.8 shows a troubleshooting flowchart that should prove handy for determining the faulty node in a Token-Ring network. Begin with the NIC. If a diagnostic disk is available, use it to determine the functionality of the NIC. Many NICs and MSAUs are equipped with diagnostic LEDs. Use the LEDs to determine the operating state of each node. If both NIC and MSAU are functioning correctly, the fault will be in either the cable or connectors. Use a cable tester or time domain reflectometer to troubleshoot cable problems.

In the event that you are not equipped with the proper test equipment and diagnostics, simple substitution with known good components can be a quick method for locating the fault. Although MSAUs are relatively expensive, spare NICs, cable, and connectors should always be kept on hand. A faulty node can also be discovered by swapping components to see if the trouble moves with the faulty device.

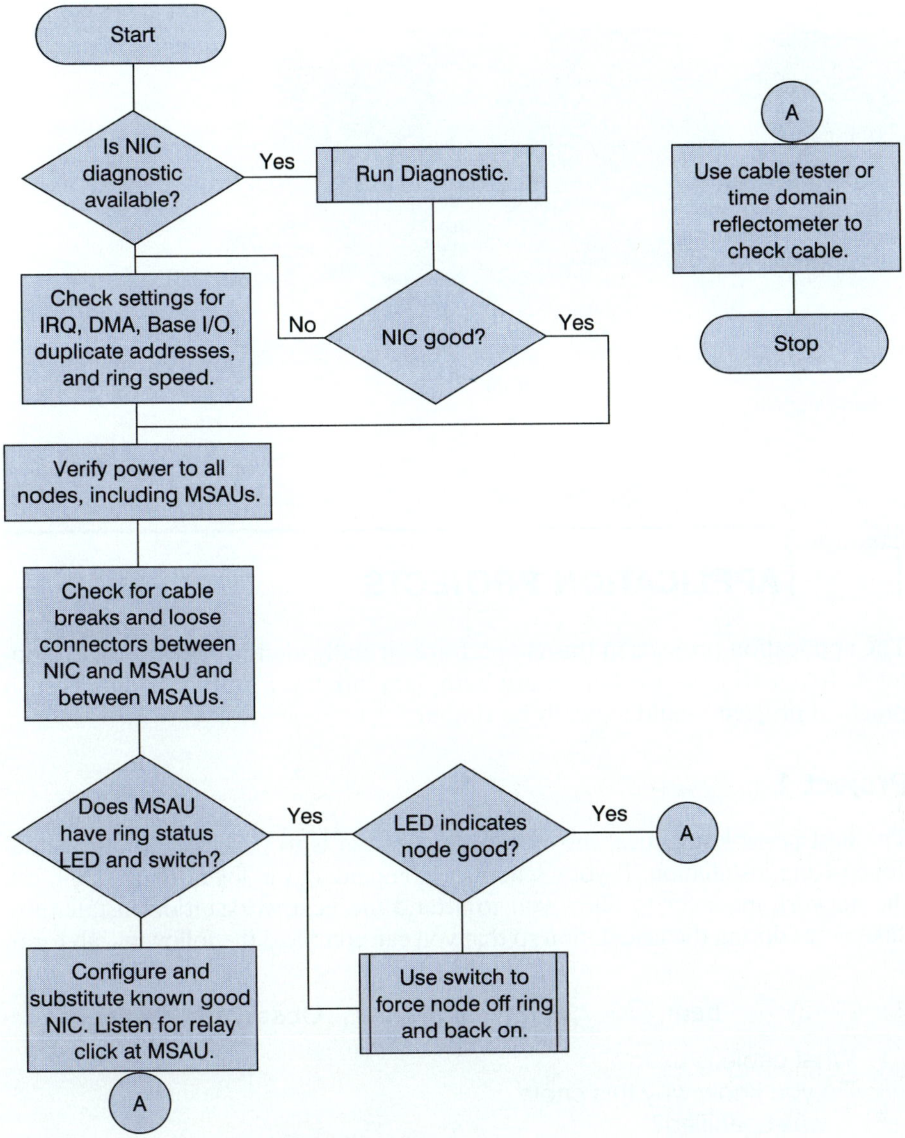

Figure 5.8 Token-Ring Troubleshooting Chart

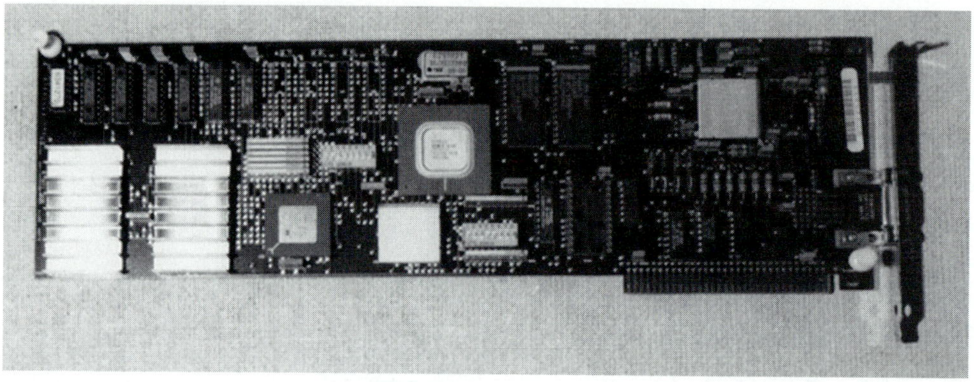

Figure 5.9 Older 4 MBPS Token-Ring NIC

APPLICATION PROJECTS

The application projects in this chapter are virtually identical to those in Chapter 4. Token-Ring and Ethernet are both data link layer protocols, and as such practical projects would logically be similar.

Project 1

The best possible practical installation application is to participate in an actual Token-Ring installation. If your school or company has a Token-Ring LAN, ask the network manager to allow you to attend the next workstation installation. Take notes during the installation so that you can complete the following lab form.

Item	Observed Result
1. What cable is used? Do you know why this cable was specified?	
2. Describe the procedure that was used to install the NIC.	
3. What is the NIC address?	
4. Is the NIC address universal or local?	
5. Which speed of Token-Ring is being used?	

Item	Observed Result
6. Why was the version of Token-Ring chosen?	
7. What topology does the LAN use?	
8. Is the segment bridged? If so, how and to how many segments? What kind of bridge is used?	
9. Is the LAN peer-to-peer or client/server?	
10. What is the file server operating system, if any?	

Project 2

Design a Token-Ring LAN to service a small office composed of an accountant, a receivables bookkeeper, a payables bookkeeper, and a general ledger bookkeeper. Your design should include

- specifications for cables, connectors, NICs, and workstations;
- drawings to show wiring and equipment placement; and
- a list of all equipment required.

REVIEW QUESTIONS

1. What topologies are suitable for Token-Ring?
2. Describe each of the fields for an IEEE 802.5 MAC frame.
3. List the duties of the active monitor.
4. Briefly discuss the steps required to insert a station into a ring.
5. What is NAUN, and how is it implemented?
6. What is the maximum hop count of bridged Token-Ring segments? Why?
7. How many stations can be connected to a single Token-Ring segment?
8. Discuss the differences between Ethernet and Token-Ring.
9. When installing a coaxial cable lobe, what kind of connector must be used?
10. On what layers of the OSIRM is Token-Ring implemented?

11. How does an Token-Ring frame designate a broadcast frame?
12. What is the data-encoding technique used by Token-Ring, and what are its characteristics?
13. What kinds of bridges may be used on Token-Ring?
14. What is the maximum practical limit to the number of workstations on a single Token-Ring segment? Why?
15. Briefly discuss the advantages and disadvantages of Token-Ring.

6

ARCNET

INTRODUCTION

ARCNET is one of the few popular LAN protocols that has never become a registered standard. Developed in 1977 by Datapoint Corporation, *Attached Resource Computing Network* (ARCNET) is a baseband token passing bus protocol that in some ways resembles the IEEE 802.4 standard. In 1981 the SMC corporation developed a single-chip LAN controller based on ARCNET, and in 1986 it introduced a new chip set that incorporated the token passing bus. Most industry-standard ARCNET applications now use this new chip set. It is probably accurate to suggest that ARCNET popularity is declining; however, there are a large number of applications still in place making ARCNET worthy of your attention.

This chapter will be concerned with the following subjects:

- Specifications and capabilities
- Physical layer topologies
- Token passing
- Frame formats
- ARCNET Plus
- Advantages and disadvantages

SPECIFICATIONS

OSI Reference

At the physical layer, ARCNET is implemented in a star topology with workstations connected to active hubs as demonstrated in Figure 6.1. The maximum distance between active hubs is 600 meters, and single workstations connected to active hubs may be up to 600 meters from the active hub port. Passive hubs may be used to extend the number of workstations connected to an active hub port. Passive hubs may not be more than 30.5 meters from an active hub and may not connect to each other. Workstations must not be farther than 30.5 meters from a passive hub. Active hubs may be connected together to extend the overall span; however, the maximum distance between workstations at opposite ends of the span cannot exceed 20,000 feet (a bit more than 6,000 meters).

SMC documentation demonstrates a method for daisy-chaining stations connected to active hubs with RG-62 coaxial cable. Up to eight nodes may be connected in this manner. An eight-port active hub, for example, would be able to support as many as 64 nodes without requiring passive hubs. In practical application, however, this technique can provide unpredictable results.

In addition, RG-59 and RG-11 (75-ohm) coaxial may be used. Both IBM Type 1 STP (150-ohm) and Type 3 UTP (100-ohm) twisted pair are acceptable. When using twisted pair, filter baluns are required to meet FCC RFI requirements. Connectors used with twisted pair include four-pin RJ-11, six-pin RJ-14, or eight-pin RJ-45. SMC uses RJ-14 connectors with DATA- connected to pin 3 and DATA+ connected to pin 4. The color insert Figure 13 shows an eight-port active hub.

Figure 6.1 Eight-Port Active with Four-Port Passive Hub

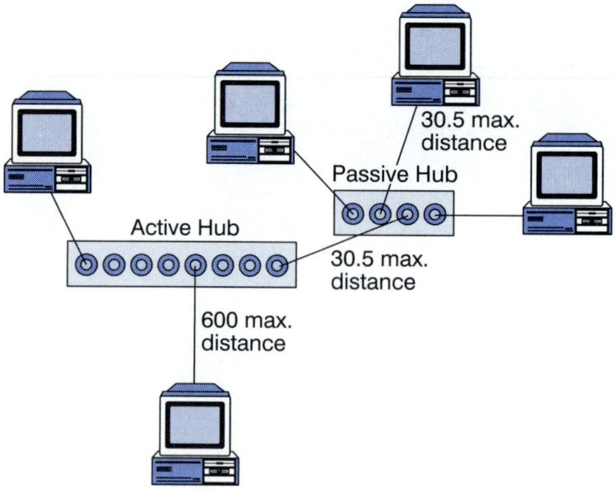

All unused ARCNET ports should be terminated in the characteristic impedance. Terminate UTP twisted pair with 100-ohm terminators, RG-62 coaxial with 93-ohm terminators, and RG-59 coaxial with 75-ohm terminators. In some active hubs, termination is automatic and an additional terminator is not required. Check the manual to be certain.

Frame Formats

As shown in Figure 6.2, ARCNET contains five different frame formats:

- *ITT (Invitation To Transmit)*—ITT is used as the token. Its primary purpose is to transfer control from one workstation to another.
- *FBE (Free Buffer Enquiry)*—An FBE frame is sent by a station that wishes to transmit data to the intended receiver to determine whether the receiving station has sufficient buffer space to allocate to the frame that will be sent.
- *PAC (Packet)*—This is the actual frame in which user data are sent. It may contain up to 508 bytes of data. Compared to other protocols, 508 bytes of data is not a very efficient size. Large file transfers would be encumbered by relatively more overhead because of this small frame size. The trade-off, however, is that small frame sizes result in fewer retransmissions when errors are encountered.
- *ACK (Acknowledgment)*—Acknowledgment frames are used to acknowledge the receipt of data frames or FBEs.
- *NAK (No AcKnowledgement)*—NAK frames are used to notify sending stations either that a packet frame has encountered a CRC error or that the receive buffer does not have room for a new packet.

Protocol Format

For any station to send a frame, it must acquire an ITT frame. ITT frames are passed from station to station in the order of their addresses. Upon receipt of an ITT frame, a station wishing to send traffic initiates an FBE frame addressed to the intended destination node to determine whether the destination is able to accept a data frame. If available, the destination node responds with an ACK frame; if unavailable, an NAK frame. Upon receipt of an ACK, the sending station assembles a data frame and transmits it to the destination.

To eliminate the necessity of passing an ITT frame to stations that either do not exist or are not powered up, a process similar to Token-Ring's NAUN must take place. Each NIC must learn its own address (by reading switch settings on the NIC) and the address of the next station in the logical "ring." The hierarchy is determined by address beginning with lowest address and ending

Figure 6.2 ARCNET Frame Formats

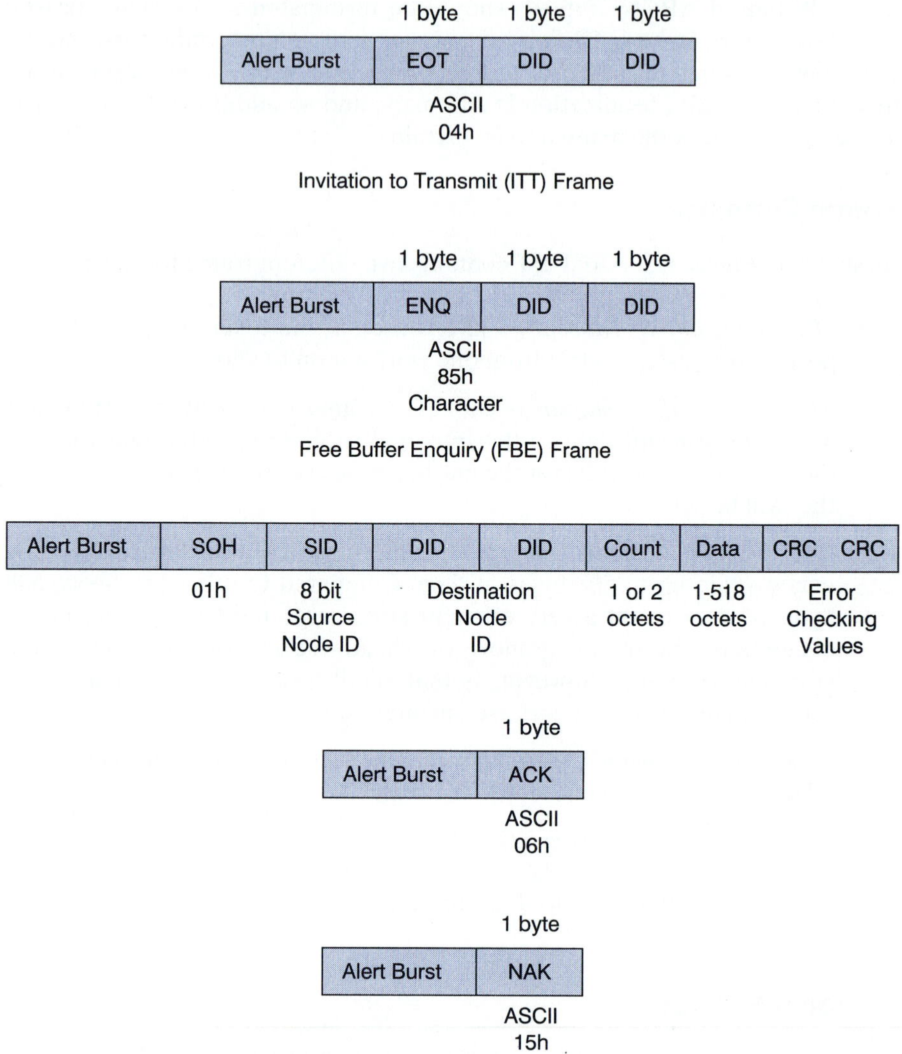

with highest address. A station's neighbor is simply the NIC with the next higher address.

Whenever a node enters or exits the logical ring, a "system reconfiguration" must take place. When a device is first powered up, it initiates the *recon* process. Recon may also be initiated by any station that has not received an ITT for 840 ms. A system reconfiguration consists of 765 repetitions of a sequence of eight logical ones followed by a single logical zero. Because of the excessively long time that a recon takes, all token passing is stopped and each NIC resets its Next ID (NID) register to its own address. A timer is started that is set to a value based on a constant (146) multiplied by 255 minus the station address (SID). In this manner, the highest address times out first and can issue the first ITT frame. Each next lowest address, in turn, sends its ITT allowing all nodes to learn their neighbor's address.

When a station is removed from the bus, its neighbor merely increments its NID register to the value of its new neighbor.

As seen in Figure 6.1, each frame begins with an *Alert Burst*. An Alert Burst is six logic one bits that serve the same general purpose as the start delimiters in Ethernet and Token-Ring frames. In fact, you may see drawings in some references that use the label Start Delimiter (SD).

Data frames in ARCNET may contain up to 508 octets; ARCNET Plus data frames contain up to 4,224 octets. In both cases, a length field is used to denote the actual number of octets in the data field.

ARCNET PLUS

A new version of ARCNET has been released that offers several improvements to the protocol:

- Bandwidth is increased to 20 MHz, more than adequate for many local area network requirements.
- Seven additional frames have been made available.
- Packet size is increased to 4,224 octets of data for supervisory functions between nodes.
- Techniques also exist to transport ARCNET Plus frames over TCP/IP for wide area networks (see RFC 1201).

Figure 6.3 shows the ARCNET Plus frame formats. Note the addition of an X to differentiate between an ARCNET Plus field and ARCNET.

- *XITT (Extended Invitation to Transmit)*—Used to pass the token from an ARCNET Plus node to a standard or unknown node
- *XTOK (ARCNET Plus TOKen)*—Token frame passed between ARCNET Plus nodes only
- *XENQ (ARCNET Plus Enquiry)*—Initiates control functions
- *XRSP (ARCNET Plus Response)*—The response frame to answer an XPAC or XENQ
- *XPAC (ARCNET Plus user data PACket)*—The user data frame between ARCNET Plus nodes. Note that the data field can be up to 4,224 octets.

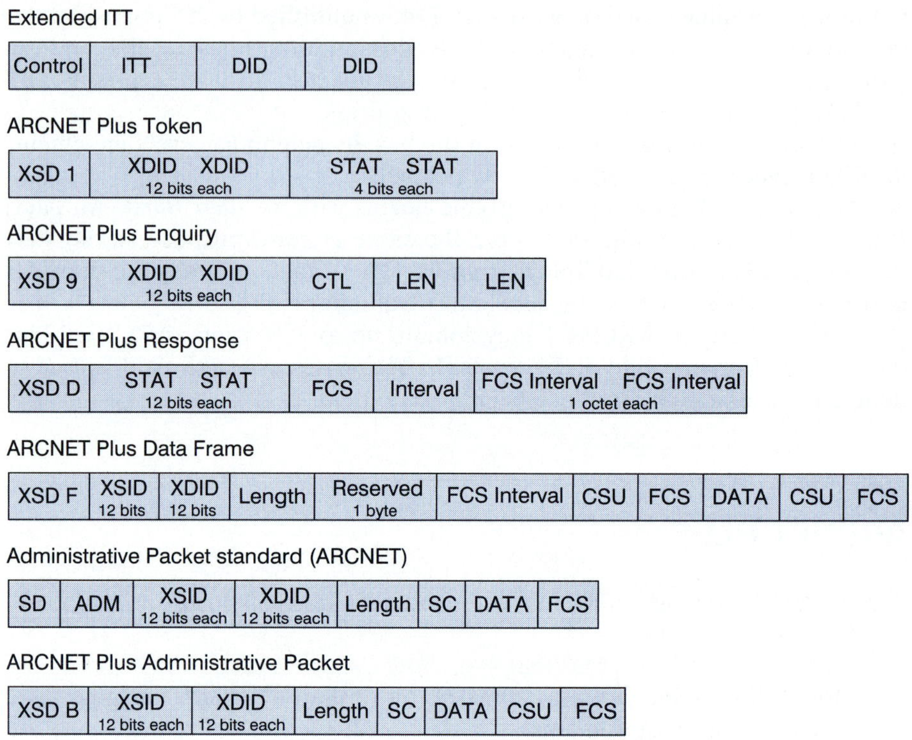

Figure 6.3 ARCNET Plus Frame Formats

- *ADM (ADMinistrative Packet)*—Administrative information frame used between standard ARCNET nodes
- *XADM (ARCNET Plus ADMinistrative Packet)*—Used between ARCNET Plus nodes to pass administrative information

INSTALLATION REQUIREMENTS

ARCNET does not offer universal addressing, which means that each NIC must have an address set on it that is unique to the network. This process is usually accomplished by setting DIP switches on the NIC. Additionally, some NICs require a mode DIP switch setting and jumpers that determine such things as IRQ number, PC buffer base address, and DMA channel number. (Color insert Figure 14 in the color insert shows an ARCNET NIC address DIP switch.) Care should be taken to prevent conflict with other devices installed in the workstation.

Even though each NIC may have a unique local address, there is a definite possibility that identical node addresses may exist on other LANs. This presents a problem when attempting to interconnect ARCNET LANs (i.e., which LAN is the address on, and how will a router distinguish between identical nodes?). RFC 1201 presents methods for transmitting ARCNET over TCP/IP by assigning the 8- or 12-bit node IDs as the least significant bits of a unique 32-bit IP address.

Active and passive hubs may be located anywhere within the distance limitation requirements. Active hubs may be stacked to increase segment length, but in no event may the maximum length of the span exceed 20,000 feet between any two nodes. SMC recommends a minimum cable segment length of 10 feet, even when nodes are immediately adjacent to one another.

ADVANTAGES AND DISADVANTAGES

ARCNET has two primary advantages:

- For small LANs of perhaps 25 workstations or fewer, it is less expensive than either Ethernet or Token-Ring.
- Using active hubs, ARCNET is able to span up to 20,000 feet between workstations at opposite ends of the overall span. This is an improvement over both Ethernet and Token-Ring.

In addition, ARCNET is probably best suited for smaller, office-type LANs that require minimal server access.

Disadvantages include the following:

- Low bandwidth (2.5 Mbps). Although ARCNET Plus provides 20 Mbps, there is not a large installed base, and support may be very limited.
- No official standard
- No universal addressing. Address fields are also quite small compared to other protocols. The eight-bit length of the Source and Destination Node ID address fields limits an ARCNET LAN to a maximum of 255 workstations (Address zero is not allowed). This shortcoming is particularly onerous if wide area protocols such as TCP/IP are in use that require unique 32-bit address fields.
- Small frame size (504 bytes of user data)

TROUBLESHOOTING

ARCNET is relatively easy to troubleshoot. Faulty nodes or cable segments may be found by simply disconnecting cable segments, one at a time, without disturbing the other workstations. This process would cause Token-Ring to stop long enough to accomplish a neighbor notification and force Ethernet into a lot of unnecessary communication to discover the disconnected port.

Most ARCNET active ports and NICs have LEDs that indicate activity on the cable. An additional LED may be available that indicates that a network reconfiguration is being performed. Ensure that the activity LED flashes when a station is turned on or frames are being sent. Different manufacturers may implement the indicators in different ways. Be certain to consult the device manual.

One of the quickest ways to disable an ARCNET LAN is for two NICs to have the same address. Because addresses are set by switches on the NICs, this problem is easy to produce. Careful attention to the logging of address settings and the switch settings themselves is the best way to prevent duplicate addresses. Note that address zero is not used and that addresses are set in hexadecimal. Switches are usually of the DIP variety. Each switch represents a binary value. Care should be taken to note the position of least and most significant bits and the switch positions for logical one and logical zero.

SMC provides for up to eight workstations, configured in a bus topology driven by a single active hub port, when using coaxial. In my experience, more than five or six workstations on the same cable segment can produce unpredictable results. For example, if one workstation is not powered up, another workstation on the same cable segment may have trouble logging in to a server. When powered up and logged on in the "correct" sequence, both workstations are able to communicate. Relocating one station to another segment eliminates the problem.

The author has used cheap "screw-on" BNC connectors on RG-62 and was forever after plagued with intermittent and unpredictable problems. Properly soldered BNC connectors will provide significantly enhanced, more trouble-free operation.

APPLICATION PROJECT

Design a local area network, using ARCNET, for a small medical clinic that consists of four doctors, a bookkeeper, receptionist, and one nurse. Provide for E-mail, a workstation that will be used as a dedicated server, and a single shared laser printer.

For the installation:

1. Make a list of node addresses that each node will be assigned.
2. List the length of each cable that will be needed.
3. Create a parts list that includes cable, connectors, NICs, and hubs.
4. Draw the layout of the installation and wire runs.

REVIEW QUESTIONS

1. Describe the topology(s) used by ARCNET.
2. What cable types are used by ARCNET?
3. Compare ARCNET to ARCNET Plus.
4. Where would you go to find more data on ARCNET?
5. What is the maximum span between two nodes on an ARCNET LAN?
6. Discuss the limitations of ARCNET.
7. Why is ARCNET considered deterministic?
8. What is the problem with using ARCNET in wide area networks?
9. How must terminators be used in an ARCNET installation?
10. If called on to recommend a LAN protocol, when would you recommend ARCNET?

7 FDDI

INTRODUCTION

FDDI is Fiber Distributed Data Interface.
CDDI stands for Copper Distributed Data Interface.

As networks grow and migrate to enterprise wide installations, demands for bandwidth, distance, and fault tolerance become overriding factors in the selection of topology and protocol. *Fiber Distributed Data Interface* (**FDDI**) does an admirable job of satisfying these requirements. Today's networks, using twisted pair and coaxial cable, are very quickly filling available bandwidth and exceeding their distance limitations. A large building or college campus, for example, could easily require high-speed, high-bandwidth data for interactive audiovisual communications as well as exceed the distance limitations of copper based wiring. Although techniques such as Fast Ethernet and *Copper Distributed Data Network* (**CDDI**) exist to supply necessary bandwidth, neither coax nor copper will be sufficient for the distances involved in interconnecting all of the buildings on campus. FDDI would be an ideal solution for solving both distance and bandwidth problems.

This chapter will be concerned with the following FDDI topics:

- Technical description and specifications
- Topology description
- Protocol analysis
- Advantages and disadvantages
- An FDDI case study

TECHNICAL DESCRIPTION

FDDI has been designed, from the beginning, as an all–fiber optic network topology and protocol. Data speeds up to 100 Mbps are easily achievable, as are distances of up to 100 km. In addition, as many as 1,000 workstations may be attached. These are impressive statistics compared to the 16-Mbps rate of Token-Ring or 10 Mbps using Ethernet. Table 7.1 shows the more important components of FDDI.

TOPOLOGY

FDDI is organized as a token-passing ring, thus allowing all of the advantages of Token-Ring such as increased throughput and as much as 90%–95% saturation. FDDI does not, however, require stations to relinquish the token after sending a frame. This means that an entire large file can be sent without waiting for other stations. Figure 7.1 depicts the dual, counterrotating ring configuration that ensures the integrity of the physical media.

More than one advantage is gained by ring redundancy. If the primary ring were to develop a break, the secondary ring would be able to substitute. If the cable suffered a break in both primary and secondary rings, the workstations adjacent to the break would immediately begin receiving on their primary rings and sending on their secondary rings. In this manner the integrity of the ring is preserved. It is also possible for both rings to be used simultaneously. In this mode, the transmission speed increases to 200 Mbps.

Physical implementation at each node connected to the FDDI ring is accomplished using a dual-port transceiver that functions as the interface converter between the fiber light source and electrical signals (usually transported via coaxial cable). Each transceiver contains ports for each fiber ring and the

Table 7.1 FDDI Parameters

Parameter	Value
Optical source	Infrared LED or laser
Wavelength	1,300 nm
Energy requirements	–20 db minimum
Fiber types	62.5/125 μm in multimode or single mode
Maximum nodes	1,000
Maximum total length	100 km
Distance between stations	2 km—multimode 40 km—single mode
Power budget between nodes	11 db

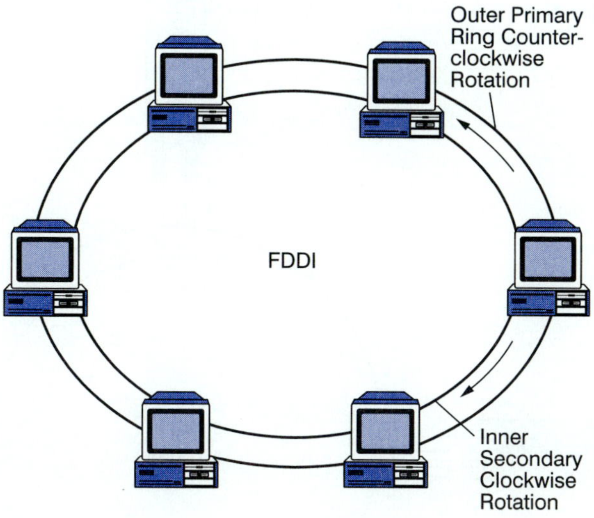

Figure 7.1 FDDI Counterrotating Ring

coaxial cables (note that coaxial is not needed if the transceiver is implemented on an NIC). In addition, the transceiver would perform the automatic reconnection process in the event of a break in the fiber link.

Workstations are connected to the ring(s) in three different modes:

- *Class A*—Attachment to both rings in either redundant failure prevention mode or a bandwidth doubling mode that uses both rings for transmission rather than redundancy
- *Class B*—Attachment to only one ring (somewhat less expensive)
- *Class C*—Implementation of the ring within a concentrator, similar to a Token-Ring MSAU, with workstations attached in a star fashion to the concentrator. This mode provides the greatest flexibility and ease of troubleshooting.

Under Class A redundancy conditions, incoming light signals are routed through the transceiver input on the outer ring, converted to electrical signals, sent to the NIC for processing, reconverted to light, and sent on around the outer ring. Simultaneously, the light signals are also directed to the inner ring and passed on (the inner ring is only acting as the redundant backup). If a break should occur in the outer ring, the transceiver merely takes its light source from the inner ring. Should the break affect both rings, the transceiver sets its input to the outer ring, and its output to the inner ring. All other nodes must detect changes and implement an appropriate process. Figure 7.2 shows ring breaks and the rerouting done by the transceivers.

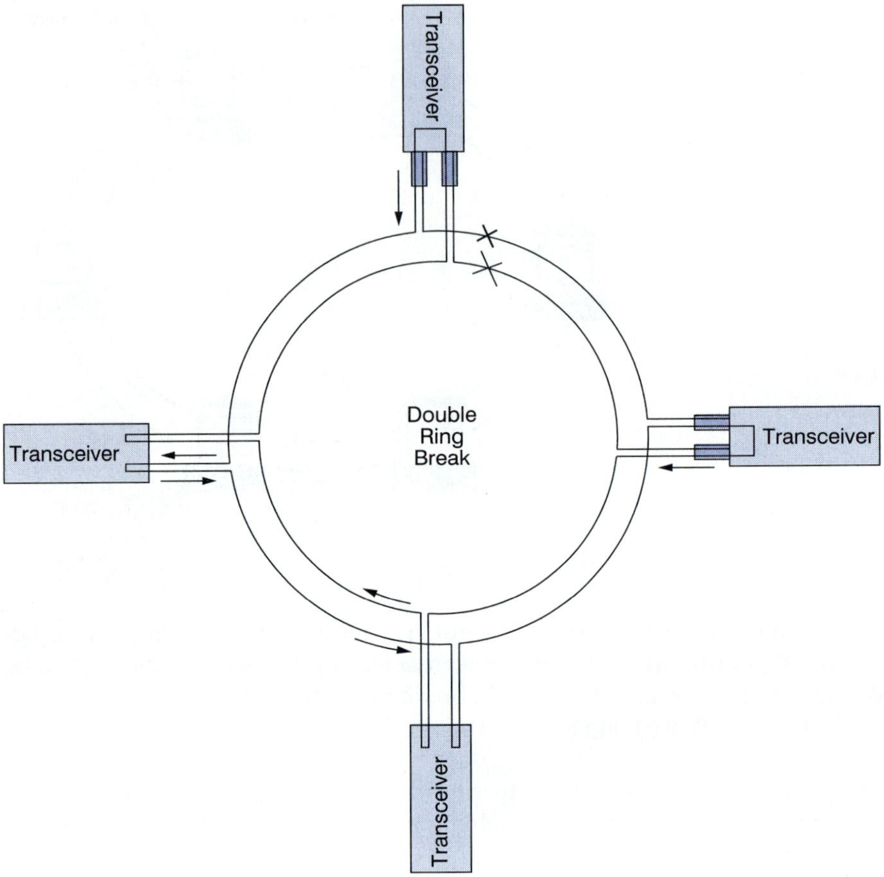

Figure 7.2
Transceiver Reconfiguration on Ring Break

PROTOCOL ANALYSIS

The FDDI protocol is divided into four separate documents:

1. The first document describes the *Physical Medium Dependent* (PMD) sublayer. This layer corresponds to the OSI physical layer. The PMD requirements include definitions for the fibers themselves, transceivers, optical power, and the Media Interface Connector (MIC).

2. Document 2 deals with the *PHYsical layer* (PHY). In FDDI the OSI physical layer is divided into two sublayers, PMD (lower sublayer) and PHY (upper sublayer). PHY covers the connection between the physical and MAC sublayer of the OSI data link layer 2.

3. The third FDDI layer is the *Media Access Control* (MAC). The FDDI MAC corresponds to the same OSI data link sublayer. FDDI frame formats are defined by the MAC.

4. The fourth FDDI document, labeled *Station ManagemenT* (SMT), covers the supervisory functions for station control and monitoring. It is the function of SMT to detect cable faults and redirect data as required. SMT is unique to FDDI and does not exist in the OSIRM. Figure 7.3 shows the construction of an FDDI MAC frame. As can be seen, the field order is identical to Token-Ring, from which most of the FDDI protocol is taken. Figure 7.4 displays the relationship of an FDDI MAC frame to the OSIRM.

FDDI uses *Protocol Data Units* (PDUs) in the same way as Token-Ring. The information field data packets can range from 128 to 4,500 bytes, and the overall frame length is limited to a maximum of 9,000 bytes.

ADVANTAGES AND DISADVANTAGES

FDDI implementation will produce numerous advantages:

- Large numbers of users (up to 1,000)
- 100-Mbps bandwidth (200 Mbps if both rings are combined)
- Very long distances (up to 200 km overall, with 2 km between workstations)
- High reliability due to redundant rings and SMT fault management
- High immunity to electromagnetic and electrostatic interference
- Efficient host attachment availability

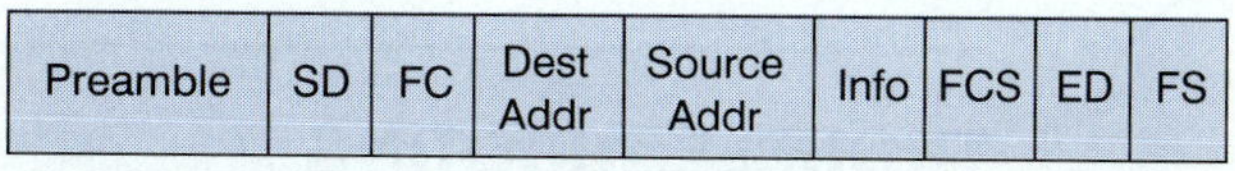

Figure 7.3 FDDI MAC Frame

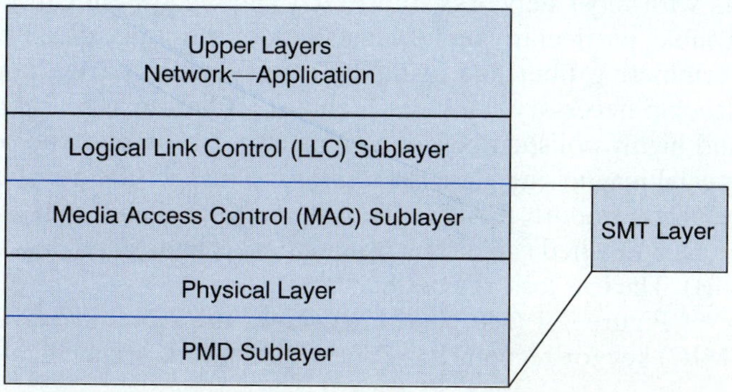

Figure 7.4 FDDI Protocol Stack

- Multimedia support due to high bandwidth
- Token prereleased at the end of a data frame

A few disadvantages also exist using FDDI:

- High cost of installation and hardware
- Existing requirements to connect to lower-speed wire-based systems
- Speed conversion problems
- No active monitor

WHEN TO USE FDDI

For FDDI to be a realistic solution, given the very high cost to implement, there should be a need for

- very high bandwidth;
- isochronous, high-bandwidth data traffic such as interactive voice and video;
- distances between stations in excess of 100 meters;
- mission-critical requirements for fault tolerance; and
- electrically noisy environments.

TROUBLESHOOTING

As with most networks, the FDDI cabling system can be a major source of trouble, particularly on new installations if not installed by experienced people. Terminating fiber and installing connectors requires training and practice to develop necessary skills. Each end of a fiber must be cut at exactly 90 degrees and highly polished before a connector can be epoxyed onto the fiber end. A special magnifying glass is necessary to inspect the polished end to ensure it is perfectly smooth. Fiber cable testers are available that ensure the confidence of each finished cable. The primary test is light signal loss measured in decibels (dB). The less loss, the better.

Figure 7.7 (see page 119) shows the ANSI *Media Interface Connection* (MIC) key for receptacles. Four combinations are available:

CASE STUDY

Let us examine the typical, multibuilding college campus shown in figure 7.5. The campus could easily cover an area of several city blocks and serve vocational programs, such as a machine shop, that are electrically noisy owing to the large number of motors that are running. There is a clear need for a fiber installation to deal with both distance and electrical noise problems. In addition, many educational institutions are installing multimedia systems that require higher bandwidth to deal with the interactive voice and video requirements of, for example, a remote classroom using a centralized CD-ROM "jukebox" for voice and video presentations or an on-line lecture delivered from a central location to remote classrooms.

It may be arguable that a college classroom is a noncritical mission because lessons might be delayed without severe consequences, but if the entire campus is shut down because the backbone distribution system for data is inoperative, the additional reliability of FDDI might very well justify its increased cost.

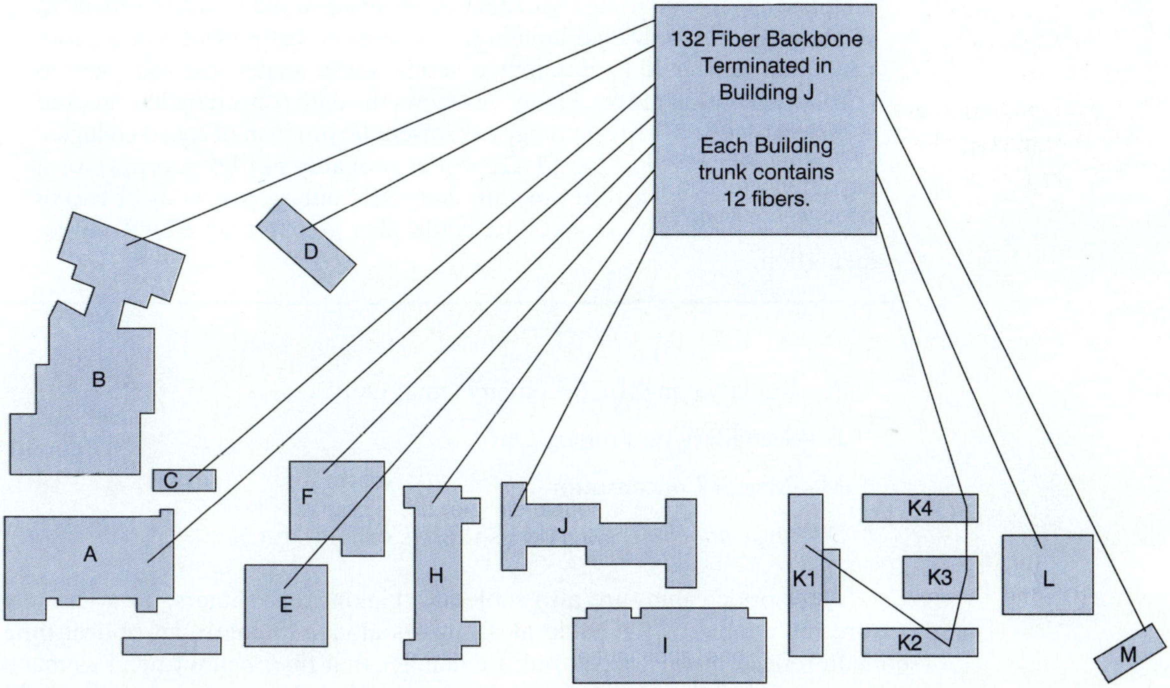

Figure 7.5 Fiber Optic Backbone Distribution

ALTERNATIVES

- A fiber backbone using Fast Ethernet switches and fiber optic data converters may be a less expensive solution.
- Within individual buildings, where electrical noise is not a problem, fiber links could be terminated in a server that will also route to copper-based local LANs if the problem of speed changes can be resolved.
- A recommendation for FDDI would probably not be appropriate if there is no mission-critical function that could not survive a day or two of downtime.
- Budgetary constraints might also preclude an FDDI implementation.
- Use wireless topologies to overcome distance limitations where high bandwidth is not required.

CONCLUSIONS

In the specific case of the college campus, there is a clear need for a fiber installation to deal with distance, multimedia traffic, and electrical noise problems. The typical campus covers a large area. It serves several vocational programs, such as machine shops, welding, and automotive, that are electrically noisy owing to the large number of motors, arc welders, and so forth, that are running.

A fiber backbone using Fast Ethernet switches would be a less expensive solution. Within individual buildings, where electrical noise is not a problem, fiber links could be terminated in a server or router that will route to copper-based local LANs. Figure 7.6 shows the data converters in a stacked configuration. Today's technology has solved the problem of speed changes.

A recommendation for FDDI would probably not be appropriate if there is no mission-critical function that could not survive a day or two of downtime. Budgetary constraints could also preclude an FDDI implementation.

- A—Primary (ring) In, Secondary (ring) Out
- B—Secondary In, Primary Out
- M—Master Concentrator
- S—*Single attachment station* (SAS) to Concentrator

Fiber optic cables are also subject to kinking and shiners. To accurately ensure the quality of the cable at all points along its length, an optical time domain reflectometer is required. Remember that fiber cannot bend as much as coax. Bend radius should not be less than 12 inches and preferably 18–24 inches where possible.

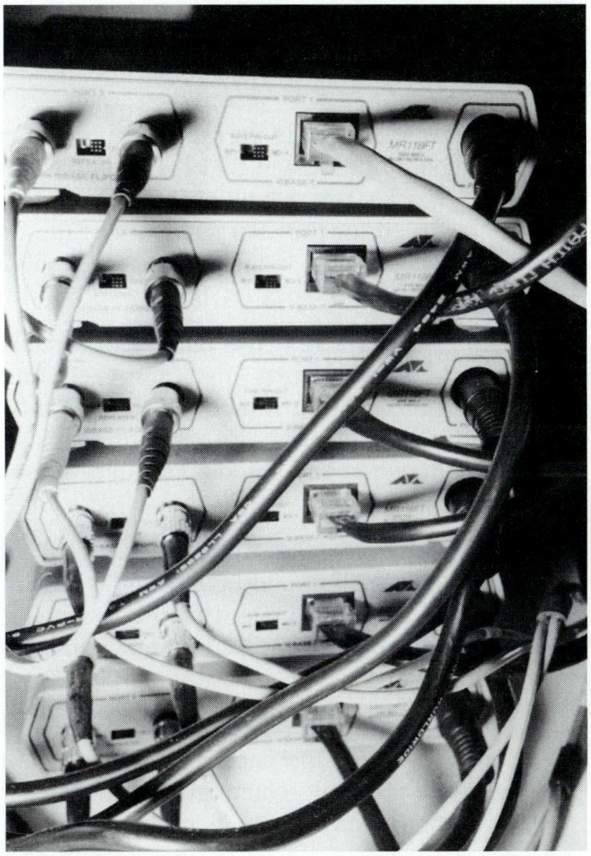

Figure 7.6 Stacked Fiber Optic Data Converters

- A—Primary (ring) In, Secondary (ring) Out
- B—Secondary In, Primary Out
- M—Master Concentrator
- S—Single Attachment Station (SAS) to Concentrator

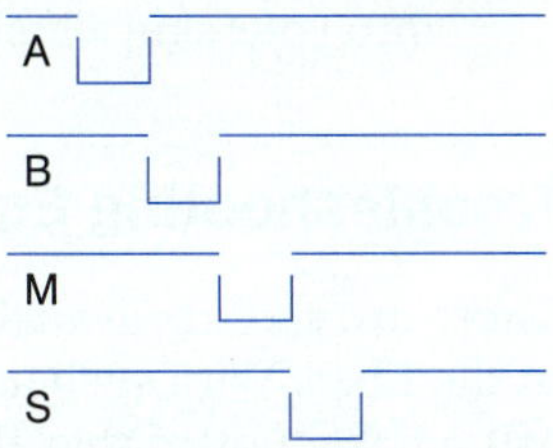

Keys are set into top of connector shell as viewed from the front of the receptacle.

Figure 7.7 Media Interface Connection

Preinstallation Considerations

There are a number of items to consider before your fiber installation begins:

- *Specifications*—Make certain you understand the specifications of the fiber you purchase and that it is suited to the requirements of your network plan. Ensure that all of the devices that connect directly to the fiber are designed for the characteristics of the fiber to be purchased. Mixing multimode and single-mode fiber can result in light loss at unpredictable places.
- *Testing*—Ensure that the factory or vendor has tested your fiber and published the results. Test each reel yourself, before you make the cuts, to ensure that it meets the published test results after shipment. Test each cut length before and after installing connectors. An optical time domain reflectometer and light loss detector are the ideal tools for this job.
- *Cutting to length*—Before making each cut, ensure that bend radii will not be exceeded. Allow additional lengths at each cable end to accommodate trimming and possibly moving the terminated end to a different location in the immediate area. Within the wiring closet, as much as 10 extra feet is advisable.
- *Protecting the installation*—In most cases, fiber is used on a backbone. You can protect the backbone by terminating it at a patch panel. The backbone fiber will remain undisturbed and any changes to configuration can be done with less expensive patch cords.
- *Personal safety*—Laser light, even low power, will damage the retina of your eye. Never look into a laser beam. Broken fiber particles can get into your skin which can cause irritation and sometimes infection.

Troubleshooting Equipment

There are sniffers available that have attachments that allow direct connection to the fiber. With such a device, the FDDI frames may be viewed directly. You will quickly notice that there is no active monitor to aid your troubleshooting. You can, however, begin your search by looking for an excess of voided or beacon frames. Frame type is determined by the value in the token Frame Control field.

FDDI tokens contain four fields:

- Preamble—16 octets
- Start Delimiter—2 octets

- Frame Control—1 octet
- End Delimiter—2 octets

    LED Source: -10 dBm to –25 dBm into 62.5/125 fiber

    LED Receiver: –20 dBm to –35 dBm

    Laser Source: 0 dBm to –35 dBm into single mode fiber

    Laser Receiver: –20 dBm to –45 dBm

Optical loss detectors measure the loss of light in decibels from a calibrated source to the opposite end of a fiber. Optical transmitters are typically set as shown in Table 7.2.

APPLICATION PROJECTS

Project 1

Examine the environment in which you are studying this book. Write a paper that determines the need (or lack of need) for an FDDI backbone. Justify your conclusions, and list alternatives that might be more cost-effective.

Project 2

If an FDDI installation is available, create a drawing that shows the topology of the installation. List the model and part numbers of the components of the FDDI installation. Answer the following questions:

1. What topology is used?
2. What class of NIC connection is used?
3. Why was FDDI chosen (if known)?
4. Is the fiber single- or multimode?

Table 7.2 Fiber Loss Measurements

LED Source: –10 dBm to –25 dBm into 62.5/125 fiber
LED Receiver: –20 dBm to –35 dBm
Laser Source: 0 dBm to –35 dBm into single–mode fiber
Laser Receiver: –20 dBm to –45 dBm

REVIEW QUESTIONS

1. What are the two modes of fiber used in an FDDI installation?
2. Briefly discuss the capabilities of each of the fiber modes.
3. Briefly describe the three classes of NIC connection to FDDI.
4. Briefly discuss the FDDI PDU.
5. List the characteristics of FDDI.
6. List the advantages of FDDI.
7. List the disadvantages of FDDI.
8. What is the maximum number of stations on an FDDI ring?
9. What is the maximum frame size in FDDI? The maximum length of the data field?

NETWARE

8

Novell NetWare

INTRODUCTION

Novell NetWare, through the mid-1990s, dominated the installed base of network microcomputer-based server operating systems. An estimated 50% of all LAN servers have NetWare installed in them. This has not always been true. The original Novell offering, based on the Xerox XNS protocols, was not well received forcing Novell into a reorganization. This may have been, in part, due to the CP/M operating system that was then installed as the microcomputer server/workstation operating system. With the introduction of IBM's PC and the MS-DOS operating system, Novell's fortunes took a major turn for the better.

The study of a network operating system rightly deserves an entire book. It is not possible to deal thoroughly with all of the features of NetWare in a single chapter. The intent of this chapter is to analyze NetWare as it applies to the relationship between NetWare and network environments:

- An analysis of the NetWare operating system as it relates to the OSI model
- An overview of NetWare's functions
- Preparation for installation of server and client software
- Upgrading to version 4.x and 5.x

Because of its well-defined, layered approach to network functions and services, it is often thought that NetWare had a great deal of influence on the ISO as it developed the OSI model. As each new model of personal computer has been released, Novell has released an improved version of NetWare. Early versions were designed to operate on 8088-based systems. By today's standards those systems were very slow and ponderous. Installation and maintenance requirements provided true job security as they were difficult and complicated. Today's versions are considerably easier to deal with, but the *Certified Novell*

CNA stands for Certified Novell Administrator and *CNE* for Certified Novell Engineer.

Administrator (**CNA**) and *Certified Novell Engineer* (**CNE**) ratings that are obtainable from Novell continue to look very good on a résumé. Table 8.1 lists the versions of NetWare and some of their more important features. The mnemonics will be explained as the chapter progresses.

PROTOCOL ANALYSIS

The major components of a NetWare LAN include the following:

- *File server*—A computer containing the NetWare operating system
- *Client*—Usually a workstation that is capable of communicating with the server
- *Router*—A software or hardware device capable of determining the location of an addressable network node. NetWare contains routing functions.
- *Communications server*—That part of NetWare used to control modems and remote communication devices
- *Print server*—A workstation dedicated to the queuing and routing printing services for the network. The NetWare server can also be a print server that controls printing requests.

The NetWare operating system is primarily based on the UNIX kernel. During installation, a unique partition is created and formatted. The system files and all other server-based files are stored in this partition. Once booted, operating system control is passed from MS-DOS to NetWare.

Table 8.1 NetWare Version Features

Version	Processor	Max Users	Features
1A, 1B, 1C	CP/M and 8088	100	Minimal
ELS I&II	80286 80386 80486	4 or 8	Minimal
2.x	80286	100	Duplexing/mirroring, fault tolerance, UPS support
3.x	80386/486	250	ODI and TCP/IP available
4.x	80386/486/Pentium	1000	Bindery changed to registry. SPX-II, VLMs, NDS
5.x	80386/486/Pentium	1000	Native pure TCP/IP, JAVA GUI

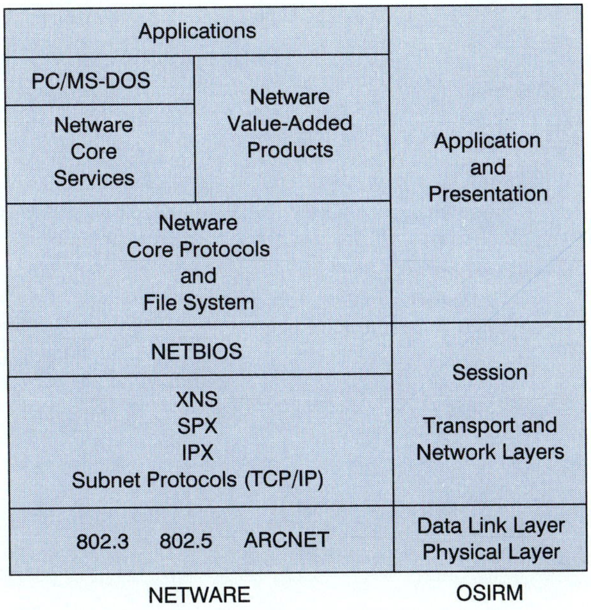

Figure 8.1 Services and Systems of NetWare

OSI Comparison

Figure 8.1 is a diagram that shows the services and systems of NetWare as they relate to the OSI reference model. The following sections describe the relationships between NetWare and the OSI model.

Physical layer, data link layer, and MAC protocols. At the physical layer are the cables and NICs for specific topologies and protocols. The MAC layer protocols for Ethernet, Token-Ring, ARCNET, FDDI, and so forth, are included in the data layer. A NetWare server can be configured for up to four MAC layer protocols in a single server.

It is the function of *Internetwork Packet eXchange* (**IPX**) to provide addressing, routing, and switching of data packets from point to point on the network. A NetWare server, configured for multiple NICs, may be used as a router because of the presence of SPX/IPX. Figures 8.2a through 8.2c show the MAC layer frames that encapsulate a *NetWare Core Protocol* (**NCP**) data packet. It is the encapsulation that provides the link between the data and network layers.

IPX is Internetwork Packet eXchange

NCP stands for NetWare Core Protocol.

Referring to Figure 8.2a, we see that the type field in an Ethernet frame would contain the value 8137h. This is the value used to specify that NetWare is the data field protocol. Both 802.3 Ethernet and 802.5 Token-Ring use the 802.2 LLC format to specify the service access points (DSAP and SSAP). Because both destination and source nodes must use the same protocol (within a local LAN), both destination and source SAPs will use the same value. In NetWare applications the value is E0h. NetWare versions 3.x and earlier lim-

Figure 8.2a NCP Data Packet Encapsulated by an Ethernet Frame

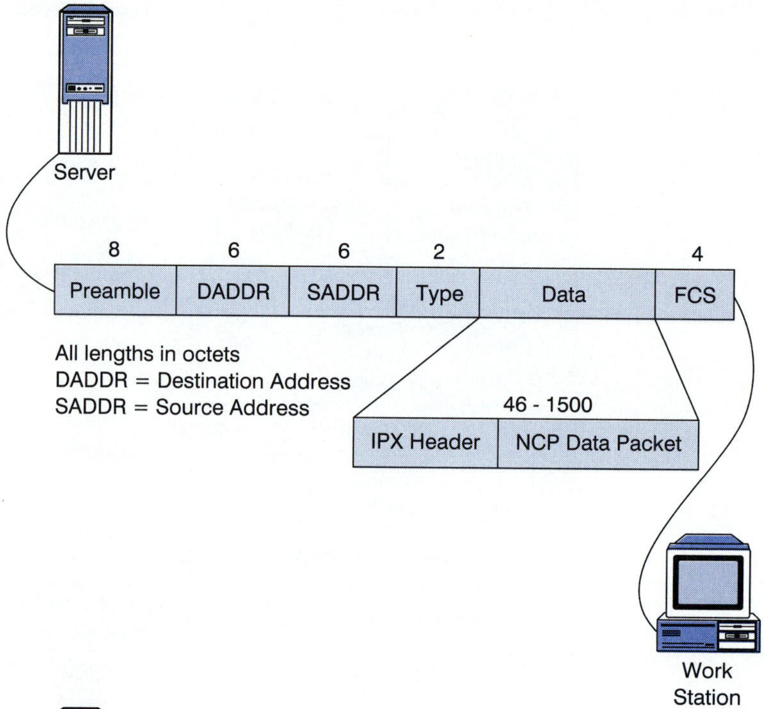

Figure 8.2b NCP Data Packet Encapsulated by a Token-Ring Frame

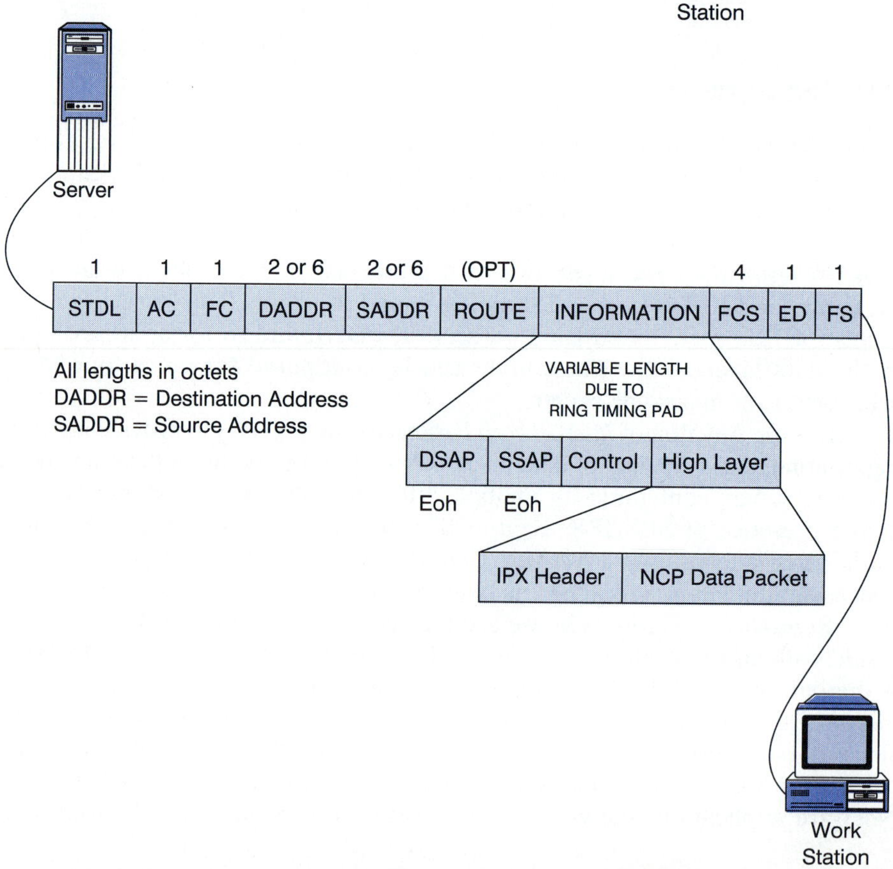

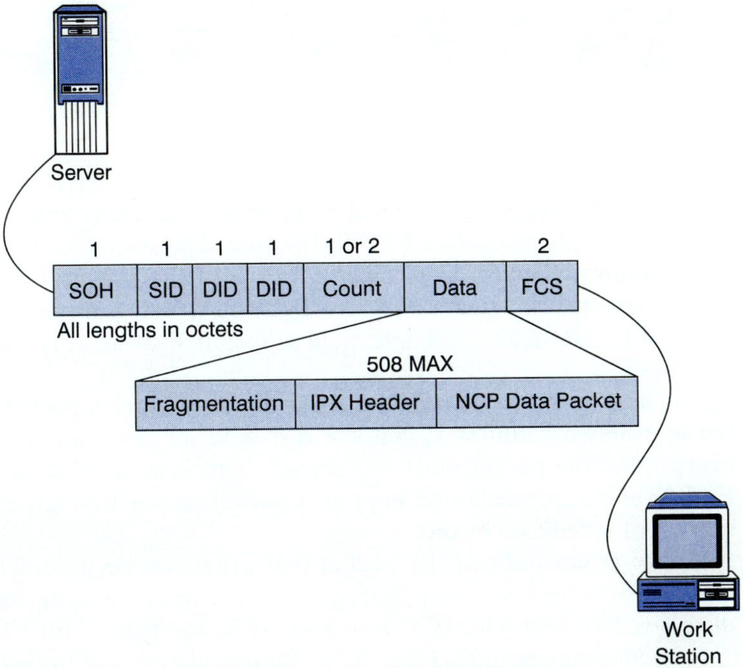

Figure 8.2c NCP Data Packet Encapsulated by an ARCNET Frame

ited data packet sizes to 576 octets, which allowed Ethernet and Token-Ring to transfer a complete NetWare packet in a single transfer. With version 4.x a sliding *window* has been incorporated that dynamically changes the size of the data packet to accommodate error rates and congestion. Longer packets are more efficient in networks with few errors and low congestion.

Figure 8.2c shows a NetWare packet encapsulated in an ARCNET frame. ARCNET is unique in that it does not entirely conform to any of the 802.x standards. ARCNET is only able to send a 508-octet data frame, but NetWare IPX assembles 576-octet packets. This results in two ARCNET frames whenever a maximum-length IPX packet is sent—thus the reason for the Count and Fragmentation fields in ARCNET frames. The count field is set to two for fragmented frames; the first frame contains 508 octets and the second up to 68 octets.

Transport and Network Layers

IPX. IPX is a *connectionless* protocol in that it provides no guaranteed delivery of packets. Most LAN installations encounter few errors, and an 802.2 LLC, if installed, will provide connection-oriented end-to-end guaranteed delivery. The IPX header contains 30 octets organized as shown in Figure 8.3. The length field contains a count value from 30 to the maximum packet size of 576 octets.

Checksum (FFFF)	Length	Transport Control	Packet Type	Destination Network	Destination Host	Destination Socket	Source Network	Source Host	Source Socket	Data Packet

Figure 8.3 IPX Header

The checksum field is used to provide conformity with the Xerox XNS header. It is always set to FFFFh because a four-octet CRC is used in the MAC frame for error detection. In fact, an IPX datagram is identical to an XNS internetwork datagram packet. Because IPX datagrams can be any length from 30 to 546 octets, a length field is included to identify the length of the data field.

The transport control field is set to zero before a packet is sent so that the internetwork router(s) can use this field for determining the number of routers that the packet must go through. This is referred to as the *hop count*. Each router represents one hop; as a packet passes through each router, the hop count is reduced by one.

Xerox has defined the packet types that can be used. The packet type field contains an 8-bit value that specifies the type. NetWare only uses four of the types: type 0 or 4 for IPX, type 5 for SPX, and type 17 for NCP.

Addressing requires three fields for destination and three for source. The *host* is the NIC physical address. This address is most often set by a switch on the NIC or is embedded in a NIC EPROM. Within a given LAN, each NIC must have a unique physical address. Ethernet and Token-Ring manufacturers consider this sufficiently important that nearly all manufacturers supply Ethernet and/or Token-Ring NICs with built-in addresses that are internationally unique so that no two NICs would ever have the same physical address. A *socket* specifies an address for NetWare processes including value-added processes. *Network* addresses are assigned by network administrators when NetWare is installed. Table 8.2 lists the various packet types and socket values.

Table 8.2 NetWare Packet Types and Socket Values

	Packet Type		Socket Values
0	Unknown	0000h	Routing information packet
1	Routing information packet	0002h	Echo protocol packet
2	Echo packet	0003h	Error handler packet
3	Error packet	0001–0BB8h	Xerox registered
4	Packet exchange packet (PEP)	0020–003Fh	Experimental
5	Sequenced Packet	0BB9–FFFFh	Dynamically assignable
17	NetWare Core Protocol		
16-31	Open (experimental protocols)		

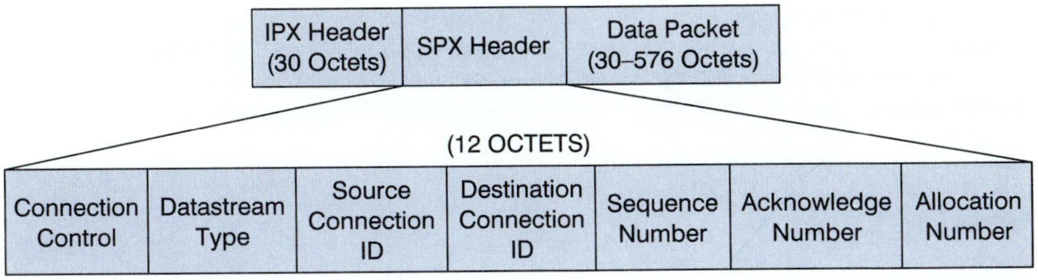

Figure 8.4 SPX Header

SPX. *Sequenced Packet eXchange* (SPX) provides the transport layer header that assumes the responsibility for the *connection-oriented* sequencing and acknowledgment of packets. NCP application and presentation layer functions generally do not take advantage of the guaranteed delivery offered by SPC because of the additional overhead caused by the necessity to create individual connections for each message. However, third-party applications are free to use SPX if desired.

An SPX frame is created by simply inserting an SPX header into an IPX header between the data packet and the IPX header. Figure 8.4 shows an SPX frame with the SPX header detail broken out.

Table 8.3 lists the functions for the Connection Control and Datastream Type fields.

The Source Connection ID identifies the source of the data packet. The Datastream Type value enables a single socket to access multiple connections (i.e., several workstations may be connected to the same NCP process at the same time).

Sequencing and acknowledgment operate in a "ping-pong" mode (see Figure 8.5). The first packet in a sequence is assigned the number 1. Packet 1 must then be acknowledged by a return packet with the *acknowledge* (ACK) bit set to 1. With windowing, more than one packet may be sent before the first acknowledgment is returned, but at some point, a timer will expire and SPX will assume the unacknowledged packet is lost and resend it.

The final field in an SPX header is the allocation number that identifies the number of data buffers available at the destination. The sender may then send packets until the sequence and allocation numbers are equal.

Table 8.3 Connection Control and Datastream Type Values

Connection Control		Datastream Type	
01-08h	Not defined	00-FDh	Client defined
10h	End of message	FEh	End of connection
20h	Attention	FFh	End of connection acknowledgment
40h	Acknowledgment required		
80h	System packet		

Figure 8.5 "Ping-Pong" Packet Sequence

Source SEND packet 1	→	Destination receives packet 1
Source receives packet 1 ACK	←	Destination SEND packet 1 ACK
Source SEND packet 2	→	Destination receives packet 2
Source receives packet 2 ACK	←	Destination SEND packet 2 ACK

Session Layer

NetWare has made Network Basic Input/Output System (NetBIOS) available at the session layer for IBM proprietary operating systems and equipment. NetBIOS is the redirector that allows a PC to be networked. It is NetBIOS, introduced in PC/MS-DOS version 3.3, that redirects network addresses to the NIC. It should be noted that NetBIOS is seldom actually implemented in NetWare installations and that NetWare's version is considered an incomplete emulation of IBM's NetBIOS.

Application and presentation layers. An important distinction of NetWare is that it must ride on top of MS-DOS. In other words, NetWare must rely on MS-DOS to execute hardware functions and BIOS system calls. This can sometimes become a performance limitation. During a given session, both workstation and server must use identical versions of MS-DOS. In NetWare 2.x versions, the workstation installation was unique for each version of MS-DOS that might be on a given workstation. This required the proper MS-DOS version to be accessed on the server for each session.

Other services at the application layer include all of the console server commands, files, and programs contained in the Public directory as well as the following:

- *NetWare Core Protocols* (NCPs), the language that clients and servers speak. The NCPs include client/server communications, file services, disk management, and directory services.
- Value-added services such as third-party E-mail packages
- PC MS-DOS
- User applications

NetWare System Calls

The system calls provide services for MS-DOS applications that run on the network. Calls are used by NetWare in much the same way as they are used in programming languages to execute subroutines used for a specific purpose. Calls included in NetWare are such things as synchronization, bindery, directory, server, connection, accounting, transaction tracking, file, message, print, and queue services.

ADDITIONAL FEATURES

System Console

When NetWare is booted, the monitor and keyboard of the server become the system console. Because MS-DOS is no longer available, only a select few commands are available on the system console that can be used to monitor or list network or server resources, monitor server health, and load additional server software packages called *NetWare Loadable Modules* (**NLMs**).

NLMs are NetWare Loadable Modules.

Volumes

Because servers tend to require large amounts of storage, NetWare includes the ability to store data on multiple hard drives. In addition, drive storage may be organized into *volumes*. A volume is created to assign a named storage area to either part of a hard drive or parts of multiple hard drives. At installation time, NetWare creates the *SYS:* volume in which the operating system files are stored along with public and login files. Specific directories include

- *System*—system files and NLMs;
- *Public*—utilities for NetWare administration and operation;
- *Login*—utilities for logging in and determining LAN resource availability; and
- *Mail*—contains a simple E-mail utility (removed in version 4.x).

Additional volumes may be created during installation. Volumes are typically installed to allow easier administration of hard drives. Volumes might be installed for APPS: (applications), USERS: (user home directories), DATA: (miscellaneous storage of shared data), or any other use deemed appropriate. Once installed, a volume becomes an additional layer in the addressable file path. For example, SYS:PUBLIC\NWADMIN.EXE would be the complete path from the SYS: volume to the PUBLIC directory, to the NWADMIN.EXE program file used to administer users and groups.

NLM

Once installed, NetWare allows additional features to be added to the operating system using specially formatted software packages, as mentioned earlier, called NLMs. These packages must be installed at the system console or during system boot and are stored in the SYS:SYSTEM directory. Once NetWare is booted, NLMs must be installed at the system console.

A typical NLM installation might be to add the TCP/IP (Internet) protocol to the operating system. The process uses the console LOAD command (e.g., LOAD A:\TCP.NLM). NLMs may also be loaded during boot if they are in the MS-DOS partition of C:.

SERVER INSTALLATION PREPARATION

Novell NetWare version 2.x can be installed in either a dedicated, server-only mode or as a shared workstation/server mode. It is almost never recommended that the shared workstation/server mode be used due to the severe performance degradation produced by having to share CPU time with the workstation. Version 3.x removed the shared workstation option requiring NetWare to be installed as a server only.

Prior to installation, a prudent network designer will carefully consider the intended use of network resources. Major considerations include the following:

- *Number of anticipated users*—How many current users will there be, and what is the estimated growth in users over the next two to three years?
- *Application software demands on server CPU time*—Many database applications rely on the server to supply some or all of the data processing. Large applications and files can consume a great deal of the available bandwidth when being transferred across the network.
- *Peak load*—That is, at what time of day will the maximum number of users access network resources?

The answers to these questions will help determine the required bandwidth necessary to accommodate peak load and growth without causing excessive response time to user requests. Bandwidth requirements are also necessary to determine which topology and MAC layer protocol you will need, as well as the point at which overly large LANs must be broken into smaller, more manageable LANs.

Server memory is another important consideration. The more memory that is available for allocation, the more efficiently the server can accommodate additional users and tasks. NetWare installation manuals offer simple formulas for calculating the amount of memory. Keep in mind, however, that it is usually more cost-effective to fill the server motherboard with the maximum memory possible when the server is purchased rather than upgrading at "retail cost" down the road.

Novell suggests the following formula, based on the size of the hard drive. The calculation determines the amount of memory needed to fully allocate (usually 4-Kbyte) blocks of allocation units to the server.

$$\frac{\text{Drive size (in Mbytes)} \times 0.023}{\text{Block size} + 4\text{ Mbytes}}$$

Based on personal experience, anything less than 8 Mbytes of main memory will be disappointing, even on small LANs. NetWare's performance improvement is quite noticeable as memory capacity is increased beyond 8 Mbytes.

Additional considerations include these:

- *Shared resource requirements*—Shared resources include printers and print servers, server-based hard disk drives, databases, files, modems, and third-party functions.
- *Security*—NetWare includes options for a log-in password, minimum password length, password life and reusability, and right to change a password. Other security features include account restrictions for time of day, day of week, number of concurrent log-ins, number of bad log-in attempts and recording, specific workstation login, transaction tracking (file integrity and audit trail), trustee assignments for directory and file access, and specific file right assignments.
- *Accounting*—NetWare includes options for user billing based on server access, file access, and file usage. Administrators should expect to spend a great deal of time managing accounting services if they are used.

CPU

Since it is the server that becomes the busiest node on a LAN, it should contain a CPU that is fast enough to keep up with user demand. Generally speaking, a current, state-of-the-art CPU should be specified for the server if budget limitations permit. By so doing, you will prolong having to upgrade your server just because user requirements increase. Even with severe budget limitations, a Pentium® machine is low enough in relative cost to become justifiable as a server platform for even the smallest networks.

Server manufacturers have begun designing their products to contain multiple microprocessors. Two modes of *multiprocessor* operation are used, symmetric multiprocessing and master/slave.

Master/slave processing utilizes one CPU chip as a master processor that can assign tasks to other *slave* CPUs. Slave processors are often dedicated to handling specific types of tasks. For example, one slave CPU might be dedicated to processing I/O tasks for peripheral devices. A second slave CPU might be dedicated to processing all requests for hard drive access.

In *symmetric* multiprocessing, all CPU chips are designed as equals. Tasks are assigned to the first available CPU. With symmetric processing, the server operating system must be capable of making the assignments and coordinating the processing of tasks.

Drives

A server's hard disk drive(s) is at the heart of the LAN. It should be fast and reliable as well as have sufficient capacity to accommodate all of the program, data, and user storage requirements. It is usually wise to overestimate drive capacity requirements by a healthy margin to ensure adequate growth accommodation. Your hard drive vendor should be willing to certify drives for Novell use.

Mirroring and Duplexing

NetWare also offers disk duplexing and mirroring. *Mirroring* is a technique in which two drives are installed, side by side in a server, such that the second drive becomes a mirror of the first and an automatic backup of the primary drive. *Disk duplexing* is similar to mirroring with the addition of a second drive controller that acts as a backup to the primary controller. Transaction tracking ensures data integrity by creating an audit trail record of all data transactions so that, in the event of a failure, only those changes made after the failure need be redone.

NICs

The type of NIC is determined by the topology and MAC protocol you have chosen. There are usually a wide range of prices from vendor to vendor for NICs. Vendor choice should be based on reliability, upgrade ability (will firmware revisions be included in the price?), and availability as well as cost. Service and maintenance availability are probably not going to be important considerations for NIC purchases because it is usually cheaper to have a few spares on hand and simply throw away bad units.

NIC preparation may include switch settings for node ID (MAC layer source address), IRQ, DMA, and base I/O addresses. The settings for each NIC should be logged for future reference as the NICs are configured and installed. Many LAN administrators create maps of their LANs that show location and configuration information. Such a map becomes a valuable tool, particularly when the LAN grows.

Peripherals

Console. Each server must be equipped with a keyboard and monitor during installation and maintenance although they may be removed when not needed to inhibit unauthorized access. The monitor and keyboard are called the *server console*, whose function is reduced to simple monitoring functions and which may be used to instruct the server to load additional software modules (NLMs) when required. The cost of the server console can be kept low by using black and white monitors and inexpensive keyboards. Use the savings for bigger hard drives, more memory, and faster CPUs!

Backup. Backups and disaster recovery must be a part of the planning process. Tape backup units are reasonable in cost and provide a relatively rapid method for backups on tape cartridges that can be stored off-site. Tape is, unfortunately, notoriously unreliable. Tapes can stretch quite easily so that restoring data often results in errors in the restored data. A more expensive solution is a removable hard disk such as a Bernoulli-type hard drive or writable CD-ROM or magneto-optical drive. The rule of thumb here is to install the fastest and most reliable backup system your budget allows and remember the old cliché, "Your data are only as reliable as your last backup!"

Printers. Printer sharing is often one of the prime reasons for networking. NetWare provides two ways to share printers and modems. Printers and modems may be connected directly to the server printer (LPT) and communications (COM) ports or connected to workstations that are configured to become dedicated (remote) print servers or communications servers. The preferred method is the remote dedicated server because this setup frees the main server CPU for internal use. More recently, printer manufacturers are providing for NICs to be installed in the printer itself so that the printer simply becomes a network-addressable node and thus a dedicated print server.

To establish a printing operation in NetWare, three objects must be created:

1. *Printer*—The logical device that consists of the software driver for the specific printer being installed on the network.
2. *Print queue*—A named area, usually in a print server, to which print jobs are sent before going to the physical printer. Print queues are responsible for spooling print jobs to printers one at a time on a first-in, first-out manner based on priority.
3. *Print server*—A PC that contains a copy of NetWare but is dedicated to serving print jobs only.

In recent years, laser printer manufacturers have incorporated the NIC and print server into the printer itself. This allows a *network printer* to be directly connected to the LAN, thus eliminating the need for a dedicated PC running NetWare as a print server. Print queues and printer drivers must still be created but are now run in a data or application server.

Modems. Modem sharing can be done by connecting modems to the serial ports on the server itself or, in a manner similar to print servers, a workstation dedicated as a remote communications server.

UPS. *Uninterruptable Power Supply* (**UPS**) service is available with 2.x versions and higher. Essentially, a battery backup device (UPS) is connected to the server

UPS is Uninterruptable Power Supply.

that monitors the UPS so that in the event of a power failure, user workstations and the server can be shut down in an orderly manner without loss of data.

WORKSTATION PREPARATION AND INSTALLATION

NIC

Just as you did for the server, the NICs used in the workstations must be configured for node ID, IRQ, DMA, and I/O base addresses and then installed in the workstation.

Workstation (Client)

ODI is Open Datalink Interface.

The NetWare diskette labeled WSGEN contains the installation programs for the client shell. A *shell* is much like a Terminate and Stay Resident (TSR) program that attaches itself to MS-DOS so that any network-addressable operations can be intercepted and redirected to the NIC. The shell is sometimes referred to as a *client redirector*. NetWare 2.x combined NETx (the MS-DOS version specific interface), with IPX to form the client-specific interface. NetWare version 3.x introduced *Open Datalink Interface* (**ODI**) that eliminates the necessity of MS-DOS version specific shells. Interestingly, NETx or IPXODI installations can be implemented on clients connected to any of server versions 2.x, 3.x, or 4.x.

Running WSGEN

WSGEN is the 2.x, 3.x client shell generator that replaces the earlier SHGEN and GENSH. WSGEN is used to link the NIC LAN driver to IPX. From any MS-DOS workstation, insert a *diskcopy* of the WSGEN diskette and execute the WSGEN program.

- You may select from the LAN drivers supplied by Novell or from the diskette supplied by the NIC manufacturer.
- Select the appropriate values for IRQ, Base I/O address, and RAM memory buffer base address.
- Finally, highlight *yes* to configure the client shell IPX.COM.

WSGEN will create an executable program file called NETx.COM where x = the version of MS-DOS being used (e.g., NET3.COM). In your AUTOEXEC.BAT or any other batch file of your choosing, enter the following lines:

```
IPX
```

NET3 (Be certain to use the WSGEN created NETx.COM. If you are using MS-DOS version 6, e.g., the line would read NET6).

F:

LOGIN

In your CONFIG.SYS file, enter the following line to ensure that all 26 network logical drives will be recognizable by the client workstation:

LASTDRIVE=Z

Running IPXODI

If your NIC driver software is written for the Novell/Apple-developed ODI specification, WSGEN is no longer required. The primary advantage of ODI is that it allows multiple network layer protocols such as TCP/IP or AppleTalk to run over the same NIC that is configured for a datalink layer protocol such as Ethernet. Multiple protocols are not possible without ODI.

Just as you did for an IPX client, you can install the appropriate commands for an IPXODI client in AUTOEXEC.BAT or your own batch file as follows:

1. Install the NIC driver by running the driver program that is supplied with your NIC. An example might be AM2100.COM (an HP Ethernet driver). This becomes a two-stage process when the ODI is installed with IPX. LAN drivers for the chip set used on the NIC are the IEEE 802.2 LLC drivers for specific NICs (AM2100 from Advanced Microdevices or 3C5x9 from 3Com are examples). ODI is also used to allow more than one protocol, such as IPX and the Internet TCP/IP, to run over the NIC at the same time. Prior to running the NIC driver, run the program LSL.COM (*Link Support Layer*), and then run the NIC driver program—for example:

   LSL.COM (if ODI is to be installed)

   AM2100.COM

2. Run IPX or IPXODI to bind IPX to the NIC driver.
3. Load the shell program NETX.COM.

A complete example of the ODI client shell installation, shown as follows, must be done each time the client is booted for use on the network.

LSL.COM

AM2100.COM

IPXODI.COM

NETX.COM

VLMs are Volume Loadable Modules.

With the release of version 4.x, NetWare has offered an alternative to NETX.COM, which is, of course, bound to the version of MS-DOS being used in the workstation. *Volume Loadable Modules* (**VLMs**) may be installed in place of NETX.COM. The VLMs may be installed on a workstation even though the server is using version 3.x or 4.x. VLMs are not bound to the version of MS-DOS and offer a significant increase in flexibility for network protocols that may be used. If you have the VLMs available, simply replace NETX.COM with VLM.EXE and you are done.

On occasion, you may wish to unload the client shell. The process must be done in reverse order by executing the appropriate command followed by /U. For example, begin the uninstall with VLM /U.

Supervisor Functions

When NetWare is first installed on a version 2.x or 3.x server, a user named *Supervisor* is created. NetWare provides for supervisor functions that determine who will have access to the network, what kind of access they will have, and the security and privileges each user is granted. Security levels include

- passwords,
- directory rights,
- trustee directory and file rights, and
- file attributes.

User creation. The user named Supervisor can create other users. This is normally done with the SYSCON or MAKEUSER utility programs. NetWare provides for four different types of users: ordinary users, user groups, group managers, and other supervisors. From an administrator's point of view, it is vastly easier to manage groups of users than it is to manage individual users. In other words, rights and privileges should be assigned to groups rather than individuals.

Trustee rights. The supervisor must grant trustee rights for access to directories and files to users, including these:

1. *Read*—Open and read files in a directory (file scan needed to see directory).
2. *Write*—Change file contents.
3. *Create*—Create new files and subdirectories, and salvage deleted files.

4. *Erase*—Delete files and subdirectories.
5. *Modify*—Change attributes and file or subdirectory names.
6. *File Scan*—Be able to see directory listings.
7. *Access Control*—Grant rights to others.
8. *Supervisory*—Grant all directory and file rights.
9. *Execute*—Prevent users from copying executable programs.

Inherited rights mask. Rights granted to any directory are passed to all subdirectories unless a user has specifically limited rights. Explicit trustee rights override the inherited rights mask. Supervisor right cannot be eliminated from the inherited rights mask.

File attributes. Set by FILER.EXE, ATTRIB.EXE, FLAG.EXE.

1. *Read Only*—The file may *not* be written to or modified.
2. *Shareable*—Access to the file may be shared by multiple users.
3. *Hidden*—The file name will not appear in a directory listing.
4. *System*—The file is either an MS-DOS or NetWare system file.
5. *Transactional*—File changes are included in the transaction tracking log.
6. *Purge*—Following deletion, the file will be purged from the system. It may not be undeleted.
7. *Archive Needed*—The file was modified after the last backup (assigned automatically).
8. *Read Audit*—The user will be charged for reading this file (not implemented in 3.x)
9. *Write Audit*—The user will be charged for writing to this file (not implemented in 3.x)
10. *Copy Inhibit*—The file must be .EXE or .COM and cannot be revoked once the copy inhibit attribute is assigned.
11. *Rename Inhibit*—The file cannot be renamed.
12. *Delete Inhibit*—The file cannot be deleted.
13. *Execute Only*—The file can only be executed. This is to prevent file copies.

Create log-in scripts. Log-in scripts are similar to MS-DOS batch files that are executed when a user logs into the network. A general form called the *sys-*

tem log-in script is always executed once NetWare has determined that a user's password and log-in name are a match. Each user may also have an individual log-in script although individual user log-in scripts generally require excessive supervisor maintenance time.

Create and change passwords. Supervisor may grant the right to change a password to users, cause the password to expire after a set period of time, or prevent the reuse of passwords.

Create directories and virtual drives. This is done using the MAP and SEARCH commands. MAP is used to assign directories to virtual MS-DOS drives and SEARCH is the NetWare equivalent to the MS-DOS PATH command.

NETWARE VERSION 4.X

On large networks there are often numerous servers. Users may have access to some or all of these servers, but without creating your own list of available resources, it quickly becomes impossible to remember where to find the resources you need. NetWare versions 2.x and 3.x *bound* all of a specific server's resources together but made no provision for binding a resource from another server. Users were required to log into each server in which they had an account and access to resources.

NetWare Directory Services

NetWare 4.x contains a global database called the *NetWare Directory Service* (NDS). With NDS, users may now view resources that are available from many servers as though they were being presented by a single source. For example, the print server might be located in the print shop with an assigned name of PS_WritersIIIsi, the user's personal directory in server Authors (located somewhere in the "Network Room"), and the E-mail server named MailServ1 (physically located at the publisher's offices in New Jersey). In 3.x, each user or group would have to be configured to show the path to each of the servers used. This often means that a network administrator must go to each workstation and configure the user for needed resources and to each server to create a user account. Version 4.x allows the 4.x server to be configured so that a single log-in to the server *Authors* would also provide the user with connections to the E-mail and print servers.

This distribution of NDS services is possible because services from different servers are listed and organized in the global database in a hierarchical manner much like a company's organizational chart. Users now see the company's resources rather than a list of cryptically named servers that may or may not contain the required resource and which the user must ATTACH to in order to use the resource. (ATTACH.EXE is the 3.x utility used to log in to additional servers.)

At version 4.x install time, an NDS tree name must be supplied. This is the name of the NDS database. Within the tree, additional *container objects* may be installed. Container objects include the following:

- *Country*—An optional object used if the tree contains servers that are installed in different languages
- *Organization*—A container or containers that denote major organizations such as companies or divisions
- *Organizational Unit*—Containers that may be used to denote departments or other subdivisions

Containers are then used to hold other objects such as groups, users, servers, printers, and volumes. Each container object can be configured for access to server resources by setting the rights to object access and any trustee assignments. Rights set at the container level then flow down to the *leaf* objects (servers, volumes, users, etc.) stored in the container.

Novell has also released NDS for use with the Microsoft Windows NT Server operating system. NT, the subject of the next chapter, will not have anything like NDS until version 5 now being referred to as "Windows 2000."

Additional 4.x Features

Other features of note are as follows:

- NetWare file system improvements such as data compression and data migration in which seldom used files are located close to off-line devices such as tape backup
- Network auditing support
- Improved memory management with suballocation of unused block space
- Improved client services
- Improved file system security
- Integrated storage management services
- Simplified installation
- Electro Text–based manuals
- Improved print services

Logging In to Version 4.x

When a 4.x server is first created, the user account ADMIN (formerly Supervisor) is created. For a user to log in successfully, ADMIN must create the user account and grant it access to *objects* that the user will have access to. Objects are the global network resources listed in the NDS database. Figure 8.6 shows a sample 4.x network used by the students, staff, and faculty at a university. Each of the servers and each of the shared laser printers would be created as objects and listed in the NDS as available resources.

Table 8.4 lists the NDS tree for the network; the tree is named StateU. Organizations (O) are StuLab (Student Lab), Elec (Electronics Department), CS (Computer Science), and Admin (Administration). Within the Electronics,

Table 8.4 StateU NDS Tree

```
[root] – StateU (name of the NDS tree)
 |____O=StuLab (an organization within the tree)
 |    |____StuLab_Printer
 |    |____StuLab_Server
 |    |____SYS: (Volume)
 |    |____APPS:
 |    |____Student (user account)
 |____O=Elec
 |    |____Elec_Printer
 |    |____Elec_Lab (server)
 |    |____OU=Faculty (an organizational unit within an organization)
 |    |    |____(faculty user accounts)
 |    |____OU=Students
 |    |____(student user accounts)
 |____O=CIS
 |    |____(faculty user accounts)
 |    |____OU=Students
 |    |____(student user accounts)
 |____O=Admin
 |____OU=ADMIN
 |    |____Groups (e.g., deans, department chairs, accounting, personnel, etc.)
 |    |____Users (user accounts)
 |____OU=Faculty
      |    |____Users
      |____OU=Staff
      |    |____Users
      |____Admin (Server)
      |____Faculty (Server)
      |____Staff (Server)
      |____Admin_Printer
```

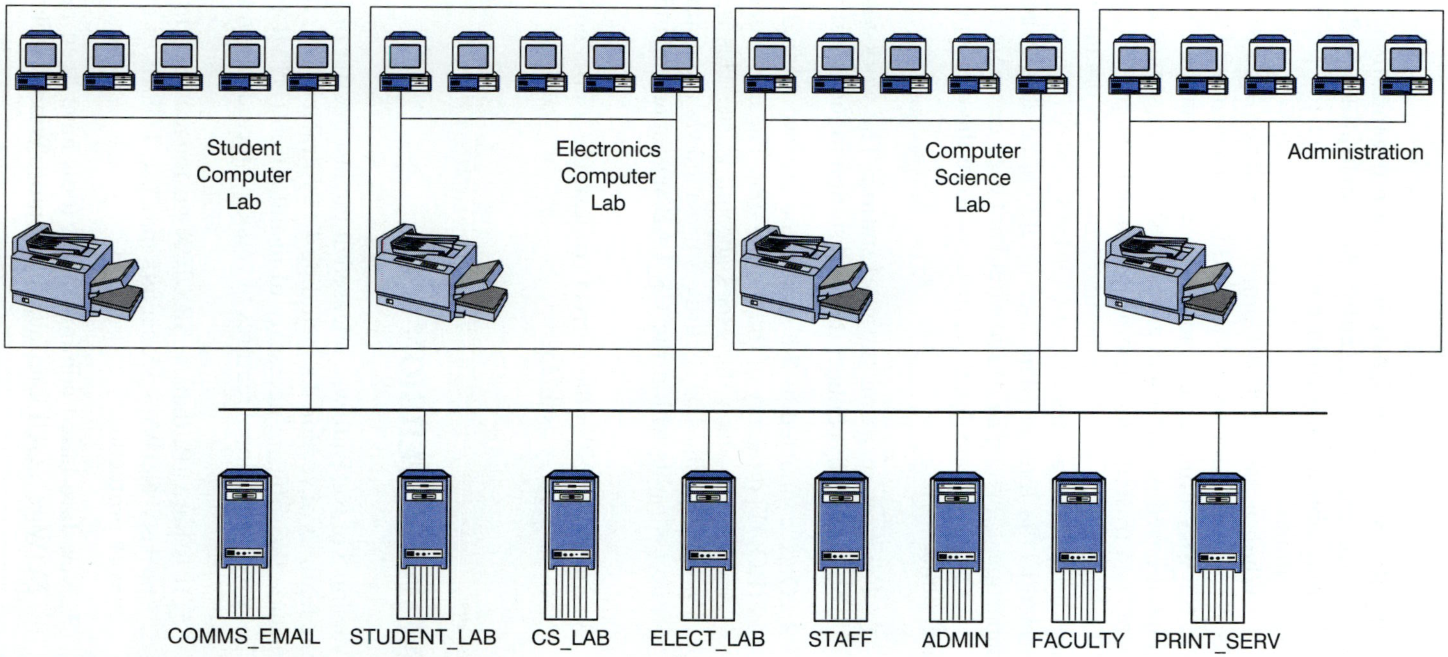

Figure 8.6 Global Resources Using NetWare 4.x

Computer Science, and Administration organizations, organizational units (OUs) are created for Faculty, Administrators, Staff, and Students. The remaining objects, shown in parentheses, are the physical servers, volumes, and printers.

When a user in the Computer Science Lab wishes to log in to the CS_Server to work on a Visual Basic program and send code lists to the PRINT_SRV print server and the laser printer in the CS Lab, access would be granted based on the users group membership(s) plus any object or property rights and trusted relationships that have been granted to objects to the user's OU. Rights may also be inherited from the CS organization. The user might also be granted access to the COMMS_EMAIL server that is, in turn, connected to the Internet. The user would *not* be able to access any of the other department servers; he or she would not even be aware that they existed.

Practically speaking, the process, from the user's perspective might occur as follows:

1. The user turns on the workstation. The workstation is configured to automatically connect the workstation to the server CS_LAB.
2. Once connected to the server, the user would find him- or herself in the [ROOT] directory of the StateU tree. The user would now need to access the OU in which the user's account exists. This is known as setting the *context.* Additional security is provided via the granting of folder and file access rights within the CS_LAB server in a manner similar to version 3.x.
3. Once located in the correct context, the user is now able to type *login* in the same way as in 3.x.

NETWARE VERSION 5.X

Version 5 of NetWare was released in the last quarter of 1998. It contains all of the features of version 4.x including 4.11 IntraNetWare. IntraNetWare releases include the software necessary to install a web (HTML) server on a NetWare file server. Additional features of version 5 include the following:

- It is pure IP; that is, SPX/IPX no longer need to encapsulate TCP/IP packets. NetWare 5.x servers may use TCP/IP as the only transport/network protocols.
- New Java-based administration tools have been made available to give NetWare a GUI interface that is more Windows-like.

TROUBLESHOOTING

Troubleshooting in any network operating system requires the knowledge of a fully trained network administrator or engineer; CNA and CNE certifications are often required. Readers of this text are strongly urged to take a class in NetWare and obtain copies of the CNA and CNE manuals available from Novell Press. It is also impossible to do justice to all of the troubleshooting skills that one must acquire to be successful as a CNA or CNE in a single chapter. In addition to troubleshooting the physical and data layer problems, a NetWare administrator must be familiar with

- network services (client services, VLMs);
- message handling services (E-mail, etc.);
- storage management services (how NetWare stores data on hard drives);
- menu systems (NetWare is a command line operating system like UNIX or MS-DOS. Menus are used to automate user access to applications and services when no graphical user interface (GUI) exists.);
- log-in scripts (automated access utilities run during the log-in process that can send greetings to the user, run startup-type programs and batch files, attach users to other servers (3.x), and often culminate in a menu);
- NDS (maintenance and sometimes troubleshooting the security of a user's access to the network);
- network connection (how clients connect to the NDS tree and NetWare servers);
- accessing files, applications, and data stored on NetWare servers;
- printing (creation and maintenance of logical Print Servers, Print Queues, and Printers);
- file system management (where and how files and folders are stored);
- file system security (rights and access to files);
- server console operations; and
- disaster recovery (backup and restore of data stored in NetWare servers). This is a truly critical function of the network administrator. Hard drives and servers do fail. Preventing the loss of data can often mean the difference between keeping the organization running and closing the doors forever.

CHAPTER REVIEW

- The major components of NetWare include the following:

  File server—a computer containing the NetWare operating system

  Client—usually a workstation that is capable of communicating with the server

  Router—a software or hardware device capable of determining the location of an addressable network node. NetWare contains internal routing functions.

- NetWare functions as they relate to the OSI reference model:

  Application and presentation layers

    MS-DOS

    Value-added products

    NetWare Core Protocols

    Server-based applications

  Session layer

    NetBIOS

  Transport and network layers

    SPX

    IPX

    XNS

    TCP/IP

  Data and physical layers

  LLC and MAC protocols: 802.2 (LLC), 802.3 (Ethernet), 802.4 (Token Passing Bus), 802.5 (Token-Ring)

- IPX is the connectionless, network layer protocol responsible for passing datagrams from one network node to another.
- SPX is the connection-oriented, transport layer protocol responsible for the end-to-end reliability, sequencing, and acknowledgment of data packets.
- NetWare installations require preparation and planning for the number of users, hard drive type and capacity, memory capacity, shared resources, security, accounting, and NIC(s).

- The NetWare server installation process includes NIC installation, hard drive partitioning and formatting, copying system 1 and 2 disks to the MS-DOS partition, running the Server program, running the Install program, loading NLMs, and binding IPX to the NIC drivers.
- The NetWare workstation installation includes running four programs: LSL.COM (if ODI is used), the NIC driver program, IPX or IPXODI, and NETX.COM or VLM.EXE.
- NetWare 4.x changes the bindery into a global *registry* that lists all of the objects known to the global network.

APPLICATION PROJECTS

Project 1

Create your own step-by-step plan to upgrade an existing NetWare version 3.x LAN to version 4.x. Include plans for both server and clients. Your plan should include the following:

1. Material requirements
    a. Material purchase orders
    b. Vendor delivery dates
2. Hardware modification/configuration requirements
3. Software modification/configuration requirements
4. Time line plan (when is each step scheduled and how long will it take to complete)

Project 2

Perhaps the most valuable project for this chapter is an actual, hands-on, network installation. If not possible, contact a Novell NetWare LAN administrator and make an appointment to attend the next upgrade or modification to the network. Take lots of notes, particularly notes on the planning and procedures that were used. Note the documentation that the LAN administrator has available.

Make a written report that includes sections for

- planning procedures,
- documentation,

- actual step-by-step procedures used, and
- your suggestions to improve the process you observed.

REVIEW QUESTIONS

1. List the major components of NetWare.
2. List the major versions of NetWare and the major features of each version.
3. List the seven layers of the OSIRM, and relate the functions of NetWare to each layer.
4. What common LAN protocols will NetWare support?
5. Briefly describe IPX.
6. Briefly describe SPX.
7. What services do NetWare system calls provide?
8. List the major considerations you should plan for prior to a NetWare installation.
9. What are the major security provisions contained in NetWare?
10. What items are created to enable printer sharing on a NetWare LAN?
11. What step(s) must be completed, during a NetWare installation, before the Install program is run?
12. What is installed by the Install program?
13. List the methods available in NetWare for sharing printers and modems.
14. What is the purpose of the server console?
15. You have been asked to recommend a server for a 100-user LAN. What features should the server have?
16. You have finished installing a new workstation on a NetWare LAN. What driver programs would you run to access the network?
17. List the improvements made in NetWare version 4.x.
18. What is the advantage of using a global registry instead of a bindery?
19. What is the version 4.x NDS?
20. What is meant by the term *context*?
21. Why are backups important?

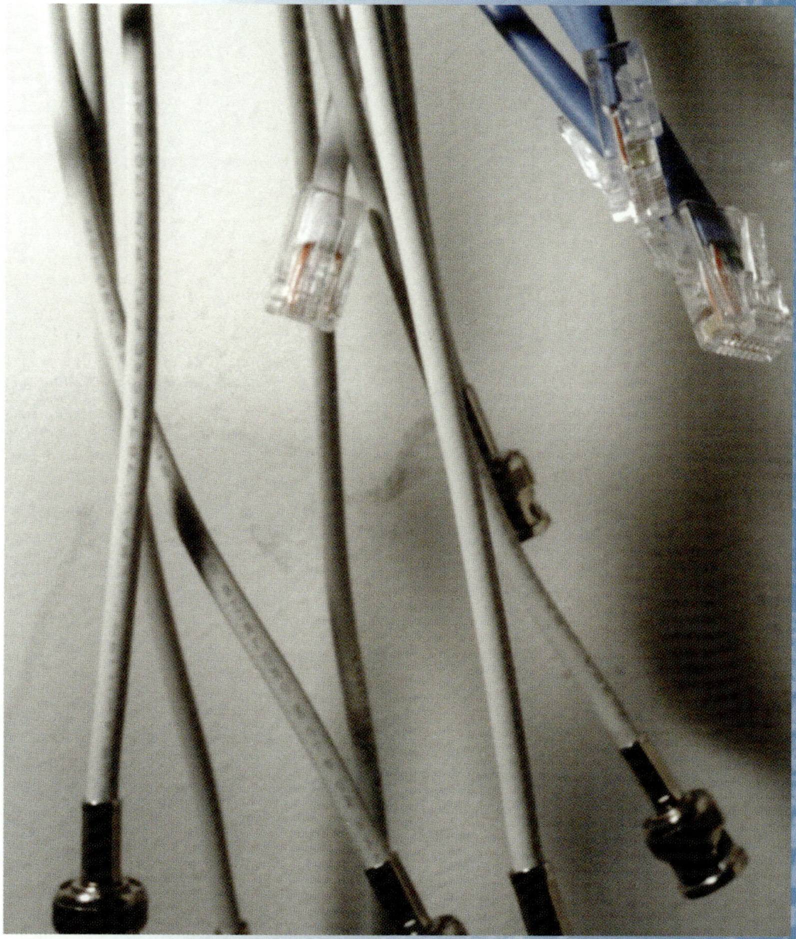

Figure 1 Category 5 plenum rated cables using RJ-45 and BNC connectors.

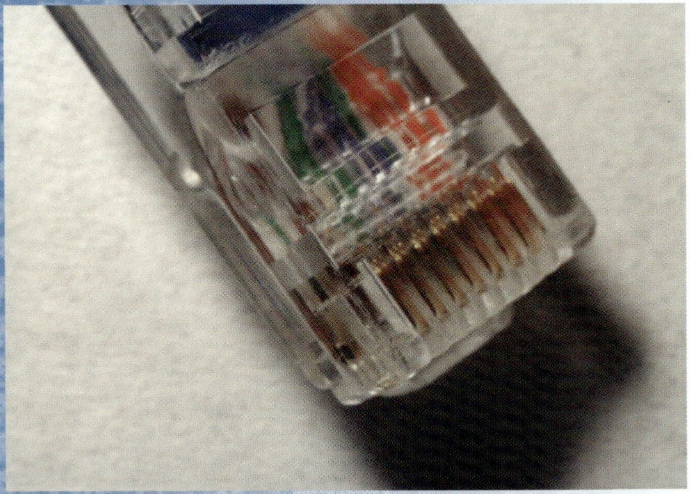

Figure 2 RJ-45 connector.

Figure 3 10Base2 "Thinnet" BNC connector and coaxial cable.

Figure 4 10Base5 "Thicknet" type N connector on double shielded "Ethernet" coaxial cable.

Figure 5 Voice grade punchdown block.

Photo courtesy AutoDesk, Inc.

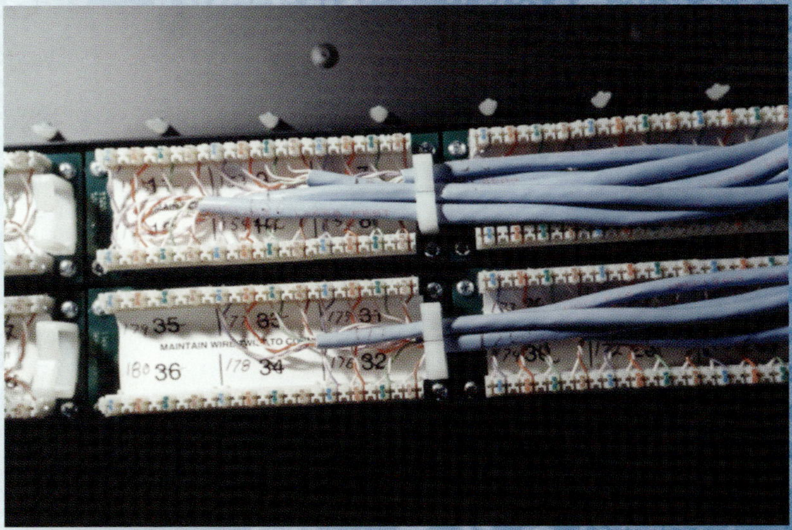

Figure 6 Data grade punchdown block.

Photo courtesy AutoDesk, Inc.

Figure 7 Well designed and installed data punchdown blocks and wiring.

Photo courtesy AutoDesk, Inc.

Figure 8 Rack mounted wire room installation including: Server (lower left), Tape backup (up from server), Router (up from tape backup), Patch panels (upper middle), and Hubs (lower middle and upper right).

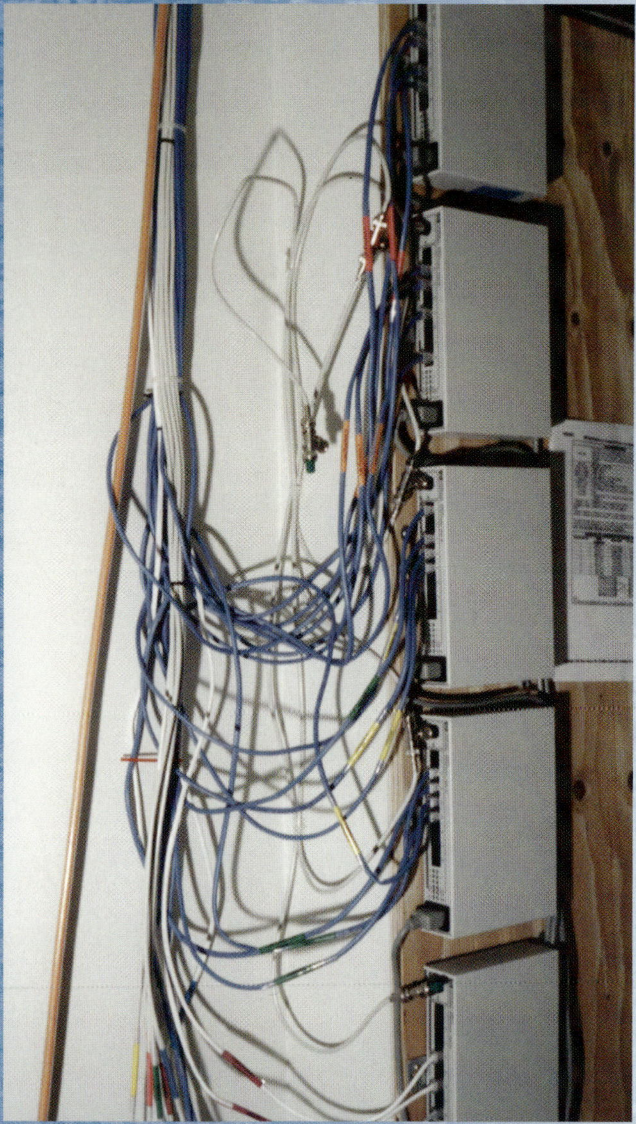

Figure 9 Stacked 8 port hubs. Note ports for 8 RJ-45 10BaseT and one 10Base2 port on each hub. The hubs are mounted on 3/4 in. plywood.

Figure 10 Multiple NIC protocols in a single server: "Thinnet" ARCNET NIC (3rd down from the top), "Thicknet" transceiver cable Ethernet NIC (3rd up from the bottom), and 10BaseT Ethernet (2nd up from the bottom).

Figure 11 Rack mounted RJ-45 10BaseT patch panel. Note that every cable has a permanently affixed label.

Figure 12 10Base5 transceiver.

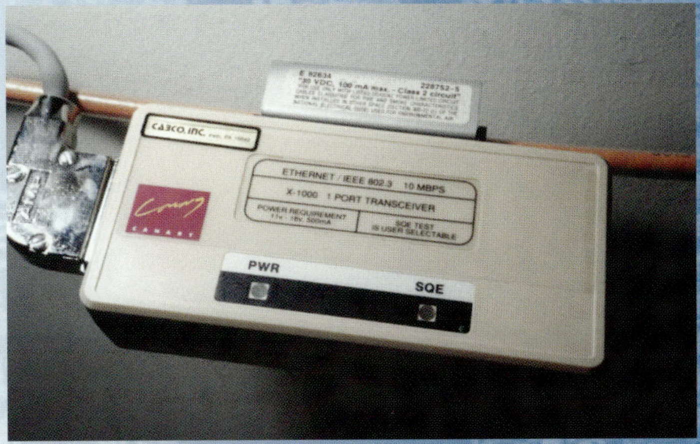

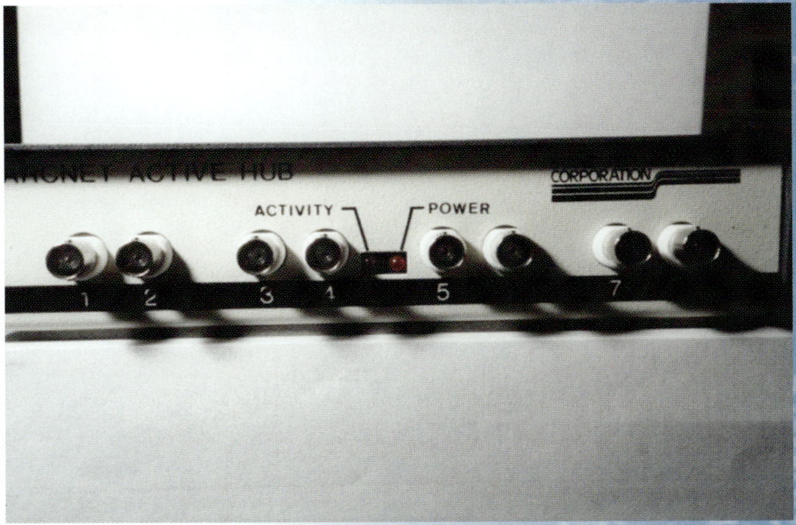

Figure 13 8 port hub.

Figure 14 ARCNET NIC. Note address DIP switch on right.

NT

9

Windows NT

INTRODUCTION

Microsoft has offered several network operating systems, beginning in 1986 with MS-NET. This was not one of Microsoft's better efforts, but it was DOS based, and IBM marketed it under the IBM PC Network Support Program label. With IBM's name attached, networked PCs became a realistic market. Network software vendors now had an opportunity to grow and prosper.

In 1988, with the introduction of the OS/2 operating system, Microsoft offered a much improved network operating system known as LAN Manager. The concepts of client and server were introduced with LAN Manager. IBM eventually took over OS/2 and LAN Manager and currently markets both. Meanwhile, Microsoft, clearly recognizing an opportunity to capture a portion of the hugely successful NetWare market, developed a new operating system based, in part, on LAN Manager and incorporating the graphical features of Windows.

The result of this effort produced *New Technology Advanced Server* (NTAS) version 3.1, first released in August 1993. Observers gave it high ratings overall but poor marks in memory usage, non-NetWare compatibility, and TCP/IP implementation. Microsoft responded with the 1994 release of version 3.5. NT was now NetWare aware, much less memory-hungry, and offered full TCP/IP implementation. Administration can be accomplished from a workstation using Windows for Workgroups and Windows 95/98 as well as from an NT Workstation machine. Reports from NT administrators showed NTAS 3.5 to be a reasonably stable and versatile platform.

This chapter will cover

- an analysis of the NT Server operating system as it relates to the OSI model,
- an overview of NT's functions, and
- installation procedures and recommendations.

PROTOCOL ANALYSIS

NetBIOS is Network Basic Input/Output Services.

Prior to 1984 and the introduction of DOS 3.1, PCs could not be networked. No method existed for the operating system to become aware that drives other than its own physical floppy and hard disks existed. IBM developed *Network Basic Input/Output Services* (**NetBIOS**) as the tool, within DOS, that could be used to intercept workstation requests for network drives.

When an application has need to read or write to a local disk, an interrupt type 21h procedure is executed by the application. It is the interrupt service routine, a part of the PC BIOS, that accomplishes the requested task. INT 21h is, unfortunately, unable to deal with nonlocal drive requests. DOS 3.1, with NetBIOS, adds a new interrupt, INT 5Ch. INT 5Ch is invoked whenever a nonlocal drive access is requested by either the application or the network interface card.

An additional feature was added to DOS that provided file and record locking so that files could be shared by nonlocal PCs. The MS-DOS SHARE command is used to set the hierarchy of directories.

Application Layer

Figure 9.1 shows NT as it relates to the OSI Reference Model. At layer 7 are the input/output (I/O) services, Named Pipes (which will be explained shortly), and user/server applications.

Presentation Layer

Layer 6, the presentation layer, provides what Microsoft refers to as the *environmental subsystem*. This is the Windows-like *graphical user interface* (GUI). A *provider interface* establishes the link between session and presentation layers.

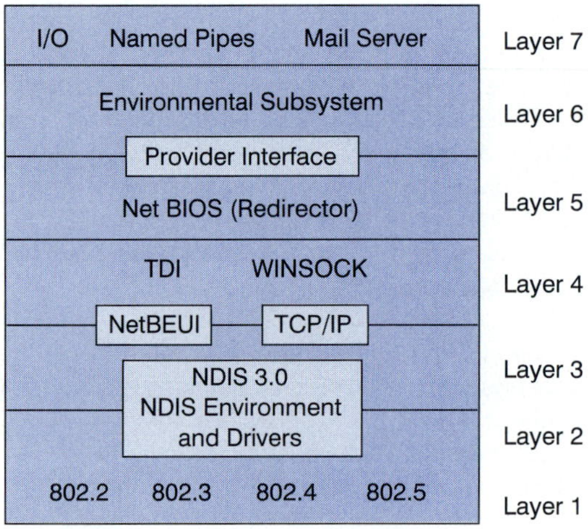

Figure 9.1 NT as It Relates to the OSI Reference Model

Session Layer

Layer 5 provides session controls and includes NetBIOS and the redirector (INT 5Ch) services. Figure 9.2 shows the relationship between the INT 21h and INT 5Ch service routines.

Transport and Network Layers

Layers 3 and 4 may be connected using one or more of several supported protocols. One of the significant features of NT Server is its ability to support multiple-transport protocols. NT is delivered with TCP/IP ready to install.

Transport services. Transport services include *Transport Driver Interface* (**TDI**) and *windows sockets* (WINSOCK). A socket is somewhat similar to the service access points (SAPs) that were presented in the MAC sublayers of the IEEE 802.2 standard. Where SAPs connect the MAC layer to other layers, sockets connect the transport layer to other layers when Windows is running.

TDI is Transport Driver Interface.

NetBIOS/NetBEUI. The distinctions between NetBIOS and NetBEUI are subtle. IBM Developed NetBIOS as a simple set of 18 commands for connecting PCs. *NetBIOS Extended User Interface* (**NetBEUI**) adds eight more commands and is also used as a transport layer protocol. It is often the preferred choice because it is, in many ways, faster and more efficient than NetBIOS. When NetBEUI is in use, NetBIOS becomes the application interface (API) that invokes NetBEUI.

NetBEUI is NetBIOS Extended User Interface.

NetBIOS was originally used as the NT default transport layer driver, but Microsoft used the nearly identical NetBEUI protocol in NT 3.1. NT 3.5 adds NWLink as a driver for both NTAS 3.5 and NT Workstation 3.5. This implementation continues in version 4.0. NWLink uses the NetWare SPC/IPX transport and network layer protocols to enable NetWare clients to connect to NT servers without having to install new client software.

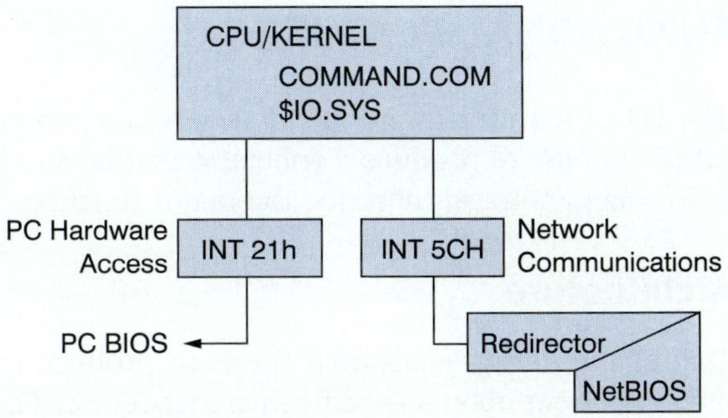

Figure 9.2 The Relationship between the INT 21h and INT 5Ch Service Routines

TCP/IP. Although TCP/IP is not normally associated with local area networks, it is rapidly becoming the de facto standard where wide area networks are concerned, primarily due to the phenomenal growth of Internet connectivity. NT contains a 32-bit "turbo" TCP/IP API that is an excellent choice for all LANs that need wide area connectivity.

Data and Physical Layers

At the data link and physical layers, NT supports a wide variety of protocols, including

- Ethernet,
- Token-Ring,
- ARCNET, and
- FDDI.

NDIS is Network Driver Interface Specification.

Network Driver Interface Specification (**NDIS**) is the glue that binds the data link layer protocol(s) to the operating system. In the previous chapter we described NetWare's Open Datalink Interface (ODI), which performs a similar function. What NDIS 3.0 adds to NT is the ability to load client software into extended memory. This is an enormous plus for conventional memory-hungry MS-DOS based programs.

NT OPERATING SYSTEM SHELL

Figure 9.3 shows the NT shell configuration. NT is a protected mode operating system in which a centric *kernel* is used to control access to system hardware. No user application is allowed direct access to hardware devices. Requests for hardware services must be processed by the kernel with data passed between hardware device and application on a time shared basis.

FUNCTIONAL FEATURES

The list of features found in NT deserves a good deal of attention. These features combine to produce a robust, versatile, and stable operating system. The following paragraphs describe the major functions on NT.

Architecture

One of the design goals of NT was to produce an operating system that was not dependent upon a specific microprocessor. Those sections of NT that must deal with hardware have been effectively isolated in the *Hardware Abstraction*

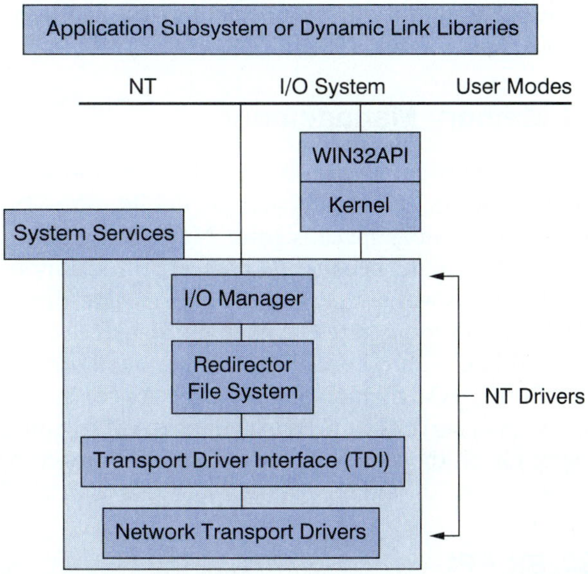

Figure 9.3 NT Operating System Shell

Layer (**HAL**) so that NT is easily ported not only to the Intel 80xxx processors but also to RISC chips.

HAL is Hardware Abstraction Layer.

NT servers can divide processing requirements among as many as 16 processors, significantly enhancing overall performance. Unfortunately, workstations are limited to two processors.

NT is a preemptive operating system. No task is allowed access to the CPU for more than a few milliseconds before it is stopped and cached away in memory. A queue of tasks is maintained in memory, each task being allowed CPU access in turn. NT provides up to 32 priority levels so that those tasks such as real time clocks or memory refresh can operate successfully.

NT is both multitasking and multithreaded. *Multitasking* simply means that more than one program may be running at the same time. An example might be a communications program running in background to receive a fax, an on-line scheduler also in background, and a word processor running in foreground grinding out this text. *Multithreading* allows multiple users to access the same program or service routine. For example, a client/server database program, running in the server, would use a supervisor program to process the multiple requests for access to the same data. Multithreading is essential to a server accessed by multiple workstations.

NT centralizes user profiles in a database called *the Registry*. Configuration and setup data for files such as .INI, .CNF, and so forth, are stored in the registry. One of the major time saving features for network administrators is the ability to save workstation CONFIG.SYS, AUTOEXEC.BAT, and .INI file data in the server. Software is available to compare a workstation's configuration to the registry database and download the correct configuration to a workstation, automatically. Unfortunately, this feature only works with NT workstations.

NT Memory Management

NT is the entire operating system. Like Windows 95, it is not an overlay of MS-DOS. To users, this means that the debilitating MS-DOS limit of 640 K of conventional memory space is gone. NT is designed to access up to 4 Gb of RAM. This is fortunate because NT itself still seems to be a bit memory-hungry. Workstations will not perform at their peak efficiency with less than 16 Mb and NT Server demonstrates its peak performance between 24 and 32 Mb of memory. Adding features such as database, mail, or Web servers mandates at least 32 Mb of RAM memory. In my experience, the addition of even a small Web and E-mail server required 64 Mb of RAM to eliminate "out of resource" messages. Given the relatively low cost of memory compared with total server cost, no NT server should be installed with less than 128 Mb of main memory.

32-Bit API

The application interface in NT is designed for full 32-bit data transfers. Programs may be written that fully use this feature. One could hope that the 64-bit API is not far in the future when 64-bit Pentium processors and PCI bus designs are commonplace. Unfortunately, NT 5.0 (now known as Windows 2000), appears to retain the 32-bit API.

Drive Management

RAID is Redundant Array of Inexpensive Drives.

Redundant Array of Inexpensive Drives (**RAID**) technology provides a six-level technique for combining multiple drives such that the system sees a single drive only. NT supports levels 1 and 5. Level 1 is a simple disk-mirroring system similar to that used in NetWare. Level 5 adds the capability of *striping* data across several disks to improve disk read/write response plus fault-tolerant parity checking to allow damaged disks to be repaired. By writing data, simultaneously, to numerous sectors on a disk that appear to the system as a single disk, any physical sector that produces a parity error can be rewritten using identical data from another identical physical sector. NT implements RAID support in software, eliminating the requirement for expensive RAID hardware. A relatively inexpensive SCSI controller and identical spaces on three separate drives are all that are required.

Plug-and-Play

An NT "wizard" called *NTDetect* will attempt to detect installed NICs during installation. NTDetect is not truly plug-and-play but does perform a similar function. Unfortunately, NICs and other plug-in devices must conform to

Microsoft's NDIS 3.0 standard. In the author's experience, this "plug-and-play" is not necessarily a blessing until you have determined that a specific vendor's product will truly "plug-and-play" in your computer. Just because the box says "plug-and-play" or "Windows 95 compatible" is definitely not a guarantee that the board will install successfully in an NT machine. In fact, software designed for Windows 95 often will not run in NT. Particular care should be given that drivers for peripheral devices are NT-compatible. Microsoft has indicated that true plug-and-play may be implemented in Windows 2000.

Peer-to-Peer

Both NT workstation and NT server are designed to connect as peer-to-peer operating systems. NT workstation is the entire operating system and does not require a server to communicate with other NT workstations. NT workstations may be configured that allow the sharing of resources. While NTAS contains a server "service," it also contains a peer-to-peer workstation service. While access to server resources requires log-on and authentication, the connection between machines is peer to peer. Unfortunately, Microsoft documentation conflicts on this issue. You will find periodic references to client/server connections in some of Microsoft's publications.

Domains

NT server allows the creation of an organizational tool called a *domain*. Users who are members of a domain can share any of the resources of the domain with a single log-on, even though resources may be spread over many servers or workstations. More than one domain may be created on the same LAN circuit. As far as the LAN protocol is concerned (e.g., Ethernet), there is only one large circuit. It is the NT operating system that is aware of different domains.

When NT server is installed, you will be given three choices: (1) Install as a *Primary Domain Controller* (PDC), (2) install as a *Backup Domain Controller* (BDC), or (3) install as a stand alone server. It is recommended that the first server installation be a PDC. An additional server or servers may be installed as BDCs. The function of the PDC is to consolidate all of the user profiles from all members of the domain in the PDC registry. User and group administration may now be done at a single machine. The PDC will automatically replicate profiles to BDCs so that if the PDC is down for any reason, a BDC can automatically take over PDC functions.

NT domains can be configured in three ways: (1) as a single domain, (2) as multiple domains with trusted relationships, and (3) as multiple trusted domains with a master domain controller. As an NT network grows, it is quite possible that PDCs on a multiple domain network might be physically located anywhere on the planet. Without a master domain controller, the network administrator would need to travel to each PDC to perform administrative tasks. A master domain controller eliminates this need.

Given the rather high cost of NT for workstations, you could achieve your peer-to-peer objectives with Windows for Workgroups or Windows 95/98 with a significantly smaller investment. These operating systems do quite well on benchmark tests and require less memory than NT to do so. This author would recommend that you apply the money you saved on workstations toward the installation of an NT server. However, it should be noted that NT Workstation provides separate user profiles that significantly improve security by requiring users to have their own account names and passwords to access their profile. The NT File System (NTFS) offers much better security than Windows 95/98.

Trust Relationships

Once the domains have been created, one domain may allow another to share resources by establishing a *trust.* Let us suppose that the "marketing" domain has created a database for sales forecasts. This is information that both the purchasing and manufacturing groups need. When the marketing domain administrator creates a trusted relationship for users of the "purchasing" and "manufacturing" domains, they will be able to log on under their own log-on and domain names and have immediate access to marketing's forecast data.

Note, however, that the reverse of a trusted relationship is not true. No trust has been created for marketing to share data in either the "purchasing" or "manufacturing" domains. The administrators of those domains would have to create the trusted relationship for marketing. Using trusted relationships relieves administrators of the need to set up each individual PDC machine for access required by members of other domains.

It would also be possible for the "marketing" domain administrator to assign permissions for access to the database files. Since "purchasing" and "manufacturing" need only to read the data, and should not be allowed to modify it in any way, the *trust* would be set up as a read only relationship.

NetWare Aware—WINNET API

A major feature of NT is that it can be made Novell NetWare-aware. By installing NDIS 3.0 and NetBIOS in any Windows workstation, the workstation may be used with a NetWare server. If both the NetWare and NT client software are loaded, the workstation can communicate with both an NT server and a NetWare server. Unfortunately, without the addition of a Microsoft client shell, the NetWare clients will be unable to communicate with NT server, nor will they be able to take advantage of the NT security and programming interfaces. Remote access and backup would also be unavailable.

By installing NWLink in an NT server together with the NetWare Client and Print Services, an NT server becomes a gateway to the NetWare server. Install a group on the NetWare server called NTGATEWAY and any NetWare client workstation is able to see all of the NetWare drives just as though it was connected directly to the NetWare server. This may sound like an ideal solution to integrating NT and NetWare. Unfortunately, there is both a time and bandwidth penalty to pay. A client must first access the NT server over the cable, then access the NetWare server, again over the cable.

SMB compatibility with LAN Manager

Server Message Blocks (**SMBs**) are used to transport data to the lower layers. This is done to maintain backward compatibility with OS/2 and LAN Manager. SMB message service is accomplished with simple broadcast datagrams. SMB is primarily used to transport data to lower levels.

SMBs are Server Message Blocks.

Named Pipes

When an NT server wishes to transport data to a client, the server generates a DOS Create that opens a connection for a client. The connection is referred to as a *named pipe*. The client is then able to generate a DOS OPEN using the name of the pipe. In essence, a connection will exist between server and client that enables direct memory address (DMA) transfers between client and server.

UNC

Universal Naming Convention (**UNC**) is used by NT to determine the path to a file location. UNC was begun in MS-Net and is also in use on the Internet. For example, the path to a server-based file called "app01" would be written as f:\\MSapps\app01 where f:\\ indicates drive f: on a server named Msapps. As shown, app01 is the shared resource name. Adding an additional backslash (f:\\MSapps\app01\) indicates that app01 is now a subdirectory of the shared directory in server MSapps.

UNC stands for Universal Naming Convention.

Mac Connectivity

For those of you who have attempted to connect an Apple Macintosh to a PC-based LAN, NT will offer a little slice of paradise. *Services for Macintosh* contains all of the software needed to extend connectivity to a Mac. In fact, Mac users will often not be aware that they are actually using resources on a PC server. Not only that, but Windows, NT, MS-DOS, and OS/2 clients are able to access LaserWriter printers. Support is available for Macs using Ethernet, Token-Ring, or FDDI on LocalTalk networks. The only possible drawbacks are that NT servers require an additional 2 Mb of hard drive space for Mac services and Mac clients will be unable to use their RAS routing protocol nor will they have remote or dial-in access.

NT VERSION 4.0

The most noticeable difference between NT 3.5 and NT 4.0 is the addition of a GUI similar to Windows 95. Additional features include the following:

- Internet Information Server (IIS) contains Web, FTP, and Gopher server engines that allow an NT server to establish a presence on the Internet.
- Remote Access Services (RASs) now include both the Point-to-Point (PPT) and Point-to-Point Tunneling (PPTP) protocols. These protocols, explained in Chapter 12, enable challenge response password security and Private Virtual Networks (PVNs).
- A network sniffer called Network Monitor comes with NT 4.0, which can be used to monitor and analyze some or all of the packets sent and received by an NT machine.
- NT 4.0 introduces Domain Name Service (**DNS**).

DNS is Domain Name Service.

- Routing Information Protocol (RIP) is provided to enable NT as a TCP/IP router.

INSTALLATION

Installing the Server

Microsoft has made the NT installation reasonably painless and informative. NT even runs a program called NETDETECT.COM that is used to detect the configuration of your server hardware. NTDETECT should not be confused with plug and play. While it does a reasonably good job, it may not detect your specific devices. To ensure compatibility, Microsoft delivers a *Hardware Compatibility Manual* with the install CD. If your device is not on the approved list, you will need to obtain the correct driver software from the device manufacturer.

NT will ask you for the license mode you desire. There are two choices: Per Seat and Per Server. This very confusing terminology really means that you need to determine how users connect to the server. Per Server licensing establishes the maximum concurrent licensed connections, and Per Seat establishes the maximum number of licensed client machines that may access the NT server.

During the setup, NT will show you the existing drive partitions and then allow you to partition other drives from E: through Z: using either the MS-DOS File Allocation Table (FAT), NT File System (NTFS), or OS/2 High Performance File System (HPFS) file system formats. The MS-DOS FAT format is of use on the C: drive so that you can boot the server from a floppy, but all other drives should probably take advantage of the much improved NTFS filing system. If you wish to reinstall or upgrade NT, you will need up to 130 Mb of FAT formatted drive space-free. NT only installs to a FAT partition that may subsequently be converted to NTFS. Incidentally, not being able to boot from a floppy is usually considered an improvement to server security. As for HPFS, there is no need for this file format unless you expect to be using OS/2.

When asked to specify protocols, install the default protocol NetBEUI first. For the local area network, it will prove much more efficient than a wide area protocol. Install routable protocols such as TCP/IP second. This is critical in NT clients since they will default to the first protocol listed in the control panel. NT Server simply responds to the protocol sent by a client if the protocol is installed in the server.

If you are installing TCP/IP, you will be prompted for a 32-bit IP address. You will need your network administrator to assign an IP address. You may use any IP address to get NT installed and change to assigned values at a later time. Refer to the chapter on TCP/IP for additional details concerning TCP/IP configurations.

The rest of the installation involves sharing server resources such as printers and drive(s) and directories with clients. This process is accomplished from within the Windows NT File Manager DISK function after setup has rebooted in the NT graphics mode.

This is not a book on NT administration (see the bibliography for additional reading); however, some common procedures to customize your server include the following:

- *Domain controller or server*—NT servers do not have to be domain controllers, neither primary nor backup, however, the *first* NT server installed in a domain *must* be a primary domain controller. Setup provides a *Windows NT Server Security Role* dialog box that allows you to choose server control type.
- *Creating the computer name*—Following Server Security Role settings, you will be given a choice of choosing a computer name. Any name up to a maximum of 15 characters is allowed with the following exceptions: No spaces (use underscores instead); avoid real names or places that might be used by a user as a log-in name.
- *Determining the server language*—The install program assumes English but at this point you will be able to choose from a large and growing list of languages, assuming you have the disk(s) that support your choice.
- *Configuring network components*—Now is the time to install Windows components such as screensavers, bitmaps, and sounds. Don't forget that these things take up valuable disk space; you may want to delete all the component files you don't actually use.

- *Configuring printers*—You are on your own here because only you know which, if any, printers will be installed. One recommendation, shared by many network administrators, is to choose printer or printer queue names that sound like the printer model. "Printer1" doesn't help much when a user is trying to figure out which Windows printer driver to select; CS_LAB_HP3SI offers at least a hint that the printer is the HPIIIsi lab printer. A distinct advantage in printer administration may be had if client workstations are also NT. A single printer driver can be installed on an NT server. NT workstations are capable of selecting the server's printer driver. Other versions of Windows do not have this capability.
- *Installing server applications*—NT servers are ideal for sharing MS-DOS applications such as diagnostic utilities. Client/server database managers such as Oracle or Microsoft SQL Server are installed and run on the NT server itself. In most cases, these programs may actually be installed from a client. Administrators may install applications over the network to clients.
- *System parameters*—You will need to know the parameters for the PC in which you will install NT. Minimum requirements for hardware include 80486 (NT 4.0) or newer CPU, 32 Mb of RAM (my recommendation), 130 Mb of free and contiguous hard drive space (version 4.0). You may wish to include an additional 130 Mb on C: to accommodate a reinstall. NT first copies install files to free space and then compiles the operating system files in the WINNT directory. If insufficient space is free on C:, NT will not reinstall. You will also want a CD-ROM drive. The bulk of the files used during the installation are on the install CD, and it is much faster than an over-the-network install, which also ties up network resources.

The installation process for NT can be done in one of three basic ways:

1. Install to a formatted hard drive partition with nothing on it.
2. Install from diskette to a formatted hard drive with MS-DOS or a version of Windows installed.
3. Install from CD-ROM to a formatted hard drive with MS-DOS or a version of Windows installed.

Installing to blank formatted hard drive. To prepare your server, format the hard drive partition that will be drive C:. You will need to boot the system from drive A: using MS-DOS then format drive C:. The NT installation process assumes that you have at least three startup diskettes, even though you will soon learn how to install from CD-ROM without the diskettes. If your install CD-ROM did not arrive with three installation diskettes, you must make them.

Several switches are associated with WINNT. Use WINNT /h to view all of the switch possibilities. Use WINNT /ox to create the install diskettes. Then boot your computer using diskette 1. The install process will guide you the rest of the way. Be certain you know the parameters for your hard drive controller(s) and NIC(s). If you already have a MS-DOS boot disk and do not wish to use the NT installation diskettes, use WINNT/b to install directly from the CD-ROM.

Remember that NT was designed to be independent of the microprocessor. When you begin the installation, you will notice that there are several subdirectories on the installation CD-ROM such as alpha, client, i386,and so on. For the sake of discussion we will assume that your server CPU is an Intel Pentium and change to the i386 subdirectory.

Installing to formatted hard drive with operating system previously installed. If either MS-DOS or any of the Windows versions are already installed on drive C:, NT can be installed as an additional operating system. From the first diskette change to the subdirectory that conforms to your server CPU and, using file manager, run the WINNT.EXE program. The remainder of the process is identical to installing to a blank formatted hard drive.

Installing directly from CD-ROM. If you are installing from CD-ROM, you can use the /b switch to install without the diskettes. From this point on, the installation is identical to previous methods.

Installing the Client

Most existing networks may not enjoy a cost-justifiable reason for upgrading to an NT Workstation client. Although the NT client is an extraordinarily stable platform, all of your network interconnect and graphical operating system needs can be achieved with the much less expensive Windows for Workgroups (3.11) or Windows 95/98. Your decision to upgrade may well be based on the cost of maintaining the much less stable Windows 3.11, 95, and 98 platforms.

One very useful feature for NT administrators is the ability to install client stations over the network. Be certain to consult your administrative guide for details to set up this possibility. Version 3.51 CD contains Windows 3.11 client installation files and version 4.0 CD contains Windows 95 installation files. Newer CD-ROMS are expected to contain Windows 98 installation files. A separate CD-ROM must be obtained for NT Workstation. To install the client over the network, simply copy the files to an NT directory that is shared and accessible by only those who will use it. Boot from an MS-DOS disk that contains the DOS based Microsoft Client files that can connect to the NT server and run SETUP.EXE from the NT client directory.

TROUBLESHOOTING

Server Support

If you expect to become a network administrator, you will want to familiarize yourself with the files that are critical to an NT installation:

- *CONFIG.SYS*—This file contains device drivers critical to your *specific* installation. If you are still using NDIS 2.0, you will need the device drivers: PROTMAN.DOS and WORKGRP.SYS to tell the network where to find PROTOCOL.INI and the bindings for NetBEUI.
- *PROTOCOL.INI*—This file contains the initialization details for:

  [network.setup]—lists version, name of network interface card (e.g. MS$3c5x9), transport, and LAN type;

  [MS$3c5x9]—details of the network interface card such as IRQ and base I/O address;

  [protman]—protocol driver name (PRTMAN$) and protocol priority; and

  [MS$NETBEUI]—details for NetBEUI.
- *SYSTEM.INI*—NT adds two sections to Windows SYSTEM.INI: [network] and [password Lists]. The information in these sections will be unique to your installation.

Remember that all of the previous three files are created or modified by the NT install. You may change them if you wish, but be certain you know precisely why you are making a change.

Now is an excellent time to install your backup device and do a full server backup. You might also wish to install and configure an *uninterruptable power supply* (UPS) at this time to prevent power source–induced problems.

Administrative Tool Set

Within the administrative tools, NT includes three applets that can be used to troubleshoot NT problems. With these applets, nearly all configuration problems can be resolved. System performance can be measured and displayed graphically and system events can be monitored for both successful events and failures.

NT Diagnostics

This tool is a much improved version of the old DOS-based Microsoft Diagnostics (MSD). Figure 9.4 shows the main screen form. Properties lists for all of the hardware devices and operational services can be displayed and printed. A

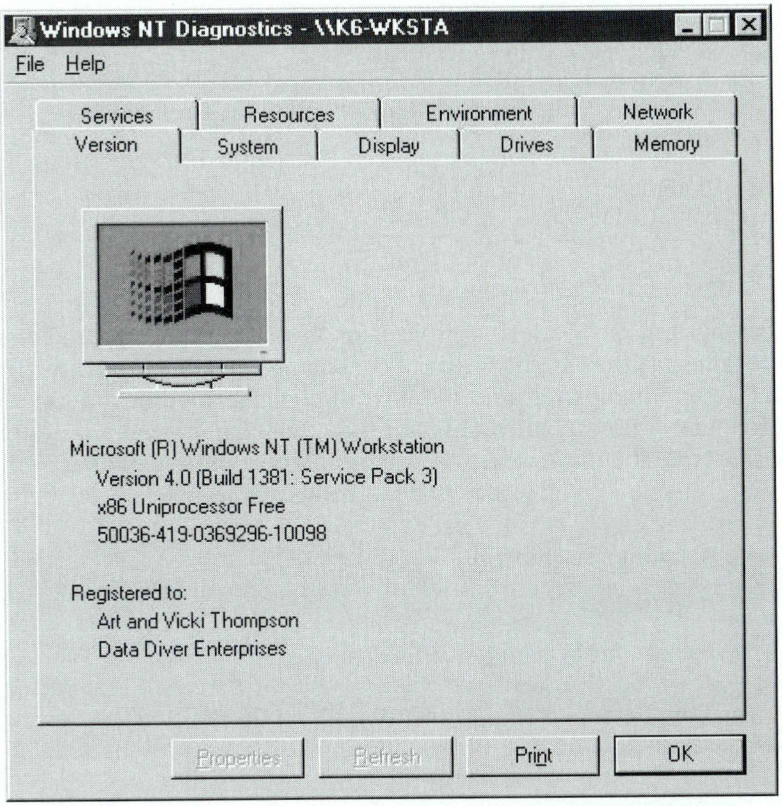

Figure 9.4 NT Diagnostics

printed copy should probably become a part of your network documentation and updated every time any server parameter or device is changed or modified.

The Network tab can be used to view statistics pertaining to network performance and usage.

APPLICATION PROJECTS

Project 1

Create your own step-by-step plan to install an NT server. Include plans for both server and clients. Your plan should include the following parts:

- Preparation
  1. Material requirements
     a. Material purchase orders

    b. Vendor delivery dates

  2. Hardware modification/configuration requirements
  3. Software modification/configuration requirements

- Time line plan (when each step is scheduled, and how long it will take to complete)

Project 2

Perhaps the most valuable project for this chapter is an actual, hands-on network installation. If not possible, contact an NT LAN administrator and make an appointment to attend the next upgrade or modification to the network. Take lots of notes, particularly notes on the planning and procedures that were used. Note the documentation that the LAN administrator has available.

Make a written report that includes sections for

- planning procedures,
- documentation,
- actual step-by-step procedures used, and
- your suggestions to improve the process you observed.

CHAPTER REVIEW

- NetBIOS is the addition to DOS that allows data transfers to or from network drives to be *redirected* to or from the network interconnect cable. Requests for drive services (INT21h) are examined and redirected to INT5Ch services for all nonlocal drives.
- Figure 9.1 demonstrates the relationship of NT to the OSI reference model.

  Named Pipes provide the I/O access to applications at layer 7.

  Layer provides the Windows graphical presentation layer interface.

  Layer 5 includes the NetBIOS redirector services.

  Transport services may be provided by the *network transport service* or *Windows sockets* (similar to service access points [SAPs]).

  Network and Transport layers are connected by *NetBEUI* (default) or TCP/IP.

  At the data and physical layers, NT supports Ethernet, Token-Ring, ARCNET, and FDDI.

- *Network Driver Interface Specification* (NDIS) binds the data link protocol(s) together and adds the ability to use extended memory.
- NT is designed to be as hardware-independent as possible. The *kernel* contains the hardware manipulation services that operate in a protected mode environment. All requests for access to hardware functions and services must be processed by the kernel.
- The architecture of NT includes a *Hardware Abstraction Layer* (HAL) that allows independence from a specific CPU. NT can currently be installed on Intel 80486 and newer, DEC Alpha, and the MIPS4000.
- NT is *multitasking* and is designed to work effectively in *multiprocessing* systems.
- NT provides for extremely large memory servers, up to 4 Gb, and eliminates the MS-DOS 640-K barrier.
- User configuration is contained in the *registry*.
- Setup configurations are contained in files ending with .INI, .CNF, etc.
- NT supports 32-bit APIs and RAID drive technology.
- NT is plug and play, assuming that server hardware is also plug and play.
- NT clients are peer to peer and do not require a server.
- NT servers can communicate with NT clients, Windows and Windows for Workgroup clients, MS-DOS clients, Macintosh clients, and NetWare servers (using the WINNET API).
- *Domains* are created as logical or organizational workgroups.
- *Trust relationships* are created to establish the sharing of resources between domain users.
- NT maintains compatibility with LAN MANAGER through the use of *System Message Blocks* (SMBs).
- *Universal Naming Convention* (UNC) allows compatibility with Internet path conventions.

REVIEW QUESTIONS

1. List and describe the NT functions for each layer of the OSIRM.
2. Discuss the functions of NetBIOS and its relationship to MS-DOS and NT.
3. What does NetBEUI add to NetBIOS?

4. What features or functions of NT make it hardware-independent?
5. What is the function of NDIS?
6. What is the NT *kernel*?
7. How does NT prevent a user application from directly accessing hardware functions?
8. What is a domain?
9. How are trusted relationships used?
10. Where does NT keep user descriptions?
11. Discuss the difference between the bindery used in Novell NetWare 3.x and the registry used in NT.
12. List the client operating systems that can communicate with NT.
13. Describe the symbology of the universal naming convention.
14. What are the memory limits supported by NT?
15. NT workstations do not require a server. Why?

VINES

10 Banyan VINES

INTRODUCTION

If you have ever seen a banyan tree, it looks as if the seed was planted high in the air with the roots of the tree branching down to the ground to take root and begin the growth of another tree. Thus it is with Banyan Systems, Inc.'s VINES. VINES takes its name from the banyan tree because its architecture creates branches for communication with network nodes in a hierarchical manner much like the directory service used by NetWare version 4.x.

VINES is in fact based on UNIX system 5.3. UNIX is a multiuser and multitasking operating system designed to enhance the portability of applications from machine to machine. With this portability added to the ability to create multiple communications links or branches, VINES lends itself very well to wide area network applications. VINES is able to accommodate a diverse set of protocols and, as you will soon see, conforms quite well to the requirements of the OSI Reference Model.

VINES supports client workstations running MS-DOS, Windows, and OS/2. Macintosh clients may also be connected but must use the Appletalk LAN protocol to communicate with a VINES server. A VINES server may be installed on an Intel x86 single or multiprocessor server. System requirements and support include the following:

- 80386 or better CPU
- 80-Mb hard drive or larger in ST506, IDE, ESDI, or SCSI formats
- 8-Mb RAM or larger—VINES ver 5.x will support up to 16 Mb (ISA bus), 256 Mb (MCA bus), 256 Mb (EISA bus)
- UPS support
- ICA (Intelligent Communications Adapter)—Up to four ICA cards may be installed in a server; however, ICA installations limit maximum memory support. ICA cards support serial communications or fractional T1. (T1 lines will be explained in the chapter on wide area networking.)

PROTOCOL ANALYSIS

OSI Reference

Figure 10.1a diagrams the relationship of a VINES client to the OSI model; Figure 10.1b shows the server as it relates to the OSI model. At the application layer, VINES offers a robust selection of services, including network printing, electronic mail, and messaging. In addition, VINES supports both UNIX and MS-DOS applications and includes a NetBIOS emulator in a similar fashion to NetWare. Third-party applications may also be added to the server.

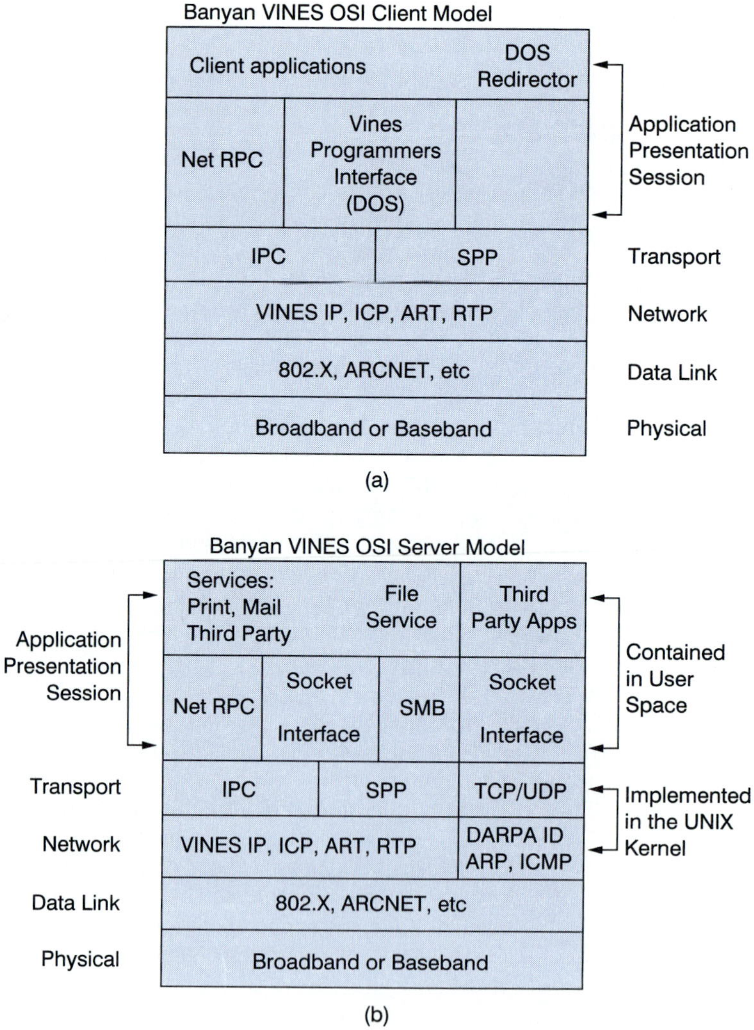

Figure 10.1 Relationship of a VINES client (a) and server (b) to the OSI model

VINES Basic Services include

- network administration;
- StreetTalk—a global naming service;
- VANGuard—provides network security;
- electronic mail; and
- PC/MS-DOS file service.

VINES Gateway Services include

- support for IBM 3270/SNA and 3270/BSC and
- asynchronous terminal emulations.

VINES Utility Services include

- network integrity and
- backup and recovery.

Note, in the client model, that VINES uses the System Message Block (SMB) and file redirector that is contained in MS-DOS.

At the session and transport layers, VINES uses their *Network Remote Call Procedure* (NetRPC). Based on the Xerox XNS Courier protocol, NetRPC provides layer independence between the transport and application layers through the use of a high-level language and compiler between the application and data link layers.

At the transport layer, VINES offers both open protocols and proprietary solutions. Open protocols include Transmission Control Protocol (TCP) and User Datagram Protocol (UDP). (UDP is part of the Internet Protocol; both TCP and IP are the subject of Chapter 13.) The proprietary solutions are *VINES InterProcess Communications Protocol* (VIPC), used for both connection-oriented and connectionless (datagrams) service. *VINES Sequenced Packet Protocol* (VSPP) provides reliable connection oriented packet transmission only. Again, these protocols are based on XNS.

The following are additional proprietary protocols:

- *VINES Internet Protocol* (**VIP**)—The network layer protocol used to encapsulate the MAC protocol on the Data Link layer. Note that VINES is also able to implement the true Internet TCP/IP protocol suite.

VIP is VINES Internet Protocol.

- *VINES Internet Control Protocol* (**VICP**)—Transport layer protocol for connection and connectionless packet and datagram transmission. ICP also resolves address conflicts and provides routing cost information where choices between routes to a destination node are possible.

VICP means VINES Internet Control Protocol.

VARCP stands for VINES Address Resolution Control Protocol.

- *VINES Address Resolution Control Protocol* (**VARP**)—This routing protocol is used between VINES servers to assign an address to any node that does not already have one.

VRUP is VINES Routing Update Protocol.

- *VINES Routing Update Protocol* (**VRUP**)—VRUP provides the periodic updates to ensure that routing tables are current in all of the routers connected to the network.

Open and industry standard protocols include TCP/IP, ICMP, ARP, and CCITT X.25. These popular public and DoD protocols are dealt with in more detail in Chapters 12 and 13 on wide area networking and TCP/IP, respectively.

At the data link and physical layers, VINES supports nearly all of the popular LAN protocols. Standards include IEEE 802.2, 802.3, and 802.5. Additional protocols include ARCNET, AT&T's Starlan, and both of IBM's synchronous protocols, SDLC (Synchronous Data Link Control) and BSC (Bisynchronous).

Serial links may be established between servers at up to 64 Kbps in either synchronous or asynchronous modes or X.25's Link Access Procedure-Balanced (LAPD) protocol. In addition, VINES servers can be configured as remote hosts to either IBM or Digital Equipment Corporation (DEC) terminals. When a VINES workstation is configured to emulate an IBM 3270 terminal, the server appears as a 3274 cluster controller that can, in turn, be linked to an IBM mainframe. As many as 96 concurrent sessions are possible.

Data Link Header Formats

Figures 10.2a, b, and c show the header formats for IEEE 802.2, 802.3, and 802.5. Because the 802.x frame formats must conform to the IEEE specifications, they appear here in exactly the same way they were presented in the chapters on Ethernet and Token-Ring. VINES simply adds its header, just prior to the data frame, as the complete packet is passed down from higher layers and assembled for transmission.

Figure 10.2a shows the Ethernet 802.3 frame format where the length field is used to determine the VINES packet type in a manner similar to Ethernet type II. VINES also supports the older Ethernet II. Figure 10.5b shows the insertion of a VINES Packet field to the Token-Ring frame, again, to determine the packet type.

VINES uses this technique of packet type field insertion in all of the Data Link layer protocols that it supports. To the designer of a VINES LAN, this means that routing must be done by a VINES server or that routers must be aware of the VINES format.

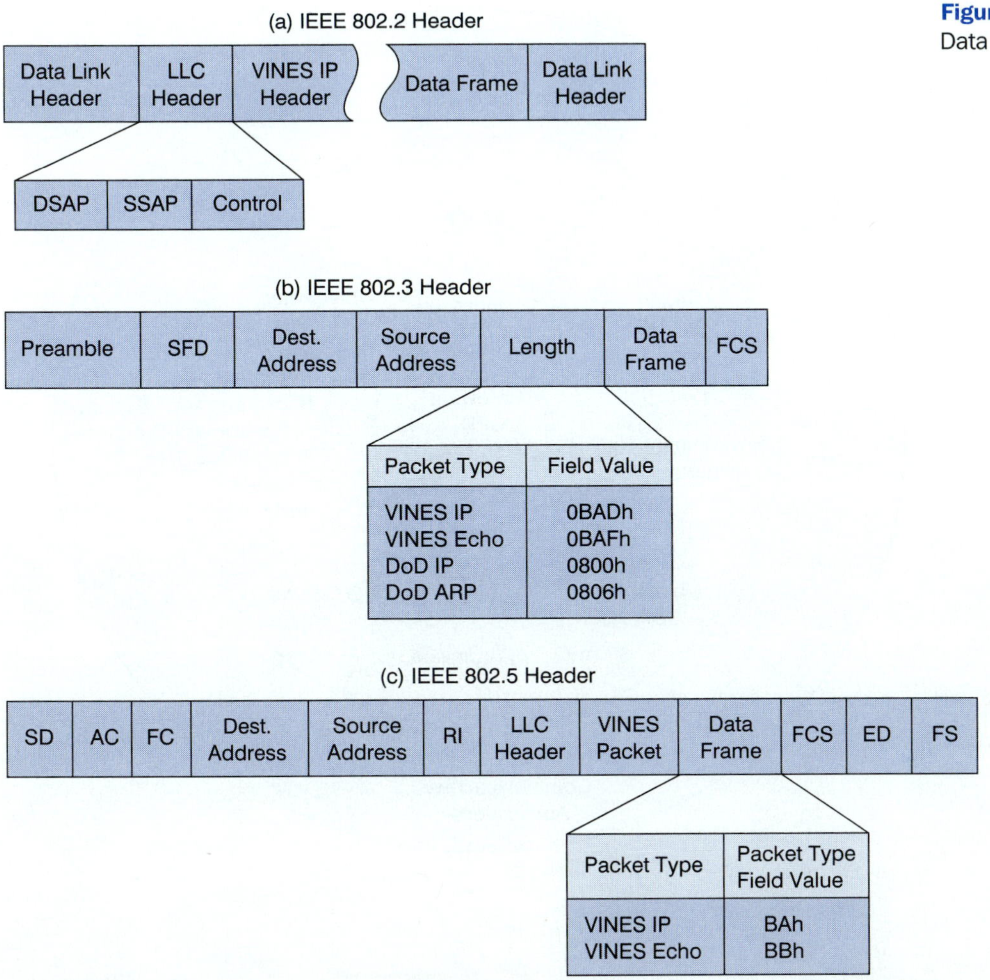

Figure 10.2a,b,c
Data Link Layer Headers

VINES AND THE UNIX KERNEL

Figure 10.3 shows the UNIX kernel. Within the kernel ring, VINES loads its device drivers for disk, LAN, tape, and so forth, plus communications drivers and user spaces.

Figure 10.4 shows the relationship between VINES and the UNIX kernel. Communication from a client is redirected to the network cable and passed to the server operating system when a request to the memory protected kernel is initiated. The kernel then causes the appropriate device driver and communication protocol to process the client request.

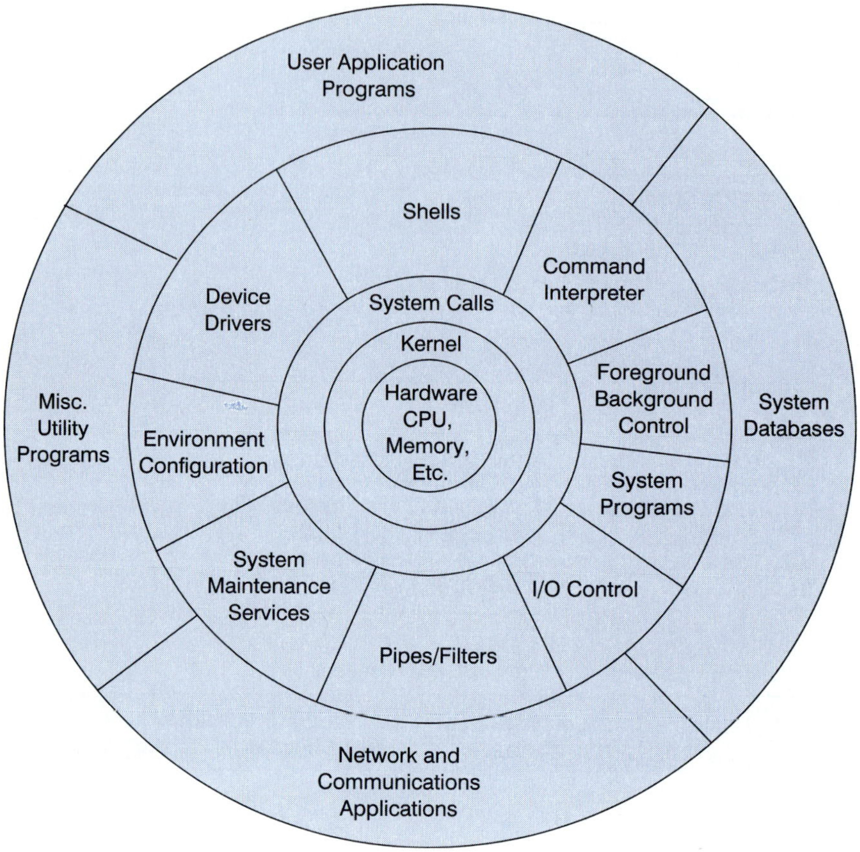

Figure 10.3 UNIX Kernel

Security

VINES provides for security in the following manner:

- Users and groups are given passwords and can be prevented from changing passwords.
- Users may be restricted to using specific workstations.
- Access to files, printing, and communications services can be restricted.
- Access to the management services for files and directories can be restricted.
- Access to other servers that are connected by serial or TCP/IP can be restricted.

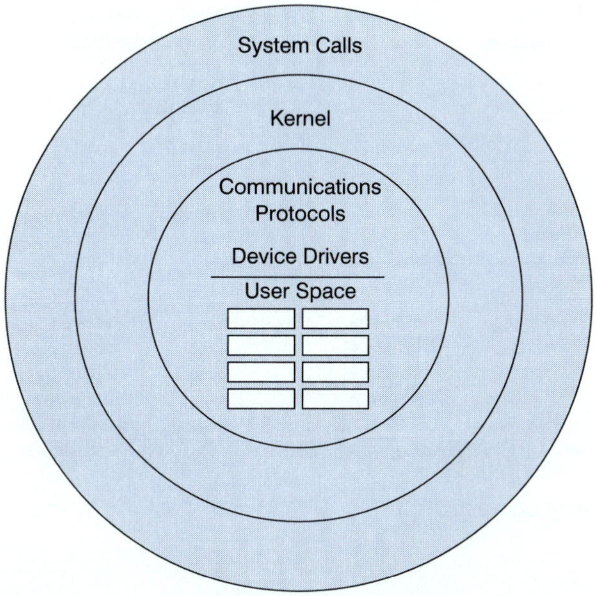

Figure 10.4 VINES Adaptation to the UNIX Kernel

StreetTalk

VINES uses a global naming service called StreetTalk in a manner somewhat reminiscent of Netware's NDS directory service. Within StreetTalk, a naming service can be used to assign names and attributes to users and resources. Servers, for example, use the naming convention ST@servername@Servers. A *Servers* group is created at install time and a name is automatically assigned. During installation, the installer assigns each server a *servername,* within the Servers group. Servernames are then used to create groups of users and resources within the Server's organization.

Figure 10.5 illustrates the StreetTalk naming convention. The two servernames are PrenHall01 and PrenHall02. Two groups exist, Editors and Authors, for which two printing resources and three users have been created. User Art Thompson is able to access the HP Laserjet *printing resource* on *server* PrenHall01 and is a member of the Authors *group* that belongs to the Seattle *organization*.

With StreetTalk, administrators are able to

- assign names to users,
- create named groups and organizations,
- assign users to groups and groups to organizations,
- assign groups to server locations,

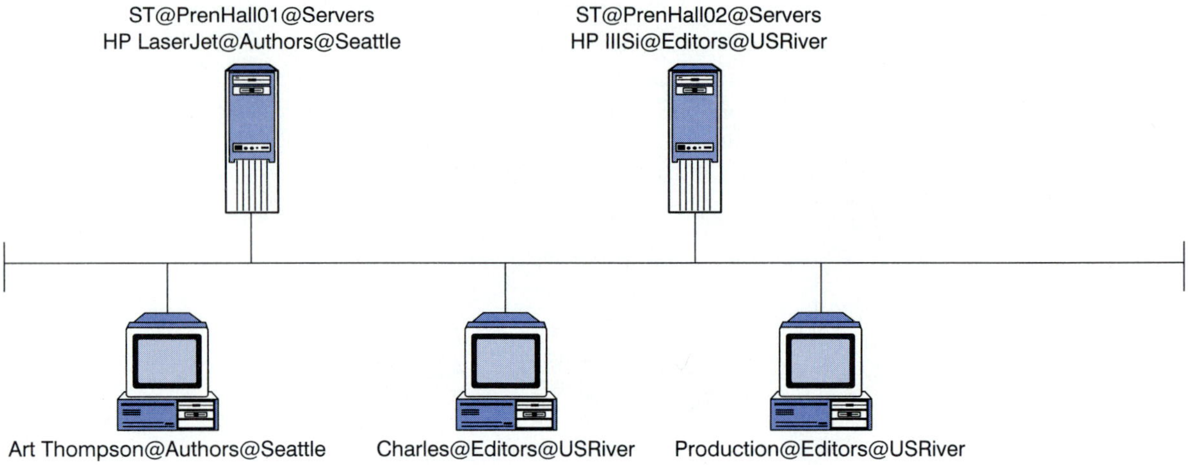

Figure 10.5 StreetTalk Naming Conventions

- locate names of groups and users, and
- create AdminLists of users assigned to be administrators for groups and servers.

Because VINES is based on UNIX, access rights to directories and files can be set for individual users, groups of users, or restricted to the creator/owner of a file or directory only. As with DOS and Windows, file attributes may also be set for read/write, read only, and so forth.

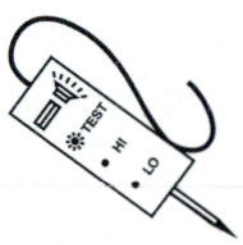

TROUBLESHOOTING

Because VINES is based on UNIX, it will be seen by the user as a command line operating system. No graphical user interface or tools are available. Because VINES does not have a large installed base of customers, few third-party troubleshooting tools are available. UNIX, and therefore VINES, is an extraordinarily versatile operating system and quite complex. Before you can effectively administer and troubleshoot VINES, you will need to master the complexities of the operating system. Unfortunately, it is far beyond the scope of this book to provide even a cursory knowledge of UNIX.

It is also advisable to master the C programming language since most of the operating system and its support shells are written in C. Much of the administration and system monitoring may be enhanced by the use of C programs and UNIX script files, which are used in a manner similar to DOS batch files, but you will have to write them yourself. If you are already proficient with UNIX, you should expect to learn VINES with relative ease.

LAN problems on VINES networks are approached with the same troubleshooting tools and equipment that one would use on any network. The problems with physical layer components and data layer protocols are the same as with any network operating system. Because VINES is so often implemented in wide area networks, an understanding of routers and router programming is essential. WAN protocols such as TCP/IP come with a few simple programs that will be of help. The TCP/IP tools will be demonstrated in Chapter 13 on TCP/IP.

During my introduction to a VINES network, it was pointed out that a network analyzer was one of the essential monitoring tools. In fact, one analyzer was permanently installed in the server wiring room, and a portable model in the form of a laptop computer was handy as well. On that installation, protocol analyzers and cable testers were the primary network troubleshooting tools.

CHAPTER REVIEW

- VINES is based on the UNIX system 5.3 operating system but has been ported to run on Intel processor–based servers.
- VINES supports MS-DOS, Windows, OS/2, and Macintosh clients.
- The UNIX kernel controls all access to the CPU and its associated hardware.
- User space and communications services reside in the protected memory space controlled by the kernel.
- Shells surrounding the kernel provide the system services and calls to device drivers required by application programs running in the outer ring.
- Client requests for server drive access are redirected to the network cable and passed to the server.
- VINES security includes user names and passwords, workstation restriction, and restrictions on access to print services, directories and files, communications services, server management, and servers running TCP/IP.
- StreetTalk is the VINES administrative tool that provides a global naming service that allows users to be assigned to groups; groups to server locations.
- VINES supports UNIX and MS-DOS applications and is equipped with a NetBIOS emulator.

- Presentation layer services are provided by NetRPC, which provides a high-level language and compiler. Routing functions are supplied by VARP and VRUP.
- VIPC and VSPP provide the transport layer sequencing and acknowledgments services.
- Data link layer support is provided for Ethernet, Token-Ring, ARCNET, and FDDI, plus IBM's SDLC and BSC.

REVIEW QUESTIONS

1. What is the operating system used by VINES?
2. List the major features of VINES.
3. What are the major functions of StreetTalk?
4. List the protocols that VINES uses at the transport and network layers, and provide a brief description of each protocol.
5. List the data link layer protocols supported by VINES.
6. Describe the naming convention used in VINES.
7. List the client operating systems supported by VINES.
8. Describe the security features of VINES.
9. What is the primary function of the UNIX kernel?
10. You are installing a VINES server. What brand of CPU would you use?

11
AppleTalk

INTRODUCTION

No collection of network operating systems would be complete without Apple Corporation's AppleTalk. The Macintosh operating system includes a twisted pair LAN interface called *LocalTalk.* The network interface that controls LocalTalk is AppleTalk. Apple has insisted on the same "ease of use" design criteria that is the hallmark of their Macintosh operating system, which is designed for plug-and-play features that include LocalTalk. Probably no other LAN is more easily installed than AppleTalk/LocalTalk. Support is available for other protocols including IEEE 802.3, 802.5 and ARCNET as well as TCP/IP. Both Novell NetWare and Microsoft NT support Macintosh connectivity and Apple provides MS-DOS and DEC VMS protocol stacks.

AppleTalk has been delivered in two phases. Phase 1 is noticeably limited in that it will only support up to 254 unique node addresses due to its 8-bit addressing format. Phase 2, released in 1989, significantly extends the number of unique nodes to 16 million by doubling the number of address bits. This is still limited, however, when compared to the 32-bit addressing used with TCP/IP and the Internet.

AppleTalk deals with both local and wide area concerns. This chapter will limit itself to a presentation of the details of AppleTalk as it relates to LANs and only offer an overview of wide area protocols. The bibliography offers several sources for those interested in the details of AppleTalk in wide area applications.

PROTOCOL ANALYSIS

OSI Reference Model

As can be seen in Figure 11.1, AppleTalk maintains conformance to the OSIRM. Phase 1 supported older versions of Ethernet in addition to LocalTalk; however, most of the common Data Link protocols are supported in phase 2 including IEEE 802.2, 802.3, and 802.5.

Both the application and presentation layers are supported by the AppleTalk Filing Protocol and Postscript services for printing. At the session layer, four protocols are used to support data transfers to lower layers, the relationship between the local network and other networks, a session open/close protocol, and access to printing devices. AppleTalk supports internal routing tables, a unique technique for sending a datagram to another node and measuring the echo that is returned, connection-oriented transaction control, and a protocol to translate names to the internal socket addresses. At the network layer the Datagram Delivery protocol facilitates communications between the addressable sockets in each of the connected nodes.

Wide Area Protocols

The following lists the wide area protocols that apply to layers 3–7 and provides a brief description. As you read each description, try to relate the information to similar protocols presented in previous chapters.

Figure 11.1 AppleTalk Referenced to the OSIRM

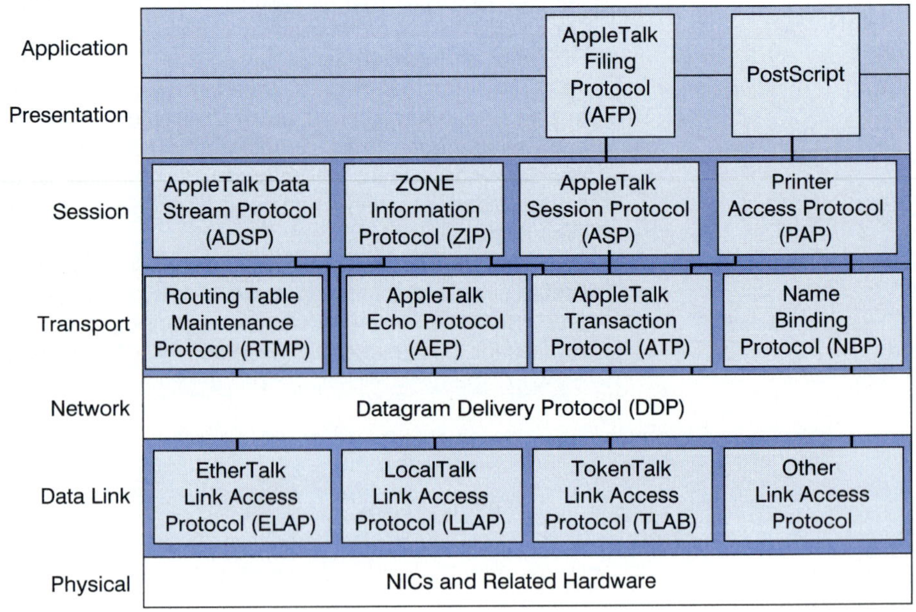

AppleTalk Data Stream Protocol (ADSP). ADSP's primary function is to establish and sequence a full duplex stream of data packets between any two AppleTalk sockets regardless of the speed of each node. Figure 11.2 shows the ADSP header. A *Source ConnID* field establishes the two-octet socket that connects the nodes at each end of the socket. Two sequencing fields follow with *PktFirstByteSeq* containing the sequence number of the first byte and *Pkt-NextRcvSeq* identifying acknowledgment of the last packet received by the identified socket. A *RecvWdw* field provides a window that is used to control the flow of data.

ADSP is AppleTalk Data Stream Protocol.

Zone Information Protocol (ZIP). AppleTalk defines a zone as a group of logically connected networks. Phase 2 provides no particular distinction for a network to belong to a zone. This makes it possible for networks to have identical numbers as long as they do not belong to the same zone. It falls upon ZIP to determine which networks belong to which zones and to provide routers with information to maintain the routing tables. In fact, ZIP is implemented within a router.

ZIP means Zone Information Protocol.

AppleTalk Session Protocol (ASP). As its name implies, ASP is responsible for opening and closing sessions between server and client. In addition, ASP can pass session commands and responses between server and client and can also determine the status at the remote end of a session in order to assure reliability.

ASP is AppleTalk Session Protocol.

Printer Access Protocol (PAP). Four call commands are used to implement the PAP protocol. PAPOpen is issued by a user to initiate a session with a network printer and PAPClose to terminate the session. During a session, clients can use the PAPWrite call to send data to the print server and PAPRead to obtain information and status. Phase 1 was limited to print sessions between Macintosh workstations and Postscript LaserWriter printers. Phase 2 allows PAP to become a general print session protocol.

PAP is AppleTalk Session Protocol.

Routing Table Maintenance Protocol (RTMP). When two or more networks are connected together by routers, AppleTalk uses RTMP to store a table of information about the routers and their various connections. The routing table must contain a list of all of the possible networks, including

RTMP means Routing Table Maintenance Protocol.

1. the address of destination network,
2. the data link port number,
3. the address of the next router in a sequence of routers,
4. the hop count (total number of routers in the path to the final destination, and
5. a reference check to the ZIT used by the routers to exchange information about which routers are currently connected.

AppleTalk Echo Protocol (AEP). AEP is similar in purpose to the PING protocol used on the Internet to determine whether a destination node is active and able to respond. In addition, AEP can be used to determine the time delay of a packet sent to and received back from the destination node.

AppleTalk Transaction Protocol (ATP). ATP is the connection-oriented protocol that provides reliable transmission of data between a client socket and a server socket to a higher-layer application. To accomplish this task, ATP uses a three-part sequence:

TReq is Transaction Request.

1. Transactions are initiated with a *Transaction Request* (**TReq**)

TResp means Transaction Response.

2. Response to a TReq is accomplished with a *Transaction Response* (**TResp**) that informs the initiator of the result of the data transmission.

TRel is Transaction Release.

3. A *Transaction Release* (**TRel**) terminates the process.

NBP is Name Binding Protocol.

Name Binding Protocol (NBP). When multiple networks are connected together, some method must exist to look up the address of a destination node that may or may not be connected and turned on. Tables could be maintained in each server but that would require a great deal of overhead and bandwidth when the servers tried to update their node ID tables. NBP uses simple datagrams to find the address of a destination node but only when requested. NBP also allows a server to be given a name that is meaningful (e.g. LAN_TECHNOLOGY) because it provides the address translation service that obtains the actual four-octet address of a server. The format is type@zone

DDP means Datagram Delivery Protocol.

Datagram Delivery Protocol (DDP). Simply stated, DDP provides the interface to all of the higher layers that enable data frames from the data link layer or a router connected to another network to be passed to or from specified sockets that connect to the higher layers. DDP is connectionless in that it relies on the transport layer to guarantee reliability. The DDP packet header includes addressing for both destination and source socket. Phase 2 extends the DDP header to include addressing for both destination and source networks.

Local Area Protocols

LLAP is LocalTalk Link Access Protocol.

LocalTalk Link Access Protocol (LLAP). LLAP is included in all Macintosh computers and LaserWriter printers. It is LLAP that allows users to connect to each other without having to deal with any other protocols or server operating systems and share the printing services. Figure 11.2 shows the LLAP header. Note that Apple uses the term *packet* to describe the actual data field(s) and the term *frame* to describe the combination of header/data/trailer.

Following the frame preamble, the LLAP header (Destination/Source/Type) has fields for a destination and source address. Phase 1 provides only 8

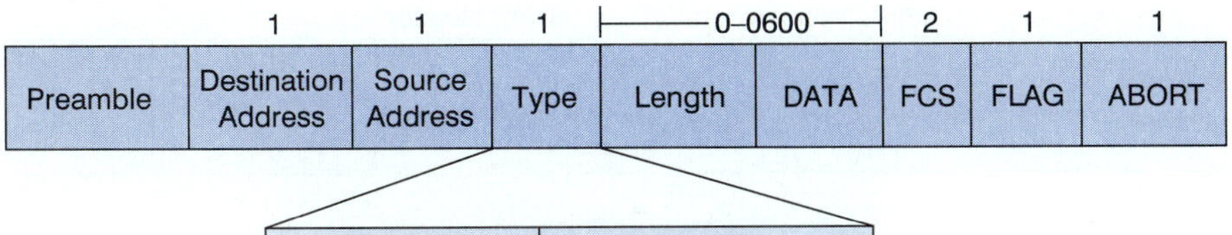

LLAP Type Values	Description
00h	Not Valid
01-7Fh	LLAP Client Packets
01h	DDP Short Header
02h	DDP Extended Header
0Fh	Experimental
80-FFh	LLAP Control Frames
81h	ENQ Packet
82h	ACK Packet
84h	RTS Packet
85h	Cts Packet

Figure 11.2 LLAP Header

bits for each field. Phase 2, however increases the number of address bits for each field to 16, allowing up to 16,515,334 unique node ID addresses.

The LLAP Type field is used to identify data packets (01-7Fh) or control packets (80-FFh). As noted in Figure 11.2, data fields may contain up to 600 octets, with the least significant 10 bits used to establish the length of the data field. Control packets do not contain raw data but can use all 600 bits for control information.

In the LLAP trailer (FCS/FLAG/Abort), a two-octet frame check sequence (FCS) field provides error checking, which is followed by a single-octet Flag that contains the value 7Eh. The final field is a one-octet Abort field containing 12 to 18 logic one bits. The combination of the Flag and Abort effectively identify the end of a frame.

EtherTalk Link Access Protocol (ELAP). Because we have already dealt with Ethernet in detail, it need only be said here that ELAP provides the protocol interface for Ethernet (phase 1) and IEEE 802.2 and 802.3 (phase 2). Figure 11.3 shows the phase 1 Ethernet frame that is used by AppleTalk. One notable difference is the length of the data field. A pure Ethernet frame could have up to 1,536 octets but is limited by AppleTalk to 600. Large data file transfers would not be as efficient on the AppleTalk LAN.

ELAP is EtherTalk Link Access Protocol.

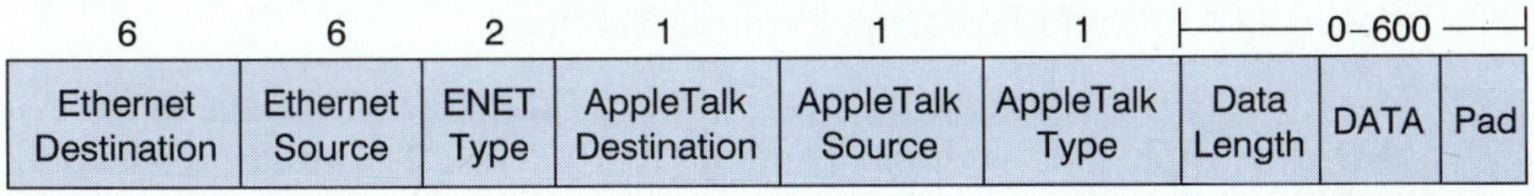

Figure 11.3 Phase 1 EtherTalk Link Access Protocol

Figure 11.4 Phase 2 802.3 or 802.4 Frame

	802.2 Header			SNAP Header			
Data Link Header	DSAP (AAh)	SSAP (AAh)	Control (03h)	Protocol SNAP (080007809Bh)	Long DDP Header	DDP Data	Data Link Trailer

Figure 11.4 demonstrates Apple's phase 2 implementation of IEEE 802.2, 802.3/802.5. As shown, the frame conforms to the LLC requirements for an 802.2 destination and source service access points. Within AppleTalk, both SAPs use the value AAh and the control field is set to 03h to indicate unnumbered information. A five-octet SNAP header is set to 080007h (Apple) followed by 809Bh (EtherType phase 2). The EtherType value would be replaced by the TokenTalk value in a Token-Ring.

TLAP is TokenTalk Link Access Protocol.

TokenTalk Link Access Protocol (TLAP). TLAP is the IEEE 802.5 interface protocol that allows AppleTalk to be implemented on a Token-Ring.

TROUBLESHOOTING

Without question, an AppleTalk LAN will be the easiest to maintain. All of the software and hardware necessary for networking is included and configured when you buy the computer. You need only add the twisted pair cables, create shares as needed, and you are finished. Adding or converting to one of the optional protocols such as EtherTalk or TokenTalk is not much more difficult. Macintosh is plug-and-play. Install the new NIC, cabling system, and software protocols, and you are once again finished. Your only truly necessary troubleshooting tool is a cable tester.

Where Macs are installed on NetWare or NT networks, your primary difficulties will be with the installation and configuration of the support software that must be installed and configured in the network operating system. Macintosh, for example, uses long filenames (up to 256 characters). NT and NetWare 4.x will support the long filenames but require special software for the Mac since the maximum length of a filename is natively different in each operating system.

CHAPTER REVIEW

- Application and presentation layer protocols include AppleTalk Filing Protocol (AFP) and Postscript Printing Services.
- Session layer protocols include AppleTalk Data Stream Protocol (ADSP), AppleTalk Session Protocol (ASP), Zone Information Protocol (ZIP), and Printer Access Protocol (PAP).

- Transport and network layer protocols include Routing Table Maintenance Protocol (RTMP), AppleTalk Echo Protocol (AEP), AppleTalk Transport Protocol (ATP), and Name Binding Protocol (NBP).
- Data link layer support is provided for EtherTalk Link Access Protocol (ELAP), LocalTalk Link Access Protocol (LLAP), and TokenTalk Link Access Protocol (TLAP).

REVIEW QUESTIONS

1. List the application layer protocols, and briefly describe each.
2. List the session layer protocols and provide a brief description of each.
3. List the transport and network layer protocols, providing a brief description of each.
4. List the link layer protocols and provide a brief description of each.
5. Draw a diagram of an EtherTalk frame.
6. Draw a diagram of an AppleTalk frame.
7. Draw a diagram of a TokenTalk frame.

CLOUD

12 Wide Area Networking

INTRODUCTION

It is becoming increasingly necessary that network professionals have an understanding of the wide area protocols that are being installed in both private and public enterprises. This chapter will present an introduction to the Internet and a simplified overview of the currently popular wide area protocols, including

- X.25,
- Switched 56K,
- ISDN,
- Frame Relay,
- ATM, and
- DSL.

Because an entire book could easily be written for each of these protocols, this chapter will supply an overview of each of the common wide area protocols. Readers are encouraged to consult the bibliography for sources that will fill in the details.

In Chapter 2 we defined the local area as confined to the limits of a building or other small area that rarely crosses public boundaries. Traditionally this has been true, but as fiber optics and wireless medium become more popular, physical boundaries are becoming much more blurred. The "public" protocols, used by the telephone companies (X.25, Switched 56, ISDN, Frame Relay, ATM, DSL) to connect users over the widest possible area, are, for the most part, data link layer protocols. We could abandon physical boundaries and distance limitations in our definitions and refer only to the protocols in use to determine wide or local area, but many LANs, confined to the limits of a building, use network and transport layer protocols so that workstations can use inexpensive dial-up lines to connect to the Internet, or to create an intranet that has the look and feel of the Internet, or because server-based applications require higher-layer protocols.

While the definition of LAN/CAN/MAN/WAN/GAN may be the subject of much discussion, readers of this text can significantly reduce the confusion factor with a thorough understanding of when, where, and how to use a protocol. This is the knowledge that you should take with you. Again, this chapter presents the overview; students are strongly urged to continue a more thorough study of individual protocols prior to actual implementation or use.

Remember that routers communicating with identical network and transport layer protocols are used to connect LANs of differing data link layer protocols. Gateways are used where differing protocols may exist at any layer. Gateways must be able to translate protocols from layer to layer and network to network.

THE INTERNET

Certainly the largest WAN, the Internet, is really a collection of smaller networks that are all connected together. In North America the fiber optic backbone for Internet connections is operated and maintained by Microwave Communication, Inc. (MCI).* Figure 12.1 shows the primary nodes on the backbone as of July 1996. At that time, MCI was using a 45-Mbps format over the fiber backbone. Migration to 155 Mbps has been accomplished using Asynchronous Transfer Mode. (ATM will be explained later in this chapter.) The migration is planned in stages from OC3 (155 Mbps) through OC12 (622 Mbps). C12 is anticipated in 1998.

OC refers to *optical carriers*. A single OC bandwidth is 51.8 Mbps. The 155-Mbps nodes use single-mode fiber optic cable. Additional nodes have been added in Seattle, northern California, San Diego, Miami, Fort Worth, St. Louis, Charlotte, New York City, Vermont, and Montreal.

All of the subnets on the Internet connect to the MCI backbone at one or all of the available nodes or through services such as UUNet and SprintLink that are connected directly to the backbone. A typical Internet connection path might be from a household analog telephone line, to a local *Internet Service Provider* (ISP), who is, in turn, connected to SprintLink, and thus to the MCI backbone itself. Networks such as EBONE (European Backbone) in other countries are also connected to the MCI backbone. These connections are usually fiber or satellite.

The Internet uses a protocol at layers 3 and 4 known as TCP/IP, which will be covered in the next chapter. Every workstation, router, server, and gateway connected to the Internet must use TCP/IP to be able to communicate. TCP/IP becomes the common protocol to all nodes on the Internet. Each node must also have a unique address.

* In 1999, MCI merged with Worldcom to become known as MCIWorldcom.

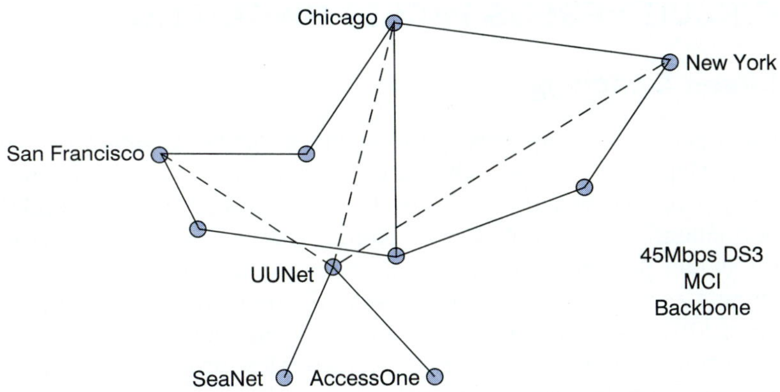

Figure 12.1 Internet Backbone

Until recently, control of the Internet in the United States was provided by the National Science Foundation (NSF). The NSF has now relinquished its control to three commercial companies and no longer supplies funding. IBM, MCI, and Merit formed a nonprofit corporation that operates the Internet backbone in the United States. IBM develops hardware and software, MCI operates the fiber optic backbone, and Merit provides the administrative functions.

A fourth organization, Internic, is charged with maintaining the registration of domain names. Rather than trying to remember a list of 32-bit IP addresses, an IP address can be registered with Internic as a *domain name*. For example, *www.microsoft.com* is a registered domain name. When a user wishes to connect with Microsoft's Internet World Wide Web server, they need only enter the domain name in the appropriate box in their software application. The Internet maintains a special *Domain Name Services* (DNSs) program installed in servers that are used to look up the real IP address. There are currently nine "root" DNS servers on the Internet. Networks connected to the Internet must install their own DNS servers for local use.

Standards for the Internet are set by the *Internet Engineering Task Force* (IETF). Representatives from private industry, the academic community, and government form standing committees that determine which standards will be used on the Internet. A particularly useful technique is used to begin the process of generating a new standard or modification to an existing standard. Any interested party may generate a *Request For Comment* (**RFC**), post it on the Internet, and circulate it to all other interested parties. Other interested parties will examine the proposal, ensure that it does in fact do what it is intended to do, and suggest recommendations and alternatives to modify the proposal. If sufficient interest is generated, the IETF will then create a committee composed of the interested parties to develop a finished product. Votes are eventually taken to adopt the RFC in its final form.

RFC is Request For Comment.

Now that you have been given a glimpse of a global WAN, we can proceed to build a knowledge base of the components that are used. We will begin with the techniques used by public communications carriers in the United States.

CIRCUIT VERSUS PACKET SWITCHING

Circuit Switching

Circuits may be temporary, permanent, or virtual. *Temporary* circuits are like your telephone—created when a call is made and torn down when the call is completed. *Permanent* circuits use the same path at all times, and the circuit is permanently connected. *Virtual* circuits may be permanently connected, but the circuit path may change to suit circuit quality or path availability. Where circuits are both permanent and virtual, connection-oriented protocols must be used to establish the connection between source and destination. Where circuits are switched and virtual, connectionless protocols are used because the switches provide the connection.

When you dial a number on your analog telephone, the telephone company central office builds a temporary circuit between source and destination by connecting the appropriate switches. You may now pass voice, data, or fax over that circuit. The circuit does not know or care what protocol is being used. Once the dial-up call is completed, the circuit is torn down, freeing the switches to be used for other calls. This temporary circuit is also referred to as *switched virtual circuit* because a second call to the same destination would not necessarily use the same circuits. It is a switched circuit because electronic switches are used to physically make the connection between source and destination.

DS0 and T1 Lines

Your analog telephone line is called a *DS0*. At the CO, a device known as a *codec* digitizes the analog information on a DS0 line by sampling the signal at a constant rate to determine the voltage available at the instant a sample takes place. Referred to as *Pulse Code Modulation* (PCM), this sampling process produces a 64-Kbps digital data stream composed of 8-bit frames of data where the digital value of each 8-bit sample represents the analog signal level at the time of sampling.

In the download mode from CO to the analog phone line, the PCM bit stream is not converted back to analog. It is, instead, sent directly into the analog line as an amplitude modulated (AM) bit stream. Retaining the pulse coding allows digital services such as caller ID to be made available to analog customers. To the human ear, the AM-modulated bit stream sounds like normal voice. V.90 modems, however, are able to translate the bit stream into data at up to 53.3 Kbps. Were it not for the loss of 1 or 2 bits per sample because of the relatively poor signal to noise ratios on most analog lines, these modems would be able to process up to 56 Kbps. V.90 modems in the upstream mode simply send pulse coded modulation bit streams straight to the CO. Owing to the poorer quality of analog lines, 56-K modems only encode a 7-bit sample rather than the standard 8-bit—thus, their limit to 56 Kbps instead of the 64

Kbps produced by an 8-bit sample. In practical application, analog lines are rarely of sufficient quality to allow even 53.3-Kbps operation.

Incoming analog signals are converted to digital by a *coder decoder* (codec). A device called a *Time Division Multiplexer* (TDM) is used to combine multiple DS0 lines into a single bit stream. The TDM combines DS0 frames from more than one call into a continuous stream of data. The combination of codec and TDM is done in equipment called *channel banks*.

U.S. telephone systems combine 24 DS0 channels, as shown in Figure 12.2a, into a 1.544-Mbps *T1* line. A standard T1 line transmits 193 bit frames. Each of the 24 DS0 channels is processed sequentially, 8 bits per channel, until all 24 channels are processed ($8 \times 24 = 192$). A final signaling bit is added to the T1 frame to make the total number of bits 193. The process is reversed when the DS0 channels are broken out at the destination end. Figure 12.2b shows the components of a T1 line.

A further technique is implemented to compact the bit streams. There is usually a quantity of dead space in voice calls in which there is nothing but residual line noise—no voice at all. A TDM can statistically remove the dead space from the data stream, including the noise, and thus compact the data. Of course, the dead space must be reinserted at the destination; however, some of the noise will have been removed, improving the quality of the transmission. To maximize the utilization of a T1 line, channel banks, between COs and

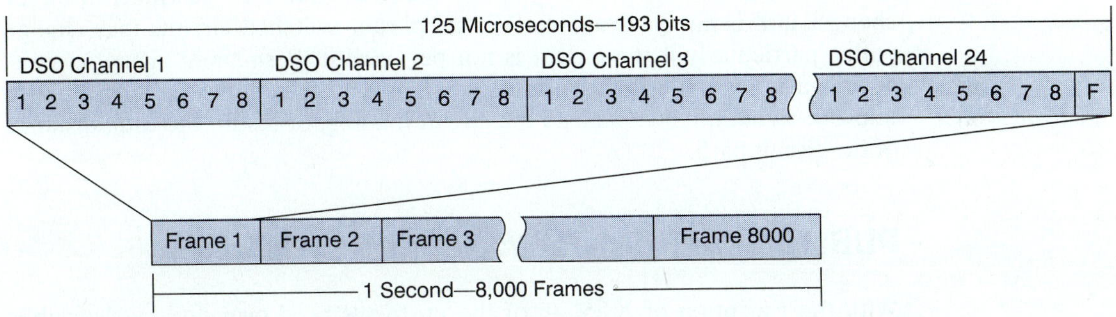

Figure 12.2a T1 Frame Format

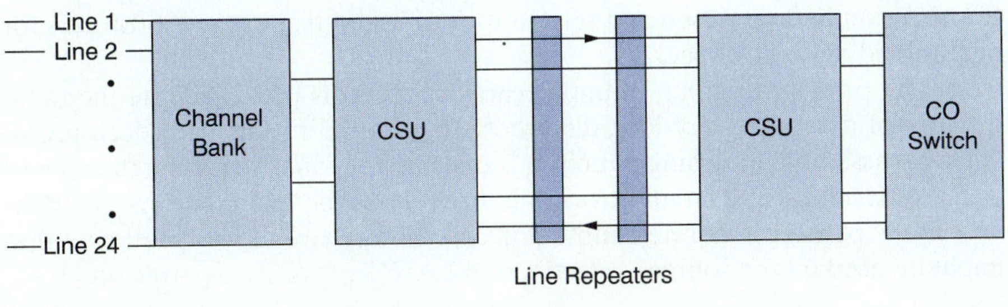

Figure 12.2b T1 Line Components

IXCs are IntereXchange Carriers.

between COs and long-distance service operators called *InterеXchange Carriers* (**IXCs**), usually service more than 24 DS0 lines in such a way as to ensure that 24 active calls are placed on a single T1. This limits the total number of T1 lines that will be required to meet normal service needs.

Note that Figure 12.2b shows two pairs of wires on the T1 line itself. This is done to enable full duplex operation in which data may be sent in either direction simultaneously. Repeaters are usually installed every 6,000 feet, primarily because that is where loading coils are installed on analog lines.

Packet Switching

Suppose that your telephone line is entirely digital. Further, it is permanently connected through the entire telephone system to its intended destination or destinations. Given these conditions, it will no longer be necessary to interpret the dialing code to determine the destination address. A destination address can be added to a packet of data sent across the circuit. Instead of dialing a new number and switching circuits to reach a new destination, we merely change the destination address inside the packet. This technique is called *packet switching*.

Packet-switched circuits may be either permanent or virtual or both permanent and virtual. A permanent circuit is usually wired through the telephone company central offices (COs), bypassing switching circuits to reduce noise and interferencc. The path between source and destination never changes and is always available. Virtual packet switched circuits may change paths, particularly if the circuit is not permanent. Permanent virtual circuits are always available, but paths are assigned by the telephone company to improve signal quality, balance the circuit loading, or lessen the total distance of the circuit path.

PUBLIC TELEPHONE SYSTEM PROTOCOLS

With the exception of X.25, all of the protocols used over and by the public telephone system are data link layer protocols. X.25 was developed when the quality and reliability of public carrier transmission lines was quite poor. Newer protocols such as Frame Relay and ATM assume that high-quality transmission lines are used and rely on user supplied higher-layer protocols for guaranteed delivery of packets.

The primary function of public carrier protocols is to facilitate the rapid delivery of data over very long distances. To accomplish this task, each protocol must assemble incoming data into frames in a manner that suits the type of transmission lines and circuits available throughout the telephone system. Public carrier protocols neither know nor care about any of the protocols that might be used on the source or destination LANs.

When a network connects to a public carrier, a *Data Service Unit/Channel Service Unit* (DSU/CSU) must be in place to first create the correctly formatted data stream (DSU) and then establish the correct electrical signal levels (CSU). CSUs usually provide the correct termination impedance; where they do not, a terminator must be added between the CSU and the transmission line.

X.25

One of the oldest wide area protocols, the CCITT X.25 standard was originally developed as a packet-switching technique that would reliably transmit data over relatively unreliable analog telephone lines. Reliability is provided through sequencing and acknowledgment at the network layer. A sliding window control is used to set the length of a packet to an optimal size for the quality of the circuit. X.25, although still in use in many networks, is being replaced by newer protocols that are both faster and more efficient.

X.25 uses the network, data link, and physical layers. Physical layer standards include these:

- X.21/X.21bis—Digital, balanced two-wire, full duplex, synchronous mode using 15-pin connector
- X.31—Semipermanent ISDN
- Vex—Analog asynchronous mode to about 56 Kbps
- RS423/RS422/V.10—Analog to 64 Kbps

At the data link layer, X.25 uses *Link Access Procedures* (LAPs). LAP is based on the *High Level Data Link Control* (HDLC) protocol originally developed by IBM. HDLC is a synchronous transmission protocol organized as shown in Figure 12.3. *Link Access Procedures—Balanced* (LAP-B) is used for the channels that carry data, otherwise known as *bearer channels*. LAP-D is used by channels for signaling.

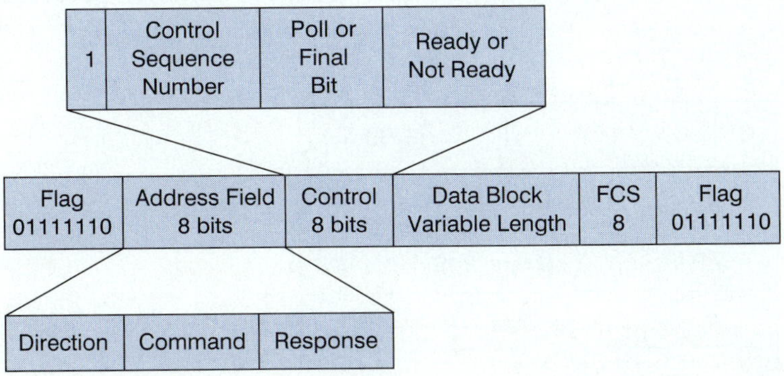

Figure 12.3 HDLC Frame Format

The network layer provides the packet formatting for *call request*, *incoming calls*, and *normal data packets*. Figure 12.4 shows the normal data packet format. The first byte in the sequence contains the *Logical Group Number* (LGN) that, together with the *Logical Channel Number* (LCD), identifies the path the data will take. The Q bit determines either user data or control packet. Direction of data is determined by the Q bit. Packet count is stored in the P(R) and P(S) fields for received and sent packets respectively. The M bit is set to 0 to indicate more packets are to follow and set to 1 to indicate the last packet in a sequence.

Switched 56K

As its name implies, switched 56K has single-channel bandwidth limitations similar to a single DS0 channel but without the out of band signaling. Out of band signaling is the 4 K at each end of a 64-K channel that is sometimes used to send digital signals to "dial up" a destination address. An analog DS0 line cannot use this space because the signals in these spaces are not strong enough to be reliably detected by the electronic circuits that receive them.

Switched 56 channels are connected to CSU/DSUs that accomplish dial-up service to multiplexers that can provide multiple DS0 channels. Because the multiplexers bypass the local telephone company office switches, switched 56K lines can connect directly to the IXC, thus eliminating a great deal of noise and interference. Lines may be either dedicated or switched.

Switched 56K usually requires an expensive T1 line even though only a single DS0 is used. This method does, however, allow for anticipated growth or for bursty traffic that temporarily requires additional bandwidth. Because Switched 56K is able to temporarily adjust bandwidth to suit demand, it is often referred to as "bandwidth on demand."

ISDN

Integrated Services Digital Network (ISDN) is a relative newcomer to wide area networking. Standardized by CCITT as I.430 and I.431, ISDN is offered as a totally digital, protocol-transparent, data link layer protocol in two forms.

Figure 12.4 X.25 Normal Data Packet

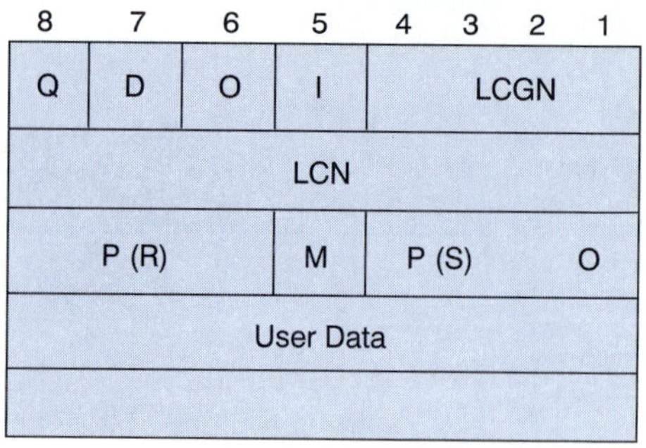

Basic Rate Interface (BRI) offers two B channels of 64 Kbps for data or voice and a 16K D channel for signaling. The BRI package is designated as 2B+D. Using the IETF-approved *Multilink Point-to-Point* (MLPPP), specified in RFC 1717, users can combine two B channels into a single 128-Kbps channel. With data compression, BRI offers the opportunity for interactive voice and video for such things as teleconferencing. For users who require additional bandwidth, *Primary Rate Interface* (**PRI**) offers 23 64-Kbps channels plus a 64-Kbps signaling channel. With PRI, the full T1 bandwidth is allocated. Both AT&T and MCI are offering ISDN over Frame Relay as a way to eliminate the need for dial-up service.

PRI is Primary Rate Interface.

Installation requirements. Perhaps the most important feature of BRI is that it will run over the existing local loop. Hardware requirements are a DSU/CSU terminal adapter and an NT-1 terminator for the local loop, as shown in Figure 12.5. A typical microcomputer user would install the ISDN interface in an expansion slot or as a stand-alone unit interfaced through RS-232C or V.35. Appropriate communications software would be installed and the system operated in the same manner as the analog modem replaced by the ISDN installation. In fact, the same communications software used with analog modems will function perfectly well with an ISDN modem so long as the modem command set (usually the Hayes command set) is understood by the ISDN terminal adapter.

An additional consideration is the speed at which the software will communicate with the serial port. You will be unable to use the full bandwidth of ISDN if your software cannot deal with the 64-Kbps data rate. RS-232C, as implemented in the 16550A UART found in PCs built after 1992, limits the serial port to a maximum of 38.4 Kbps. In many cases, there is insufficient cable shielding and grounding to allow more than 19.2 Kbps. The easiest solution to this problem is to install the terminal adapter in an expansion slot and avoid the need for RS-232C. Users of external terminal adapters are well advised to interface to the PC with V.35.

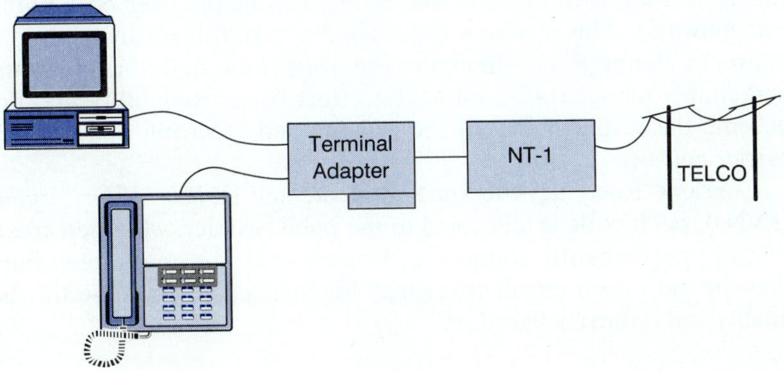

Figure 12.5 Typical ISDN Installation

ISDN services and applications. ISDN BRI can operate at roughly 27 times the rate of a 2,400-baud modem. With this much bandwidth, standard services for voice, data, and graphical images are easily implemented. E-mail, fax, interactive games, and music are commonplace. With data compression, voice and video teleconferencing is a practical reality. Technical writer John Peter Barlow has commented, "Compression techniques are continuing to evolve so it's reasonable to expect that we will have VHS-level quality." All of this "VHS-level quality" can be made available over the copper-based POTS (Plain Old Telephone System) local loop that is already connected to every house that has telephone service. ISDN can be effectively applied to a diverse variety of applications such as telecommuting, telemedicine, Internet access, distance learning, teleconferencing, and simultaneous voice and fax or data.

One of the adverse effects of successful telecommuting has been the need to operate the network around the clock. Network administrators are finding it increasingly difficult to shut down the network for maintenance or backups without getting calls from disgruntled users, even at 3:00 in the morning. This may require trained technicians on duty 24 hours a day, seven days a week.

Some consider ISDN as simply a stepping stone to the all fiber networks envisioned by the service providers. This may cause some managers to delay the implementation of telecommuting. When the cable companies are able to compete with the RBOCs, they will be able to deliver higher-bandwidth and perhaps lower-cost services than ISDN. TCI, for example, currently delivers up to 30 Mbps to a shared neighborhood cable at about $39/month.

Frame Relay

One of the biggest impediments to high throughput has been the necessity to guarantee the delivery of data. Public networks were the culprit. They were noisy and unreliable so long as copper was the primary transmission medium. With the introduction of fiber optics, a great many of the barriers to reliable data transmission have been eliminated.

One of the first services to take advantage of high-quality digitized public carrier transmission lines, Frame Relay is available over both public and private networks. This service was designed to take full advantage of "clean" fiber networks. Frame Relay eliminates the overhead required to guarantee delivery and simply passes traffic on a best effort basis. Reliability and flow control become the responsibility of the sending and receiving nodes, not the public carrier network.

Frame Relay networks are implemented as *Permanent Virtual Networks* (PVNs). Each node is identified to the public carrier, who then creates circuits that are permanently connected. Connections are guaranteed but virtual in that the path each circuit takes may be changed at any time to ensure signal quality and reduce congestion.

Frame Relay provides scaleable bandwidth to T1 speeds over the permanent virtual circuit. The cost of Frame Relay service is quite reasonable and is billed on a "pay as you go" basis. Users subscribe to a *Committed Information Rate* (CIR), a guaranteed bandwidth for which the user is generally billed on a flat-rate basis. Whenever traffic exceeds the CIR, additional charges may be incurred. With some RBOCs, off-peak hours have no tariff over subscription bandwidth usage.

Frame Relay requires a T1 line, a *Frame Relay Access Device* (FRAD), or router using store and forward packet-switching techniques. Figure 12.6 shows the setup of a Frame Relay PVN. Each of the FRADs represents an addressable node on the Frame Relay network. What is not shown is the capability of the FRAD to integrate differing protocols into the Frame Relay data stream. For example, the high school might use ISDN for Internet access and the all digital telephone system, switched 56K to send voluminous reports to administration, and X.25 to the state mainframe. All of these protocols would be aggregated into a single data stream, one frame at a time.

Because of the integration of protocols, packets must be stored temporarily, while frames are constructed and queued. It is this store-and-forward feature that makes Frame Relay unsuitable for isochronous (real-time) traffic, although voice over Frame Relay can be made to work reasonably well.

Frame construction. Figure 12.7 diagrams the construction of the frame used in Frame Relay. Each frame begins and ends with a single-octet *flag* to ensure that receiving equipment is able to synchronize to the frame timing. Data are limited to 4,096 octets or fewer and may be encapsulated by other protocols such as X.25 or ISDN. In fact, ISDN and Frame Relay are closely associated. Both services are part of the *Switched Multimegabit Data Services* (SMDS) system offered by most of the public networks.

As you can see, a maximum of 12 octets is required for frame addressing and control. Compared with the 4,096 octets of data that can be passed in a single frame, overhead represents less than 0.3% of the total bandwidth.

The following list describes the contents of the address field.

- *Data Link Connection Identifier* (DLCI)—DLCI is a 10-bit value (6-bit msb + 6-bit lsb; *msb* and *lsb* mean most and least significant bit, respectively) that identifies the node (FRAD or router) to which the frame is to be sent. What this translates to is a total network of 1,024 nodes before a new PVN must be created.
- *Command/Response Indicator* (C/R)—Not currently used, may be set to 1 or 0
- *Forward Explicit Congestion Notification* (FECN)—Frame Relay has no way to control flow other than to discard frames when congestion occurs. The FECN bit is set to notify receiving nodes that congestion is high and

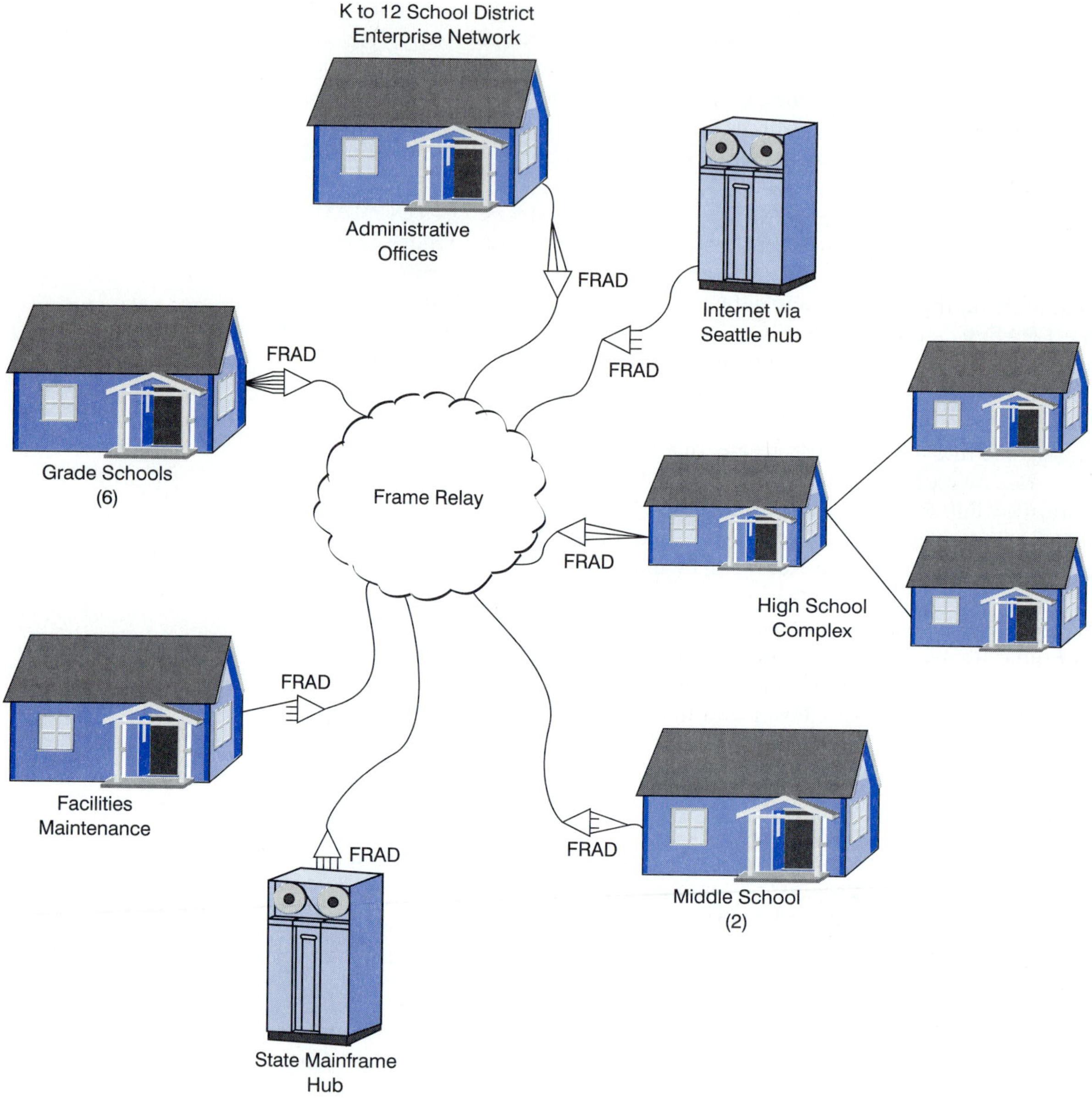

Figure 12.6 Typical Frame Relay Permanent Virtual Network (PVN)

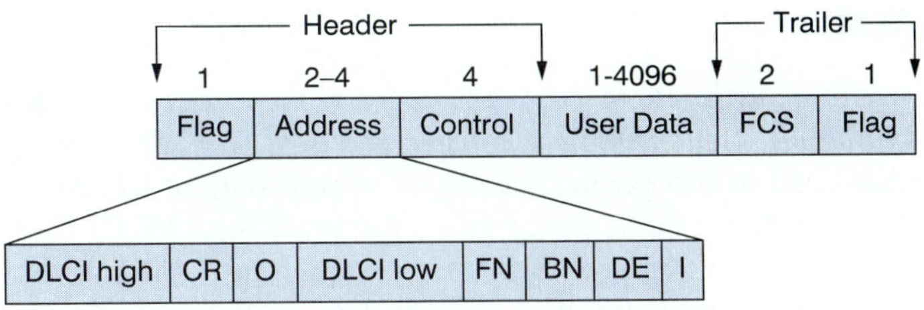

Figure 12.7 Frame Relay Frame Construction

that frames may be discarded. It is left to the receiving node to control data flow.

- *Backward Explicit Congestion Notification* (BECN)—BECN is set by the receiving node to notify the sender that congestion exists. The sender may now adjust the flow of packets until a frame is returned with BECN reset to 0.
- *Discard Eligibility Bit* (DE)—Sending nodes can set this bit to notify the network to discard this frame, during congested periods, before other more critical frames.
- *Extended Address Bit 0* (EAB0)—May be used to extend the DLCI address range if the carrier offers extended address service.
- *Extended Address Bit 1* (EAB1)—Used for the same purpose as EAB 0

Figure 12.8 displays the control field. When Frame Relay needs to send control or messaging frames, the control field is used under *Local Management Interface* (LMI) extension framing. Two types of messages may be sent: STATUS_INQUIRY and STATUS. Users request status from the network with STATUS_INQUIRY; the network responds with STATUS.

The control field is further divided as follows:

- UIF—unnumbered information frame
- PD—protocol discriminator
- CR—call reference (set to null)
- MT—message type

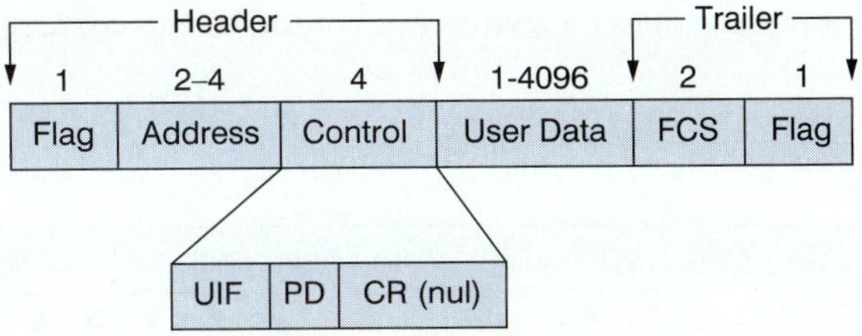

Figure 12.8 Frame Relay Control Field

ATM

As fiber optic cable replaces copper, new very high-speed services become available. *Asynchronous Transfer Protocol* (ATM) is being offered as a high-speed cell or fast packet technique to pass data at 622 Mbps or more. ATM was designed to be the transfer mode for *broadband* ISDN (B-ISDN). This genuine bandwidth-on-demand technology will support full multimedia data, including voice, video, imaging, and framed data as well as low-speed X.25. ATM is the first service that combines both packet/cell switching and circuit switching.

Figure 12.9 shows the details of the 53-octet cell for *User Network Interface*. Five octets comprise the header, leaving 48 octets for data.

ATM is a connection-oriented protocol that consists of virtual channels and virtual paths. ATM switching equipment requires connections between incoming and outgoing virtual channels. The information to identify the channel is contained in the three *Virtual Channel Identifier* (VCI) fields. Routing information is supplied by the two *Virtual Path Identifier* (VPI) fields. Up to 256 paths may be identified with the 8 bits in the VPI fields. Each path may then accommodate up to 65,536 channels using the 16 bits in the VCI fields.

Calls may be prioritized in the *Call Loss Priority* (CLP) field in a manner reminiscent of Frame Relay's discard eligible (DE) bit. *Generic Flow Control* (GFC) determines the access that terminals sharing the ATM network will have. With GFC, terminals can be guaranteed equal access to the available bandwidth. The final field, RES, is reserved.

Figure 12.10 demonstrates the virtual channel and path structure of an ATM network. Channels are fed into an ATM multiplexer that identifies the virtual path, then aggregates all of the channels and paths onto the common transmission path through the network. The process is reversed as the paths and channels are demultiplexed.

ATM layers. The ATM protocol is described in three layers. The *physical layer* in an ATM network is not defined for ATM. Instead, ATM relies on other protocols to define the physical media. ATM is normally implemented, at the physical layer, using fiber optic cable. However, it will also run over STP, UTP, and coaxial cable.

An *ATM layer* is defined to connect the physical layer to the *ATM Adaptation Layer* (AAL). The ATM layer generates the five-octet header when passing data to the physical layer. Conversely, incoming data have the header removed by the ATM layer. Cells arriving at an end point are sent to the AAL. Cells arriving at a switch are routed to the correct bit stream in an ATM multi-

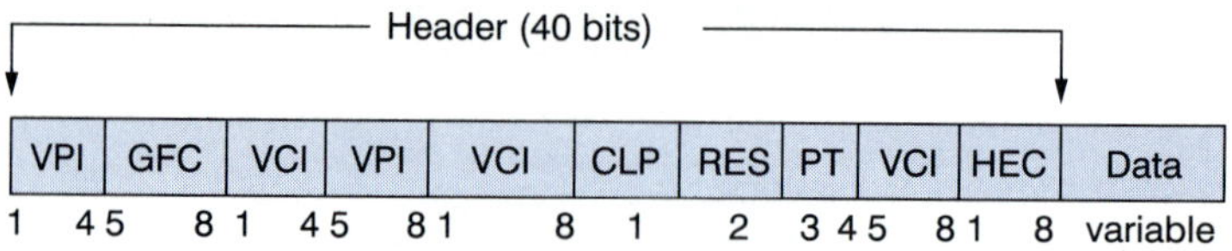

Figure 12.9 ATM User to Network Cell

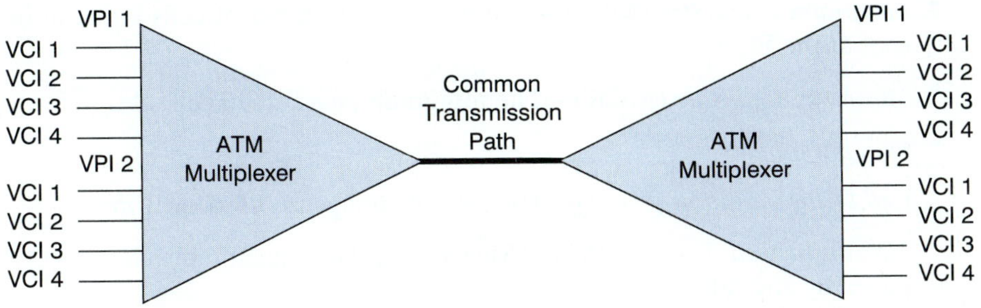

Figure 12.10 ATM Channel and Path Multiplexing

plexer, and a *Virtual Channel Connection* (VCC) is created to connect two channels together.

The ATM adaptation layer connects the ATM layer to higher layers in the protocol stack at an end point in the ATM network. Format conversion is made to add data from an incoming ATM cell to a packet used in the higher layer protocol. Outgoing data is taken from a higher-layer PDU, 48 octets at a time, and sent to the ATM layer for the addition of an ATM header.

Four classes of service are established in the ITU-T standard. Table 12.1 shows class as it relates to timing and type of connection. Having different classes of service allows ATM to adapt a class of service to suit the type of traffic being sent. For example, isochronous traffic such as voice and video would use class A to maintain critical timing and connection. Non-real-time data could use Class C or D depending on whether a connection needs establishment.

Quality of service. Certain types of traffic such as voice and video are very time-sensitive. ATM provides a mechanism for negotiating the *Quality of Service* (QoS) at the time of connection. A set of parameters are provided that constitute a *Source Traffic Descriptor* that, along with cell delay variation tolerance and a conformance definition, characterize an ATM connection. Traffic parameters include the following:

- *Peak Cell Rate* (PCR)—The maximum rate at which cells may be created and sent
- *Sustainable Cell Rate* (SCR)—The average rate at which a continuous stream of cells is sent

Table 12.1 ITU-T ATM Application Classes

Class	Bit Rate	Type of Connection	Timing Relation Required	AAL Type(s)
A	Constant	Connection Oriented	Yes	AAL1 AAL2
B	Variable	Connection Oriented	Yes	AAL2 AAL5
C	Variable	Connection Oriented	No	AAL5 AAL3/4
D	Variable	Connectionless	No	AAL3/4

- *Maximum Burst Size* (MBS)—The maximum number of cells that can be sent at the PCR
- *Minimum Cell Rate* (MCR)—The minimum guaranteed cell rate
- *QoS parameters:*

  Cell Delay Variation (CVD)—The rate of change in cell delay times

  Maximum Cell Transfer Delay (Max CTD) The maximum delay experienced by any cell

  Cell Loss Ratio (CLR)—The ratio of delivered cells to cells not delivered

Several categories of service are available for different types of traffic:

- *Constant Bit Rate* (CBR)—CBR is intended for real-time traffic that cannot tolerate variable bit rates or delay. CBR is characterized by a continuously available PCR for all cells. Typical applications include videoconferencing, video on demand, and interactive voice and video.
- *Real-time Variable Bit Rate* (rt-VBR)—This QoS category is intended for time-sensitive applications that can tolerate some variation in cell transfer speed but must be delivered with minimal delay and delay variation. rt-VBR is appropriate for voice and video. Traffic parameters include PCR, SCR, and MBS.
- *Non-real-time Variable Bit Rate* (nrt-VBR)—Most useful for bursty traffic that is not sensitive to delay and delay variation, nrt-VBR is suitable for statistical multiplexing of connections. Traffic parameters are PCR, SCR, and MBS. Typical applications include data and file transfers for such things as banking or order processing systems.
- *Available Bit Rate* (ABR)—No QoS parameter is negotiated with this service. Traffic sources must have the ability to adjust their information rates when the network requires a change. Traffic parameters specify the maximum required bandwidth and minimum useable bandwidth using PCR and MCR, respectively.
- *Unspecified bit rate* (UBR)—UBR negotiates no service guarantees nor guaranteed bandwidth. Cells are sent on a best-effort basis and may be subject to a great deal of statistical multiplexing. Traffic is expected to be noncontinuous and bursty.

Digital Subscriber Line (DSL)

DSL technology is currently being implemented by the RBOCs to allow fully digital, high-bandwidth data links over both fiber and copper. DSL is perhaps most notable for its ability to extend the bandwidth of the local loop that connects an analog telephone to a CO. Current modem technology allows up to 56 Kbps over the local loop. DSL technology is expected to increase the available bandwidth to as much as 9 Mbps down and 640 Kbps up.

Initial experimentation by AT&T, using the technology of the time, indicated that, for reasonable quality human voice transmission, a maximum analog bandwidth of 3,300 Hz between 300 Hz and 3,400 Hz was possible over twisted pair wire at up to 18,000 feet. More recently, it has been discovered that digital signaling techniques can extend the usable bandwidth up to 9 Mbps over the same analog line. To an analog telephone customer, this means that a single telephone line can be used, simultaneously, for both voice calls and data transmission.

DSL technologies are available for more than the local loop. The xDSL family includes the following:

- *High-bit-rate Digital Subscriber Line* (HDSL)—Characterized by either a duplexed 1.544 Mbps or 2.048 Mbps data rate over two- or three-pair copper, respectively. HDSL is limited to 15,000 feet or 4.5 km.
- *Symmetric Digital Subscriber Line* (SDLC)—Occupies the same bandwidth as HOSL but uses only a single pair and limits maximum distance to 10,000 feet or 3 km
- *Asymmetric Digital Subscriber Line* (ADSL)—Used over the local analog loop. This DSL technology is asymmetrical because it offers a higher download data rate than upload data rate. Data rates may be from 1.5 to 9 Mbps over the entire 18,000 feet of a local loop in a download mode from CO to the local loop. Data uploaded from the end of the local loop to the CO has a useful bandwidth between 16 and 640 Kbps. If the local loop is limited to 12,000 feet, upload data rates up to 1.544 Mbps may be had.
- *Rate Adaptive Digital Subscriber Line* (RDSL)—Adds the ability to change data rates to suit line conditions to the ADSL rate characteristics.
- *ISDN Digital Subscriber Line* (IDSL)—Uses the ISDN BRI rate to 144 Kbps over the 18,000-foot local loop. This includes the two 128-Kbps B channels plus a 16-Kbps D channel. Termination is into an IDSL interface rather than an ISDN voice switch.
- *Very High-speed Digital Subscriber Line* (VSDL)—In a downstream mode, data rates are between 13 and 52 Mbps over a distance of 1,000–4,500 feet. Upstream data rates are between 1.5 and 2.3 Mbps. VSDL requires a fiber optic feeder and ATM to function.

Implementation considerations. Because DSL technologies are designed to run over the local loop, some additional consideration of local loop characteristics is necessary. When the telephone system was digitized in the late 1960s and early 1970s, the local loop was left as an analog circuit. T1 service was initiated that used repeaters to clean up a local loop and render it capable of passing digital signals at up to 1.544 Mbps. The following problems may be encountered on the local loop:

- Analog local loops often use loading coils to balance the lines and extend them to as much as 30,000 feet. Loading coils literally send digital signals to ground.
- Bridge taps were installed on some local loops to tap off a branch of the local loop to serve multiple users rather than running a new local loop. Bridge taps cause digital signals to be reflected back to their source.
- Special amplifiers are installed on some local loops to extend their length. Digital signals stop at these repeaters.
- It has been a common practice to use different gauges of wire on local loops. Mismatched gauges cause impedance mismatches that produce reflected signals. If not too severe, reflected signals usually cause voice transmissions to sound hollow or echoed. These same mismatches can destroy digital data.

T1 service introduced the use of remote terminals to extend the length of a T1 line. Unfortunately, DSL signals stop at remote terminals. All of these listed local loop and T1 problems must be resolved before DSL can be implemented. According to Belcore, 80 to 85 percent of all U.S. analog customers live within the 18,000-foot limitation. For these customers, DSL will be an attractive choice. It is unknown whether the RBOCs will do anything to allow the remaining 20 percent of their customers access to DSL technologies.

Current ADSL installations differ in actual installed bandwidth and in cost. US West in Olympia, Washington, is, for example, providing up to 200-Kbps ASDL service to customers. For about $60 per month, a user can lease the ADSL service, an ADSL modem, and an Internet service provider.

TROUBLESHOOTING

The term *Point Of Presence* (POP) is used in telecommunications to determine the legal boundaries for the responsibility of maintaining equipment and transmission lines. For example, the POP for your residential telephone line is on the outside wall of your residence where the telephone company mounts its termination box. The termination box and all lines and equipment back to the CO are the responsibility of the telephone company. All lines and equipment from the termination box into and inside your house are your responsibility.

From a troubleshooting point of view, if a problem is not on your side of the POP, you are obligated to inform the CO, and they are obligated to provide troubleshooting and repair according to the terms of your contract. Your primary troubleshooting effort must then be to determine that all is correct up the POP. The techniques for doing so are no different than those presented in previous chapters with the exception of routers and gateways.

At the physical layer, devices called *Data Communication Equipment* (DCE) are connected between *Data Terminal Equipment* (DTE) devices. A DTE (computer, router, gateway, or FRAD) sends digital data to a DCE (modem or DSU) that converts the data to analog tones, in the case of a modem, or the correct frame type for digital public carrier protocols, in the case of a DSU. Modems send the tones in a common format to another modem, which then converts the tones back into digital data and outputs the data at its DCE port for use by a DTE. DSUs connect to CSUs that set the correct electrical characteristics for the public carrier's transmission lines. CSUs may also contain the transmission line terminator; if not, then a CSU must be connected to the correct terminator and the terminator connected to the transmission line.

Because routers and gateways operate at both LAN and WAN layers of the OSIRM, network analyzers must be capable of capturing all of the protocols used and presenting an analysis that determines the health of your network. Problems encountered with the use of routers and gateways include these:

- *Protocol mismatches*—Many routers are capable of using more than one LAN or WAN protocol. This is usually accomplished by simply installing and configuring an appropriate expansion slot. Where multiple protocols are aggregated into a single data stream output, data speeds and addressing conflicts may result.
- *Routing protocol configuration*—As always, protocols must be correctly configured whenever any equipment is installed or replaced.
- *Routing path problems*—WANs very often connect multiple networks. A major administrative task is to determine the correct path through all of the routers on a WAN to the intended destination. In many cases, there are opportunities for a packet to take more than one route. Network administrators must determine what routes exist and which are the most cost-effective to use. Time to route and cost to route often conflict. It may be faster to route over a T1 line but much cheaper over fractional T1 or Frame Relay. Routing protocols such as *Open Shortest Path First* (**OSPF**), once correctly configured, can automate the pathing decision. ATM, while not specifically a routing protocol, can be used to determine least cost path.

OSPF means Open Shortest Path First.

- *Filtering problems*—For security purposes, routers can filter certain addresses to allow only authorized users access beyond a router into or out of a LAN. Hackers exist to try to discover ways to defeat filtering, making eternal vigilance mandatory.
- *Security problems*—Although primarily concerned with unauthorized access, the administrator of a network must also ensure that no inadvertent security "holes" are introduced into the network.

CHAPTER REVIEW

To repeat the opening caution at the beginning of this chapter: You have been presented a simplified overview of commonly used wide area protocols. Much of the detail has been left out in the interest of time and space. Readers are encouraged to explore the details by referring to the bibliography.

Protocols presented here include the following:

- X.25—Characterized as a packet-switching protocol based on the High Level Data Link Control Protocol (HDLC). X.25 Network and Transport protocols for Logical Group Number (LGN) and Logical Channel Number (LCN) are used to address and route packets.
- TCP/IP—This is the protocol developed for the Internet. TCP is the connection-oriented transport layer protocol that is responsible for sequencing and acknowledgment of IP datagrams; IP is the network layer protocol used to transmit encapsulated data frames in the form of IP datagrams.
- Switched 56K—A protocol characterized by its single DS0 bandwidth without the use of the 4-Kbps band edges. Switched 56K usually requires a T1 line and is often referred to as scaleable bandwidth on demand since multiple 56-Kbps signals can fill the T1 line. DSU/CSU service units are required at each end of a switched 56-K line.
- ISDN—A protocol that allows all four wires of an analog DS0 line to be used in such a way that an aggregate of up to 128-Kbps bandwidth is possible. BRI ISDN uses digital transmission techniques for two 64-Kbps B channels and one 16-Kbps signaling channel. PRI ISDN allows 23 BRI channels to be run over a T1 line.
- Frame Relay—A telephone company–based service that establishes a permanent virtual circuit for all routers or FRADs to connect to the Frame Relay cloud. Frames are sent through the network on a best-effort basis; no effort is made to guarantee delivery. FECN and BECN are used to forward and backward notify Frame Relay nodes of congestion and the possible discard of frames. Bandwidth is scaleable with users paying a flat rate for a committed bandwidth and additional fees for bursty traffic in excess of the committed rate. Owing to the store-and-forward nature of packet assembly, Frame Relay is considered unsuitable for isochronous traffic with the possible exception of low-quality voice.
- ATM—Asynchronous Transfer Mode is one of the newest developments in high-speed transmission protocols. Bandwidths in excess of 650 Mbps are currently capable over fiber optic cable. The ATM protocol creates a 53-byte cell into which packets of data are placed for transmission, thus

combining both packet- and cell-switching techniques. Multiple channels of data can be multiplexed onto a single ATM circuit. Because ATM is a data link protocol, each input channel can be of a different protocol. Only the source and destination nodes associated with a specific ATM channel must share identical protocols.

- Routers are used to connect LANs. Each LAN may use a different data link protocol because the MAC header is stripped at the router input and the data frame is encapsulated by the routing protocol. Routers connected to each other must use identical network and transport layer protocols.
- Gateways are used when none of the layers have common protocols. This allows any LANs that the gateways can interpret to communicate with each other.
- Telephone company services to user premises are most often provided on either 64-Kbps DS0 analog lines or 1.544-Mbps T1 digital lines.

Circuit switching is done by physically connecting a circuit when a call is placed and disconnecting the circuit when the call is finished.

Packet-switching circuits are permanently connected and calls are routed based on the address contained in the routing packet.

REVIEW QUESTIONS

1. Contrast the differences between public and private WANs.
2. Which of the protocols in this chapter are public protocols?
3. Define the term *packet switching.*
4. Contrast the terms *packet switching* and *circuit switching* as they relate to WAN protocols.
5. Which of the seven OSI layers are commonly used for wide area connectivity.
6. Describe the difference between the Internet and an intranet.
7. When and why would you use a gateway?
8. Must routers connect to each other using the same protocol? Justify your answer.
9. Describe the difference between a permanent and a virtual circuit.
10. Describe the characteristics of a DS0 line.
11. Describe the characteristics of a T1 line.
12. Give a brief overview of the characteristics of each of the following protocols:
    - X.25
    - Switched 56K
    - ISDN

- Frame Relay
- ATM
- xDSL

13. What is a PVN?
14. What is a router?
15. What is cell switching?
16. Why are public carrier protocols at the data link layer?
17. Why would you *not* use multimedia voice/video over Frame Relay?
18. What is meant by the term *bandwidth on demand*?
19. What is a FRAD used for?
20. Describe the term *multiplexing*.
21. What is the purpose of a CSU/DSU?
22. To what equipment would you connect a DSU?
23. What are the components of a channel bank, and what is each component used for?
24. Describe T1 service.
25. What are the implementation issues when converting DS0 analog service to digital?

www.prenhall.com

13 TCP/IP

INTRODUCTION

TCP/IP is Transport Control Protocol Internet Protocol.

With the explosive growth of the Internet, *Transport Control Protocol Internet Protocol* (**TCP/IP**) has become a de facto standard for transport and network layer protocols. TCP/IP, originally developed in the early 1970s by Vinton Cerf and Robert Kahn, can trace its origins to the Defense Department Advanced Research Projects Agency Network (ARPANet), which formed the foundation for what we now call the Internet. IP provides connectionless routing of datagrams using a "best effort" technique to determine shortest path and routing around congestion or bad circuits. IP must rely on TCP for connection-oriented sequencing, acknowledgment, and flow control.

TCP/IP is really a suite of protocols. At the Network layer, protocols include the following:

IP is Internet Protocol.

IGMP means Internet Group Management Protocol.

- *Internet Protocol* (**IP**)—Handles Internet routing
- *Internet Control Message Protocol* (ICMP)—Used by IP to pass error messaging and information required by another router or host system
- *Internet Group Management Protocol* (**IGMP**)—Used to send messages to multiple destinations
- *Address Resolution Protocol* (**ARP**)—Provides address translation between IP and layer 2 protocols
- *Routing Information Protocol* (**RIP**)—Used to determine path through one or more routers to destination network
- *User Datagram Protocol* (**UDP**)—UDP is used by the application layer to send messages between host computers. UDP is a datagram service that does not include reliable delivery.

At the transport layer, Transport Control Protocol is used as the connection-oriented transport protocol that provides sequencing and acknowledgment of packets. Packets are assembled and disassembled in convenient sizes. Timers are used to determine whether an acknowledgment is overdue.

The TCP/IP protocol suite also includes a number of utility protocols that facilitate file transfers, E-mail, and network management:

- *Telnet*—Used for remote log-on to a host system. Telnet causes a PC to become a remote terminal to the host system. Since many of the Internet hosts are UNIX based, users may need to become familiar with the UNIX operating system.
- *Bootstrap Protocol* (**BootP**)—Used to determine the IP address of a station that does not know its own address. Internet service providers (ISPs) often use BootP to assign an IP address to remote log-on hosts.
- *File Transfer Protocol*(**FTP**)—As the name implies, used to pass files between hosts
- *Simple Mail Transfer Protocol* (**SMTP**)—An electronic mail protocol
- *Simple Network Management Protocol* (**SNMP**)—Used to create and maintain a set of tables within nodes connected to the network that provide status information about a node

Figure 13.1 provides a graphical display of two networks connected by routers as they relate to TCP/IP. Each network is connected to its own router's NIC using the data link layer protocol in place on the local network. Both routers then use TCP/IP to communicate with each other. A greatly simplified explanation of the process is that to send a packet from the Ethernet LAN to the Token-Ring LAN, the Ethernet LAN's router must remove the Ethernet header and trailer and replace it with a TCP/IP header and trailer before the packet can be sent to the Token-Ring router. The Token-Ring router then adds a Token-Ring MAC header and trailer to the packet before sending it around the local ring.

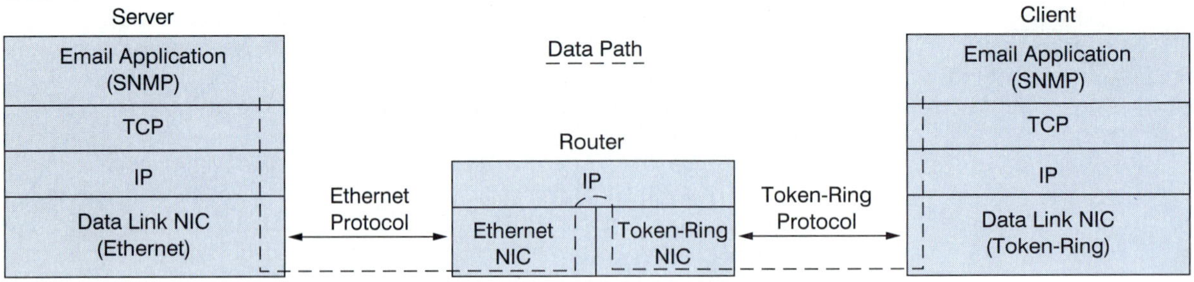

Figure 13.1 Connecting Networks with TCP/IP

IP

IP Addressing

IP addressing is accomplished with a 32-bit address. The Internic registers these addresses and assigns them to a classification system based on the number of host computers that may be used at each IP *network ID* address. The most significant bits of a 32-bit IP address are used to determine the network ID; the remaining bits are used to determine the node or *host* ID. A network address is the net ID of a router or gateway with host addresses for each node connected to the network. For example, a Class A address, shown in Figure 13.2, would have its most significant bit set to 0 and use the next 7 bits to identify the *net ID*. A Class B address would have a net ID of 10xx and use the next 14 bits; a Class C address 110x, and use the next 21 bits, and so forth.

As you can see, the actual IP addressing scheme is based on binary values. To make it easier for humans to read, a decimal dot notation was created. If a 32-bit IP address were divided into 8-bit groups, the binary number 11111111 would have a total decimal value of 255. We can then look at an entire 32-bit address, using decimal dot, as 0.0.0.0 through 255.255.255.255. Table 13.1 shows the complete list of Class A-E IP addresses using decimal dot notation.

Note that the owner of a Class A license could have a single network, perhaps centered around a mainframe server, to which 2^{24} (16,777,216d, the maximum value using the least significant 24 bits) host systems could be connected. A total of 128 Class A licenses could be issued assuming that 0.0.0.0 is a possible address. In practice, addresses using all ones or all zeros are not used.

Subnet Masking

RFC 950 discusses the concept of *subnet addressing*, now a requirement on the Internet. The purpose for a subnet is to further divide a network ID into a sub network ID, hiding the internal details of a network from external routers. To

	Net ID	Host ID
Class A	0 x x x x x x x	24 bit Host ID
Class B	1 0 x x x x x x + 14 bits	16 bit Host ID
Class C	1 1 0 x x x x x + 21 bits	8 bit Host ID
Class D	1 1 1 0 x x x x + 28 bits	(Class D is reserved as the multicast ID)
Class E	1 1 1 1 x x x x + 27 bits	(Class E is reserved for future use)

Figure 13.2 IP Address Scheme

Table 13.1 IP Address Classifications

Class	Address Range
A	0.0.0.0–127.255.255.255
B	128.0.0.0–191.255.255.255
C	192.0.0.0–223.255.255.255
D	224.0.0.0–239.255.255.255
E	240.0.0.0–247.255.255.255

cause a Class C net ID to only use its eight least significant bits for host addressing requires a technique called *subnet masking*. Within each host on a Class C network, a default mask value of 255.255.255.0 is applied to the entire 32-bit address using a logical AND operation. The result is to effectively mask out all but the eight least significant bits of the address. Default masks used for Classes A and B would be 255.0.0.0 and 255.255.0.0 respectively; however, it is possible to identify subnets using any mask value that is within the assigned class of host IDs.

Why, you may ask, have we gone to all this trouble? The primary reason is to reduce the number of entries that an administrator must program into a router. By using a subnet mask, we need only make a single entry in a router table for each net ID (router) connected to our local router. Without subnet masking, an entry for every host would also need to be made.

Figure 13.3 demonstrates the application of a subnet mask to class C IP address, 192.104.45.1. Using a logical (Boolean) AND, logical ones are ANDed to every address bit to be masked, resulting in a network ID of 192.104.45.0.

IP Datagrams

Figure 13.4 shows the format of an IP datagram. The first 32 bits of the IP header includes a 4-bit *version field* that is set to reflect the version of TCP/IP in use. The version currently used is 4. A second 4-bit field determines the *length* of the header *without* any data. IP assumes 32-bit words so that 4 bits would allow a maximum of sixteen 32-bit words or 64 bytes. *Type of service* (TOS) is the 8-bit field that identifies one of the previously mentioned TCP/IP applications. Bits 16–31 are set to the *total length* of the datagram. A combination of header length and total length determines the point at which an IP datagram begins and ends. Total possible length of an IP datagram is 65,535 bytes.

Figure 13.3 Subnet Masking

Class C address	192	104	045	001
Subnet mask (255.255.255.0)	11000000	11010000	00101101	0000001
	Network ID			Host ID
AND result =	11000000	11010000	00101101	00101101
	192	104	045	0

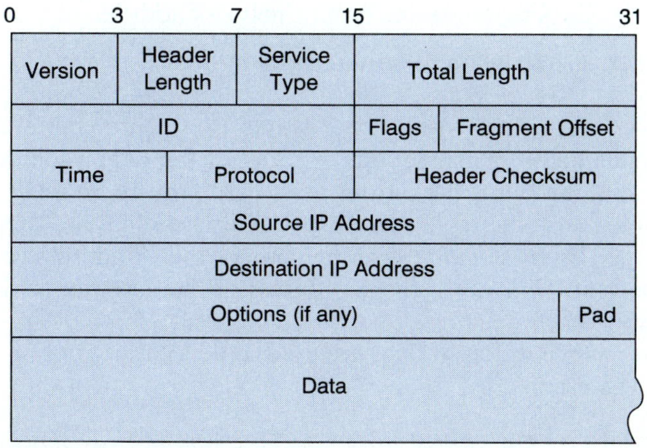

Figure 13.4 IP Header

Three-bit *flags* are used to identify datagram events. When a datagram that exceeds the maximum total length is transferred, it must be broken into *fragments,* each of which is a flag event. Each fragment is identified, usually sequentially, in the 13-bit ID or *identification* field as a 16-bit value that identifies each portion of a fragmented datagram. A *fragment offset* value is the number of bits between the beginning of a datagram and the start of the current fragment. It is entirely possible that only the last fragment is received and all other fragments discarded. For this reason, an 8-bit *time to live* (TTL) field is set so that if the timer expires without an acknowledgment that the datagram has been received, IP can resend the datagram.

The 8-bit *protocol* field identifies the protocol that sent the datagram. These are data link protocols such as Ethernet or Token-Ring. Following the protocol value is a 16-bit checksum that is composed of the 16-bit "ones complement" of each of the 16-bit words in the header. No data is included in this checksum.

IP addressing is accomplished with 32 bits for both source and destination. Discussions are currently underway to expand the number of IP address bits to 128. Because of the vastly greater than anticipated growth of the Internet, the number of unique IP 32-bit addresses will be exceeded in the relatively near future.

When IP sends a datagram, it first looks at the destination address to determine whether it is connected to its host. If so, the datagram is sent directly. If the destination is beyond the current network, the datagram must be sent to a local router. It then falls on the router and its internal lookup table to pass the datagram on to other routers connected to the WAN. At the network layer, IP has a routing table that it can refer to find

- destination IP address,
- IP address of next hop router,

- flags to determine host or network address,
- specification of next network interface.

Table 13.2 shows an example of a router table entry. Different router manufacturers may set up their routing tables in a somewhat different arrangement, but all of the entries must exist, and IP, running in the router, must be able to use the table correctly. Column headings are supplied for clarity.

The *destination* heading denotes the IP address to which the packet is to be sent. *Gateway* is the IP address of the gateway or router that will forward the packet.

Five different flags are used to denote the routing method or mechanism to be used:

U—The router is up, meaning that the IP address shown in the GATEWAY column is local and will not go to a router.

G—The packet will go to the router or gateway address shown in the GATEWAY column.

H—The packet is to be routed to a host directly, not to a network.

D—The indicated route is a redirected route.

M—A redirected route that has been modified.

The REFCNT or reference count field is used to indicate the number of active uses for each connection to a destination. This is done because TCP maintains a connection to the destination until all packets in a session are sent.

The USE column contains the total number of packets sent along the route. Routes may be used by more than one source. However, if a single source were to send 10 packets to the gateway, the USE value would be 10.

The final column shows the intended use for the packet. These entries are sometimes proprietary to the specific router or network in use. In the example shown, emd0 is used for an Ethernet destination.

In many cases, a packet must travel through more than one router to be delivered to its final destination. Each router that a packet travels through is referred to as a *hop*. In its control of packet transmissions, TCP must keep track of the hop count or number of routers through which a packet has traveled. Limitations of up to nine hops are usually applied to prevent packets from hopping around large meshed networks forever.

Table 13.2
Router Table Entry

Destination	Gateway	Flags	Refcnt	Use	Interface
139.246.016.004	139.246.016.010	U	4	14509	emd0

IP Routing

Address Resolution Protocol. One of the problems encountered in wide area networking relates to the difference in addressing schemes between data link and wide area protocols. Ethernet, you may recall, uses 6 octets (48 bits) for an address, whereas IP uses only 32 bits. Neither protocol is aware of the other's addressing schemes.

Address Resolution Protocol (**ARP**) was developed to deal with the differing address format problem. Essentially, ARP dynamically generates a map that lists a host IP address and its corresponding data link layer NIC address. All of this process is normally done without user preparation or intervention.

ARP is Address Resolution Protocol.

Where a host exists without any device such as a hard drive to store its IP address, a protocol known as *Reverse Address Resolution Protocol* (RARP) is invoked. During the boot process, RARP first reads the host NIC address then makes a request to the network for an IP address to be used while the host is operational. In such cases, a special server is usually set up to process RARP requests.

Routing Information Protocol. Routing Information Protocol (**RIP**) is implemented as a message in a *User Datagram Protocol* (**UDP**) datagram. (UDP is actually a Transport Layer Protocol and will be explained in the section on TCP.) Each message consists of up to 504 bytes and is inserted immediately following the UDP header, as seen in Figure 13.5a. Five fields, shown in Figure 13.5b, are used to determine *command, version, address family, IP address,* and *metric.*

RIP means Routing Information Protocol.

UDP is User Datagram Protocol.

Figure 13.5a RIP Message in a UDP Datagram

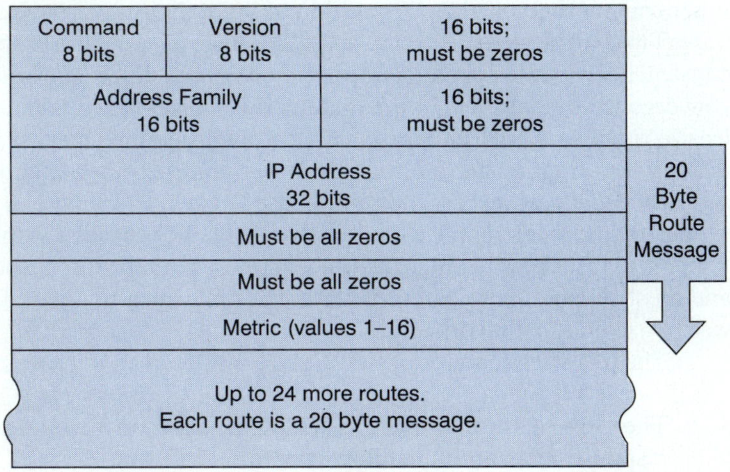

Figure 13.5b RIP Message Format

Commands may be either a *request* (1) or a *reply* (2). Requests ask for a routing table or portion of a routing table; replies contain the requested table information. Version is usually 1, although there is an RIP version 2. Twenty bytes are used to specify an address family, normally IP (2), an IP address, and a metric. Metrics, in practice, become the hop count. Using RIP, up to 25 different routes or hops can be specified.

RIP uses five different operations:

- *Initialization*—Used to request complete routing tables from all of the routers connected to the network
- *Request received*—The response to an initialization
- *Response received*—Indicates that the response has been validated and may be used to update the routing table and that modifications to the routing table may proceed
- *Regular routing updates*—At, usually, 30-second intervals, all routers exchange their routing table information to add any changes that have been made. Doing so significantly reduces the usable bandwidth. For this reason, RIP is often criticized as too inefficient.
- *Triggered updates*—When routes are changed, updates may be triggered. In this case only the changes are communicated.

Open Shortest Path First. Developed to overcome the limitation of RIP, Open Shortest Path First (OSPF) is a *link-state* protocol rather than a *distance-vectored* protocol such as RIP. Whereas RIP only concerns itself with the distance to a destination in terms of hop count, OSPF actively runs periodic tests to determine for itself the status of its connection to other routers. OSPF does not exchange routing tables. Instead, it sends its own status information to other routers that use the information to build their own routing tables.

The ability of a network's routers to accomplish a table construction/update is referred to as *convergence*. In most cases, the faster the convergence the better. Unfortunately, the shortest path is not necessarily the least-cost path. A path through a T1 line might be the shortest and fastest, but the cost of a fractional T1, although slower, may be much cheaper. Conversely, a two-hop path using T1 lines will cause a packet to arrive at its destination sooner than a single hop via the fractional T1. For these reasons, OSPF allows a separate router table entry for the least-cost path, fastest response time path, and most reliable path. These table entries may also be made for each IP service in use on the network.

The following features of OSPF are considered an improvement over RIP:

- The cost of route can be calculated based on throughput, round-trip response time, and reliability of path.

- The cost to route can be entered for each IP service.
- Loads on equal cost paths may be balanced to prevent delays on congested paths.
- Table updates can be made by broadcasting to all routers in a single message.
- Authentication can be implemented using passwords. Unfortunately, the passwords are sent in clear text.

Internet Control Message Protocol

When conditions such as errors or queries need to be communicated to other IP stations, an *Internet Control Message Protocol* (**ICMP**) datagram is generated by IP. ICMP datagrams may be processed by TCP as well as IP. There are 18 types of ICMP messages. However, to prevent a condition known as a *broadcast storm* in which ICMP errors are sent in response to broadcast messages, ICMP error messages are never sent in response to the following:

ICMP stands for Internet Control Message Protocol.

- ICMP error
- Datagram to IP broadcast address (broadcasts are sent to all stations)
- Datagram sent as a data link layer broadcast
- A fragmented message
- A datagram without a source address

ICMP is also able to request a time stamp from another host. The response is generally given as the number of milliseconds that have transpired since 0000 UTC (formerly Greenwich Mean Time).

Transmission Control Protocol (TCP)

TCP is the connection-oriented protocol that IP and User Datagram Protocol (UDP) rely on for reliable delivery of packets and datagrams. Reliability is assured by the following methods:

- Data are passed in packet sizes based on decisions made by TCP.
- TCP segments are sent as IP or UDP datagrams.
- TCP sets a timer when it sends a data segment. If the timer expires before an acknowledgment is received, TCP assumes the segment is lost.
- TCP maintains its own header checksum.
- TCP receiving stations send acknowledgments for each segment sent.

- Receiving stations discard duplicate segments. This can happen if a sending timer expires but the receiver actually got the initial segment.
- Flow control is established by the TCP receiving station, which will not allow the sender to overrun its buffer space.

Figure 13.6b shows the TCP header encapsulated in an IP header. When the packet is passed to the router, the IP header is read first, followed by the TCP header. The router now has all of the information required to reliably send the packet to its destination.

From Figure 13.6a, you will observe that the TCP header begins with 16-bit port numbers for source and destination. TCP uses ports to identify the sending and receiving applications. Some port numbers are reserved for specific uses. For example, TCP UDP datagrams use ports 67: and 68:; World Wide Web servers use port 80:, and so forth. Port numbers, Service Access Points (SAPs), and sockets all serve similar purposes, each in its own environment. A socket is the combination of IP address and port number.

Microsoft Windows uses sockets in combination with *named pipes* to provide communications from the data link layer to higher layers within the operating system. Socket values are given an alphanumeric name. Applications may then refer to a socket by name rather than numeric value.

Figure 13.6 (a) TCP Header and (b) Entire IP Datagram

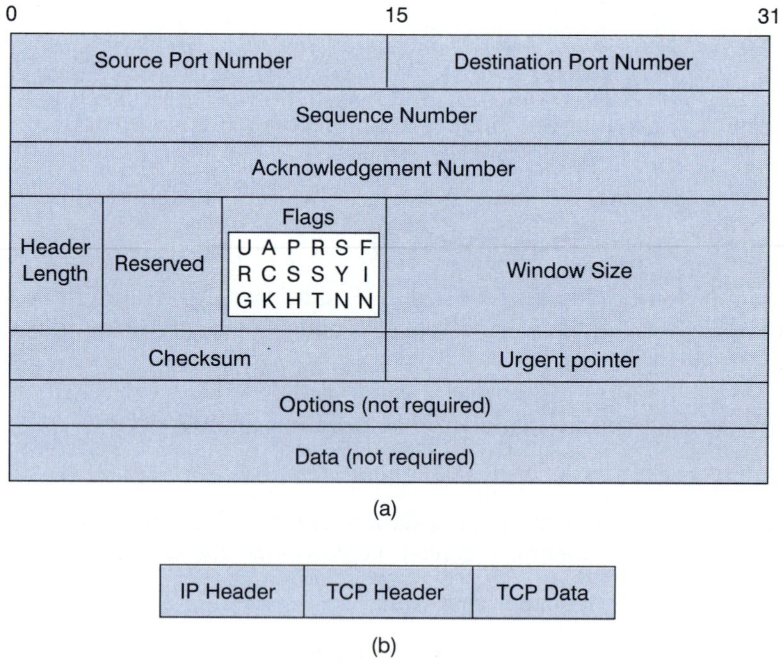

Sequence and acknowledgment numbers follow the port numbers. Each 32-bit value allows data streams with up to 2^{32-1} segments before the counter resets to zero and resumes the count.

As with IP, TCP provides a 4-bit field for the header length in 32-bit words and a 16-bit field for the TCP header checksum. There is a 6-bit "reserved" field.

TCP flags consist of the following:

- *Synchronize* (SYN)—SYN is set to initiate the beginning of a sequence.

  Acknowledge (ACK)—ACK is set to indicate that the 32-bit acknowledgment number is valid.

- *Urgent Pointer* (URG)—URG is set to notify the receiver that the data are urgent. It falls upon the receiver to act on this knowledge.

- *Push* (PSH)—Push indicates to the receiver that it should pass all of the data being collected in a sequence to the receiver's processing function.

- *Finish* (FIN)—The FIN flag indicates that the sender has no more data to pass. FIN can be used to terminate a TCP session.

- *Reset* (RST)—Causes the connection to be reset to starting values. This flag is used when a segment is lost and the entire data stream must be resent.

An option field is available that is most commonly used to set the size of segments and for the windowing process. In most cases, larger segments are preferable because they reduce header overhead. Unfortunately, long segments may also produce *fragmentation*, a case in which segments arrive out of sequence owing to congestion or bad paths. Reducing segment length can reduce fragmentation.

User Datagram Protocol (UDP)

UDP datagrams are used by TCP to cause a single IP datagram to be sent. UDP datagrams are sent on a "best effort" basis with no guarantees of delivery. UDP's value is that it limits its maximum data size to 512 bytes or less and can supply a foreign IP and port address in addition to the local IP address and port values. UDP datagrams are most often used by such applications as RIP, DNS, BootP, SNMP, and others where maximum packet size is critical. Where guaranteed delivery is critical, TCP should be used.

Figure 13.7 describes a UDP header. Note that UDP supplies its own checksum and that the data field may contain zero bytes. It is implied that foreign IP address and port values are communicated in the data field and that applications using UPD datagrams are constructed accordingly.

Source Port Number (16 bits)	Destination Port Number (16 bits)	UDP Length (16 bits)	UDP Checksum (16 bits)	Data (may be zero length)

Figure 13.7 UDP Header

DOMAIN NAME SYSTEM

To send a datagram to an IP destination, the IP address of the destination must be known. Can you imagine trying to associate all of the 32-bit IP address values with the names of each individual host? Would it not be far easier to remember a host name such as www.spscc.ctc.edu than its IP address?

The Domain Name System (DNS) was created to allow users to enter a structured host name in a datagram or E-mail address field and then allow the application to look up the associated IP address in a distributed database. The DNS database is distributed because DNS servers may be located throughout the network with each host configured to use its local DNS server.

To use DNS, an application must invoke a *resolver* that either requests or provides the correct IP address for a given host name before TCP/IP can send either UDP or IP datagrams. On the Internet, host names and their associated IP addresses must be unique. In the United States, the Internic organization is currently responsible for registering host names and assigning their IP addresses and license class. A hierarchical DNS has been established that is similar to that shown in Table 13.3a. Table 13.3b shows several of the current "generic" domains.

For all countries except the United States, a country suffix follows the domain name. Domains in Australia would have an .au suffix applied; .uk is used for United Kingdom, and so forth. There is currently some discussion that would require a .us suffix for U.S. domain names. In addition, non-U.S. countries sometimes form second-level domains beneath their country code. For example, .ac.uk indicates an academic institution domain in the United Kingdom.

A move by a private company is under way to add additional primary domains above and beyond the current generic domains. Primarily motivated by commercial concerns, the suggested new domains would allow commercial enterprises to obtain domain names that were organized by the markets in which their products were sold.

FILE TRANSFER PROTOCOL (FTP)

FTP, as its name implies, is used to transfer copies of files from hosts that can have different operating systems. Text files may be copied in either ASCII or EBCDIC. You may recall that ASCII and EBCDIC are character oriented (7- or 8-bit characters). Binary transfers (non-character-oriented files) are sent as either *image file type* (continuous streams of bits with an 8-bit byte size) and *local file type* (where the size of a byte is specified by the sender).

Table 13.3a Domain Name Hierarchy

Top-level domains: COM EDU GOV INT MIL NET ORG —— Country

Second level: (name of organization or company)

Additional levels: (sub organizations)

Example: **www.spscc.ctc.edu/cis/athompson/**

Where: www = name of server

spscc = sub organization

edu = top level domain

/cis/athompson = file hierarchy on the server

Table 13.3b Generic Domains

Domain	Description
COM	Commercial companies
EDU	Educational institutions
GOV	Government organizations (U.S.)
INT	International organizations
MIL	U.S. military
NET	Networks
ORG	Nonprofit organizations

To copy a file using FTP, a *control session* must be initiated between a client and an FTP server. Once connected, the client initiates an active open to TCP port 21 to enable the control connection. This connection remains active until terminated by the client. A *data connection* is established each time a file is copied. Many data connections may be initiated while the control connection remains active.

An example of this process is shown in Figure 13.8. Note that the control connection requires a log-in name and password. Some FTP servers allow *anonymous* log-ins. In most cases, the log-in name is "anonymous," and although there is no password, common etiquette requires your E-mail address as the password. The *GET* command is used to initiate a data connection to copy a file (in the example shown "bcoral.htm", an ASCII type file) from the FTP server to the host client. Conversely, a *PUT* command initiates a data connection to copy a file from client to server.

Table 13.4a lists the commonly used FTP commands. Note that STOR is the equivalent of GET and RETR is the equivalent of PUT. In the UNIX operating system FTP commands are uppercase. In the file transfer example shown in Figure 13.8, Windows NT was the operating system where commands are not case-sensitive. Table 13.4b uses the HELP command to list all of the commands available on a particular server.

Figure 13.8 FTP Session

```
C:<\\>\>WINNT>ftp www.westsound.com
Connected to www.westsound.com.
220 www.westsound.com FTP server (Version 6.00) ready.
User (www.westsound.com:(none)): thompson
331 Password required for thompson.
Password:
230 User thompson logged in.
ftp> ascii
200 Type set to A.
ftp> get bcoral.htm
200 PORT command successful.
150 Opening ASCII mode data connection for 'bcoral.htm' (3289 bytes).
226 Transfer complete.
3353 bytes received in 0.89 seconds (3.76 Kbytes/sec)
ftp>
```

Table 13.4a Common FTP Commands

Command	Description
ABOR	Abort transfer(s) underway
LIST	List file directory (ls in UNIX)
PASS	Password on server
PORT	Client IP address and port
QUIT	Log off and terminate control session
RETR(GET)	Copy file from server to client
STOR(PUT)	Copy file from client to server
SYST	Obtain system type from server
TYPE(ASCII/BIN)	Specify file type
USER	User name on server

Table 13.4b FTP Command List

```
ftp> help
Commands may be abbreviated. Commands are:

!          delete       literal    prompt       send
?          debug        ls         put          status
append     dir          mdelete    pwd          trace
ascii      disconnect   mdir       quit         type
bell       get          mget       quote        user
binary     glob         mkdir      recv         verbose
bye        hash         mls        remotehelp
cd         help         mput       rename
close      lcd          open       rmdir
```

TELNET

Prior to the time that PCs were networked, nearly all mainframes, minicomputers, and UNIX systems supplied simple terminals for use on the desktop. Terminals have no ability to execute programs and must therefore rely on programs running in a controlling computer for all transactions. Mainframes, minis, and even UNIX systems are not all compatible with each other. TELNET was developed to remotely connect a terminal from one system to a differing system using a common format for the terminal emulation.

As with FTP, a TELNET session is created, using TCP/IP as the common protocol, between a client and a TELNET server. A log-in shell is created for the client that allows the client to log on as an ordinary user. Once connected, the client "sees" the server in the same manner as any other terminal or PC connected to the server. PCs are made to look like dumb terminals through the use of terminal emulation software and may then create TELNET sessions themselves.

Figure 13.9 demonstrates a TELNET session used to log onto a UNIX mail server for the purpose of checking mail. The session was initiated from my home via an Internet service provider (ISP). Note that a DNS server was used to resolve the domain name of the mail server. The actual IP address could have been used if known.

During the log-on process, the client will be asked for a password. There is nearly always a time limit, usually one minute, in which to respond. Failure to respond successfully within the time limit will result in the connection being terminated. Unfortunately, TELNET sends password characters in clear text (unencrypted). This represents a severe security problem. In many systems, a home directory is set up for specific user and host names. Then when a known user from the proper host logs in, no password is requested. This is a somewhat better procedure from a security view but still considered poor security.

The TELNET protocol specifies *Network Virtual Terminal* (NVT) ASCII, the 7-bit version used in the United States. The end of a line of characters is terminated with the ASCII characters for linefeed and carriage return (denoted as \r\n). The NVT form of ASCII is also used in FTP, SMPT, and Finger. Once connected, client and server may negotiate to change from NVT to a mutually acceptable format. TELNET provides for four transmission modes:

- *Half duplex*—Originally the default NVT mode but rarely used today because of full duplex use in most servers
- *Character at a time*—Used in Rlogin, a UNIX application similar to TELNET
- *Kludge line at a time*—Assumed whenever either an ECHO or SUPPRESS GO AHEAD option is not in effect during half duplex operations. In half duplex, a GO AHEAD must be received by a client before

Figure 13.9 TELNET Session Used to Log onto a UNIX Mail Server

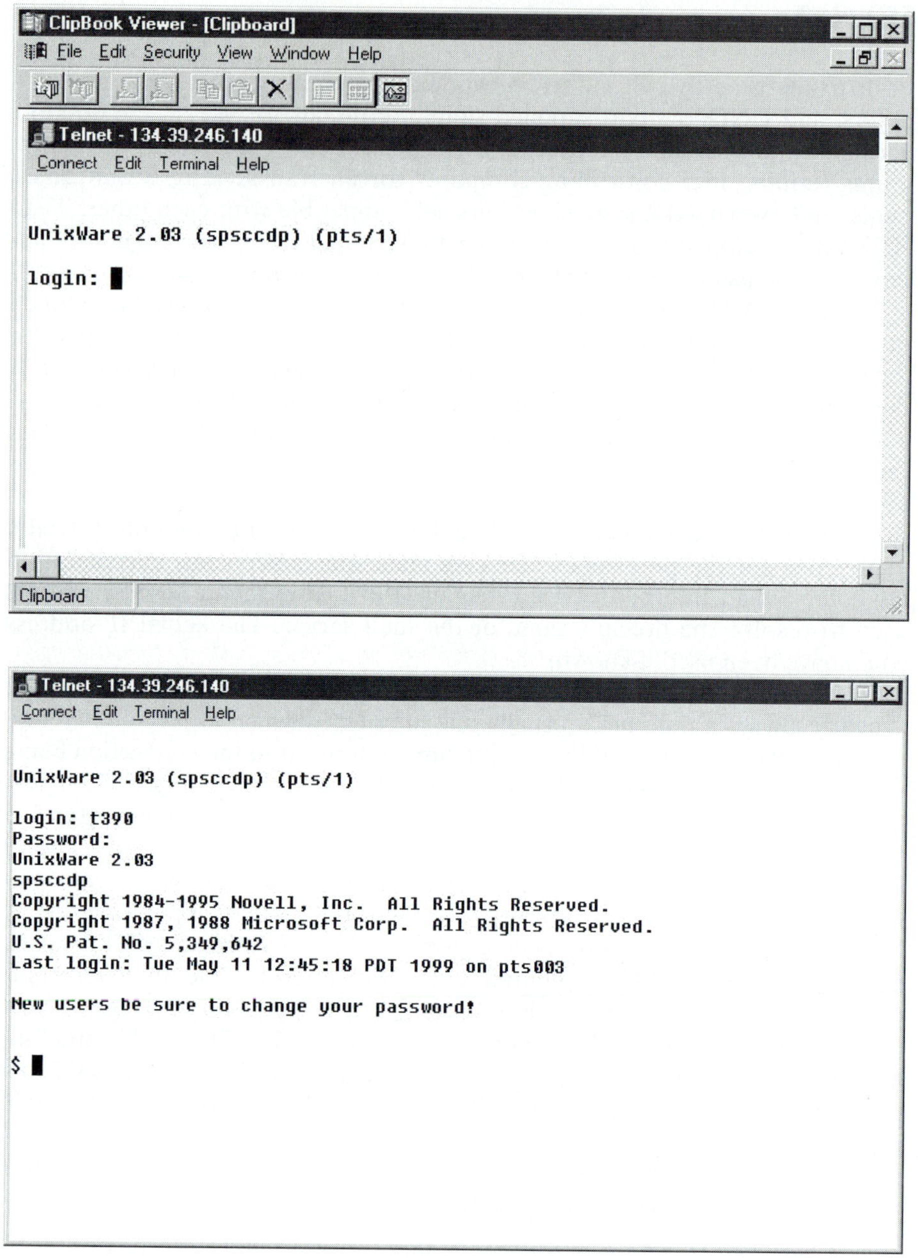

it can send its transmission to the server. To ECHO means to cause the character sent to be echoed back to the client's display screen.

- *Real line at a time*—Negotiated during initial session connect, this mode corrects deficiencies in kludge line at a time. Real line mode is most commonly in use today.

BOOTP

Using RARP, you were shown how an IP address could be obtained by a diskless system. BootP was created to allow a diskless system to "bootstrap" itself and connect to a server using UDP datagrams. Until recently, dial-up users connecting to the Internet made use of BootP to either obtain an IP address or make the ISP server aware of a previously issued IP.

More recently BootP is being replaced with *Dynamic Host Protocol* (DHCP). DHCP has the added advantage of being able to assign an IP address from an available pool of address on a first come, first serve basis. The need for a client to configure an IP address is eliminated and a more efficient use of the ISP's available IP addresses can be had.

Figure 13.10 shows the format for a BootP request. Port 67 is used for the server and port 68 for the client. Two ports are used so that a BootP server can broadcast when necessary.

SIMPLE MAIL TRANSFER PROTOCOL (SMTP)

As its name implies, SMTP is the protocol used to send and receive electronic mail over TCP/IP. To use E-mail, one must install a third-party program capable of formatting to SMTP requirements. Known as *user agents*, E-mail programs exchange mail with E-mail servers using *Message Transfer Agents* (MTAs). The MTA runs in the mail server. MTAs also exchange mail with each other.

To send an E-mail, a client generates the E-mail message, formatted to SMTP requirements, then transfers the message to the MTA server that holds the client's E-mail account. Based on the destination address contained in the E-mail message, the MTA will contact the MTA in which the destination account is located. For the addressee to read the message, a user agent program must be run. The addressee logs onto the appropriate MTA and retrieves any messages that are being stored on the MTA.

The SMTP protocol uses 13 commands: DATA, EXPN, HELO, MAIL, NOOP, RCPT, RSET, TURN, SAML, SEND, SOML, QUIT, and VRFY. All commands are sent using ASCII. A typical command sequence for sending a message is shown in Figure 13.11. Note that the client has already connected to the MTA and that responses from the MTA are in italics. The last line of the

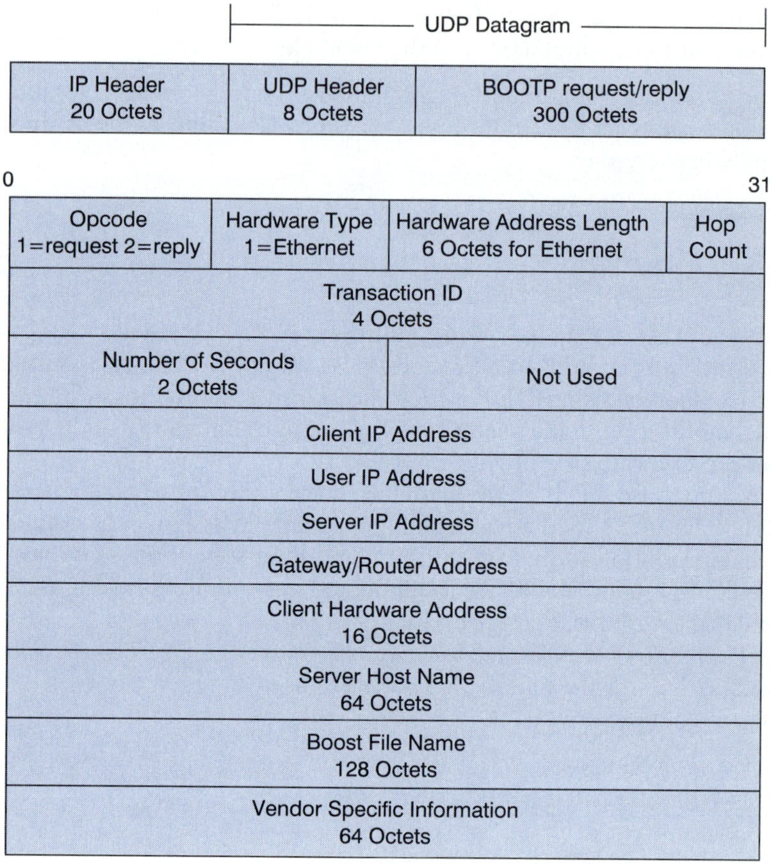

Figure 13.10 Format for a BootP Request

message must be a period on a line by itself and is shown on the line below "This is the message."

E-mail messages must be formatted in a specific manner and are composed of three parts:

- *Envelope*—Used by MTAs to determine delivery address. In the example shown the envelope consists of

  MAIL From: <thompso@mail.spscc.ctc.edu>

  RCPT to:<thompson@westsound.com

- *Header*—E-mail headers may consist of up to nine fields, separated by blank lines and formatted as follows:

  Received:

  Message-ID:

HELO mail.spscc.ctc.edu
mail.spscc.ctc.edu., you rang?
MAIL From:<athompso@spscc.ctc.edu>
<athompso@spscc.ctc.edu> . . . Sender ok
RCPT To:<thompson@westsound.com>
<thompson@westsound.com> . . . Recipient.ok
DATA
Enter mail, end with "." on a line by itself
This is the message.
.
Mail accepted
QUIT
mail.spscc.ctc.edu sending mail
thompson@westsound.com sent
"User agent sent message"

Figure 13.11 User Agent/MTA Interaction

From:

Date:

Reply-To

X-Phone

X-Mailer

To:

Subject:

- *Body*—This is the main content of the message. By default, ASCII is used. However, newer formats such as *Multipurpose Internet Mail Extensions* (MIME) and *Hypertext Markup Language* (HTML) are being used on the World Wide Web to facilitate transfer of multimedia and HTML documents. Note that a single line transferred by a DATA command cannot exceed 1,000 bytes.

SIMPLE NETWORK MANAGEMENT PROTOCOL (SNMP)

As the Internet began to grow, network administrators began looking for tools that would manage the TCP/IP protocols that connected a wide variety of network equipment produced by a multitude of vendors. ISO standardization of a management protocol has been under development for more than 10 years and is still not fully standardized. The need for a standardized management tool was so urgent that the Internet developers introduced a simple but usable interim manager, SNMP.

A complete management system should consist of three major components:

- A *Management Information Base* (MIB) that defines the types of information that network nodes will maintain.
- The *structure of management information* that defines the structure of the variables in an MIB.
- The protocol used to transfer information over the network, in this case, SNMP.

SNMP is composed of three basic software elements. An SNMP *manager* may reside within a server or in a remote workstation. The second software element is the *agent* that resides within a network node device such as a router, print server, workstation, and so forth. The third software element is the *protocol* that the manager and agent use to communicate with each other—namely, SNMP.

In essence, the manager has the capability to poll an agent for information about the status of the agent's host node. Agents are responsible for reporting node status in the form of variables called scalars. A scalar variable might indicate that a node device is down or experiencing a large number of retries or perhaps describe the routing table in a router or gateway. Network administrators may then query agents for usage statistics in an effort to determine the operational status of the network. Using only 12 management data types, SNMP messages can be sent to describe the status of a node.

Messaging Protocol

SNMP uses only five message operator types:

1. *get-request* (PDU type 0)—Sent by the manager to fetch the value of one or more specified variables
2. *get-next-request* (PDU type 1)—Sent by the manager to fetch the next variable in a table of variables (scalars)
3. *set-request* (PDU type 2)—Sent by the manager to set the value of one or more variables
4. *get-response* (PDU type 3)—Used by the agent to respond to get-request, get-next-request, and set-request operators
5. *trap* (PDU type 4)—Sent by the agent to notify the manager of an agent event

Figure 13.12a shows the flow of the SNMP operators, and Figure 13.12b diagrams the placement of an SNMP frame within an IP packet.

Management Information Base (MIB)

The MIB is a database of information that is maintained by the agent. It is divided into groups with names such as *system, at, interfaces, ip,* and so forth. These tables contain the information that the manager needs or defines.

SNMP uses 12 different data types to define variables:

- *INTEGER*—Integers are defined as unrestricted, IP forwarding flag, or minimum and maximum values.
- *OCTET STRING*—A string of 0 or more bytes
- *DisplayString*—A string of ASCII bytes
- *OBJECT IDENTIFIER*—The IP objects in mnemonic format (i.e., Cityu.edu.mgmt.mib)

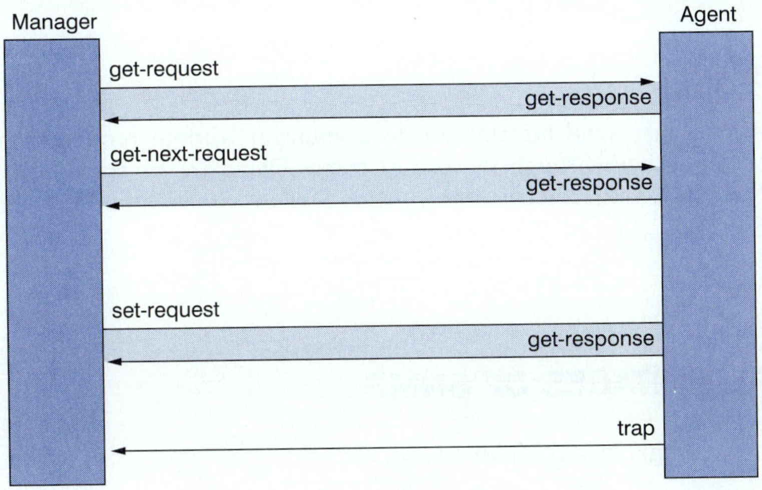

Figure 13.12a Flow of the SNMP Operators

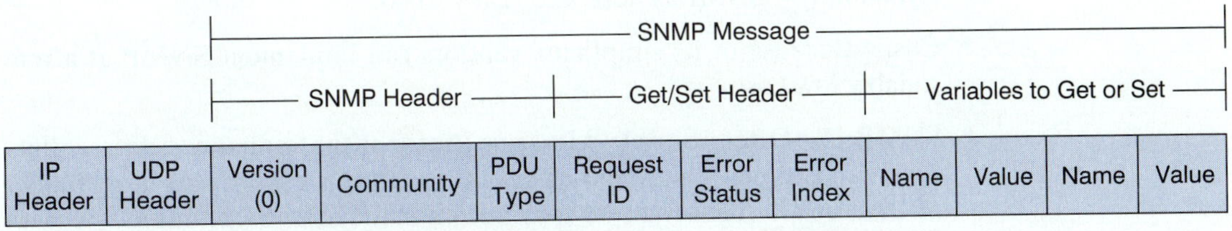

Figure 13.12b SNMP Message Encapsulated by IP

- *NULL*—No value
- *IpAddress*—A four-octet string using the IP addressing convention (i.e., 142.50.20.1)
- *PhysAddress*—The physical MAC address (6 bytes in Ethernet or Token-Ring)
- *Counter*—A nonnegative, incremental, wrap-around counter with values between 0 and 2^{32}–1
- *Gauge*—A latch-at-maximum-value counter that may increment or decrement between 0 and 2^{32}–1
- *TimeTicks*—Counter that counts time in 0.001-second increments
- *SEQUENCE*—A C language–type structure that is used in an MIB to define (1) udpLocalAddress (the local IP address); (2) udpLocalPort (the local port number in range 0-65535)
- *SEQUENCE OF*—Vector definition with all elements having the same data type

Traps

Agents may send information to a manager without request. This process is accomplished through the use of traps. There are six traps*: coldStart, warmStart, linkDown, linkUp, authenticationFailure, egpNeighborLoss*, and *enterpriseSpecific.*

ADVANTAGES OF SNMP

- Simplicity—It is easy to use.
- Support—More than 30 vendors currently support SNMP.
- Availability—SNMP is here and ready to go.
- Cost—Because of its simplicity, vendors can implement SNMP at a reasonably low cost.
- SNMP II—Offers Simple Message Protocol that enhances data collection with two new commands: get-bulk-request that retrieves large blocks of data and inform-request that allows managers to communicate with each other.

DISADVANTAGES

- OSI is developing a more full featured management standard called *Common Management Information Protocol* (CMIP). However, only a few vendors are currently supporting CMIP, and even though it was begun in 1979, it is not yet fully standardized.
- SNMP has a rather large overhead in that managers and agents use a significant portion of available bandwidth to communicate with each other.
- SNMP must run over TCP/IP; however, SNMP II with SMP will allow SNMP over IPX, AppleTalk, and so forth.
- SNMP is a proprietary protocol and not an official standard and may lock a user into a specific vendor's application of SNMP.
- A number of the vendors who have developed their own proprietary management packages offer only limited versions of SNMP in the hope that you will find their offerings worth the additional cost.

TROUBLESHOOTING

Packet InterNet Groper (PING)

PING is a utility application that queries an IP address to determine whether the addressed host is actively connected to the network. Figure 13.13 lists the format for using PING. Upon receipt of a PING request, the "pinged" host responds with a brief message, as shown in Figure 13.14. The response can be used to identify the round trip response time to receive the reply and *Time To Live* (TTL) field contents from the IP header.

Periodic PING reports can be generated and logged. Over time, the data can be used to generate a graph that will show trends in the response time to access various hosts such as routers and gateways connected to WANs. Sudden increases in response time or no access at all are clear indications of trouble.

Traceroute

TCP/IP is, after all, a wide area protocol. Because routers and gateways are often the cause of "traffic jams," there is a need to test the response time of packets that travel across a WAN. Traceroute is a utility application that will measure the time through each router and show the domain names and associated IP addresses of each hop.

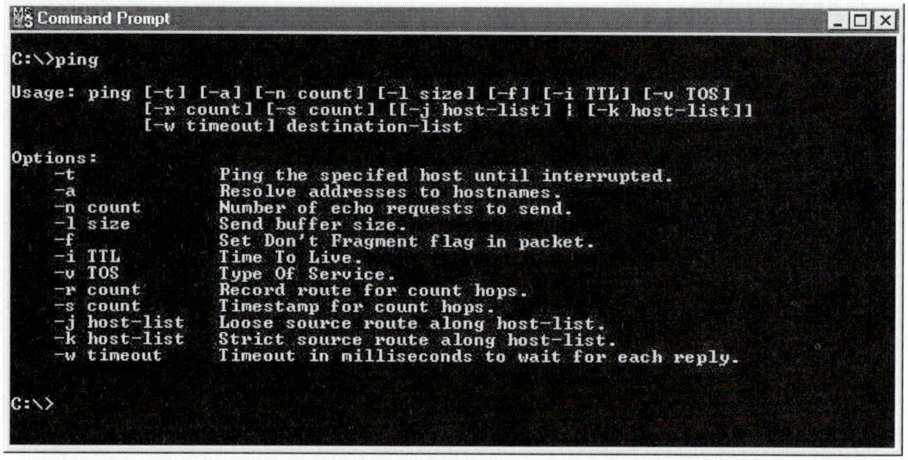

```
C:\>ping

Usage: ping [-t] [-a] [-n count] [-l size] [-f] [-i TTL] [-v TOS]
            [-r count] [-s count] [[-j host-list] | [-k host-list]]
            [-w timeout] destination-list

Options:
    -t             Ping the specifed host until interrupted.
    -a             Resolve addresses to hostnames.
    -n count       Number of echo requests to send.
    -l size        Send buffer size.
    -f             Set Don't Fragment flag in packet.
    -i TTL         Time To Live.
    -v TOS         Type Of Service.
    -r count       Record route for count hops.
    -s count       Timestamp for count hops.
    -j host-list   Loose source route along host-list.
    -k host-list   Strict source route along host-list.
    -w timeout     Timeout in milliseconds to wait for each reply.

C:\>
```

Figure 13.13 Ping Command Format

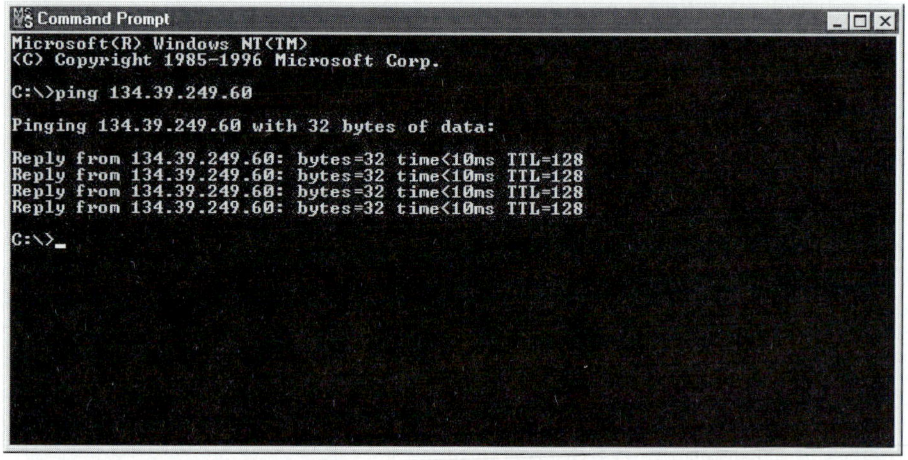

```
Microsoft(R) Windows NT(TM)
(C) Copyright 1985-1996 Microsoft Corp.

C:\>ping 134.39.249.60

Pinging 134.39.249.60 with 32 bytes of data:

Reply from 134.39.249.60: bytes=32 time<10ms TTL=128
Reply from 134.39.249.60: bytes=32 time<10ms TTL=128
Reply from 134.39.249.60: bytes=32 time<10ms TTL=128
Reply from 134.39.249.60: bytes=32 time<10ms TTL=128

C:\>_
```

Figure 13.14 Ping Response

TECHTIP

IP can sometimes be used to trace routes by using the return route (RR) option in the IP header. Unfortunately, an IP header has room for nine IP addresses only. On today's Internet a nine-hop limit would be completely inadequate.

The Traceroute response shown in Figure 13.15 was achieved by TELNETing from the author's home, through a local ISP and into a UNIX server at a community college. You can see in Figure 13.15 that Traceroute has a maximum of 30 hops, after which the test packets are assumed lost. Note also that the time through the westsound.com routers was much longer than the other routers encountered. This may be due to servers that are being used to route packets within the ISP's LAN rather than dedicated routers. When using Traceroute, one must also be aware that a trace may not always take the same path. This is particularly true on the Internet and over WANs that use the public telephone system between routers.

Finger

Where information about a user account at a particular host is desired, the Finger protocol may be used. One might wish to know whether a particular user is logged on or if a particular host is connected and running. Figure 13.16 "fingers" a user account at the University of Western Australia that has been set up to provide the inventory in a Coke machine. (If you like sickeningly sweet soft drinks, try the Redeye.)

```
Command Prompt

Tracing route to clipper.spscc.ctc.edu [134.39.241.9]
over a maximum of 30 hops:

  1     *        *        *     Request timed out.
  2   180 ms   180 ms   181 ms  gw.westsound.com [206.129.4.11]
  3   210 ms   181 ms   190 ms  su16.s11-6.c1.sea.ixa.net [204.194.9.25]
  4   191 ms   200 ms   190 ms  905.Hssi5-0.GW1.SEA1.ALTER.NET [137.39.136.5]
  5   190 ms   190 ms   191 ms  104.ATM2-0.XR1.SEA1.ALTER.NET [146.188.200.50]
  6   181 ms   180 ms   200 ms  195.ATM9-0-0.BR1.SEA1.ALTER.NET [146.188.200.65]

  7   190 ms   200 ms   191 ms  137.39.23.26
  8   190 ms   200 ms   190 ms  fe4-0-0.wes-br3.nw.verio.net [129.250.31.118]
  9   190 ms   181 ms   200 ms  fe1-0.wes-br4.nw.verio.net [129.250.31.119]
 10   201 ms   190 ms   200 ms  hssi3-0.sea-br2.nw.verio.net [198.104.194.49]
 11   200 ms   200 ms   211 ms  fe9-1.sea-br1.nw.verio.net [204.200.8.5]
 12   191 ms   190 ms   210 ms  wak20-gw.nw.verio.net [204.200.241.1]
 13   200 ms   230 ms   211 ms  seauw3-FE0-0-0.wa-k20.net [198.32.170.26]
 14   231 ms   230 ms   210 ms  S-Puget-Sound-7206.ctc.edu [168.156.1.98]
 15   220 ms   231 ms     *     clipper.spscc.ctc.edu [134.39.241.9]
 16   250 ms   250 ms   251 ms  clipper.spscc.ctc.edu [134.39.241.9]

Trace complete.

C:\>_
```

Figure 13.15 Traceroute Response

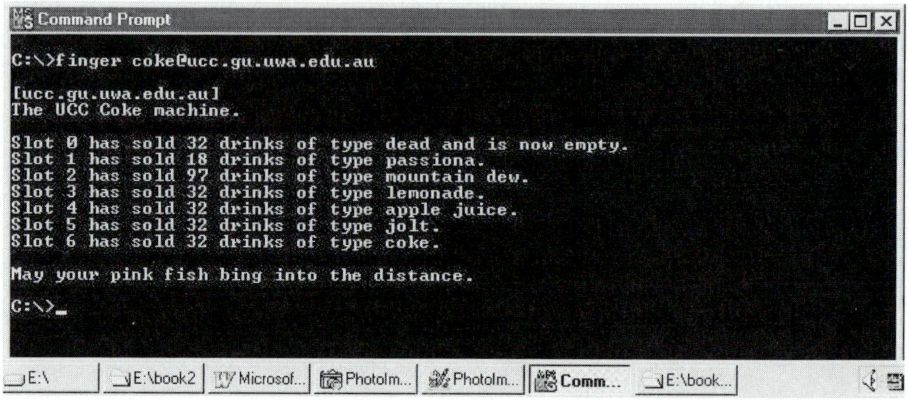

Figure 13.16 Finger Protocol Example

CHAPTER REVIEW

- TCP/IP—This is the protocol developed for the Internet.
- TCP is the connection-oriented transport layer protocol that is responsible for sequencing and acknowledgment of IP datagrams.
- TCP can use UDP to send unconnected datagrams most often containing control information or requesting status information.
- IP is the connectionless network layer protocol used to transmit encapsulated data frames in the form of IP datagrams. Application data transfers are most often sent as IP datagrams.
- IP routing protocols include ARP, RARP, RIP, and OSFP.
- TCP/IP is composed of many subprotocols, including IP, ICMP, IGMP, TCP, UDP, Telnet, BootP, FTP, SNMP, SMTP, and others.
- Files may be transferred with FTP.
- ICMP is used to communicate network problems to client hosts.
- TCP uses UDP to send informational datagrams.
- BootP and DHCP are used to connect remote users to gateway servers.
- TELNET is used to remotely log on to a host computer.
- E-mail is sent using SMTP.
- Information about network health may be obtained using SNMP.
- Protocols that may be used for troubleshooting include PING, Traceroute, and Finger.

REVIEW QUESTIONS

1. Why is TCP/IP referred to as a *suite* of protocols?
2. Which protocols are included in TCP?
3. Which protocols are included in IP?
4. Why is TCP connection oriented?
5. How does IP send datagrams?
6. Create a drawing that demonstrates the process of sending a TCP/IP packet between LANs connected by routers. Show all of the protocols used at each layer by each node in the network.
7. How does IP create its address field?
8. Describe the process of *subnet masking*.
9. Describe each of the fields in an IP header.
10. How many bytes may be in an IP datagram?
11. How does IP deal with routing information?
12. Discuss the attributes of ARP.
13. Discuss the attributes of RIP.
14. How does OSPF improve on RIP?
15. What is ICMP used for?
16. What are sockets?
17. What are named pipes?
18. How do sockets and named pipes relate to each other?
19. What methods does TCP use to "guarantee" delivery of packets? What is UDP used for?
20. Describe the DNS system.
21. What is FTP used for? Provide an example.
22. List three protocols that could be used to troubleshoot a TCP/IP network. Describe how each protocol would be used.
23. Which protocol is used to remotely log onto a host computer?
24. Which protocol is used to *connect* a dial-up user directly to a gateway server?
25. Which protocol is used to send E-mail?
26. Describe the features of SNMP.
27. Where would you use SNMP? Where would you limit use of SNMP?

14

Small Network Design

INTRODUCTION

The design of a network includes much more than a technical design process. In fact, the technical design is sometimes the least important aspect. Networks are most often installed for three basic reasons:

- *Organizational needs.* For a network installation to be desirable to senior management, it must usually be demonstrated to *reduce costs, increase productivity,* or *establish a technological or competitive edge*.
- *Political advantage.* Whenever a department or group can demonstrate success by using a network, other departments will soon be demanding the resources to install their own network. Success may or may not be forthcoming, but many managers would consider it politically dangerous to be left out of the successful network. In such cases, the technical merits of the design are often secondary to the image of the network as a tool for success. In fact, the success of the network—indeed, its initial acceptance—may be based more on political considerations than any other.
- *Technical superiority*. It is quite possible to make a technical case for the network, particularly when it can be demonstrated that the installation of a network will provide a competitive edge over a company's competitors. In such cases, the design's technical merits may receive more attention. It is becoming much more difficult to specify new technology, for the sake of new technology, unless it is needed to retain a competitive edge over competition.

The prudent designer will keep all of these requirements in mind when designing the network. As well, keep in mind that someone, perhaps yourself, is going to have to maintain the network. There is, perhaps, nothing worse than trying to continuously play catch-up to a network that is inadequately designed, poorly installed, or both.

DESIGN PROCESS

The design process consists of eight distinct categories as shown in Table 14.1. Each phase is examined to determine the needs of a particular design's requirements. Begin with phase 1 and work your way through the process, carefully examining each step to determine the requirements for your network. At the end of each phase, a written report to management is created that summarizes the key points of the process, offers alternatives and recommendations, and an opportunity for management to return suggestions, recommendations, and authorization to continue the project.

Phase 1: Organizational Strategy and Needs Analysis

Phase 1 in any network design must be an analysis of the needs that the proposed network must satisfy. Such an analysis should include an identification of the problem that the network is to solve. Identify the cause(s) of the problem and the objectives that must be achieved if the network is to solve the problem. It is crucial that your analysis of needs is aligned with the strategic goals of your organization if management is to give its support to the project.

Factors that are often considered during a needs analysis include

- need to improve communications,
- increase productivity,
- replace old or obsolete hardware or software,
- improve data/document flow,
- establish technical edge,
- expand capacity,
- keep up with competition,
- reduce costs,

Table 14.1 Design Process Categories

1. Organizational strategy and needs analysis
2. Technical requirements
3. Availability analysis
4. Alternatives
5. Cost-benefit analysis
6. Final selection and design
7. Design review
8. Implementation

- consolidate and/or increase security of data storage,
- reduce and/or improve control of inventory,
- conformance to vendor/supplier/customer requirements, and
- allow future growth.

No matter how carefully a network is designed, if its users are not pleased, for whatever reason, the network administrator will not be a popular person. Therefor, a careful analysis of user requirements must be included in the needs analysis. Users should be interviewed to determine

- task functions,
- document form and flow,
- message/data volume,
- recommended improvements or changes, and
- organizational rules.

Following the interview process, a consolidation of the results can be done to point out areas of common interest and priority. Results should also be compared to the organizational rules set down by management to ensure that the end result conforms to these rules. Follow-up interviews are appropriate to deal with anomalous needs or activities.

The final step in the needs analysis should be a written report to management outlining the results of the survey and analysis. Don't be surprised if management sends you back to find out why people aren't doing things the way management thought they were. Although you may well be required to deliberately design to management specifications rather than user needs, your analysis will still provide a great deal of information on methodology and flow that will indicate more effective solutions.

Phase 2: Technical Requirements

With organizational needs and user requirements established, the technical requirements of the network may be addressed. A traffic analysis should be done that determines the minimum acceptable bandwidth requirement. Factors such as number of users, message quantity and length, peak load times, and maximum acceptable response time are analyzed to determine the minimum bandwidth requirement. LANs that appear too congested may have to be segmented by bridges and/or switches or redesigned to use faster protocols.

An engineering design lab, for example, might pass very large drawing and specification files between client and server, a large bandwidth requirement. An office staff, on the other hand, typically passes messages of shorter length, needing less bandwidth than engineering. Departments connected to large databases will require more bandwidth than those that primarily use the network for electronic mail and small application file service.

With a clear understanding of bandwidth requirements, the designer is able to choose a suitable protocol and topology. Whereas Ethernet might be suitable for office traffic and electronic mail, Token-Ring might be the better choice for a client/server database that employs 200 users processing insurance forms. FDDI might be the better choice for the engineering lab and is perhaps a good choice for the backbone that connects multiple servers together. Figure 14.1 demonstrates the use of multiple protocols and topologies.

Each component of the network should be considered in terms of its suitability for the intended operations. Whereas a 486 CPU might serve effectively as the server for a small office Ethernet LAN, the large client/server database could require the capacity of a mainframe just to store the data. Individual, high-speed multiprocessing servers would then be connected to the front-end processors of the mainframe. Certainly, it would make no sense to install FDDI to the engineering workstations and server if the server itself were not able to meet the processing demands.

Workstations are equally worthy of analysis. Older 386 workstations may be suitable for word processing or print servers. High-speed RISC-based engineering workstations are often fully justified in the drafting department. Many

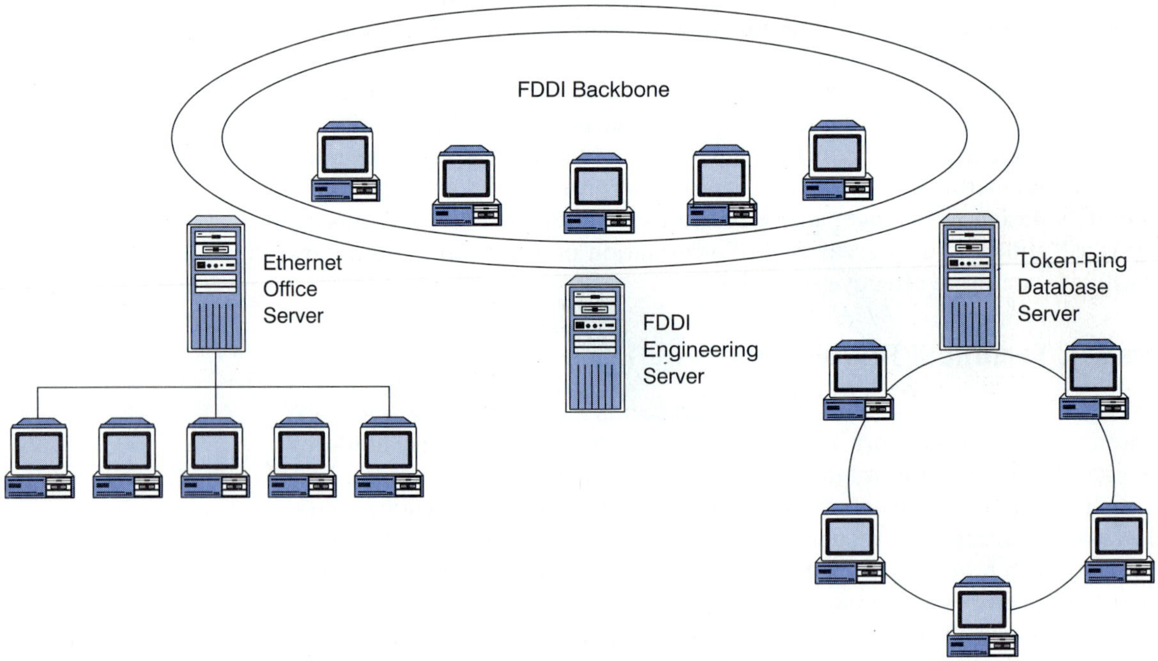

Figure 14.1 Multiple Topologies and Protocols on a Common Backbone

LANs have incorporated diskless workstations (sometimes called *network PCs*) for security reasons and as a way of reducing costs. Many large organizations are installing *intranets* that have the look and feel of the Internet but may not actually connect to the Internet. Powerful application and file servers contain all of the software needed by users who are still empowered to do creative computing but who no longer need large, expensive PCs on the desktop. The computing power is distributed among the servers.

The selection of the physical wiring plant is most often dictated by the selection of protocol and by the physical restraints of the LAN environment. Where electrical noise and interference is high, such as elevator shafts and around electrical machinery, shielded cable or fiber optics should be specified. Elevator shafts are also subject to vibration. Any electronics, particularly disk drives, located near elevators or other sources of vibration, should be shock mounted.

Phase 3: Availability of Equipment

A great deal of money may be saved if part of the design process includes a survey of existing equipment that is suitable and already in place. This is particularly true when your objective is to upgrade a current network or replace an older legacy system. Much of the wiring may be suitable and need not be replaced. Category 5 UTP cable, for example, easily accommodates 100-Mbps Fast Ethernet. For 10-Mbps Ethernet, older category 3 UTP is entirely satisfactory. There would be no good reason to replace the coaxial network cabling on local networks if the older LAN can be either bridged to a newer LAN or simply connected to a high-speed backbone by adding a high-speed NIC to the server.

Be aware of the political considerations regarding older equipment. The finance vice president might well get by on an old 386 workstation if the only need is for E-mail, but if personal assistants get new Pentiums, how do you think the VP might feel? Interdepartmental rivalries are another political consideration. You might want to specify new Pentiums for all of the vice presidents and then let the president decide to downgrade them to 486 machines.

Phase 4: Alternatives

Every section of your design should include an analysis of alternative solutions. Such an analysis becomes the justification for the selection of specific items in the design. If alternatives have been identified in advance, it is much easier to make intelligent decisions. Be certain to outline the advantages and disadvantages of each alternative.

We all have personal preferences that tend to bias our thinking. One way to minimize bias is to attach a weighted value to each design requirement during the alternative analysis process. A weight is assigned to each design item that reflects its overall value to the objectives for the finished design. For example, in a design whose objective is "reasonable" response time and "minimum" cost, response time might be given a weight of 3 and cost a more important weight of 4. Each alternative is then multiplied by its weighting factor and a sum of all the weighted criteria produced.

As shown in Figure 14.2, a weighting process not only reduces bias but also makes a complicated decision process somewhat easier. Note that when cost receives the highest weight, ARCNET has the highest score. When bandwidth and congestion are more highly valued than cost, Token-Ring and FDDI are the preferred choices. Care should be taken to use realistic weights based solely on a factual evaluation of each choice as it compares to other alternatives.

Alternative analysis should include the following items:

- *Second sources for equipment and software*. If one supplier cannot meet a delivery date, a second source may. If the primary vendor discontinues support or products, a second source can prevent a potential disaster. If no second source exists, a careful analysis of need is in order. Do you really need the item badly enough to risk a single vendor?
- *Identify alternate protocols*. Often only senior management is aware of future plans that may render current designs obsolete before they are implemented. If presented with protocol choices that include growth opportunities beyond current plans, management will be better able to make their decisions.
- *Identify alternatives for hardware and software*. Hardware and software decisions should be based on several factors. NICs, for example, should be identical and from the same vendor, if possible, to prevent protocol

Figure 14.2 Weighted Alternative Method

Attribute	Rank	ARCNET	Ethernet	Token-Ring	FDDI
Bandwidth	3	2	3	4	5
Congestion	2	4	2	5	5
Initial cost	5	5	4	3	1
Ease of installation	1	4	5	2	1
Cost of maintenance	4	4	5	3	3
Totals (rank * weight)		**59**	58	55	43

Attribute	Rank	ARCNET	Ethernet	Token-Ring	FDDI
Bandwidth	5	2	3	4	5
Congestion	4	4	2	5	5
Initial cost	3	5	4	3	1
Ease of installation	1	4	5	2	1
Cost of maintenance	2	4	5	3	3
Totals (rank * weight)		53	50	**55**	**55**

incompatibilities. This violates the single-source precaution, but if xyz Corp. guarantees "NetWare" and 3Comm 3C5x9 compatibility, you can buy from xyz and still fall back on 3Comm as a second source.

- *Service.* Determine the warranty, maintenance, and training support supplied by each vendor.
- *History.* Most vendors are willing to supply lists of customers willing to discuss their experiences with the vendor. Your goal is to discover the vendor's reliability and reputation. Try to obtain the names of unhappy customers, if possible. Determine the vendor's reputation for dealing with problems when they do occur.

Phase 5: Cost-Benefit Analysis

As alternatives are examined, the cost of each item should be compared with the benefits it provides. A product that does not provide an adequate solution to the problem is not justified even though it may have a low cost. Conversely, it may be thoroughly justifiable to specify a high-cost item if its benefits provide the best possible solution. This may be particularly true when growth is factored in. The prudent network designer looks ahead for at least 3–5 years and deliberately creates a design to accommodate anticipated growth.

Phase 6: Finalize the Design

Up to this point, most of your design is contained in lists and written reports to management. Perhaps a few preliminary drawings have been made. In other words, phases 1–5 are primarily confined to collecting information that is appropriate to the design criteria, analyzing the data, and the all-important process of gaining management's support and agreement to continue the project.

Now you are ready to actually complete the final "approved" design. Several activities must take place:

- Drawings should be made that detail the layout of the network.
- Worksheets and records are filled in with the details for configuration of hardware and software. A master network manual is begun that details the design and any changes or revisions in the design.
- Security of the network is often critical. A small office LAN may need little or no security, but where information stored in servers and workstations must be confidential, operating systems that require log-in names and passwords must be selected. Any time a network node allows ingress or egress from the immediate premises, security is potentially compromised. Routers, gateways, communications servers, and modems should be protected by firewalls that prevent unauthorized use of the network.

- Disaster recovery plans must be written and made a functional part of the network. If you have ever lost the data on your hard drive, you will appreciate the huge cost in time and lost opportunity. Backup and recovery systems, however, can be prohibitively expensive. Your analysis should weigh the cost of losing data against the cost of recovering it. Remember also that recovery times, particularly on high-capacity, multigigabyte-server drives, can require a great deal of time.
- Redundancy of equipment such as servers, disk drives, and power supplies is indicated whenever downtime cannot be tolerated. Side-by-side servers allow a secondary server to take over automatically in the event of a failure of the primary server. *Redundant Array of Inexpensive Drives* (RAID) systems are an excellent method for providing both security and redundancy to data storage drives. Redundant, "hot swappable" power supplies and disk drives provide redundancy for critical equipment. If a wide area link is critical, routers, or gateways may also need redundancy.
- Network management includes both the people who manage the network and the hardware and software tools they need to keep the network functioning smoothly. At minimum, the network manager should have a cable tester for each type of cable in use and cable assembly and repair tools readily available. Some type of performance-checking software should also be available. On large networks, particularly where multiple protocols must coexist, the expense of a network analyzer can be justified. Management of large networks can be made more efficient through the use of *remote monitoring* (RMON) agents that allow the network manager to maintain the software configurations for each node on the network from a remote site.
- Timetables and schedules for design completion, procurement, and implementation should be completed and published. A formalized project management process should be started in parallel with the start of the design process. This is particularly necessary when dealing with large projects.
- Lead times for critical items should be ascertained in advance. Expensive items such as servers, routers, and gateways are not always sold off the shelf.
- Finalized hardware and software lists should be completed.
- Vendor selection must be made. This is often done through a competitive process that begins with a *Request For Proposal* (RFP) that outlines the network requirements for vendors who then respond with their solutions to the design requirements. Responses to RFPs are then evaluated and one or more vendors selected.
- Training is often a critical part of the design process that must take place before the network is fully operational. Training manuals may need to be written. Vendors often supply training on their own hardware and software.

Phase 7: Design Review

Given the complexity of even a simple LAN, a thorough review of the design at all levels of the project is a must. Every phase of the project should be reviewed to ensure that nothing has been left out. Changes to the design should also be reviewed and approved prior to acceptance to ensure that all of the drawings, lists, and records are correctly updated.

A successful technique known as a *structured walkthrough* is used by many systems analysts to ensure that a design meets its intended objectives before submitting the design to management or committing to implementation of the system. You may also hear this process referred to as *proof of concept*. A structured walkthrough requires three individuals in addition to the designer:

- *Walkthrough coordinator*—This person is responsible for ensuring that the designer and design peer adhere to goals and objectives set down for the walkthrough. The walkthrough can be done in stages as each phase of the design nears completion.
- *Designer peer*—This individual should possess skills similar to those of the designer. The peer's primary responsibility is to evaluate each phase of the design looking for errors, omissions, and improvements. The peer should feel free to offer any suggestions or criticisms at any time. Most designers feel an intense ownership in their designs and often consider criticism as a personal attack. Peer reviewers should avoid personal criticisms and the walkthrough coordinator should be prepared to mediate disputes.
- *Note taker*—Having someone dedicated to documenting the walkthrough ensures adequate documentation and frees others to concentrate on their assigned tasks.

Phase 8: Implementation

It is an easy temptation to view implementation as the work of other departments, vendors, or subcontractors. To take this view, particularly when the design replaces a legacy system, is to invite inevitable problems with schedules.

As each phase of the installation is completed, it must be tested for proof of concept and any deficiencies corrected. Acceptance testing is a critical phase in the design process and should be addressed with care. Performance factors such as response time and useable bandwidth should be specified in the RFP and measured during acceptance testing. Vendors should be required to demonstrate successful implementation, particularly with new and unproven technology and critical components.

CASE STUDY

Smith, Smith, Halverson, Jones, and Black are a Portland, Oregon–based law firm that has contracted with you to recommend a design for a local area network to be installed in their new building. The firm will occupy all three of the floors in an older warehouse-style brick building that is currently under renovation and scheduled for occupancy in approximately six months.

The firm expects to continue its 12% annual growth rate. Currently, the firm consists of 5 senior partners, each of whom has a personal assistant. There are also 5 general partners and 27 associate attorneys. An office manager supervises 5 paralegals, 15 secretaries, 1 accountant, 1 bookkeeper, and 1 receptionist.

The third floor will be occupied by the senior partners, their personal assistants, a large conference room, and the law library. The second floor is to be occupied by the general partners, associate attorneys, and the paralegals, with the secretarial pool, accounting, and reception on the first floor.

The primary goals of the network are to enhance communications, automate attorney billable hour reporting, consolidate the client files, and provide quick access to a large legal database. Toward these ends the firm would like all employees to be connected for Email. The partners have asked that the library be equipped with workstations that are capable of accessing both the company's legal database as well as the Internet for legal research. You have also been requested to offer suggestions that might improve the stated goals.

You have been asked to use existing software and hardware where possible. Currently, hardware consists of several 80286 and 80386 clones, some dot matrix printers, and three laser printers. Most of the secretaries are using WordPerfect version 5.1 for MS-DOS and maintain their own client lists. Accounting is using an older DOS-based version of Peachtree.

The following is a proposal, submitted by the son of one of the general partners, who is taking a course in network design. As you read the proposal, consider each section as it relates to the eight design phases previously discussed. Note any deficiencies and be prepared to offer alternatives and suggestions of your own.

Network Design Proposal
for
Smith, Smith, Halverson, Jones, and Black

PROPOSAL TO MANAGEMENT

Overview

Networking

The proposed network organization revolves around the enterprise workgroups that currently exist [see Figure 14.3]:

- Senior partners and executive assistants
- General partners and associate attorneys
- Secretarial and paralegal
- Accounting

The network will consist of three centrally located file servers to which individual users will have access on an "as need" basis. The server labeled Accounting will contain all of the accounting applications and financial database information, which may include the billable hour reports from attorneys. The server labeled Applications will contain all of the word processing, client database, office management applications, electronic mail, "groupware" scheduling and communications, and any other shared applications that are deemed appropriate. The third server is suggested as a client/server database that will contain any and all legal information and resources that might be used by attorneys.

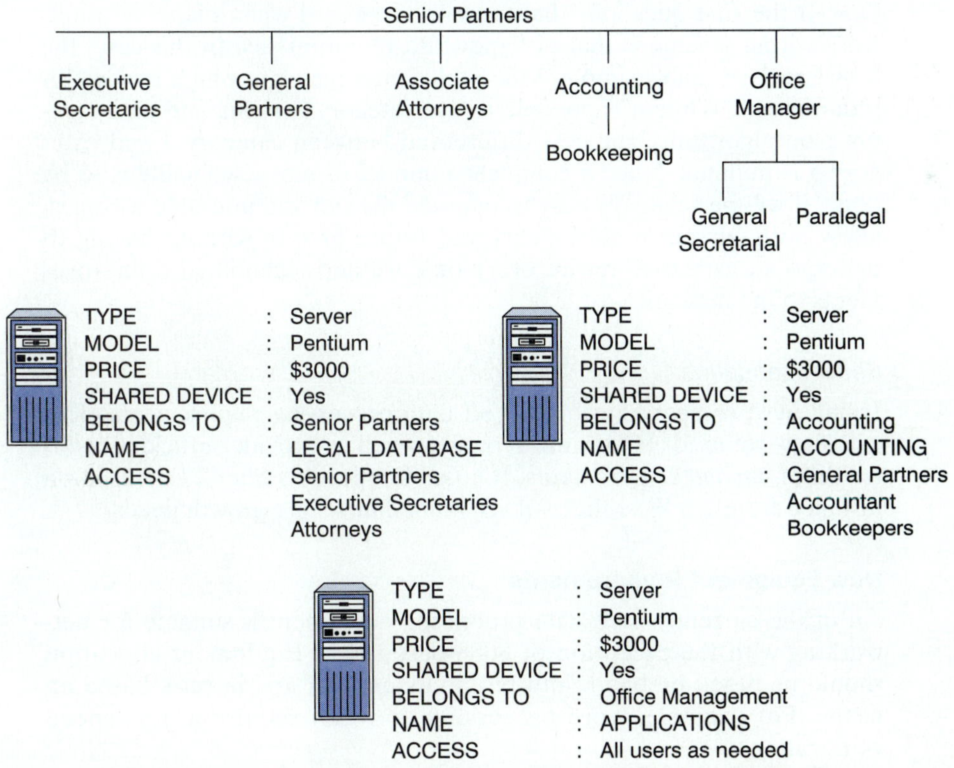

Figure 14.3 Smith, Smith, Halverson, Jones, and Black Organizational Chart

Each user is anticipated to have a suitable networked workstation on their respective desks. This will, of course, require the purchase of additional equipment. It is recommended that the 8088-based PCs be upgraded to allow standardization of Microsoft Windows as the operating system. However, all of the printers are perfectly useable. Laser printers should be installed on the network in a shared mode, where applicable, and on individual desks as required. Dot matrix printers may be shared or assigned to local workstations.

New installations should include the following:

- A law library kiosk of four or more workstations and a shared laser printer with connection to the Internet for research.
- The main conference room wired so that notebook computers can be networked during conferences. Wireless LAN technologies are ideal for this purpose, although they are admittedly expensive. A fiber optic network connection is also recommended that will allow video teleconferencing in a large screen presentation format.

Physical Installation

One of the first questions that must be answered when planning a network wiring scheme is that of bandwidth requirements. In this case, the answer is reasonably simple. Video teleconferencing is a high-bandwidth requirement. While it is possible to use category 3 wiring and data compression algorithms, the cost differential between category 3 and category 5 is minimal. Since a complete remodel of our new facility is to be done, it will be relatively easy to upgrade the old and unusable wiring to allow both current requirements and future growth without having to undergo an expensive rewire every time we add technological improvements to the network.

Recommendation

Install new, category 5 cable for all data processing requirements. This will allow room for bandwidth growth as well as provide sufficient bandwidth for current requirements. If possible, specify a fiber T1 connection installed from US West that will accommodate future growth needs.

New Equipment Requirements

All of the currently used data processing equipment is suitable for networking with the exception of 8088-based PCs. Equipment allocation should be based on bandwidth requirements that are, in turn, based on usage. For example, word processing does not require a high-speed workstation.

Recommendations

Workstation Usage	Computer Equip. Model	Quantity	Cost (est.)
Network servers	Pentium 200 based computers	4	$10000 each
Attorney teleconferencing workstations	Pentium 200 based computers	49	$ 1500 each
Secretarial workstation	Pentium 166 based computers	32	$ 1100 each
Accounting/bookkeeping	Pentium 166 based computers	3	$ 1100 each
Wireless conference room	$1200 per hookup plus $5000 for large screen teleconference display.		

Software Considerations

Each network server will require an operating system. Choices must be made to determine whether the interfaces will be graphical (Windows, etc.) or text (MS-DOS) based. In addition, the communications server will need appropriate software to interface with US West services and the choice of client/server database will need to be made.

From a management perspective, it is sometimes wise to "standardize" employee use of application software packages. Issues such as licensing, support, and training are more easily managed, and there are potential cost savings. Unfortunately, individual users become very attached to applications with which they are comfortable and highly productive. From the network manager's point of view, any properly licensed application currently in use that is network-compatible can be easily installed in a server and shared by all. If standardization is desired, policies may be implemented to provide an "approved list" for future software purchases. We need not spend additional money on standardized software until it is needed.

Recommendations

- Server operating system: Microsoft NT

  NT offers excellent security, graphical interface, group scheduling and E-mail, and network management support. In addition, licensing costs are less than those of Novell NetWare, NT's strongest competitor.
- MS-DOS-based applications need not deal with the graphical interface if they do not wish to. Automatic menuing can be programmed to allow MS-DOS users to "see" screen forms they are used to.

- Windows for Workgroups, Windows 95, or Windows NT can be installed in each workstation, as requested, for graphical interface. You may wish to encourage a migration to the Windows environment so that the excellent workgroup scheduling and conferencing software can be used by all employees.

Alternative

Microsoft NT licenses are less expensive than NetWare; however, it should be noted that NT is a new system and does not have a long history of stability even though there are no reports of instability as yet. NetWare is a proven stable platform with a large installed customer base and a relatively good supply of trained administrators. There is significant support and third-party software available for NetWare.

- Legal research server: Numerous databases exist for legal research and can be purchased and installed as needed. The current CD-ROM "jukebox" technology presents an ideal storage media for this type of data. It is also possible to combine the legal and accounting servers into a single unit although hard-drive capacity may soon be filled. Total savings by combining servers is estimated to be $3,500.
- Users should be allowed to continue using their preferred applications so long as they are properly licensed and are network compatible. Future purchases should come from an approved and standardized list.
- E-Mail: The Internet service that is selected will provide an E-mail format for external Internet use. Internally, any of the commonly available packages such as Microsoft Mail or Lotus CC:Mail would be suitable. Arrangements have been made to provide some "evaluation" samples. Standardizing on a Windows interface would provide both internal and dial-up E-mail service as well as "groupware" services.

Telecommunications

A fourth server is recommended that will replace the current, outmoded, and overloaded PBX system. By converting telecommunications to a network-based format, significant improvements, such as teleconferencing, fax on demand, and automatic call routing can be made to the overall communications effort.

- Workstations can be configured to access networked fax and data modems, eliminating the need for most of the stand-alone fax and data modems. An Internet service provider and the Internet will be accessible from the workstation without the need for modems in workstations.
- Remote access via modem from home or elsewhere will be possible through the communications server. Microsoft NT contains an excellent remote access service.

User Training

- The network manager will create and implement a training program for all users prior to moving into the new facility.
- A temporary "training LAN" should be set up and users scheduled for training and practice as needed.
- Written user manuals should be distributed prior to training sessions and will become the basis for training.
- No additional equipment or software cost is anticipated for this training although some productivity will be lost if training occurs during normal work hours.

Network Design

Figure 14.4 shows an overview of the preliminary network design.

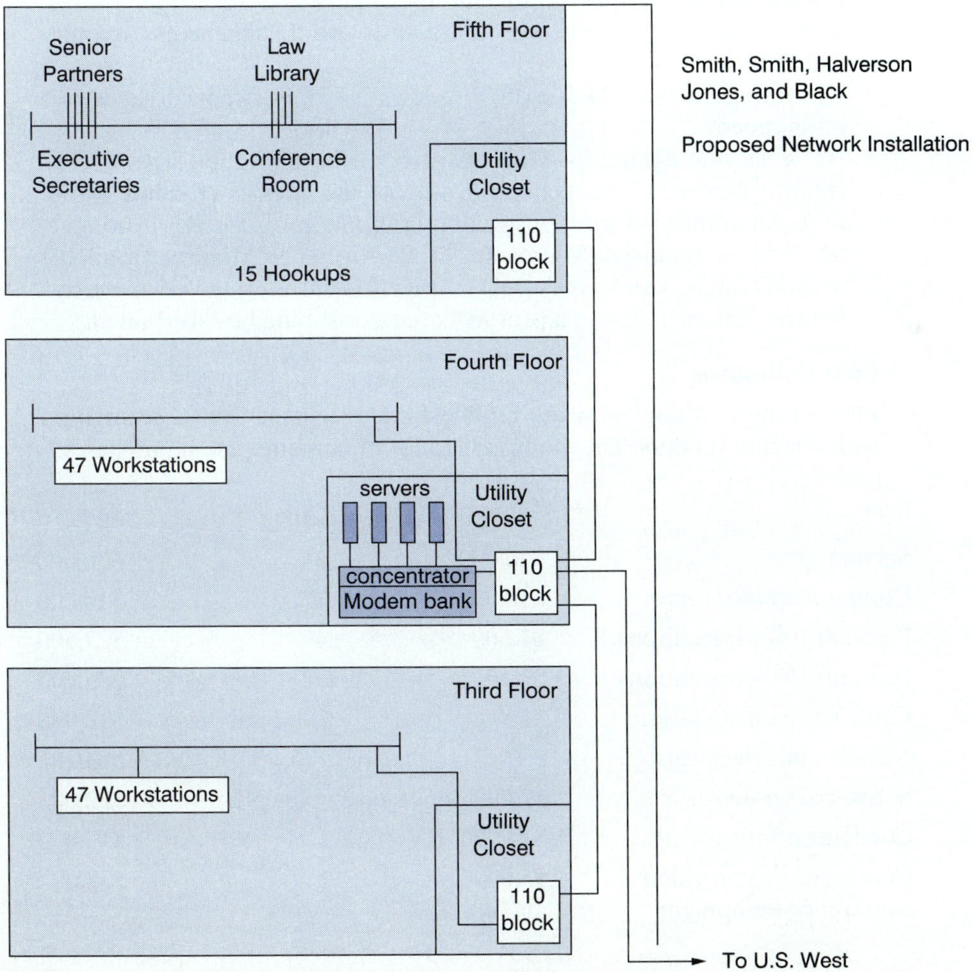

Figure 14.4 Preliminary Design

- Protocol—The network workstations will be connected using the time tested Ethernet protocol. Ethernet is relatively inexpensive and very easy to maintain.
- Topology—All workstation network nodes connected via 10BaseT using category 5 cable terminating in RJ-45 connectors and 110 blocks as appropriate. Communications server to teleconferencing link recommended in 100BaseTx over category 5 cable.
- LAN Segmentation—All network nodes will be centrally connected to an intelligent concentrator located in the first-floor utility room. The use of an intelligent concentrator will provide equipment security, improved maintenance and network management, increased flexibility for upgrades and improvements, and isolation of network segments. Incoming lines from US West will converge at the concentrator.
- Security—All incoming access shall be through firewall security with domain access and passwords required. Users shall be assigned server access on an "as needed" basis. Passwords and domain access accounts will be required.
- Operating system—Microsoft Windows NT Advanced Server is recommended.
- Network management—Concentrator to be equipped with SNMP (Simple Network Management Protocol) and RMON (Remote Monitor). An additional cable tester and crimping tools for RJ-45 connectors will be required. Microsoft NT Performance Monitor (available with NT at no extra cost) will be used for monitoring server performance. Rental access to a protocol analyzer should be ascertained.

Cost Estimates

Please note that the below are retail estimates and subject to negotiation with selected vendors. The following is a list of new equipment purchases.

Item	*Estimated Cost*	*Quantity*	*Total Cost*
Servers	$10,000	3	$30,000
Communications server	$10,000	1	$10,000
Pentium 200 workstations	$1,500	49	$73,500
Pentium 166 workstations	$1,100	32	$35,200
Cable wiring installation	$100 per drop	109 total drops	$10,900
Network interface cards	$80	113	$9,040
Software (server)	$2,000 per 10 users plus NOS		$22,600
Concentrator	$17,000	1	$17,000
Conference room video conference equipment	$5,000	1	$5,000

Item	*Estimated Cost*	*Quantity*	*Total Cost*
Conference room wireless LAN	$1,200/hookup	10	$12,000
Total			$225,240

Alternatives

- There are 18 workstations, currently in use, that will be suitable for network use. Use of this equipment will reduce the above cost by approximately $14,300.
- An additional $10,000 can be saved by combining the legal and accounting servers into a single unit.
- If faster access to the Internet is deemed necessary, an additional T1 line and router can be installed in the second-floor wire room. Anticipate a minimum cost of $2,000 for the router plus $300–$500 to install a T1 line. Monthly service charges for T1 service can be as low as $30/month to as much as $1,200/month depending on bandwidth and class of service.

CASE STUDY DISCUSSION QUESTIONS

1. Considering each of the eight design phases, which of them were adequately addressed?
2. Which of the design phases were *in*adequately addressed?
3. Can you offer additional alternatives that would be appropriate to the design?
4. Does the proposal adequately justify the cost of the design?
5. What recommendations would you make to either lower the cost or improve the benefits of the design proposal?

Training for network administrators and users is often begun during the implementation phase. Training should be given a good deal of careful thought during the design. It does no good to install a network no one knows how to use or maintain effectively. A new network often requires additional staffing. Sufficient lead time should be designed in to accommodate the hiring process and any training the new employees might require.

Because of the truly explosive growth of networking and telecommunications, an interesting anomaly has begun to appear in many organizations. Referred to as *absorption gap*, the ability of individuals to absorb the knowledge of all of the new innovations in a timely manner is increasingly more difficult. Designers may be wise to carefully consider the rate at which people can truly learn what they need to know about the new network.

CHAPTER REVIEW

- The three basic reasons for installing a network are as follows:
  1. Organizational needs
  2. Political advantage
  3. Technical superiority
- The design process includes eight steps or phases, each of which requires a written report to management.
  1. Organizational strategy and needs analysis
  2. Technical requirements
  3. Availability analysis
  4. Alternatives
  5. Cost benefit analysis
  6. Final selection and design
  7. Design review
  8. Implementation
- Items included in a traffic analysis include the number of users, message quantity and length, peak load times, and maximum acceptable response time.

  Prudent designers should remember that political considerations often supersede technical and organizational requirements.
- In choosing alternatives, be careful to minimize personal bias. Bias should also be kept out of written reports as much as possible.
- Alternative analysis should include second sourcing, alternate protocols, alternative choices for hardware and software, and service/support/training alternatives.
- All designs must include a cost-benefit analysis.
- Security should be considered at ingress/egress points and for the environment that contains servers, routers, gateways, and telecommunications equipment.
- Disaster recovery plans should include a cost-benefit analysis that weighs the cost of lost data and opportunity against the cost of rapid and accurate backup and recovery systems.
- Requests For Proposals (RFPs) are written for submission to vendors.

- Design reviews should include structured walkthroughs.
- Design implementation must include acceptance testing.

REVIEW QUESTIONS

1. List the eight phases of a network design process and the key tasks that must be accomplished in each phase.
2. What is the final step in each of the phases?
3. Why are political values important to a network designer?
4. Why must the designer evaluate organizational needs?
5. List the 12 factors that are considered in a needs analysis.
6. List the five requirements that should be considered in user interviews.
7. What are the factors included in a traffic analysis?
8. What is the end result of a traffic analysis?
9. When would you recommend shielded cable?
10. When would you recommend fiber optic cable?
11. When would you recommend using old, voice quality twisted pair?
12. Why is personal bias a problem for network designers?
13. How can you help minimize bias?
14. List the four categories of alternatives that should be included in your report.
15. How much additional capacity should you design into a network and why?
16. Where would you begin designing security into your network?
17. What are RMON agents used for?
18. What is RAID?
19. What is an RFP used for?
20. Describe a structured walkthrough.

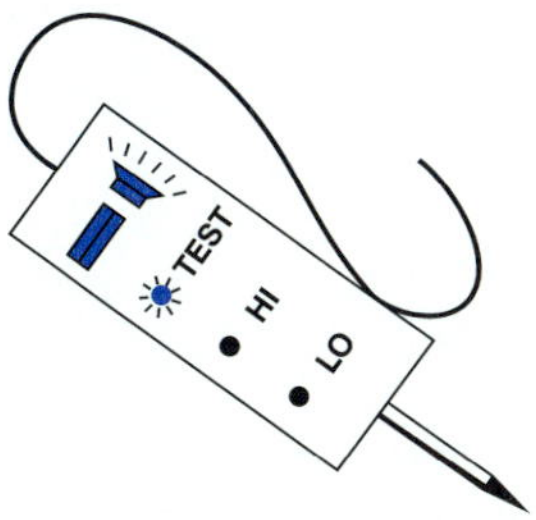

15

Network Performance Tuning and Troubleshooting

INTRODUCTION

Network administrators can save a great deal of time and effort if they make a few relatively simple observations and calculations before the network is designed and installed. First, determine who will use the network and how they will use it. From the previous chapter you will recall that the traffic analysis done during the design stage will supply the necessary information to enable a reasonably accurate estimate of bandwidth requirements.

Following installation, these same observations should be reviewed periodically to ensure that the intended design parameters continue to be met. One thing is for certain: few networks remain static. One must always consider the eventuality of growth in both the demand for network services and the number of network users.

Topics covered in this chapter will include

- measuring and estimating network traffic,
- effects of bridging and routing,
- measuring and estimating performance, and
- server tuning.

PERFORMANCE TUNING

Measuring and Estimating Network Traffic

Several useful measurements of network traffic can be made. For example, certain hours of a normal workday, such as 8 A.M., when everyone is trying to log on, can be used to determine the degree to which the available bandwidth is being used. Referred to as *peak load,* these measurements or estimates should be made for peak hour of the day, day of the week, week of the month, and month of the year. In the design of new networks, peak message load combined with frame header and trailer overhead are the values that will determine the amount of bandwidth the network will need. Be certain to provide a generous-reserve bandwidth to accommodate growth.

Ethernet

From Chapter 4, you will remember that Ethernet is a probabilistic protocol. We can calculate the overhead for each frame passed but must collect empirical data from the cable to measure true throughput since there is no effective way to predict collisions.

From Figure 15.1, you can see that each Ethernet frame contains 26 bytes per frame, not counting the data field. These 26 bytes are called *overhead*. Each Ethernet frame must have a minimum of 46 data bytes and may have up to a maximum of 1,500 data bytes. A minimum Ethernet frame would then contain a total of 72 bytes; a maximum frame, 1,526 bytes.

Some relatively simple math can now be used to calculate the required bandwidth in bits per second.

$$\text{Bit rate in bits/second} = \frac{\text{frames/message} * \text{frame size} * 8 \text{ bits/byte} * \text{activity frequency}}{3600 \text{ seconds/hour}}$$

Typical activities would include such things as E-mail transfers, print jobs, program and data downloads, and saving data to the server. Unfortunately, the number of frames per message is an estimate that might be off by as much as 50% if accurate measurements cannot be taken. Activity frequency can be observed and recorded, time permitting, but is still subject to error simply due to changing job requirements.

Table 15.1 shows a form loaded with some typical activities. A network designer would create this form for every job activity and every user on a pro-

Figure 15.1 Ethernet Frame Format

Preamble	Destination	Source	Type	Data	FCS
8 OCTETS	6 OCTETS	6 OCTETS	2	46–1500 OCTETS	4

Table 15.1 Traffic Bit Rate Estimation Form

Job Activity	Message Size (bytes)	Frames/ Message	Frame Size (bytes)	Number of Activities/Hour	Total Bit Rate (bits/second)
Download program					
Download graphic					
Download data					
Receive E-mail					
Send E-mail					
Print text data					
Print graphic image					
Upload data					

posed network. At periodic intervals, following installation, it would be prudent to compare actual measurements to estimated values to track growth of the network.

Each activity will need to be analyzed to determine the average number of bytes per message. For example, downloading or saving graphical images would produce considerably larger message sizes than simple E-mail datagrams. You might expect that data entry personnel, engineers, and CAD operators would require more bandwidth than, say, word processors, managers, or bookkeepers.

Table 15.2 lists some relative values for bit rate requirements for common job activities. While you should not assume that these are typical values, you can relate the total bit rate requirements to the available bandwidth of your network.

With a resulting bit rate total in excess of 4 Mbps, it is clear that a single 4-Mbps Token-Ring, 2-Mbps ARCNET, or 1-Mbps AppleTalk segment would be entirely unsuitable. A 10-Mbps Ethernet LAN would be 43% saturated with a bit rate of 4.33 Mbps (4.33/10). Given the probabilistic nature of Ethernet, it is usually recommended that *saturation levels should not exceed 30%-40%.* Thus, our example, although it may be marginally suitable for today's use, would allow no growth whatsoever and might not even be able to accommodate peak loading periods without excess collisions.

Table 15.2 Traffic Bit Rate Estimates

Job Activity	Bit Rate (Bits/second)
Managers	90,105
Bookkeepers	115,000
Secretaries	165,415
Engineers	1,850,412
Drafters	2,116,740
Total estimated bit rate	4,337,672

One method that could be used to alleviate congestion would be to break the network into two segments by installing a bridge or switch. Engineering, Management, and Bookkeeping might be put on one segment and Drafting and Secretaries on the other. The Drafting/Secretaries segment would now be at 22.7% saturation; Engineering/Management/Bookkeeping, 23.2% saturation. Each segment is now well below the maximum recommended saturation rates and could grow to nearly double its respective bit rate usage without adversely affecting performance.

Token-Ring

Token-Ring is a deterministic protocol that offers two important features to the network designer. First, bit rates can be accurately calculated because there are no collisions to contend with. The absence of collisions provides the second advantage in that saturation levels can easily be taken to as much as 90%–95% with no reduction in response time. Where 10-Mbps Ethernet LANs cannot provide effective bit rates in excess of 4 Mbps, on a busy segment, Token-Ring will perform admirably with an effective bit rate of as much as 15.5 Mbps on a 16-Mbps ring.

Designers must then weigh bandwidth requirements and traffic types against both the useable bandwidth of a given protocol and its cost. Where Token-Ring might be thoroughly justified for the high-bandwidth usage of engineers, drafters, and graphic designers, its cost might be considered prohibitive for the local office network consisting of managers, secretaries, and accounting.

From Figure 15.2 you can see the overhead of the three types of Token-Ring frames. A standard token consists of 3 bytes; an abort token, 2 bytes. Without the optional routing field, Token-Ring data frame overhead is 21 bytes. The routing field need only be included in overhead calculations for a single segment. Where frames are routed to other segments, the maximum size of the routing field is 18 bytes, which provides for a 2-byte description of each route and a maximum of 16 hops.

The data field can contain anywhere from 1 to 4,500 bytes for a 4-Mbps ring or 18,000 bytes on a 16-Mbps ring. This means that overhead as a percentage of data sent can range from a minimum of 0.01% for an 18,000 data byte frame to 2,100% when only 1 data byte is transferred.

Bridging and Routing Effects

As LANs grow, the installation of bridges or switches to separate segments and routers to connect to other networks introduces a new set of problems for network designers and administrators. Bridges and routers introduce delay into the equation. Delay can be caused by the wide area link operating at a slower speed than the local network or by the delay caused by insufficient buffers in the bridge or router itself.

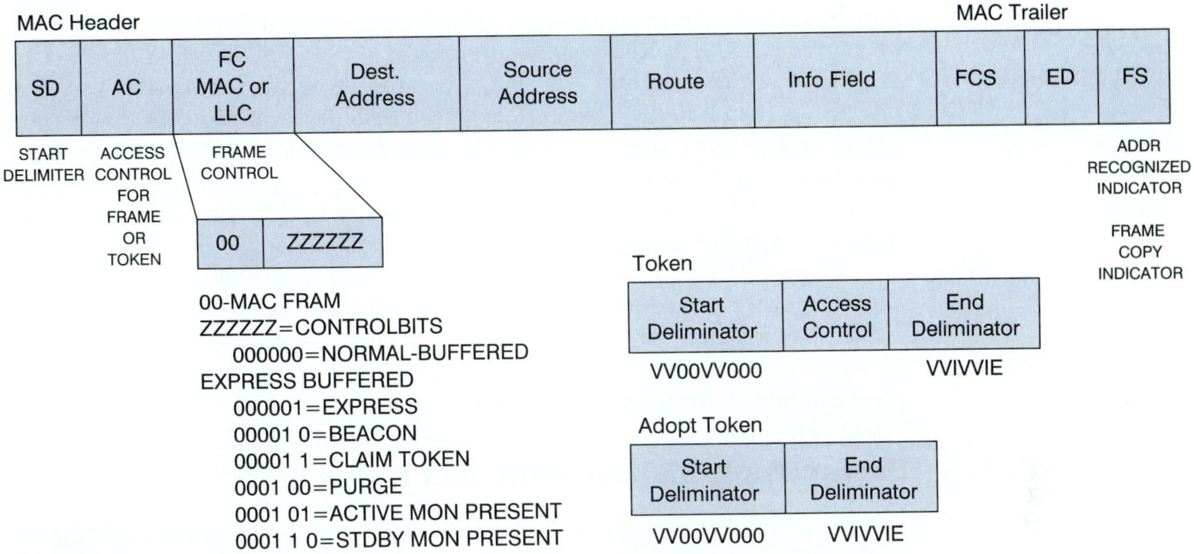

Figure 15.2 Token-Ring Frame Format

Higher-bandwidth protocols such as Fast Ethernet or ATM might cure the delay problem but will only do so at significantly increased cost. The cure for insufficient buffers is simply to add more memory to the bridge or router if possible. The purchasing decision for one of these components should include the ability to expand memory as the network grows.

Another method used to reduce queuing delay is to add additional lines between bridges or routers so that each device is capable of passing frames from its input queue to the first available line. Keep in mind, however, the cost of adding and maintaining the additional lines, particularly if they are being leased.

One of the most common methods used to minimize queue delay is to filter the source and destination addresses so that addresses on a local segment cannot be passed to a remote segment. Nearly all bridges and routers support this feature.

As the utilization of the network server increases, queuing delay will become increasingly noticeable. Up to 50% server utilization, the queue delay is usually tolerable, but as utilization approaches 100%, queue delay can approach infinity for a single-server, single-bridged line. The rule of thumb is to reduce the size of a network segment or increase the bandwidth of the line(s) connecting segments whenever server utilization exceeds 50%.

Most of the cures that will improve throughput and response time over wide area links must be weighed against significantly increased costs. The cost of maintaining a 1.54-Mbps T1 line, for example, often exceeds $800 per month in addition to the cost to install the line. Adding memory to a bridge may be a relatively lower cost, say, $4–$5 per megabyte for DRAM, considerably more if high-speed SRAM is required.

One of the currently available wide area protocols that can be very cost-effective is Frame Relay. Frame Relay is the datalink layer protocol that is transparent to transport layer protocols. In each LAN segment a router or FRAD must be connected to a T1 line, but billing is done on a pay-as-you-go basis, and most of the RBOCs do not charge for oversubscription data rates during off peak hours. With Frame Relay, users have scaleable bandwidth on demand.

A no-cost technique for more effective use of available bandwidth is to simply require nonessential traffic to be delayed and sent during off-peak hours. Any job that can be batch processed can be scheduled for transmission at night. Summary reports, database reconciliations, and system backups are ideal candidates for off-peak-hour processing.

Server Usage Measurement and Tuning

Server factors that can affect a network's performance typically include the following:

- Speed of server and workstation computers—CPU and I/O speed affect data transfer rates. Insufficient RAM limits the number of concurrent processes and may cause excessive page swapping between memory and disk subsystems.
- Disk subsystem speed and storage capacity—Disk drives are among the slower computer components; improving disk speed improves network performance. The fastest disk subsystems currently available are *Small Computer System Interface* (SCSI), *Enhanced Small Devices Interface* (ESDI), and *Integrated Device Electronics* (IDE). The amount of permanent data and program storage is directly related to the size of the hard drive.
- Server bus characteristics—The older *Industry Standard Architecture* (ISA) bus runs at 8-10 MHz using 8- or 16-bit data transfers. *Extended industry standard architecture* (EISA) and IBM's *Microchannel Architecture* (MCA) improves bus speed to 10–12 MHz with 32-bit data transfers. The newer Intel-designed *Peripheral Component Interface* (PCI) allows 64-bit data transfers at the same speed that the CPU can transfer data to RAM, typically 33 MHz using standard architecture or 100 MHz in some high-performance servers.
- Specially designed multiprocessor servers, such as those offered by Digital Equipment, IBM, Compaq, and Hewlett-Packard, will significantly improve the server's overall processing capability. Recently there has been a trend in some of the larger shops to employ very high-speed, high-storage capacity mainframes as servers where more traditional PC style designs cannot meet demands.

- Adapter speed, bus width, and network protocol will all affect network performance. Switching to 10/100-Mbps Ethernet hubs is a relatively low-cost way to increase bandwidth over existing category 5 wiring. Workstations that need the increased speed can install higher-speed NICs; those that do not can retain their 10-Mbps NICs.
- Replacing hubs with switches is also a relatively low-cost method for improving performance, particularly on Ethernet segments. An all-switched segment eliminates collision problems and enables all nodes to utilize maximum available bandwidth. This would more than double throughput on a 10-Mbps Ethernet LAN.

TUNING THE SERVER OPERATING SYSTEM

Increasingly, network operating systems are reducing the number of parameters that can be changed to improve performance. The claim is that, over time, empirical data indicate optimal settings for many of a server's parameters, thus eliminating the need to fine-tune them. This section will point out those that can be changed in current versions of NetWare and NT, but do not be surprised when future versions lock you into "optimized" values.

Tuning NT

NT comes equipped with a utility called *Performance Monitor*. Performance Monitor provides information concerning these elements:

- *Cache*—the rate at which pages are cached to disk and the effective "hit rate" of instructions in the CPU high-speed RAM cache
- *Logical disk*—the read/write cache activity to determine hard disk performance
- *Memory*—disk partitions and volumes
- *Paging file*—server RAM usage looking for memory bottlenecks
- *Physical disk*—disk performance for both single- or RAID drive systems
- *Process*—application sessions
- *Processor*—CPU performance
- *Redirector*—requests for server access and errors
- *Server*—server/network performance
- *System*—the local system and file performance

Performance Monitor will maintain event logs and provide alerts when important events occur. Screen views are presented in chart, log, alert, and report windows.

A program, only available to administrators, called *DISKPERFI,* can be run to record disk activity that Performance Monitor uses to calculate performance. Based on the results, NT allows the following parameters to be adjusted to improve performance:

- *Create stripped sets*—Stripped sets are sets of partitions from several disks that are combined into a single logical volume. Performance is increased because a stripped set can issue concurrent requests to different disk drives rather than waiting for a single serial disk read or write.
- *Delete partitions*—remove unused partitions or combine partitions to balance I/O controller and volume activity
- *Create paging files*—Normally, excess page swapping is an indication of insufficient RAM. Increasing the number of pages that can be stored in main memory, assuming enough RAM is available, will reduce the number of page swaps to slow hard disks.
- *Balance I/O across drivers*—allows disk activity to be balanced so that no one I/O controller is over used
- *Cluster size*—As hard drive capacities exceed 500 Mb, cluster size on NT machines is automatically incremented. If your server is used to store very large files, this can be an advantage. If, on the other hand, your server is more often used to pass smaller files, you can significantly increase drive space usage by creating smaller partition sizes before installing NT. Leave all but C: unformatted so that volume sets may be created from free space on unformatted partitions.

Tuning NetWare

One of the first NetWare server performance decisions to be made deals with hard disk block, volume, and partition sizes. During installation, you will be queried as to your preferred block size. In NetWare, blocks may be 4 K, 8 K, 16 K, 32 K, or 64 K. NT does not allow the administrator to set block sizes; however, the NTFS disk format provides a built-in method for faster access to large files.

Selecting a particular block size depends on the type of data stored in the server. In servers where the average size of files exceeds 64 K, the percentage of overhead is minimized by using large block sizes. Where files are typically 1–2 K, using a 64-K block would result in a great deal of wasted drive space. In a typical single server LAN, block size is usually set at either 4 or 8 K to strike a balance between small and large file sizes. Whichever block size you select, remember that block size may only be changed by reinstalling NetWare. Version 4.x of NetWare provides for a subblock allocation of file storage so that relatively empty blocks can have unused bytes allocated to storage for other files.

The NetWare Monitor NLM can be run on the server console to monitor performance statistics in a text base presentation format. When the performance results indicate the need for tuning, a user with supervisor privileges must log in from a workstation and use the SET command to change the required parameter. In version 4.x, at the console, the SERVMAN.NLM can also be loaded to set some of NetWare's variables.

The following parameters can be modified by the SET command:

- *Memory performance*—NetWare creates buffer areas in memory that can be changed, dynamically, to suit current NOS demands. A primary buffer area called the *file cache buffer* pool is created that serves buffer storage to other processes on request and to which a finished process will return buffer space no longer needed. Server memory is divided into three different pools:

    1. *Permanent memory*—Used for long-term requirements such as directory and packet receive buffers.
    2. *File cache buffers*—These buffers store the current most frequently used files. A movable pool requests file cache buffers for dynamic system file allocation and hash tables. A second nonmovable pool holds the NLMs that are currently loaded.
    3. *Alloc memory*—This memory pool stores short-term processes such as NLMs, queue management tables, drive mappings, SAP tables, service request buffers, open/lock files and semaphores, and user connection information.

- *File system performance*—NetWare provides for the caching of frequently used files in RAM to improve performance. In addition, disk writes are delayed for the most opportune write time by first writing to RAM and then putting the actual disk write process into a background operation. File-caching parameters may be set to optimize performance.
- *System processes*—Several parameters such as preemption and time-out are used to control the timing of network events. Maximum and minimum service processes and searches may also be set.
- *Threshold and warning parameters*—These parameters generate warning messages when thresholds set for other parameters are exceeded. They have no direct effect on performance rather; they are used to alert the system administrator of impending performance problems.
- *Communications performance*—The number of receive packet buffers may be adjusted as can the timing parameters for network communications.

A second management tool is the SERVMAN NLM. SERVMAN provides the following capabilities:

- NetWare opsys parameter viewing and configuration
- Views and updates SET parameters in STARTUP.NCF and AUTOEXEC.NCF files
- Views disk volume information
- Views LAN adapter, device driver, and partition information
- Views network information
- Configures IPX/SPX parameters

At this point, take a look at the bibliography for additional references. It is considerably beyond the scope of this book to provide the specific details for all of the SET command parameters. A word of caution is also in order. Changing the parameters of any network OS can also adversely affect performance. A good rule of thumb is to monitor and record or log performance characteristics on a regular, or even continuous, basis but make no changes unless genuinely poor performance is noted. If you are not certain of the effect of a particular parameter, get help before proceeding because it is entirely possible to cause permanent damage that could only be cured by reinstalling the entire server! *In all cases, make parameter adjustments only after making a full backup of the server.*

TROUBLESHOOTING

Because troubleshooting sections have been included in preceding chapters, my purpose here is to summarize troubleshooting techniques, procedures, and equipment. Most troubleshooters will tell you that prevention is the most effective tool they have. Nothing is more irritating, not to mention time-consuming, than the continuous repair of poorly installed connectors, wiring, hardware, and software.

Numerous preventive measures may be taken to reduce the number of network failures:

- A good Uninterruptable Power Supply (UPS) can save not only time but also the cost of replacing equipment damaged by voltage surges or brownouts.
- Take the time, during installation, to ensure that all of the hardware and software components are correctly installed and accurately recorded in

your master network record. Being able to quickly find a faulty cable or workstation will save countless hours.

- A great deal of time may be saved if the troubleshooter can quickly refer to accurate documentation for the determination of hardware and software configurations. Develop the habit of carrying a notebook with you to record the solutions to problems, solutions that fail to fix the problem, and data that will need to be logged in permanent records.
- Where data stored on servers are critical, you may be able to justify the cost of drive-mirroring or RAID systems that contain hot swappable drives and power supplies. Replicating data to other servers or server mirroring can prevent downtime and data loss.

Documentation

In your master records, it is essential that you document the following:

- Switch and software settings for all hardware devices including: NICs, workstation and server motherboards, and any other plug-in boards that might affect the network.
- A major part of documentation is the labeling of each end of all the cable runs with corresponding entries in the master record.
- Note workstation configuration file contents such as AUTOEXEC.BAT, CONFIG.SYS, WIN.INI, and SYSTEM.INI. Also record the IRQ, DMA, and base I/O address settings for each of the device controllers in a workstation, CPU type, and memory quantity and style.
- Record network OS configuration files: NET.CFG for NetWare workstations and the AUTOEXEC.NCF and STARTUP.NCF files in NetWare servers. With NT, be certain to keep a backup of the registration database and all of the .INI files.
- Create and maintain a map of the physical location of each network component. A number of software packages will make this a much easier process, particularly those that contain SNMP and RMON agents.

Develop a troubleshooting plan for your help desk personnel. This should include a list of Frequently Asked Questions (FAQ) and answers as well as a flowchart that allows the troubleshooter to ask a series of logical questions that can lead to quick resolution. Figure 15.3 shows a sample troubleshooting chart. Some of the questions may seem too obvious, but to the untrained user they may not be. Be prepared to do some hand holding with your users. A little personal one-on-one training, early on, with a new user can pay big dividends in fewer calls to the help desk.

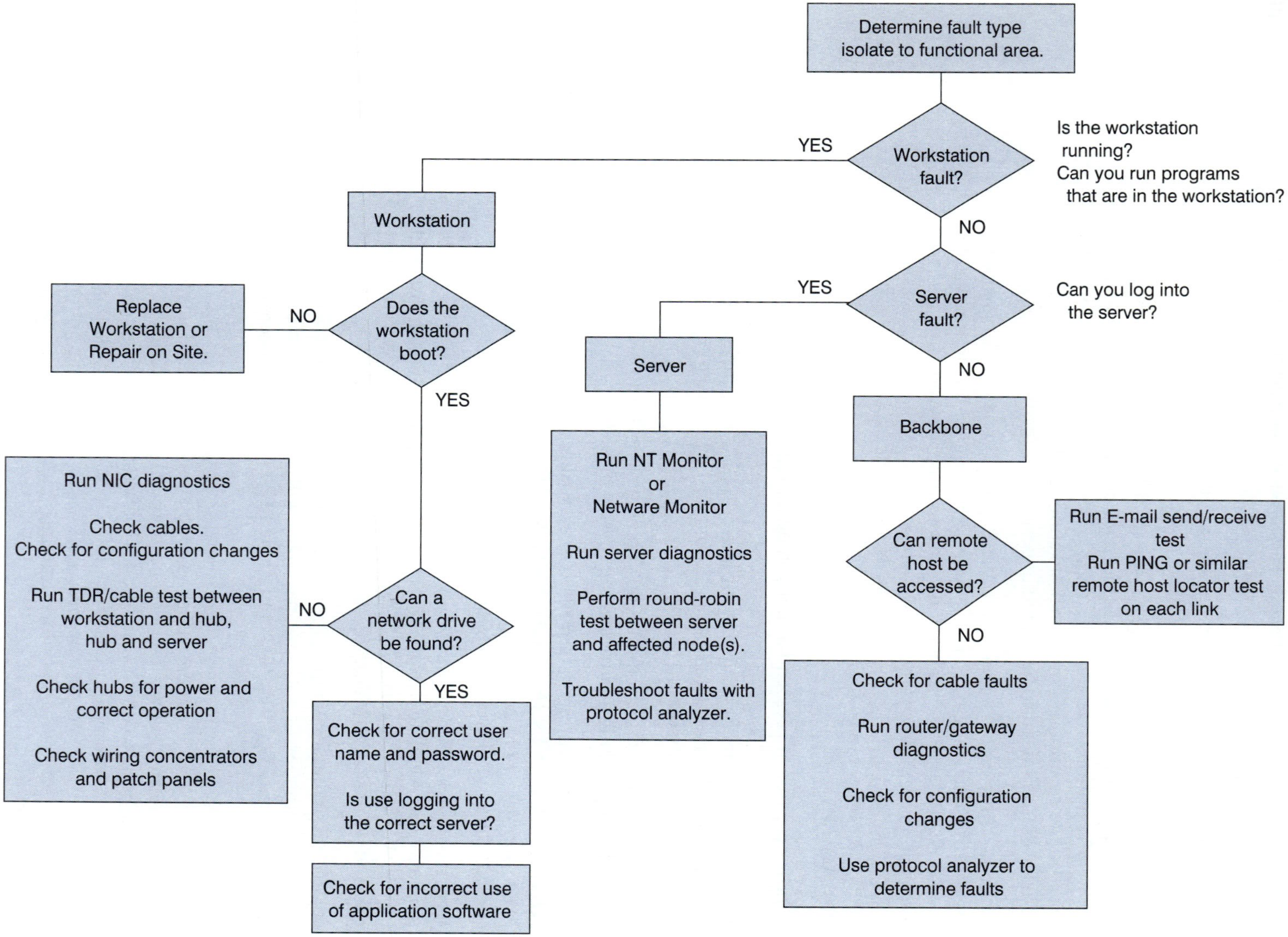

Figure 15.3 Simple Troubleshooting Tree

Test Equipment

There is no substitute for experience and proper test equipment when troubleshooting or tuning networks. Techniques that work well in one application may not provide the same results in others. Keep in mind that changes to one parameter of a network may adversely affect another. Much of the time, particularly in the absence of proper test equipment, the network administrator is reduced to a "best guess" at parameters such as user and cable activity. Therefore, empirical testing must be done. You take your best guess at the parameters, make a modification, and then observe and record the results. With common protocols such as Ethernet, Token-Ring, and TCP/IP, a great deal of empirical data already exist that you may use as a guide.

Let me repeat: there is no substitute for proper test equipment. Small office networks might get by with a simple cable tester, but a properly equipped network manager would also have a time domain reflectometer for each cable type including fiber optics, if used, plus a multiprotocol analyzer that is capable of capturing data for each protocol in use. These are not inexpensive items. Expect to pay in excess of $2,000 for a professional-quality cable tester or time domain reflectometer (TDR) and $15,000–$35,000 for your protocol analyzer. The cost justification for expensive test equipment is the estimate of the cost of downtime when the network fails (and it will!), plus the cost of lost opportunity and productivity when users sit idly by waiting for you to return a network to service.

Troubleshooting tips for wiring, Ethernet, Token-Ring, ARCNET, and FDDI have already been presented in their respective chapters. Therefore, the rest of this section will focus on the use of network protocol analyzers to capture data that will, in turn, allow a network technician to quickly identify problem areas. You will soon see that troubleshooting and fine-tuning a network without a protocol analyzer is similar to tuning your car's engine with a blindfold on.

Remember that protocol analyzers are generally capable of identifying each of the fields in an individual frame or packet, compiling selected statistics about the data being passed on the network, and identifying damaged frames and packets. With a protocol analyzer, one could capture statistics such as peak load and peak load times, peak users, and network saturation. Maximum and average frame size could be monitored and recorded. Overhead statistics could be analyzed to determine the percentage of the traffic that is local compared to that of packets from other networks. One could determine the statistics for router delay, internetwork response time, or the average number of unacknowledged packets or time-outs on transmitted packets.

Perhaps the greatest value provided by a protocol analyzer is the identification of defective frames and packets. A jabbering Ethernet NIC, for example, could be identified quickly and its node ID displayed on screen. Beaconing, common to Token-Ring, can be easily traced to the offending workstation. Packets containing encapsulated frames can be displayed to determine which of the protocols is responsible for a transmission error. In the hands of a skilled operator, the protocol analyzer is a truly formidable instrument.

Figure 15.4
Time Domain Reflectometer

CHAPTER REVIEW

- Traffic measurements include peak load, overhead, and congestion.
- Bandwidth calculations include frames per message, frame size, number of bits per character, and activity frequency.
- Traffic estimates should be made for each type of data transfer that will take place on the network. The traffic analysis begins with an analysis of job activities that includes interviews with potential users.

- High-bandwidth activities include graphics, multimedia voice and video, application downloads, server backups, and large file transfers.
- Low-bandwidth activities include E-mail, small file transfers, and data entry.
- Bridges and routers are nearly always congestion or choke points that produce delay in delivery and response times.
- Adding memory to bridge and router buffers and to servers can often reduce congestion and delay.
- Running batch-processing jobs and server backups during nonpeak load hours can significantly improve bandwidth utilization.
- Factors that improve network performance include faster processors and more memory in servers, workstations, bridges, and routers; faster disk drives; high-speed bus systems; multiprocessor servers; and higher-bandwidth physical media.
- Network operating systems can be tuned to maximize performance on specific segments. Block sizing, buffer allocation, RAM, and disk drive utilization are the main targets for performance tuning.
- NetWare uses the MONITOR.NLM to display and record performance statistics in a character-based format.
- NT uses PERFORMANCE MONITOR to display and record performance statistics in a graphical display format or log.
- The NetWare SET command is used to modify memory performance, file system performance, system processes, threshold and warning parameters, and communications performance.
- The NetWare SERVMAN.NLM can be used to view and configure NetWare parameters.
- Complete, accurate, and current documentation of all network parameters is one of the most effective tools used to maintain the network.
- Network test equipment includes cable testers, time domain reflectometers (TDRs), and network analyzers.

REVIEW QUESTIONS

1. Define the term *peak load*.
2. How many bits, in an Ethernet frame, are considered overhead? Why?
3. How many bits, in a Token-Ring frame, are considered overhead?
4. Why is overhead important to network designers and managers?
5. What is the formula for calculating bandwidth?

6. List three types of traffic that typically require high bandwidth.
7. What are the typical saturation rates for Ethernet and Token-Ring?
8. Why is the saturation rate of a Token-Ring higher than Ethernet?
9. Discuss the congestion and delay problems associated with bridges and routers.
10. What cures are available that can be used to reduce congestion and delay?
11. List five factors that affect a network's performance.
12. List the 10 performance factors that can be monitored using NT's Performance Monitor.
13. What are the five disk system performance factors that can be tuned on an NT server?
14. Why do striped sets improve performance?
15. Discuss the factors involved in setting the block size during a NetWare installation.
16. List the five parameters that can be modified using the NetWare *SET* command.
17. List the six functions of the NetWare SERVMAN.NLM.
18. What is the most important *first* step that must be done before changing a server parameter?
19. List the five essential things that should be documented on all networks.
20. Support your opinion concerning the creation of a written troubleshooting plan.
21. What is a network analyzer used for?
22. What is a TDR used for?

16 Network Administration and Security

MANAGING NETWORKS

There are four primary job classifications common to networks: network designers and engineers, network administrators, network technicians, and network support personnel. In many organizations, particularly smaller networks, some or all of the duties of each of these jobs falls on a single individual. This book is primarily aimed at administrator, technician, and support personnel but has necessarily included a glimpse at the responsibilities of the designer and engineer.

A *CNA* is a Certified Novell Administrator. A *MCP* is a Microsoft Certified Professional. A *CNE* and a *MCSE* are a Certified NetWare Engineer and a Microsoft Certified Systems Engineer, respectively.

This chapter will focus on the duties of the network administrator in a generalized sense. Readers interested in additional information are encouraged to enroll in courses leading to professional certifications such as Certified Novell Administrator (**CNA**) or Microsoft Certified Professional (**MCP**). The ultimate network certifications are Certified Novell Engineer (**CNE**) and Microsoft Certified Systems Engineer (**MCSE**). These certifications are becoming indispensable credentials for network professionals.

Responsibilities of the Network Administrator

Among the more common duties of network administration are

- installation of software and upgrades including network and client operating systems, applications, and utilities;
- adding new users and groups and maintaining the user database;

- creating and maintaining log-in scripts, menus, and icon groups;
- maintaining network security, assigning log-in IDs and passwords;
- making backups and implementing restores as needed;
- providing documentation, training, and user support;
- routine monitoring and maintenance of binderies and registration data bases, cable runs, and performance data; and
- providing justification to management for current and future network expenditures.

Managing users. When a network operating system is first installed, only one user is able to use it. NetWare 3.x names that user *supervisor*; NT and NetWare 4.x use *administrator* and *admin,* respectively. These users are granted the highest level of access to the operating system, including the right to create additional user accounts. No other users exist until a network administrator creates them.

The management of user accounts necessarily becomes one of the primary duties of a network administrator. You might imagine what it is like to manage a network with 1,000 users. There would undoubtedly be a daily requirement to either create a new account or update an existing account because a user was moving to a new location on the network or needed access to a different volume, server, or application.

NetWare is designed to accommodate four distinct user types:

- *Supervisor/admin*—Has all rights and privileges; can create and delete other users, modify user accounts and assign access rights for directories, files, and users.
- *Workgroup manager*—Created by supervisor to manage specified users and groups; can assign access rights to directories assigned by supervisor, create and delete users in assigned groups.
- *Manager*—Similar to workgroup manager but cannot delete users in assigned group.
- *User*—Not allowed to create or delete other users or change their own access rights; may, however, be given the right to grant their rights to other users

Microsoft NT user functions are, in many ways, similar to NetWare. An NT administrator is equivalent to a NetWare supervisor/admin. NT also allows the use of group accounts that may be managed by users who are members of the administrator, server operator, or account manager groups. NT also provides for *enterprise administrators* who manage the domain controllers in an NT multiserver/multidomain network. Between domains, users are granted *trusted relationships* for access to specified drives, directories, and files in another domain.

Nearly all shared resource computing environments grant some common rights and attributes to users and files. From MS-DOS you will remember that file attributes include Read Only, Hidden, Archived, and System. Network operating systems provide these basic file attributes and add others as well. It is through the assignment of file and directory rights, attributes, and access permissions that security on network resources is maintained.

This section will use terminology from NT and NetWare running on PC-based machines to describe attributes and rights. Be aware that different systems may use different naming conventions but the concepts will be similar. When using the term *attributes,* I will be referring to files and directories. The term *rights* is applied to users but may also be applied to files and directories. In general, rights determine what a user is allowed to do with files and directories to which access has been granted. Table 16.1a shows a list of the attributes available in NetWare. Attributes in NetWare apply to both files and directories. Although Microsoft documentation is not always consistent, for the most part, NT uses the term *permissions* to describe the access level that a user will have to shares, folders, and files. Access is determined at two levels: share level and folder/file level. NT then assigns rights to folders and, if in an NTFS partition, files as well. Table 16.1b lists the permissions available in NT.

NT adds ownership of files and directories as an attribute. Users who are owners may change permissions on any files or directories they own. This

Table 16.1a NetWare Attributes

Attribute	Definition
Archive	File contents changed since last backup
Copy Inhibit	Cannot copy or move file or directory
Delete Inhibit	Cannot delete file or directory
Execute Only	Applies to .exe/.com file extensions only. Copy, move, and read are inhibited.
Hidden	Hidden files and directories not displayed
Purge	Identifies file or directory as deleted but not removed from system
Read Only	May view contents but cannot change contents
Rename Inhibit	Cannot change file or directory name
Shareable	Allows multiple users to access file or directory simulaneously
System	Identifies files that are part of the operating system
Transactional	Used with transaction tracking to ensure that file updates are only made as complete transactions, partial updates caused by power failure not made

Table 16.1b NT Permissions

Permission	Definition
Read	Allows file or directory contents to be read
Write	Allows creation of subdirectories or files and changes to a file's data
Execute	Allows display of directory's attributes, permissions, and owner Allows execution of program files and display of attributes, permissions, and owner
Delete	Allows deletion of file or directory
Change Permissions	Allows changes to files or directory
Take Ownership	Allows changes to the ownership of files or directories
No Access	Not able to view contents of directory or any of its subdirectories
List	Allows viewing of file names and subdirectory names
Add	Allows files and subdirectories to be added to a directory
Add and Read	Allows file and subdirectory names to be viewed and changed Allows viewing data in files, running applications, and adding files and subdirectories
Change	Allows files and subdirectories to be viewed and changed or deleted
Full Control	Allows unlimited access, including changing permissions
Special Access	Determined by individual permissions granted by an owner

includes granting or denying access to other users, including administrators. Administrators can, however, seize control of a file or directory and override the owner's permissions. Administrators should probably consider security overrides as an invasion of privacy; not to be undertaken without good cause. Deleting files belonging to a user who has been deleted from the network is one good cause.

Table 16.2 is the list of available rights. NetWare is designed so that rights granted to any specific directory will be automatically *inherited* by all of the files and subdirectories contained in the specified directory. NT files and subdirectories do not automatically inherit permissions. Permissions must be explicitly assigned by either the owner or administrator.

Managing groups and domains. One of the more tedious jobs of the network administrator is the maintenance of users' access to servers and server files. Imagine the workload of a 1,000-user network if each user had to have a customized log-in script and menu! Suppose, however, that all of the users could be

Table 16.2 NetWare Rights

Right	Definition
Read	Allows file to be read and executed
Write	Allows files to be written to
Create	Allows new files to be created or files from other directories to be copied to the current directory
Erase	Allows files to be deleted
Access Control	Allows user to grant other users inherited rights to files and subdirectories in which the user has rights
File Scan	Allows files and subdirectories to be listed
Modify	Allows file and subdirectory names and attributes to be changed
Supervisor	Allows rights equivalent to Supervisor/Admin.

assigned to logical workgroups such as accounting, office, engineering, finance, management, and so forth. Your workload will be considerably reduced if you are only required to maintain rights for a few groups rather than each user.

Trustee assignments (NetWare) or *trusted relationships and shares* (NT domains and servers) for each group can be assigned that give all members of a group the same access rights to files and directories. The need to maintain rights for individual users is thus eliminated. A commonly suggested arrangement for group file and directory access is to give the group the same name as the primary directory or volume to which they are granted access. For example, members of the office group would be granted access to a directory or volume named *office*. Figure 16.1 shows a directory tree that depicts the group's access to office applications on a NetWare server.

In both NT and NetWare, *log-in scripts* can be created to automate routine chores such as identifying drives that the user will be accessing, displaying messages, or opening menus and launching applications. Two types of log-in scripts are available, the individual log-in script and a system log-in script that is executed whenever a user logs into a server. NetWare 4.x provides for container and profile (group) log-in scripts. The prudent NetWare administrator creates a system, container, or profile log-in script that executes all of the script requirements common to the group or container. Users are left to main-

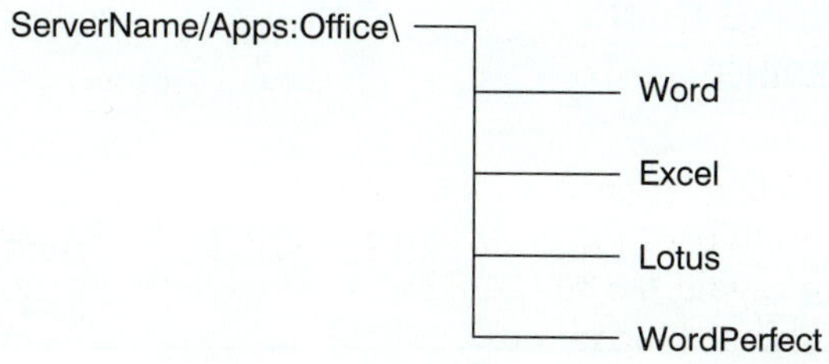

Figure 16.1 Directories Organized by Group Name

tain their own log-in scripts, if desired. Table 16.3 lists a sample default system log-in script.

Comments following the semicolons have been inserted to show the meaning of each of the script command lines. A REM script command would be used in an actual script file. The command MAP is used to declare a path in a specific NetWare volume/directory, in this case volume SYS:. The MAP INSERT commands are used to declare search paths in a manner similar to the MS-DOS PATH command. In the case shown in Table 16.3, the server would first search the current subdirectory and, if the executable file is not found, then search the PUBLIC subdirectory. The second search, S2, is used to find a copy of a COMMAND.COM file, compatible with the user's workstation, that has been stored in the server. Many more commands are available for creating log-in scripts. Time and space prevent more than a brief exposure to this powerful resource.

NT log-in scripts are much more akin to common DOS batch files and are limited to user log-in scripts. NT does, however, contain the ability to set system policies that determine access to desktop parameters, the control panel, and so forth. System policies are an effective method for preventing configuration damage caused by inquisitive but untrained users.

UNIX operating systems have a very powerful scripting capability that can take on many of the common programming constructs such as if-then-else-elsif and looping constructs similar to while-do and do-until. Menus can be constructed using a case construct. In addition to basic shell scripts, a more robust

Table 16.3 NetWare Default System Log-in Script

WRITE "Good%GREETING_TIME,%LOGIN_NAME."	;Display a greeting to user
MAP DISPLAY OFF	;Turn of map display to screen
MAP ERRORS OFF	;Don't show error reports
MAP *1:=SYS:	;First map is to root of vol SYS
MAP #2:=SYS:%LOGIN_NAME	;2nd map is to user's directory
IF "%1"="SUPERVISOR" THEN MAP *1:=SYS:SYSTEM	
MAP INSERT S1:=SYS:PUBLIC	;First search PUBLIC subdirectory
MAP INSERT S2:SYS:%MACHINE/%OS/%OS_VERSION	;Then search for opsys version
IF MEMBER OFFICE THEN	;Test for group membership
MAP O:SYS:OFFICE	
IF MEMBER OF ENGINEERING THEN	
MAP P:=SYS:ENGINEERING	
END	
END	
MAP DISPLAY ON	;Turn map display back on
MAP	;List the current map

method for automating scripts is available called Perl. Perl is somewhat reminiscent of the C or Pascal programming languages; however, its output is designed to run in a UNIX shell environment. Perlscripts may also be run in NT.

Support. One of the highest costs of a network is the cost of knowledgeable people who must be available to provide support to the users of the network. Support requirements can range from simple problems such as "I forgot my password" to the infamous, "The &%#@ network is down!" The cost to fix the password problem is limited to the salary of the support person for the time it takes to change a password and perhaps the time of the employee who is waiting for a new password. A network that is down owing to a hard drive crash in its server is significantly more costly. In this scenario all users are idle until the drive is replaced and its data restored.

Support personnel are often part teacher, part technician, and part public relations. They must be knowledgeable of not only the network but also each of the applications used on the network. New users will nearly always need some training in network access and the applications that they will use. Perhaps the most important skills support people possess are people skills.

Support personnel must be able to resolve problems quickly with both hardware and software. They must also provide their solutions to users who are often not at all happy that the problem occurred. Somehow, support must fix the problem and keep the "customer" happy with the network at the same time.

Properly staffed "help desks" should include a supervisor (often the network administrator or manager), a product specialist for each of the software applications used on the network, a technician or troubleshooter who can find and repair both hardware and software faults, and often a documentation clerk. Don't be surprised if you discover that, as administrator of a small LAN, you are *it* for all of these jobs!

Documentation. Perhaps the least enjoyed of all of an administrator's duties, complete and accurate documentation of all of the details of a network, is one of the most important tasks. Logs, charts, and records must be maintained in a timely and accurate manner. Good documentation is seldom appreciated until the network goes down and you have to physically locate the jabbering Ethernet NIC or a break in a Token-Ring. From management's viewpoint, the

Table 16.4 Minimum Documentation List

1. Cabling and wiring
2. Workstation and server hardware configuration
3. Workstation and server software configuration
4. Router and gateway configuration
5. Service and warranty agreements
6. Backup and recovery plan

biggest disaster is a downed network, an administrator on vacation, and no documentation that would enable someone to step in to resolve the problem. The following subsections describe minimum documentation requirements.

Cabling and wiring. Begin documentation of your wiring plant during installation. As each cable is run, label each cable end with a cable number that describes its physical location. Immediately make an appropriate entry in a chart similar to Figure 16.2. To make life a bit easier, you might create a code for cable numbers that suggests where the cable is run. One concept is to create a grid pattern for each floor in a building similar to grid coordinates on a map. A typical cable number might be A5B1F3W22J44 in which A5 represents the grid location or room number for the cable end you are putting the label on. B1 represents the building number, F3 the floor number, W22 the actual wire number (cable number 22), and J44 the grid number at the opposite end of the cable. At the opposite end of the cable, the label would read J44B1F3W22A5. Figure 16.2 shows this cable run as the first entry.

Figure 16.2 Cabling Chart

Wiring Chart

Building __1____
Floor __3____

Cable Number	Start Location	End Location	Length	Patched To	TDR Reading	Comments
W22	A5	J44	47m	NW4I_Bothell	.03db	

Workstation and server hardware configuration. Each workstation and server should be documented to show the configuration of the hardware installed in them. Figure 16.3 shows a sample form that could be used to record the workstation information; Figure 16.4 shows the server equipment log. One chart for each machine should be used. Some organizations make periodic inspections as part of a preventive maintenance program to ensure that machines are properly configured.

In the space marked "Other," you might record an IP address, Subnet mask, and the Default gateway settings if your network is running TCP/IP. Additional hardware components could be added to this minimum list such as mouse, modem, and so forth.

Workstation and server software configuration. One of the most time-consuming duties of the network administrator is the installation, configuration, and maintenance of software. Legal requirements exist that prohibit the use of unlicensed copyrighted software. Conformity to both software and hardware configurations must be maintained, and software installations must be standardized across the network. Software containing viruses must be detected and removed from the network.

User training should include such topics as the proper use of licensed software, virus protection, and the potential disasters caused by configuration changes. Administrators are usually charged with the responsibility of ensuring

Server Log

Server Name____________ Asset #________ Location________

Administrator____________ Phone________

Device	Quantity	Capacity	S/N	Purchase Date
CPU				
Memory				
Hard Drive				
NIC				
Parallel Ports				
Serial Ports				
Other:				

Figure 16.3 Server Equipment Log

Figure 16.4 Workstation Equipment Log

Workstation Log

Workstation________________ Asset #_________ Location_________

User______________________ Phone__________

Device	Quantity	Capacity	S/N	Purchase Date
CPU				
Memory				
Hard Drive				
NIC				
Parallel Ports				
Serial Ports				
Other:				

that users follow software policies. Needless to say, users with perfectly good intentions will install unauthorized software or modify configurations. The administrator must now become both diplomat and police officer, for to allow the use of unauthorized software may result in destruction of data (viruses), conflicting configurations that may degrade network performance, or financial liability due to illegal use of unlicensed software.

One helpful technique may be to install all software on workstations from preconfigured master installations on network servers. If nothing else, the administrator is assured that correct versions and configurations are installed on workstations if the installation must be downloaded from a server. Additional protection against unauthorized copying is afforded if disk or CD copies of software are not available to users.

Windows NT Workstation has a capability that can check a user's desktop profile and download the correct configuration to the workstation. NT also allows policies to be set that disable user access to the control panel, run command line, and the start menu. Remember that SNMP is used by TCP/IP to acquire the information contained in MIB tables in nodes connected to the network. Remote monitoring agents (RMON) can be installed that allow a network manager to download the configuration of workstations and note any deviation from normal settings. This is a real help to the network administrator/manager but is only recommended for use in routers and gateways because SNMP can require too much of the available bandwidth if installed in workstations.

A log of authorized software programs installed in each workstation and server should be maintained. Many organizations conduct periodic inspections to ensure that unlicensed or unauthorized software has not been installed. There are programs available that can search a workstation for unauthorized software. Suggested software configuration files that should be recorded and backed up in a safe place include the following:

- *MS-DOS*—AUTOEXEC.BAT, CONFIG.SYS
- *Windows*—All .ini files including WIN.INI, SYSTEM.INI, and the registry
- *Network*—Netware DOS and Windows 3.x clients: STARTNET.BAT and NET.CFG, AUTOEXEC.NCF, STARTUP.NCF; NT DOS clients: SYSTEM.INI

Fortunately for the network administrator, a number of very good programs are available that help automate many of the record-keeping functions, configuration monitoring, and software maintenance requirements. *PC* magazine maintains a listing of network management and documentation shareware that can be downloaded from its Web site. Many of the network hardware vendors offer proprietary management software.

Router and gateway configuration. If your network has wide area connections, you can expect to spend much of your time maintaining the connecting points to the wide area. Routers must be programmed to know the addresses of all of the other routers they are connected to as well as the MAC addresses on their local network segment. Documentation should exist that records all of this data so that it can be quickly reproduced if needed. Maps of the overall network should be made and maintained. Fortunately, there is a reasonably large choice of software available that will be of significant help.

Intranets are enjoying a great deal of attention. An intranet is a private version of a wide area network that resembles the Internet. TCP/IP is used at the transport and network layers, and browsers are used to access resources in exactly the same manner as if the user were connected to the worldwide Internet.

Both the Internet and intranets have given rise to a specialty occupation that deals exclusively with the interface that users "see" when they access a server. A language known as *HyperText Markup Language* (HTML) is used that presents a "page" or screen display in which links to available resources are provided. Simply clicking with a mouse on one of these links causes a new connection to be made to the requested resource. Resources may be servers and/or specific directories or files. Needless to say, all of these resource locations must be documented.

Service and warranty agreements. An important item for documentation is a list of all the service and warranty agreements that exist. Many organizations contract to third parties or vendors for the maintenance of equipment. It is critical that the network administrator keep an up-to-date record of all of the service agreements that includes contact names and phone numbers as well as the details of the agreement.

Whenever a piece of hardware or software fails, the warranty list should be referenced to determine who is responsible for providing the fix. Keep your list of warranties current and accessible and you will undoubtedly save your organization a great deal of money.

DISASTER RECOVERY

Every network should have a backup and recovery plan in the event of catastrophic failure. It is one thing to lose a file, quite another to lose an entire hard drive on a critical server. It is very realistic to suggest that the loss of a company's database might well mean the end of the company. A backup and recovery plan should include, at a minimum:

- a schedule of backup times,
- a record of backups,
- location of backups, and
- method used to restore data.

A real cost is associated with making backups and restoring data. One should carefully weigh these costs against the value of the data and the lost opportunity costs associated with downtime. A backup and recovery plan that offers fault tolerance and rapid, automatic restoration of lost data will be considerably more costly than one that is done manually.

Regardless of the methodology, backup media and a copy of the backup and recovery plan should be kept in a secure place. Many organizations contract to third parties for secure storage that includes protection against fire and other natural disasters.

Where the cost of downtime is sufficiently expensive, arrangements can be made to shift processing capabilities to third-party networks that have excess capacity. An example of this scenario is the Weyerhaeuser mainframe that was designed for excess capacity. Weyerhaeuser contracts to a number of organizations for use of its mainframe in the event of a downed network. Processing is merely shifted from the damaged network to the Weyerhaeuser mainframe. A less costly approach to ensuring continuous network activity might be to install redundant access lines across the wide area and redundant servers and RAID hard drive systems for critical operations.

It is usually recommended that more than one backup be stored. For example, a backup plan might require backups of server hard drives to be made every worknight at 2 A.M. Five sets of backups are in storage at any given time. Referred to as "grandfathering" backups, this process is done on the assumption that backups can contain errors that have been perpetuated from one backup to the next. Grandfathering hopefully will provide a backup made before the error was created.

A technique that can save time and storage costs is to do incremental backups over a period of time. An incremental backup only backs up files that have been changed or created since the last backup. One might do incremental backups for a week then do a full backup every Friday night. Several of the full backups could be grandfathered and stored along with the daily incrementals.

NETWORK SECURITY

General Security Precautions

Access to computer networks should be controlled on an as-need basis. One might suggest that students, for example, should have no access to the university administrative network. Having made this declaration, a case can be made where students, faculty, and administrators might require E-mail and Internet access, in which case all of the networks would have to be designed to communicate with each other. A potentially severe security problem now exists because any user from either the school or the Internet would have the ability to attempt access to an unauthorized server. In addition, anyone with a telephone can call any modem connected to the network and attempt access. This section will offer some remedies to improve network security.

Three descriptions are commonly used to classify those who would attempt unauthorized access to computers and networks:

- *Phreaks*—Phone phreaks generally confine their activity to simple access of telecommunications networks in an attempt to keep from having to pay the normal tariff. In many cases their only objective is to collect telephone numbers connected to modems, routers, and gateways. While relatively harmless, these activities are usually illegal, particularly when tariffs are avoided, and the federal Department of the Treasury will prosecute if the access is across state lines.
- *Hackers*—Hackers are those who would "break into" a network for which they have no authorized access. There is a general assumption that hackers only break in but make no attempt to do any damage to data. Again, in addition to an obvious invasion of privacy, unauthorized access to computers and networks is illegal. Any attempt to copy information, even though nondestructive, can be considered theft. Keep in mind that the median age of a hacker is 14.
- *Crackers*—Crackers are perhaps the worst offenders. Not only do they illegally hack into a network, but they also attempt to modify or destroy

data. Those who would inject viruses into computers should properly be considered crackers.

Perhaps the only certain method for preventing unauthorized access to your network is to turn off the modem(s) and router(s). Because that approach is rarely practical, the security recommendations described in the following sections are suggested. Remember, however, that good security requires constant vigilance and concern for security issues.

Remote Access Protocols

One of the easiest entry points for a hacker is through a dial-up line connected to a modem. A simple telephone call is made to attempt to connect to the modem and gain access to a network. Using a protocol that requires authentication of authorized users is a first step in protecting the network from unauthorized use. Additional measures may be taken that include password and data encryption, authentication servers that are used for no other purpose, and packet-filtering devices that only allow packets from authorized users into or out of a network.

SLIP

Serial Line Interface Protocol (SLIP) (see Figure 16.5) was the first of the modem access protocols used by Internet service providers to authenticate TCP/IP packets. SLIP was a relatively efficient protocol in that it added only a small number of octets (two) in its header and trailer format to the overhead of an IP datagram. Unfortunately, SLIP provides no error detection, addressing, or encryption.

PPP

Point to Point Protocol (PPP) improves on SLIP by adding address, control, protocol identification, and error correction fields. Figure 16.6 describes a PPP formatted IP packet.

PPP has the following features:

- The PPP *flag* field enables timing synchronization.
- A single-octet *address* field is usually set to all ones since PPP is normally used to connect a single dial-up user to a single modem connection. Addressing of packets is done by IP.

Figure 16.5 SLIP Format

Header	IP Packet	Trailer
11000000 |	data	| 11000000

Flag	Address	Control	Protocol	IP Packet	FCS	Flag
01111110	1 octet	1 octet	2 octets	data	16 bit CRC	01111110

Figure 16.6 PPP Format

- The *protocol* field specifies one of three protocol types:

  Link Control Protocol (LCP)—used to negotiate connections to remote host. Negotiated items may include packet size, connection quality, encapsulation format, and authentication format. Authentication may take the form of Password Identification Protocol (PAP) or Challenge Handshake Authentication Protocol (CHAP).

  IP Control Protocol (IPCP)—used to negotiate for IP address(es) issued from a pool of IP addresses by remote host following authentication by LCP.

  Network Control Protocol (NCP)—used as the transport protocol following authentication and connection by LCP and IPCP. Each layer in use has its own NCP format.

- The *Frame Check Sequence* field is the 16-bit error detection process.

An additional feature of PPP is that it is capable of encrypting data frames. Depending on the type and level of encryption, PPP can establish very secure links over public access networks.

PPTP

Point to Point Tunneling Protocol (PPTP) is the most recent of the remote access protocols defined by the Internet Engineering Task Force (IETF) in RFC 1171. PPTP provides on-demand, multiple-protocol support for Virtual Private Networks (**VPNs**). PPTP is an extension to PPP that requires two connections to be made. The first connection is to the remote access host using PPP. A second connection is then made over the PPP connection to a PPTP server on a private LAN.

VPNs are Virtual Private Networks.

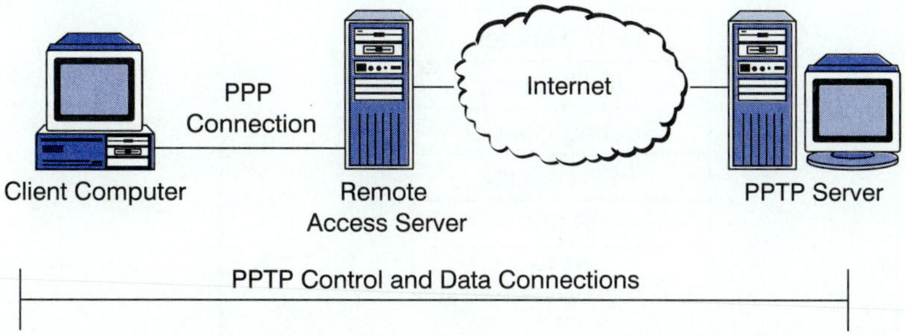

Figure 16.7 PPTP Connections

A typical example of a PPTP installation would be a client computer running PPP and PPTP to access an Internet Service Provider (ISP) and the Internet. Figure 16.7 demonstrates the protocol usage.

The concept of *tunneling* is introduced in PPTP to denote that once the PPP connection is established, a PPTP connection is created that "tunnels" through the remote access network to access the PPTP server somewhere on the Internet. When viewing the actual packets, you will see the PPP packet encapsulated by the PPTP packet. Figure 16.8 outlines the format of a PPTP packet using IP.

Log-in Names

Each user on a network server must be issued a log-in name. Customarily, this is a first initial followed by last name (e.g., athompson). Log-in names should be unique (i.e. no two the same on a given server). There may be two athompsons but not both on the same server. In practice, it is probably wise to have no two athompson log-in names anywhere in the enterprise. This will avoid E-mail addressing problems.

Some network administrators have begun issuing user names that are not common names in an effort to make log-in names as difficult for a hacker to discover as possible. Names that are random combinations of letters, numbers, and symbols and at least eight characters long make discovery as difficult as possible.

Passwords

- All network access should require a password.
- Passwords should be issued by network administrators only.
- Passwords should contain at least eight characters and use a combination of upper- and lowercase letters, numbers, and/or punctuation and special characters.
- Passwords should *not* be composed of dates, names, or words from the dictionary.

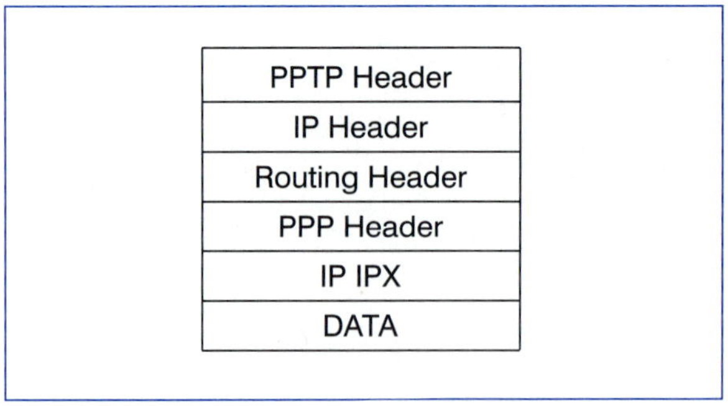

Figure 16.8 IP Datagram Encapsulated by PPTP and PPP

- Passwords should be changed on a frequent but random basis.
- Passwords should *never* be reused.

Domain Names

Microsoft NT allows for the creation of domains. Domains are nothing more complicated than workgroup names. For example, within the Administration network, domains could be established for each business workgroup. Examples might be Administrators, Receivable, Payables, Student_Records, and so forth. The use of domain names adds an additional level of security. Users must log in with user name, domain name, and password. Some administrators use domain names in the same way that user names and passwords are assigned, again, to make unauthorized access as difficult as possible.

NetWare version 4.1's Organizaton (O) and Organizational Unit (OU) offer a somewhat similar compartmentalization. Users must log into the organization or organizational unit in which their account exists. Rights are then inherited from the parent container. A potential hacker must then know the correct context of a user account as well as the user's account name and password.

One of the major concerns for a security-conscious network administrator is user conformance to security policies. Hackers will tell you that the three most likely places to discover a password and account name are (1) a sticky note pasted to monitor or back of keyboard, (2) the right-hand side of middle desk drawer, and (3) the inside cover of the user training manual. If security is to be maintained effectively, users will need regular reminders regarding security policies, and administrators will need the backing of management to enforce the policies. Continual vigilance is your best protection.

Firewalls

Entry points to networks through modems, router and gateway connections, and the Internet are particularly vulnerable to those individuals who would do damage to the network and the data it contains. Firewalls are security devices that are set up at entry points to a network as an additional security feature. They are designed to allow anything to leave the network, but nothing can enter that is not specifically authorized.

For example, a teacher at home may need to call in to her network to obtain or update a lesson plan. To do so, she would need to know the firewall password, and her software would need to know the address of the firewall node and be granted access as an authorized format as well. Once connected to the firewall, she could log in to her assigned network using log-in name, domain or organizational context, and password.

Firewalls should not be considered as substitutes for other security procedures. Viruses, for example, may be transported in E-mail that is not normally protected by the firewall.

Virus Protection

A computer virus is usually a small piece of code that attaches itself to executable programs, batch files, or macros. Whenever these items are run in a computer, the virus code is also executed. Results of a virus may be as benign as an unwanted message or graphic displayed on the monitor or as fiendish as the complete destruction of all data in memory and on the hard drive.

Regular checks should be made to detect the presence of viruses. Several good virus detection programs exist from vendors such as Central Point, Symantec, F-PROT, and McAfee. No files from external sources should be allowed onto the network until they have been screened for viruses. This means that anything arriving via external equipment attached to the network must be immediately scanned for contamination. This can be done automatically using software designed for the purpose. Users should be discouraged from copying personal software to network disks, but they will inevitably do so. Workstations should be regularly scanned for virus contamination and unlicensed programs.

Recently, a number of viruses have shown up in documents attached to E-mail. Macros such as those used in word processors seem to be the actual carrier. The virus is often not detected during an E-mail virus scan but is activated when the document is loaded and viewed.

Open Access Systems

You may wish to designate a system for "open" access—a student-operated bulletin board, for example. In such a case, *no* physical connection should exist to networked systems. Many organizations have elected to install World Wide Web pages but have done so using outside Internet service providers to prevent access to internal networks. A library kiosk with Internet access open to anyone should be considered as an extreme security breach point. Consider issuing passwords on an as-need basis with automatic expiration of passwords on logout to anyone not cleared for continuous access.

CHAPTER REVIEW

- The four primary network job classifications include administrator, technician, engineer, and manager.
- Network administrator responsibilities include installing and upgrading hardware and software; managing domains, workgroups, and users; creating and maintaining log-in scripts, menus, and icon groups; maintaining security, backup, and recovery; creating documentation; providing training and support; and monitoring performance.

- User, workgroup, and domain management requires Supervisor (NetWare 3.x) or Administrator (NetWare 4.x and NT) privileges or *manager* privileges for specified domains and workgroups.
- Attributes and permissions are assigned to files and directories.
- Rights are assigned to users.
- Workgroups and users are granted *trusted relationships* (NT) and *trustee assignments* (NetWare) for access to logical drives, directories, and files.
- Log-in scripts are used to automate commonly used functions during the log-in process. Well-thought-out log-in scripts are an effective way to minimize much of administration of users.
- Support is one of the highest-cost items in the maintenance of networks.
- An effective support desk helps minimize the cost of user training and can facilitate user acceptance of the network.
- Documentation includes cable records and labels, hardware and software configurations and addressing, and warranty information. Third-party software is available to ease this task.
- Backups should be done on a regularly scheduled basis and a record maintained. Backup and recovery systems are evaluated in terms of cost versus time to recover.
- Network security problems increase with the size of the network and its access to public networks. Hackers, crackers, and phreaks are criminal elements who intentionally violate security. Users can unintentionally violate network security if not properly trained and supervised.
- Security procedures include passwords, log-in names, domain names, and firewalls to prevent unauthorized access. Networks should be scanned regularly for viruses. Open access systems should not be connected to networks containing sensitive data.

REVIEW QUESTIONS

1. List the seven major functions of network administration.
2. Discuss the importance of documentation to a network administrator.
3. What are the three professional certifications available for NT and NetWare professionals?
4. What privilege level(s) must a network administrator have to perform all functions in NetWare and NT?
5. List the four distinct user types in NetWare.

6. What is an *enterprise administrator*?
7. Define *attributes, rights,* and *permissions,* and show how NetWare and NT use them.
8. List the NetWare file attributes.
9. List the NT file permissions.
10. List the NetWare user rights.
11. Define *trustee assignment* and *trusted relationship.*
12. What are log-in scripts used for?
13. How can log-in scripts be used to reduce administrative workload?
14. Describe the duties of a network support department.
15. Describe a properly staffed support department.
16. List the six functional parts of a network that require good documentation.
17. List the three types of network criminals, and give a brief description of what they do illegally.
18. List the five areas in which network security is a consideration.
19. What is a firewall?
20. How can you maximize the effectiveness of log-in names and passwords in terms of network security?
21. Describe a backup and recovery plan suitable for your school's open computer network lab.
22. What kind of security would be appropriate to an open network lab?

Appendix A

Installing NetWare Version 3.x

1. Configure and install the server NIC.
2. Partition the hard drive (both drives if mirroring or duplexing) for a small (10- to 15-Mb) active MS-DOS partition. Leave the rest of the drive(s) unpartitioned. NetWare will install its own partition in the unused drive space. Use an additional 10 Mb for the MS-DOS partition if you expect to load NLMs from the MS-DOS partition or are using third-party NLMs.
3. Format the drive(s) for use with MS-DOS including any extended MS-DOS partitions.
4. Boot the computer and copy the SYSTEM disks to a subdirectory on drive C: named NWSERVER.
5. Change to the NWSERVER subdirectory and Type SERVER↵.

At this point, the program SERVER will switch the active partition to the NetWare partition and present a series of menus that will guide you through the rest of the installation process as noted in Table A.1. Figure A.1 shows the four menus displayed when the SERVER program is executed.

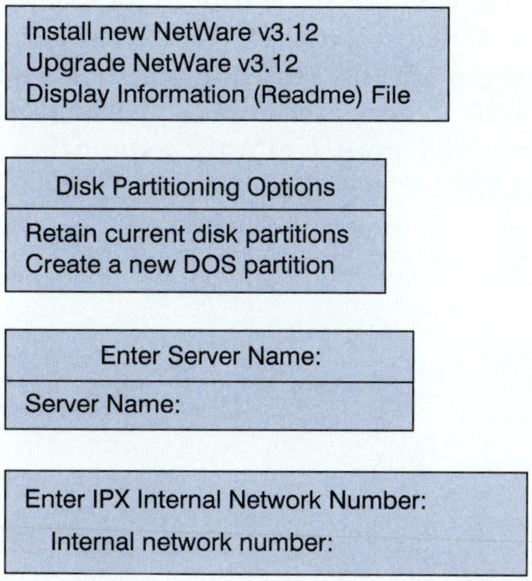

Figure A.1 NetWare v3.12 Initial Installation Menu

Table A.1 SERVER Program Execution and Disk Driver Installation

1. Enter the name of the server. This may be any name you choose provided it is a single group of connected characters. (e.g., ACCOUNTING or LAN_TECHNOLOGY). Be certain no other server of the same name will be connected to your LAN. *Note:* some server-based applications such as SQL may restrict you to 8 or 11 character server names and further restrict characters that may be used. You need not be overly concerned with this issue since the server name can easily be changed and specified in the AUTOEXEC.NCF file that contains commands used to load and bind protocols, mount hard drive volumes, and load any other NLMs that are desired during the boot process.
2. Enter the internal network ID number. This number is only used internally but must be unique if other servers are accessible. NetWare generates its own pseudorandom internal network number. You may use your own number, chosen from a list of network numbers assigned to servers. The only critical point is that no two servers that might communicate with each other may have the same internal network number. Whatever the numbering plan that you choose, *write the network number down!* Server-based applications such as SQL require you to supply the internal network number during installation. Load the hard disk driver. NetWare comes with drivers for most applications such as ISA, IDE, SCSI, and so forth. NetWare provides several generic drivers, and most NIC manufacturers provide drivers with their NICs.
3. Load the LAN driver (NIC driver). This driver must conform to the MAC protocol the MIC is using.

At the <Server Name>: prompt you must now LOAD the INSTALL program. It will prompt you to install the items shown in Table A.2. Figure A.2 shows the NetWare menus that are displayed to guide you through the process.

The final stage of server installation binds the NIC driver to IPX and configures the system for automatic server booting as shown in the sample AUTOEXEC.NCF file. When finished, the server will automatically boot on drive C: in the MS-DOS partition and execute the AUTOEXEC.BAT file, which, in turn, executes the SERVER program to switch to the NetWare partition and boot NetWare as configured by the AUTOEXEC.NCF and STARTUP.NCF files. Table A.3 lists the required bindery procedures.

Install Options
Disk options
Volume options
System options
Product options
Exit

Available Disk Options
Format (optional)
Partition tables
Mirroring
Surface text (optional)
Return to main menu

Volumes
Accounting
Engineering
SYS

Available System Options
Copy system and public files
Create AUTOEXEC.NCF file
Create STARTUP.NCF file
Edit AUTOEXEC.NCF file
Edit STARTUP.NCF file
Return to main menu

Figure A.2 INSTALL Menus

Figure A2 Installation Items

1. Disk options
   - Disks may be formatted, partitoned, mirrored, and have a very extensive surface analysis run.
2. Volume options
   - Each volume in NetWare is a virtual root directory. NetWare must install the volume SYS: at a minimum.
3. System options
   - Install the system and public files. (You can go for coffee if you are installing off a CD-ROM, or you can feed the server all the rest of the NetWare diskettes).
   - Create the AUTOEXEC.NCF NetWare configuration file and a STARTUP.NCF file (optional). These files serve similar functions during the server boot process to the AUTOEXEC.BAT and CONFIG.SYS files when MS-DOS boots. Figures 8.3a and 8.3b show samples of the two files. Note that the server name and the imported NIC driver (AM2100) are choices made by the installer. Interrupts, DMA channels, and I/O addresses must conform to the MS-DOS requirements and must *not* conflict with other hardware devices that may be installed in the server.

Figure A3.a Sample AUTOEXEC.NCF File

```
File sever name LAN_TECHNOLOGY
IPX internal net 2
Load AM2100 port=300 int=9 dma=5 frame=ethernet802.3
Bind IPX to AM2100 net=c
Mount all
```

Figure A3.b Sample STARTUP.NCF File

```
Sample STARTUP.NCF File
Load ISADISK port=1f0 int=E
```

4. Load any NetWare loadable modules (NLMs). NLMs add functions to the NetWare operating system for such things as:

• Tape backup	Fax	Modems	UPS
• Data base servers	Routing	Gateways	LanAnalyzers

   You will also want to keep up with NetWare NLMs that offer upgrades or patches to fix known bugs. NLM patches such as LIBUP9.EXE and Start3 may be obtained in the Compuserve Novell forum or from your NetWare vendor. NLMs are stored in either the sys:\system subdirectory of NetWare or in the MS-DOS partition on server hard drive. If not stored in the system subdirectory, you must use the LOAD command either at the system console or in the AUTOEXEC.NCF file to load the NLMs.

Table A.3 Finalizing the Installation Process

1. Bind the IPX to the LAN driver(s) and mount the system volume (SYS:).
2. Create AUTOEXEC.BAT with a last line that executes the SERVER program.
3. Create CONFIG.SYS—You need to also configure CONFIG.SYS for extended (XMS) memory operation if your server has more than 640 K of memory.

Installing NetWare 4.x

The version 4 installation is much improved over version 3.x. All of the necessary procedures are included without leaving the install program. The initial procedure is virtually identical to version 3.x; however, all version 4.x installations must be done from a CD-ROM. To prepare for the installation, perform the following:

1. Configure and install the server NIC.
2. Partition the hard drive (both drives if mirroring or duplexing) for a small (15- to 20-Mb) active MS-DOS partition. *Note:* Many administrators set the DOS partition size to as much as 100 Mb. This is strictly up to the individual. Leave the rest of the drive(s) unpartitioned. NetWare will install its own partition in the unused drive space.
3. Format the drive(s) for use with MS-DOS including any extended MS-DOS partitions.
4. Install MS-DOS on the formatted partitions.
5. Install the device driver for the CD-ROM.
6. Reboot the computer and access the CD-ROM. Type *Install* ↵.
7. The install program will now create the NWSERVER directory and copy all necessary files. Following the file copy, SERVER.EXE is executed and INSTALL.NLM loaded automatically.

An additional change to version 4.x concerns the way in which the automated boot procedure is executed. Two new files have been added to the SYS:etc directory that supplement the old AUTOEXEC.NCF and STARTUP.NCF files. *netinfo.cfg* is the file that supplements AUTOEXEC.NCF, and INITSYS.NCF supplements STARTUP.NCF. These files can be edited from the system console using EDIT.NLM. If you are upgrading from 4.1 to 4.11, much of what was configured in autoexec.ncf will be copied to NETINFO.CFG and converted to remarks in AUTOEXEC.NCF.

The INSTALL.BAT file on CD-ROM is located in NETWARE.40\ENGLISH (or other language(s) shown). The following should be considered before beginning the install:

- It is probably wise to run a backup of your installation before beginning an upgrade. If upgrading, be certain to back up your server data because you will be prompted to change partitioning. If you do change the hard drive partitions, all data on the drive is forever lost, and you don't want to have to explain where mega- or gigabytes of mission-critical data went, do you? Be certain you leave at least 60 Mb in the NetWare partition for the SYS: volume.
- In most cases you will probably wish to do a custom installation. Simple installation limits you to one organization and up to three organizational units. Simple installation may also prevent future installation of additional volumes utilizing hard drive free space.
- Version 4.x asks you to specify a locale. The screen form displays the locale information in the workstation. Accept the defaults unless you intend to change the workstation setup to new values.
- You will be able to choose between the old MS-DOS 8.3 file-naming convention or NetWare file-naming, which allows extended lowercase filenames. Remember that any files transferred to an MS-DOS workstation will not be able to use the extended lowercase feature.
- Ensure that volume SYS: contains at least 50 Mb; 60–100 is probably a better idea since you will probably be adding files to SYS: if for no other reason than during an install of a server-based application.
- If you choose file compression, remember that once activated, NetWare compression can not be turned off.
- You may choose to disable subblock allocation, but the default is enabled. If server performance is more critical than volume storage capacity, disable this feature.
- The default for the new data migration feature is off. Be certain you have a *high-capacity storage system* (HCSS) such as a jukebox installed if you select this option.
- You will be given the choice of installing one or more of four file groups on the server: (1) NetWare 4.x DOS utilities, (2) NetWare 4.0 OS/2 utilities, (3) NetWare 4.0 Windowing utilities, and (4) Setup a Network Directory for Client Install and Upgrade. At minimum, the DOS/Windowing utilities should be installed; you will find them quite useful.
- At approximately step 40 in the installation process, you will be asked to specify a server context. Here is where you will indicate the primary organization name (company or department name). If you have previously selected "simple installation," you will be limited to one organization container and up to three optional organizational unit containers. INSTALL creates the initial server objects, but NETADMIN or the Net-

Ware Administrator must be used to modify the NDS tree after the installation is complete.

Note that the first server installed in an NDS container is considered the master. Subsequent servers installed in the same context will have Read/Write copies of the Master partition. To envision this process, think of an organization chart for the school network shown in figure B.1. We might install the first server with a context ID of ADMIN and make all of the other servers shown in the drawing suborganizational units. We could now show the network organization in a manner identical to the organization of the school shown in Figure B.1.

A user would see the partitions for which access has been granted. A computer science faculty member might see login partitions: [Faculty] [CS_LAB] [COMMS_EMAIL] and no others, even though access to E-mail might send and receive mail for [ADMIN] users.

- After you have saved the organizational information, INSTALL will report the common server name in format cn=servername_volumename.
- You will then be asked to note the information that pertains to the

  directory tree name,

  directory context, and

  administrator name (ADMIN is the default but it can and, for security purposes, should be changed).
- At approximately step 45 (depending on your specific installation), you will be given several options to

  create a registration disk,

  upgrade v3.1x print services,

  configure communications protocols,

  copy on-line documentation from the CD-ROM,

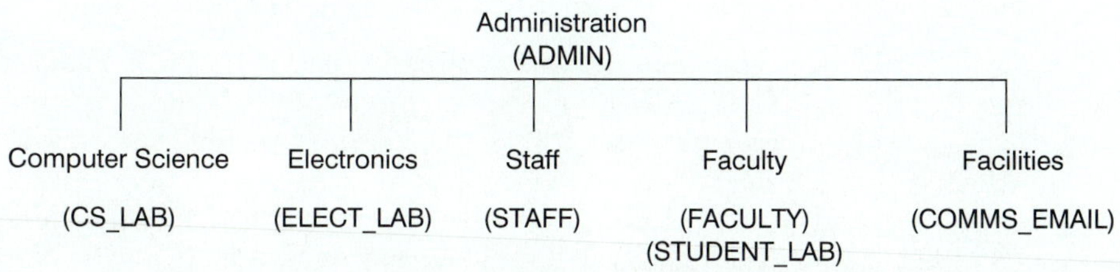

Figure B.1 Organizational Chart Showing the Hierarchy of NetWare 4.x Servers

copy computer-based training files,

create optional diskettes,

install additional language(s),

install NetWare for Macintosh,

install NetWare for NFS (NetWare File System), and

install NetWare for SAA (IBM System Architecture software for SNA networks).

All in all, NetWare 4.x installation is a much improved process with significant advantages not available in version 3.x.

Appendix C

Installing Microsoft NT 4.x

Like NetWare 4.x, NT 4.x installs from CD-ROM. Preparation is similar to a NetWare installation with some important differences:

- An MS-DOS-formatted partition of at least 130 Mb must be created on the hard drive (both hard drives if mirroring). In practice, depending on installation needs, you may need as much as 150 Mb; 200 Mb is preferable so that additional space is available when needed.
- NT comes with three install diskettes (which can be made from files on the CD-ROM if not supplied with the CD). Disk 1 contains a boot loader that boots a Windows 95 DOS operating system. Disks 2 and 3 contain the necessary files to detect the hard drive(s) and CD-ROM and load their respective device drivers. To begin the installation, insert disk 1 in the A: drive and turn on the system power. The remainder of the installation is totally automated although, as you will soon see, you will be asked a number of questions. *Note:* It is also possible to run an installation without the diskettes. In such a case, you must be able to access the CD-ROM. Change to the CD-ROM directory that corresponds to your hardware type and run WINNT.EXE. For example, change to the I386 directory if your server contains an Intel CPU.
- To make the install diskettes from files on the CD-ROM, change to the appropriate directory for your hardware CPU type. If using Windows 3.x or Windows 95/98, type *winnt /ox*. If using Windows NT, type *winnt32 /ox.*

During the automated installation, you will be asked to supply information and make decisions about the type of installation you require:

- Whether you are doing an upgrade from an existing NT installation
- Confirmation of the detected hardware
- Which partition to install NT on
- Which file system to use. It is usually better to select FAT because you can convert to NTFS from FAT but not the reverse.
- Which folder to install NT in

Information Collected by the Setup Program

- Setup type: typical, portable, compact, or custom
- Name and organization of licensee
- Registration of CD-ROM key (found on the back of the CD-ROM case)
- Licensing mode—If in doubt, choose *per server* to begin. You can convert to *per seat* following installation, if desired, but not the reverse.
- Computer name—15 characters or less
- Type of server—Choose PDC if first server on a network, BDC if second server on a network, or member server if adding resource servers to an existing domain.
- Password for user administrator
- Emergency repair disk—In my opinion this is always done. There is no good reason not to.
- Components to be installed
- Whether to install Internet Information Server

During installation, you will be asked to configure the network options. Items you should know in advance for this process include the following:

- How the computer is connected to the network (i.e., modem or direct connection via NIC)
- Whether to search for and configure a NIC (my preference) or to install the NIC driver from diskette
- Protocols to be used—Choose from TCP/IP (default), NWLink IPX/SPX Compatible, NetBEUI, and AppleTalk. If you choose TCP/IP, you will need to know its install parameters for IP address, subnet mask, and default gateway. If DHCP, DNS, or WINS servers are used, you will need to supply their IP addresses as well.
- Network services—Default services include computer browser, NetBIOS interface, RPC configuration, server, and workstation. You may click on *Select from List* for other services.
- Network adapter (NIC) setup—May include interrupt request (IRQ) value, direct memory address (DMA) channel number, and I/O port address.
- Order on protocol bindings—Determines which protocol is used first when contacting other devices on a network
- Domain or workgroup configuration and name

If you installed Internet Information Server (IIS), you will be prompted to specify which options to install: WWW, FTP, and GOPHER. IIS also needs time zone, date, and time as well as the video adapter driver and its configuration. At the end of the setup process, your video parameters are displayed. You may or may not elect to change them, but you must run the test pattern at least once before setup will conclude the installation and reboot the machine for the final time.

Glossary

10Base2 Thinnet RG58 Cable and connectors—runs at 10 Mbps
10Base5 Thicknet RG8 Cable and connectors—runs at 10 Mbps, longer distances than 10Base2
10BaseT Cabling standard using Level 5 UTP and RJ-45 connectors—100 meters, 10,000 or 1000 Mbps
100BaseF 100-Mbps baseband specifications for fiber optic cable
100BaseFX Fast Ethernet specification for multimode fiber physical layer
100BaseT4 100-Mbps category 5/5/3 physical layer specifications
100BaseTX 100-Mbps category 5 or STPP type 1 physical layer specifications
10Broad36 Broadband specifications for CATV 75-ohm cable
802.1 IEEE-defined standard for OSI layers 3 to 7
802.2 IEEE-defined standard for the LLC sublayer of OSI layer 2
802.3 Baseband CSMA/CD (Ethernet) MAC sublayer standard
802.4 Token passing (common) bus MAC sublayer definition
802.5 Token passing ring MAC sublayer definition
802.6 MAN MAC sublayer definition
AC Access Control—Token-Ring frame field
ACK Acknowledgment
ADSL Asynchronous Digital Subscriber Line
AEP AppleTalk Echo Protocol
AH Application Header
ALPS Automatic Line Protection Service
ANSI American National Standards Institute
APPC Advanced Program to Program Communications interface
ARP Address Resolution Protocol
ARPANET Advanced Research Projects Agency NETwork
ARU Audio Response Unit
ASCII American Standard Code for Information Interchange
ATM Asynchronous Transfer Mode
ATP AppleTalk Transaction Protocol
AUI Coaxial Interface connector
Bandwidth Measurement of maximum rate or frequency of a transmission medium
Baseband Physical media in which entire bandwidth is used
BERT Bit Error Rate Tester
BISYNC Character-oriented synchronous data frame
BKERT Block Error Rate Tester

Boadband Physical media in which a data stream does not occupy the full bandwidth
BPDU Bridge Protocol Data Unit—A data unit passed between spanning tree bridges
BRI Basic Rate Interface—ISDN 2ea 64-Kbps channels + 1ea 16-Kbps control and signaling channel
Bridge A device to connect two LANs at the data link layer
Broadband Analog transmissions containing multiple channels
Brouter Combination bridge and router
CAN Rules that define the syntax and semantics used for communication
CBEMA Computer and Business Equipment Manufacturers Association
CCITT Consultative Committee for International Telephone and Telegraph
CDDI Copper Distributed Data Interface—compliant with FDDI protocols
CDM Code Division Multiplexing
CDPD Cellular Digital Packet Data
CLNS Connection-less Network Services
CM Label on a cable that identifies it as communications cable
CMP Plenum rated communications cable
CMR Riser rated communications cable
CNA Certified Novell (or NetWare) Administrator—Novell NetWare professional rating
CNE Certified Novell (or NetWare) Engineer—Novell NetWare professional rating
CO Central Office
CODEC CO circuit that converts analog voice to digital 64-Kbps DS0
Common Bus Topology that connects devices to a common cable
CONS Connection Oriented Network Services
Convergence Routers talking to each other to establish route maps and map changes—time-consuming
CPE Customer Premis Equipment
CRC Cyclical Redundancy Check—mathematical method used for error checking
CSMA/CD Carrier Sense Multiple Access with Collision Detection
DCA Document Content Architecture
DCE Distributed Communications Equipment—also used as Data Communications Equipment
DDP Datagram Delivery Protocol
DDS Digital Data Service
DIA Document Interchange Architecture
DID Direct Inward Dial—PBXs are DID.
DLCI Data Link Connection Identifier
DLL Dynamic Link Library
DNS Domain Name Service
DQDB Distribute Queue Dual Bus
DS0 64-Kbps channel

DSAP Destination Service Access Point—the address of a PDU destination
DSS Distributed System Sniffer—network analyzer
DSU/CSU Data Service Unit/Control Service Unit
DV Distance Vector—calculates router hops (eight routers, seven hops max)
DXI Data Exchange Interface
E1 European T1—2.048 Mbps
ECSA Exchange Carriers Association
ED End Delimiter—Token-Ring frame field
EIA Electronic Industries Association
ELAP EtherTalk Link Access Protocol
E-mail Electronic Mail
ESF Extended Super Frame—used to monitor T1 performance
FAC Frame Address Control
FCS Frame Check Sequence
FDDI Fiber Distributed Data Interface
FDL Facility Data Link—4-Kbps open control channel
FDM Frequency Division Multiplexing
FIPS Federal Information Processing Standards Group
Frame The unit of transmission in a data link layer protocol
Frame Relay Packet frame switching that supports permanent virtual circuits
FS Frame Status—Token-Ring frame field
FTP File Transfer Protocol
Gateway A device for connecting different architectures
Gauge The diameter of the conductor in a cable
GCS Global Communications System
GOSIP Government OSI protocols
GUI Graphical User Interface
HAL Hardware Abstraction Layer
HCSS High Capacity Storage System
HDLC High-level Data Link Control—frame protocol developed from SDLC
HDSL High-rate Digital Subscriber Line
HPPI High Performance Parallel Interface—speeds to >2 Gbps
HSCS High Speed Circuit Switching
HSSI High Speed Serial Interface
Hub Point of access to network
ICMP Internet Control Message Protocol
ICS IBM Cable System
IEC International Electromechanical Commission
IEEE Institute of Electrical and Electronic Engineers
IGMP Internet Gate Management Protocol
IGRP Internet Gate Routing Protocol
Impedance Measure of the resistance to the flow of alternating current in ohms
IPX Internetwork Packet Exchange—NetWare packet exchange protocol

ISA Industry Standard Architecture
ISDN Integrated Services Digital Network
ISO International Standards Organization
IXC Inter-eXchange Carrier
LAN Local Area Network—network confined to area that is limited by cable length requirements
LAP-B/D Link Access Procedure-Balanced (X.25 version of SDLC)/Digital (ISDN) and Frame Relay
LATA Local Access Transport Area
LDM Limited Distance Modem
LEC Local Exchange Carrier
LLC Logical Link Control—sublayer of layer 2 that connects to higher layers
Local Loop Connection between phone and CO
LPDU LLC Protocol Data Unit
LSAC Low Speed Access Circuit
LSRP Link State Routing Protocol—open shortest path first.
LU6.2 Protocol that interfaces APPC
MAC Media Access Control—a sublayer of the IEEE 802.2 standard
MAN Metropolitan Area Network—networks generally confined to a city-sized area
Manchester coding The format used to send electrical signals down a cable
MAU Media Access Unit
MCP Microsoft Certified Professional
MCSE Microsoft Certified Systems Engineer
Medium The composition of the physical layer transmission line; may be cable, fiber, or air
MII Media Independence Interface—used in 100BaseT as an interface between MAC and the cable
Modem Modulator Demodulator—translates digital to analog to digital for use on voice networks
MPP Multiple Parallel Processor
MSAU Multi-Station Access Unit
NAK No Acknowledgment
NAUN Next Address Upstream Neighbor—Token-Ring address of station from which tokens are received
NCP Network Core Protocol
NDIS Network Driver Interface Specification—used by NT
NDS NetWare Directory Service—global database in NetWare v4.x
NetBEUI NetBIOS Extended User Interface—Microsoft implementation of NetBIOS
NetBIOS Network Basic Input/Output Services—data link layer services for session control (see also NetBEUI)
NH Network Header
NIC Network Interface Card—the circuit board that interfaces between devices and a physical medium

NLM Network Loadable Module
NSP Name Service Protocol
NTAS New Technology Advanced Server—Microsoft NT server software
NWLink NetWare Link—NT method for communicating with NetWare servers using SPX/IPX
ODI Open Datalink Interface—NetWare interface that eliminates DOS-specific shells
OSF Open Systems Foundation—creator of the OSIRM
OSPF Open Shortest Path First—a routing protocol
OSIRM Open System Interconnect Reference Model—ISO-defined model for networking
OTF Open Token Foundation
Packet The unit of data passed across the network layer
PAD Packet Assembly Data
PAP Printer Access Protocol
PBX Private Branch Exchange—CPE switching system
PC LAN P PC LAN Program
PDA Personal Digital Assistance
PDN Packet Data Network
PDU Protocol Data Unit—the address, control, and data section of an LLC frame
PH Presentation Header
Pilot Core program for OS/2
Polling Technique used to query a device to determine its availability or need for service
POP Point Of Presence
POTS Plain Old Telephone System—the analog telephone lines connected to most homes
PPP Point-to-Point Protocol—replaces SLIP
PRI Primary Rate Interface—ISDN 23ea 64-Kbps channels + 116-Kbps channel
Protocol Rules that define the syntax and semantics used for communication
PTT Postal Telephone and Telegraph—many countries have government-owned PTT systems.
RAID Redundant Array of Inexpensive Drives
RBOC Regional Bell Operating Companies
RFC Request For Comment—a technical paper that invites response for proposed new standards
RFC/RFP Request For Comment/Request For Proposal
RIF Routing Information Field—contains source routing information
Ring Topology that connects devices in a closed electrical ring
RIP Routing Information Protocol—distance vectoring connectionless at application layer
Router An intelligent addressing device to connect LANs or WANs at the network layer

RS Recommended Standard
SAA System Applications Architecture
RTMP Routing Table Maintenance Protocol
SAP Service Access Point—subaddressing to connect specific LLC type to MAC and higher layers
SD Start Delimiter—Token-Ring frame field
SDLC Synchronous Data Link Control
SFD Start Frame Delimiter
SH Session Header
SLIP Serial Link Interface Protocol
SMB System Message Block—commands used by NetBIOS for communicating with remote devices
SMTP Simple Mail Transfer Protocol
SNA System Network Architecture
SNADS SNA Distribution Services
SNI Subscriber Network Interface
SNMP Simple Network Management Protocol—protocol for network analysis
SONET Synchronous Optical NETwork
Source routing Method by which a router knows addressing; see RIF.
Spanning Tree A bridging protocol used in transparent bridging of Ethernet LANs
SPX Sequenced Packet Exchange
SQL Structured Query Language
SRB Source Route Bridge—bridging techniques used in Token-Ring
SRDM Sub-Rate Digital Multiplexing
SRP Source Route Protocol—IBM
SSAP Source Service Access Point—the address that is the source of an LLC PDU
Star Topology that connects devices to a central hub
STM STation Manager
STP Shielded Twisted Pair
STP (bridges) Spanning Tree Protocol—learning bridge
T1 Telephone system standard trunk; contains 24 DSO channels running at 1.544 Mbps
T3 Telephone system extended trunk; 672 DSOs, 45 Mbps
TCP/IP Transport Control Protocol/Internet Protocol—developed by the Department of Defense for ARPANET
TDI Transport Driver Interface—NT transport layer service
TDM Time Division Multiplexing
TDR Time Domain Reflectometer
TH Transport Header
Thicknet Ethernet cable standard—50-ohm RG8 coaxial cable and connectors
Thinnet Ethernet standard cable—50-ohm RG58 coaxial cable and connectors
TLAP TokenTalk Link Access Protocol

TRE Token-Ring Extender
TRel Transaction Release
Treq Transaction request
Tres Transaction response
UART Universal Asynchronous Receiver Transmitter—the integrated circuit used to manage RS-232C ports
UDP User Datagram Protocol
UNC Universal Naming Convention
UPS Uninterruptable Power Supply
UTP Unshielded Twisted Pair
VLM Volume Loadable Module
VPDS Virtual Private/Public Data Service
VPN Virtual Private Network
VRU Video Response Unit
WAN Wide Area Network
WINSOCK Windows Socket—addressable pipeline to Windows transport layer services
X.25 Packet switching protocol
XNS Xerox Network Systems
XTP Express Transfer Protocol
ZIT Zero Information Table

Annotated Bibliography

Books and Articles

Banyon® Systems, Inc. *VINES Installation Guide.* Westboro, MA: Banyon®, 1992.
Installation procedures for the VINES operating system.

Banyon® Systems, Inc. *VINES: Planning a VINES Network.* Westboro, MA: Banyon®, 1992.
VINES services, software, security; StreeTalk Naming Service.

Chappell, Laura A., and Dan E. Hakes. *NetWare® LAN Analysis.* 2nd ed. San Francisco: SYBEX®, 1993.
NetWare 3.2 basics.

Congressional Office of Technology Assessment. *Report: Saving Energy in US Transportation.* Washington, D.C.: Government Printing office, July 15, 1994.
Justification for telecommuting.

Fitzgerald, Jerry. *Business Data Communications*. 4th ed. New York: Wiley, 1993.
Telecommunications in Wide Area Networks

Hecquet, Marc. "How Telecommuting Transforms Work." *Training,* November 1994, p. 56.
Telecommuting justification; ISDN.

Held, Gilbert. *Ethernet Networks.* 2d ed. New York: Wiley, 1996.
Ethernet design, implementation, operation, and management.

Held, Gilbert. *Local Area Network Performance.* New York: Wiley, 1994.
Performance measuring and tuning for LANs.

Kendall, Kenneth E., and Julie E. Kendall. *Systems Analysis and Design.* 3d ed. Upper Saddle River, NJ: Prentice Hall, 1995.
System analysis and design.

Layland, Robin. "ISDN Takes Small Steps to the Big Time." *Data Communications,* July 1995, pp. 21–22.
ISDN trends and applications.

Miller, Mark A. *LAN Protocol Handbook.* San Mateo, CA: M&T, 1992.
Protocol analysis for IEEE 802.x, ARCNET, NetWare, NetBios, AppleTalk, VINES.

Miller, Mark A. *LAN Troubleshooting Handbook.* New York: M&T, 1993.
Protocol analysis and troubleshooting techniques for cabling, ARCNET/ARCNETPlus, Ethernet, Token-Ring, and FDDI.

Minasi, Mark, et al. *Mastering Windows™ NT Server 3.5.* San Francisco: SYBEX®, 1995.
NT server and NT client: theory and installation.

Minasi, Mark, et al. *Mastering Windows™ NT Server 4.0.* San Francisco: SYBEX®, 1996.
NT server and NT client: theory and installation.

Pastore, Michael A. *Microsoft® Windows NT®.* Seattle: Peanut Butter Publishing, 1995.
Preparatory guide for the Microsoft certified professional.

Quittner, Joshua. "Telephone Service That Rings of the Future." *Newsday* (1992).
ISDN applications.

Rains, Alvin L., and Michael J. Palmer. *Local Area Networking with Novell® Software.* Danvers, MA: Boyd & Fraser, 1994.
NetWare installation and administration.

Ramos, Emilio, et al. *Data Communications and Networking Fundamentals Using Novell NetWare® (3.11).* New York: Macmillan, 1994.
Administration of NetWare 3.11.

Spohn, Darren L. *Data Network Design.* New York: McGraw-Hill, 1993.
Wide area network protocols: Frame Relay, ISDN, Switched 56K, SNA.

WAN design.

Sterling, Donald J., Jr. Technician's Guide to Fiber Optics. New York: Delmar, 1993.
Fiber optic theory and FDDI specifications.

Stevens, Richard W. *TCP/IP Illustrated, Volume 1: The Protocols.* Reading, MA: Addison-Wesley, 1994.
The TCP/IP protocol suite.

Siyan, Karanjit. *NetWare: The Professional Reference.* 3d ed. Indianapolis: New Riders, 1994.
Novell NetWare versions 3.x and 4.x: theory and installation.

Windows® NT Resource Kit. Redmond, WA: Microsoft Press, 1995.
Planning, installing, and technical support.

INTERNET AVAILABLE REFERENCES

RFC 1157 [Case, et al. 1990]—Simple Network Management Protocol (SNMP)

RFC 1171—Point to Point Tunneling Protocol (PPTP)

RFC 1201—ARCNET over TCP/IP

RFC 1213 [McCloghrie and Rose]—Management Information Base (MIB-II)

RFC 1213 [Rose and McCloghrie 1990]—Structure of Management Information Base (SMI)

TCP/IP protocol suite information.

RFC 959 [Postel and Reynolds 1985]—File Transfer Protocol

gopher://noc.mmac.wis.edu

ISDN papers

http://www.alumni.caltech.edu/~dank/isdn

Background information on ISDN.

http://www.bst.bls.com/bbs/isdnintr.html

Bell South rate information.

http://www.combinet.com/isdn.html

ISDN backgrounder.

http://www.microsoft.com/ntserver

"Understanding PPTP," a white paper in the Microsoft NT archives covering Point to Point Tunneling Protocol (PPTP).

http://www.pacbell.com/isdn/book/isguide-8.html

Usage information.

http://www.combinet.com/eff-isdn.html

Background information on ISDN.

Index